TALK ABOUT ASSESSMENT

Strategies and Tools to Improve Learning

Author

Damian Cooper

Reviewers

Karen Adams, Newfoundland
Donna Anderson, British Columbia
Dale Armstrong, Alberta
Sherry Bennett, Alberta
Mark Cassar, Ontario
Kathy Collis, Manitoba
Roz Doctorow, Ontario
Alix Harte, Ontario
Tanis Marshall, Alberta
Leonora Scarpino-Inglese, Ontario
Otto Wevers, Ontario
Darlene Waldbauer, Manitoba

NELSON

NELSON

Talk About Assessment: Strategies and Tools to Improve Learning
First Edition

Author
Damian Cooper

Director of Publishing and Customer Solutions
Beverley Buxton

General Manager, Professional Learning and Assessment
Deborah Millard

Senior Publisher, Assessment
William Allan

Executive Managing Editor, Development
Cheryl Turner

Product Manager
Jennifer White

Program Manager
Joanne Close

Developmental Editor
Jessica Pegis

Researcher
Mary Rose MacLachlan

Editorial Assistant
Amanda Davis

Executive Director, Content and Media Production
Renate McCloy

Director, Content and Media Production
Lisa Dimson

Senior Content Production Manager
Sujata Singh

Content Production Editors
Marcel Chiera
Joyce Funamoto

Copy Editor
Elizabeth Salomons

Proofreader
Gail Copeland

Indexer
Laurie Coulter

Production Manager
Cathy Deak

Production Coordinator
Kathrine Pummell

Manufacturing Coordinator
Kathrine Pummell

Design Director
Ken Phipps

Compositor
Rachel Sloat

Photo/Permissions Researcher
Mary Rose MacLachlan

Printer
Transcontinental Printing Inc.

Reviewers
The authors and publisher gratefully acknowledge the contributions of the following educators:

Karen Adams, Eastern School District, NL
Donna Anderson, SD #68 Nanaimo/Ladysmith, BC
J. Dale Armstrong, University of Alberta, AB
Sherry Bennett, Greater St. Albert Catholic District, AB
Mark Cassar, Dufferin-Peel Catholic District School Board, ON
Kathy Collis, Winnipeg School Division, MB
Roz Doctorow, Educational Consultant, ON
Alix Harte, Toronto District School Board, ON
Tanis Marshall, Edmonton Public, AB
Leonora Scarpino-Inglese, Dufferin-Peel Catholic District School Board, ON
Otto Wevers, Toronto District School Board, ON
Darlene Waldbauer, Interlake School Division, MB

Dedication

To my parents, Doug and Alice Cooper

Talk About Assessment is the culmination of my almost thirty years as an educator. It is an attempt to capture the passion that I feel for helping teachers improve their craft and thereby helping students reach their potential.

I want to take this opportunity to thank all of the remarkable educators and students who have made, and continue to make, my work a labour of love. In particular, I wish to thank Grant Wiggins and Lars Thompson for inspiring me. I am indebted to Ken O'Connor who has been a friend and colleague in learning for many years. Special thanks go to Jorge Mendoza, Jackie Fenez, and Jane Lind for their significant contributions to this resource.

David Steele, sincere thanks for the opportunity. To Jessica Pegis, my editor, I wish to say a huge "Thanks" for your wise counsel, patience, and skill. I would also like to thank the whole team at Thomson Nelson, and in particular, to express my gratitude to Joanne Close, Cheryl Turner, Amanda Davis, Sue Selby, Bill Allan, Deborah Millard, and Mario Flandja.

For the video footage contained in the DVD, I wish to thank staff and students at The Northwest Catholic District School Board and the Dufferin-Peel Catholic District School Board, especially Mary-Catherine Kelly, Meghan Martens, Kim Savoie, Jennifer Gaudry, Cheryl McCallum, Stacy Montgomery, John-John Skillen, Liz Perozzo, Linda Orsini, AnnaMaria Del Monte, Laura Tonnelly, Astrid Cardoz, and Mark Cassar.

To my partner, Nanci, thank you for your constant love, encouragement, and understanding. And thank you for being my critical friend.

And finally to my son Chris, thanks for providing me, albeit unwittingly, with so many wonderful stories to share with educators over the years.

General Contents

Foreword

When I started teaching over 30 years ago, I gave very little thought to my assessments. Like most teachers, I worried a bit the night before I was to give a test about what should be on it; I gave little thought to either the validity of the tasks or the need for formative assessments. I never did a pre-test. All that changed when I began working for Ted Sizer as one of the first staff members of the Coalition of Essential Schools. Ted dumped a problem in my lap: "Well, the key Coalition principle is 'diploma by exhibition of mastery'. Figure out what that means and help our folks make it happen in their schools!" I didn't have a clue.

I slowly began to realize that thinking through the assessment before teaching was vital: how could you end up with excellent performance if you didn't ensure that teaching led to it? I certainly knew this as a coach; why hadn't I thought like a coach when teaching in the classroom? And so began the journey, a road lately taken, not just less travelled. Better late than never, of course.

When I began my own work in assessment reform over 20 years ago, it seemed like a quixotic quest. The world of assessment was the world of statistics; and I, like most teachers, didn't care much for the esoterica of stanines and standard deviation. Indeed, "measurement" courses in schools of education were typically taught by professors with a mathematics background, not pedagogical expertise. Few teachers paid much attention to that world—and, indeed, why should we have paid attention? The world of measurement had little to do with the classroom, and was typically of interest only to large-scale testing directors and a small band of policymakers.

How times have changed! Fifteen years ago I was sharply criticized by one of my founders for using such highly arcane words as "rubric" and "performance assessment." Now, every state and provincial standards documents refers to them, the typical teacher ponders the alignment of goals and assessments, and most educators understand that "teaching" is not sufficient to cause learning: attempts by the learner to learn and perform causes learning, and formal feedback is essential to the process. In other words, the important distinction between assessment *of* learning and assessment *for* learning has become common parlance in educational circles.

Talk is not action, however. The longstanding prior focus on only the most highly technical and external test forms of assessments over the decades can be said to have led to a lack of teacher savvy and sensitivity in assessment over time. That emphasis on summative tests has led many teachers to (wrongly) conclude that assessment is what you do after teaching and learning are over. In short, though awareness is greater, the need to greatly improve teacher repertoires in assessment is inarguable, to judge from classroom observation, discussions with educators, and formal research.

So, much more needs to be done, and Damian Cooper's fine book is a wonderful addition to the literature since it is so clear and practical. "Clear and practical" is high praise in a world of past complicated or abstract treatises on the subject of assessment: so few books on assessment actually help teachers to be better assessors while also helping them think more carefully about the role assessment should play in education. The book is a delightful blend of theory and practice on assessment *for* learning and assessment *of* learning.

What makes the book so strong? The rock-solid principles upon which the book is based—his clear and concise account of the "big ideas" of assessment; the countless practical tools for improving one's classroom practice; the constant focus on vignettes that involve the realistic details of the interplay of instruction and assessment; the self-assessment questions and tools for systematically thinking through one's practice; and the many scoring rubrics and tasks for adoption or adaptation. In short, a thorough and useful tool box for improving a very important part of one's repertoire. I wish I had had it in 1972. I would have been a far better teacher.

Grant Wiggins
Hopewell, NJ
2006

Introduction

The genesis of *Talk About Assessment* can be traced back to certain pivotal experiences in my childhood and in my career as an educator. Growing up in England in the sixties, I had first-hand experience of an educational system whose purpose was to "sift and sort" students into those who would progress to higher education, and those who would not, based on the results of a single *written* test—the 11+ Examination. By contrast, my first taste of schooling in Canada was in a very large, composite high school that offered, under the same roof, programs as diverse as "Two-Year Trades and Commerce" and "Five-Year Arts and Science." I soon found myself questioning the practice of closing doors of opportunity to youngsters in their teens, or even earlier.

Upon becoming a teacher, one of my first assignments was at a composite high school whose mission was to integrate students of all backgrounds and educational aspirations into a single learning community committed to realizing each student's potential. During the course of a typical day, I worked with students preparing to go directly to the world of work, students planning to go to community college, as well as students in their final year of school before going to university. And because students were able to move easily from one level of program to another, *ongoing assessment* by all of the teachers in the school was critical to ensure that everyone was working at an appropriate level of challenge, toward an appropriate post-secondary destination. It was at this school that my understanding of the importance of alternatives to written assessment became abundantly clear. Not all students were able to express their learning through the written mode; I quickly came to realize that some students show their best work by "doing," while for others, *talk* is an effective way to assess their understanding.

Several years later, I worked in a school for students demonstrating a range of learning disabilities. Once again, it was imperative that I explore every possible teaching and assessment strategy known—as well as invent some of my own!—in an attempt to unlock the potential of each student. The key to success in teaching and learning, I began to realize, was to find ways to *engage* students, regardless of their ability. And how *does* one engage the reluctant or struggling learner? Through one-on-one *talk*. I was coming to appreciate something that Grant Wiggins would point out to me many years later: that the word *assess* comes from the Latin *assidere*, meaning "to sit with."

Through my work as a teacher, and more recently as a consultant, I have observed that students consolidate their understanding of new concepts when they have opportunities to *talk* about new learning with their classmates; that teachers can learn far more about students' misconceptions and learning challenges when they *talk* to them individually or in small groups; and that teachers improve and refine their craft by *talking* with other teachers about what works and what doesn't work, and by having the chance to observe their colleagues teach. Hence the title of this resource, *Talk About Assessment: Strategies and Tools to Improve Learning*.

About the Text

The text of *Talk About Assessment* is divided into two parts. *Part 1: Strategies to Improve Learning* invites you to work with your colleagues as you learn about sound practices in classroom assessment, program planning, grading, and communicating with students and parents. *Part 2: Tools to Improve Learning* contains planning templates, model units, as well as a sampling of rubrics, checklists, and other tools for you to use.

Talk About Assessment reflects the seminal work of Grant Wiggins and Jay McTighe, *Understanding By Design* (ASCD, 1998), which introduced educators across Canada and the United States to the "backward design process" for curriculum planning. This approach to design is reflected in all components of this resource.

The "Backward-Design" Process

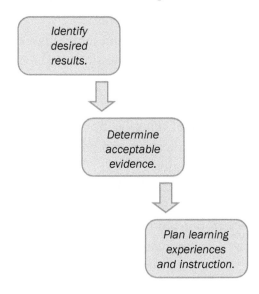

Introduction

Talk About Assessment is organized around eight big ideas—statements that capture the broad, enduring principles of sound assessment. They reflect current research in assessment, as well as the most important principles for guiding practice.

Eight Big Ideas

1. Assessment serves different purposes at different times: it may be used to find out what students already know and can do; it may be used to help students improve their learning; or it may be used to let students and their parents know how much they have learned within a prescribed period of time.
2. Assessment must be planned and purposeful.
3. Assessment must be balanced, including oral, performance, and written tasks, and be flexible in order to improve learning for all students.
4. Assessment and instruction are inseparable because effective assessment informs learning.
5. For assessment to be helpful to students, it must inform them in words, not numerical scores or letter grades, what they have done well, what they have done poorly, and what they need to do next in order to improve.
6. Assessment is a collaborative process that is most effective when it involves self-, peer, and teacher assessment.
7. Performance standards are an essential component of effective assessment.
8. Grading and reporting student achievement is a caring, sensitive process that requires teachers' professional judgement.

About the Other Components

The **CD-ROM** contains all of the tools from Part 2 of the book so that you and your grade-team colleagues can adapt or modify them before printing them for your own use.

The ***Talk About Assessment: DVD*** contains ten video-clips featuring teachers and students in real school and classroom situations *talking about assessment*. Descriptions of the clips are listed on the next page. In addition, video icons directing you to specific clips appear beside related sections in the text.

DVD Video-Clips

Clip #1: Grade 7/8 Mathematics
Focus: Using effective oral questioning techniques, including self-assessment as part of assessment for learning

Clip #2: Grade 3/4 Science
Focus: Involving students with special needs in co-operative group learning

Clip #3: Grade 5/6 Science
Focus: Establishing performance standards; managing class presentations

Clip #4: Team Planning Session
Focus: Developing a unit using a backward design process

Clip #5: Grade 5/6 French Immersion Science
Focus: Using effective oral questioning techniques; using strategies to promote student ownership of learning

Clip #6: Three-Way Conferencing
Focus: Involving students in a reporting conference with a parent

Clip #7: Grade 2 Language Arts
Focus: Facilitating effective peer feedback; selecting work for inclusion in a portfolio

Clip #8: Grade 3 Mathematics
Focus: Conducting one-on-one assessment interviews

Clip #9: Team Marking Session
Focus: Using anchor papers and rubrics to increase assessment reliability

Clip #10: Grade 7 Mathematics
Focus: Balancing oral, performance, and written assessment

In both the text of *Talk About Assessment* and the DVD, you will find numerous examples of teachers and students *engaged* in learning and assessment experiences. You will notice how good assessment is often indistinguishable from good teaching—that students typically "show their best stuff" when they feel safe, know the standards for quality work, receive feedback to help them improve their performance, and are taught the skills of self and peer assessment.

Assessment and grading are perhaps the most difficult aspects of our work, and there are no simple solutions or panaceas to the challenges that we face. But by working together and constantly talking about our own experiences, we can improve our practice, and thereby improve learning for our students.

I hope that this resource will inspire you and your colleagues to engage in lots of *Talk About Assessment*, as well as provide you with strategies and tools that will help you and your students learn together more effectively, more efficiently, and to have fun while doing so!

Damian Cooper
Mississauga, Ontario. August 2006

PLANNING, ASSESSING, AND COMMUNICATING: A VISUAL JOURNEY

The following graphic representation illustrates the significant assessment checkpoints that occur during a typical term. The corresponding sections in Part 1 of *Talk About Assessment* have been indicated to help you connect your learning with your current practice.

Although these checkpoints appear in a linear fashion, teaching and learning is a cyclical process. Similarly, while the list of Contents that follows is linear in appearance, you will find yourself dipping into the *Strategies* and *Tools* according to specific needs you have at various times throughout the year. Section 1 provides background information that informs all Checkpoints.

Checkpoint 1: Team Planning (Section 3)

- developing long-range plans for each subject
- developing or modifying program units
- selecting resources
- identifying critical assessment tasks for grading and reporting

Checkpoint 2: Assessment *for* Learning— Diagnostic (Initial) Assessment (Sections 1 and 2)

- assigning a variety of oral, written, and performance tasks to assess students' current skills and levels of understanding
- conferencing with individual students
- examining information about individual students to make instructional decisions (e.g., grouping students, remediation, possible special education requests)

Checkpoint 3: Assessment *for* Learning— Formative Assessment (Sections 1 and 2)

- providing students with frequent feedback about what they are doing well, what they are struggling with, and how to improve

- teaching students how to self- and peer assess to improve the quality of work that is submitted to you, and to help students understand your standards for quality work
- communicating informally with parents regarding individual student's needs
- communicating with in-school resource teachers to support high-needs students

Checkpoint 4: Assessment *of* Learning (Sections 2 and 3)

- scheduling assessment of learning opportunities to determine what students have learned to this point. This may include culminating tasks, formal one-on-one student interviews, examining portfolios, and so on.
- ensuring all students have completed all essential evidence of learning to this point

Checkpoint 5: Grading and Reporting (Section 4)

- examining the sample of evidence for grading for each student. The sample will include an appropriate balance of "write," "do," and "say" tasks.
- determining the summary grade for each student and asking, "Does this grade capture the trend in this student's achievement?"
- composing anecdotal comments using a "Strengths, Needs, Suggestions for Improvement" model

Checkpoint 6: Parent/Teacher/Student Conferences (Section 4)

- preparing records to support report card grades
- gathering and sharing samples of students' work with parents
- reiterating to parents each student's strengths, needs, and suggestions for improvement

BIG IDEAS
in Section 1

1. Assessment serves different purposes at different times: it may be used to find out what students already know and can do; it may be used to help students improve their learning; or it may be used to let students and their parents know how much they have learned within a prescribed period of time.

3. Assessment must be balanced, including oral, performance, and written tasks, and be flexible in order to improve learning for all students.

Section 1

Assessment Basics

Chapter 1 introduces eight Big Ideas that provide the foundation for *Talk About Assessment*. These ideas help to simplify and clarify the challenging task of classroom assessment. This chapter also discusses some key assessment terms and gives you the opportunity to assess your current practice.

Chapter 2 explores the different purposes for assessing student learning. It addresses familiar approaches such as diagnostic, formative, and summative assessment. The chapter also explains the critical distinction between assessment *for* learning and assessment *of* learning.

Chapter 3 considers challenges associated with adapting assessment for students with special needs and for second-language learners. It provides advice on managing these situations in ways that benefit learners, parents, and teachers.

Chapter 1

The Big Ideas of Assessment

SIMPLE BUT DEEP: THE BIG IDEAS OF ASSESSMENT

In an article that appeared in *Educational Leadership* (Richard Strong et al., March 1999), three highly respected educators likened education reform to Japanese *haiku* because, like these three-line poems, education reform needs simplicity and depth. Likewise, assessment reform must be simple and deep: simple to implement, so it will be embraced by busy teachers and administrators, and deep, so it will be sustainable.

Deep means two things in this context: far-reaching, involving everybody—teachers, students, administrators, and parents or guardians—because only then will it result in lasting change and profound, in the sense that the reform must have a significant impact on student learning. If you are going to spend the time and effort to implement significant changes to your current assessment practice, then you need the assurance that these changes will work.

This first chapter introduces you to eight Big Ideas about assessment. Every recommendation in *Talk About Assessment* can be traced back to these Big Ideas. They are not particularly complex, nor are they difficult to remember or implement. In this sense, they are simple but deep. The Big Ideas will be examined in more detail later in this chapter. For now, simply scan them to discover how simple they really are.

Eight Big Ideas

1. Assessment serves different purposes at different times: it may be used to find out what students already know and can do; it may be used to help students improve their learning; or it may be used to let students and their parents know how much they have learned within a prescribed period of time.
2. Assessment must be planned and purposeful.
3. Assessment must be balanced, including oral, performance, and written tasks, and be flexible in order to improve learning for all students.
4. Assessment and instruction are inseparable because effective assessment informs learning.
5. For assessment to be helpful to students, it must inform them in words, not numerical scores or letter grades, what they have done well, what they have done poorly, and what they need to do next in order to improve.
6. Assessment is a collaborative process that is most effective when it involves self-, peer, and teacher assessment.
7. Performance standards are an essential component of effective assessment.
8. Grading and reporting student achievement is a caring, sensitive process that requires teachers' professional judgement.

Improving Assessment Practice: Strategies for Success

Now that you have read the Big Ideas, you may be wondering about the practical side of changing your assessment practice. The following strategies will help you to maximize your chances for success.

Solicit the support of your principal or vice-principal

This will ensure that changes you make to your current practice are consistent with district and school policies. This is also a good way to raise awareness of your work among staff. Your principal or vice-principal may be able to provide you with time or resources to help you plan and implement the changes you wish to make.

Do not work alone!

Team up with a colleague who teaches the same grade or subject. You've heard all the clichés about teamwork before, but if you plan and implement changes to your teaching and assessment practice with colleagues,

you will

- be better able to face and overcome challenges
- increase your access to resources and support systems
- solve logistical problems with more ease
- have more fun!

Michael Fullan uses the term *implementation dip* (2001, pp. 40-41) to describe the phenomenon of school reforms that typically cause things to get worse or "dip" before eventually leading to significant improvement. If you are working alone on an initiative, you may be more likely to abandon what you are doing when the implementation dip occurs. Working with others will help you to solve any difficulties you may have, often because other teachers have experienced the same problems themselves. Working as a team will also increase your access to resources and provide you with a support system.

Tell your students about changes you are going to make

Inform students when you are going to try a new strategy, such as one-on-one conferencing, and tell them, "*We're* going to try something different this term." Most students respond favourably and with offers of help when they know that the whole class—teacher and students as a learning community—are going to explore new territory together.

Inform parents or guardians that changes are coming

Parents or guardians sometimes consider themselves experts in education because they may have experienced 12 or more years of education first-hand. Be proactive and let them know ahead of time what you intend to do. For example, inform parents if you are going to introduce peer assessment as an alternative to collecting and formally marking first drafts of student work. When parents feel that they are a part of the process, they may well provide you with an additional source of support.

Now it's time to take a closer look at the Big Ideas of Assessment.

BIG IDEA 1 Assessment serves different purposes at different times: it may be used to find out what students already know and can do; it may be used to help students improve their learning; or it may be used to let students and their parents know how much they have learned within a prescribed period of time.

Assessment has two over-riding functions: to inform instruction and to communicate information about achievement. The first function includes **diagnostic assessment**, which enables the teacher to ascertain what students currently know and can do, as well as **formative assessment**, which provides students with feedback to help them improve their learning. The second function informs students and their parents how well they have learned. This involves judging the quality of student work and using letter grades, scores, or achievement levels to describe that quality. Later in this chapter, you will have opportunities to explore these related but different functions of assessment.

BIG IDEA 2 Assessment must be planned and purposeful.

In the past, program and lesson plans clearly identified teaching objectives, instructional approaches, and resources, but offered little in terms of assessment strategies and tools to judge the quality of student work. During my own teaching career, I saw nothing wrong with leaving the "evaluation" column of my program plans blank until I had taught a course for a couple of years! Times have changed, though, and outcomes-based learning and **backward design** (see Introduction, page ix) have clarified the questions that must be posed *before* teaching begins:

1. What do I expect students to know and be able to do at the end of this unit, term, or year? (**curriculum question**)
2. How will I determine whether they have learned these things? (**assessment question**)
3. What series of lessons will be most effective in enabling students to demonstrate they have learned these things? (**instruction question**)

Assessment must be balanced, including oral, performance, and written tasks, and be flexible in order to improve learning for all students.

Provincial and locally developed curriculum documents include a broad range of learning outcomes. These outcomes, or learning targets, prescribe knowledge and understanding, skills, and attitudes or dispositions.

To adequately assess whether students have acquired these learning targets, a broad range of assessment strategies must be used. This means that some of the assessments you select or design will require students to perform or demonstrate their skills; some will require students to speak and present; and others will require students to write about what they know and understand. Balanced assessment plans contain all three kinds of tasks—what *Talk About Assessment* refers to as *write*, *do*, and *say* tasks.

Flexibility is also essential in assessment because you may need to adapt or modify your planned assessment approach for any number of reasons. For example, some students may require an alternative approach to compensate for a particular exceptionality. Other students may just be learning English or French, so a flexible approach will be necessary to prevent a language bias from interfering with the assessment information you gather. Flexibility could also take the form of an extended deadline for a student experiencing extenuating circumstances at home.

Flexibility does not mean a lack of clear expectations. Effective teachers provide their students with succinct guidelines about assessment. Flexibility is reflected in the professional judgement that such teachers demonstrate when applying these guidelines to an individual student, a group of students, or sometimes to the whole class when a specific situation demands it. I advocate the mantra, "Be firm but fair."

Assessment and instruction are inseparable because effective assessment informs learning.

Effective teachers are constantly assessing their students' learning in informal ways by listening, observing, and conferencing with them, and then using the information they gather to adjust instruction to maximize learning. When more formal assessment has occurred, such as a major project or a test, effective teachers carefully analyze the results and adjust subsequent instruction to address the learning gaps.

Balanced assessment plans contain all three kinds of tasks—what Talk About Assessment refers to as write, do, and say tasks.

For assessment to be helpful to students, it must inform them in words, not numerical scores or letter grades, what they have done well, what they have done poorly, and what they need to do next in order to improve.

Marks, scores, and letter grades alone do not provide students with the information they need to improve their work. They are merely symbols that represent degrees of quality. Too often, however, these symbols become the sole focus of assessment. Assessment information that improves learning provides students with clear and specific direction about what to do differently to improve the quality of their work.

 Assessment is a collaborative process that is most effective when it involves self-, peer, and teacher assessment.

Assessment is not something that teachers *do* to students; it is a collaborative process involving students, teachers, and parents. Everyone has a role to play if the quality of students' learning is to improve. Assessment strategies such as student work portfolios and three-way conferencing are highly effective because they maximize the potential for collaboration and help students plan for future learning.

 Performance standards are an essential component of effective assessment.

Whether assessment is being used to further student learning or to describe the quality of polished work, teachers, students, and parents need to know the standards being used to identify quality work.

During the past decade, most provinces have moved away from **norm-referenced standards**, by which student work was judged against how other students performed. Instead, **criterion-referenced standards** are being used. For each assessment, a set of pre-determined **performance criteria** are identified and student achievement is measured against those criteria. The use of **rubrics** and student **exemplars** are indicative of jurisdictions where criterion-referenced standards are in place.

Assessments designed for ranking are generally not good instruments for helping teachers improve their instruction or modify their approach to individual students.... The assessments best suited to guide improvements in student learning are the quizzes, tests, writing assignments, and other assessments that teachers administer on a regular basis in their classrooms.

THOMAS GUSKEY, 2003

BIG IDEA 8 Grading and reporting student achievement is a caring, sensitive process that requires teachers' professional judgement.

The summary of learning that appears on a report card should not come as a surprise to the student, teacher, or parents.

Someone once said that any teacher who could be replaced by a computer ought to be! But we all know that effective teachers will never be replaced by computers because one of the essential characteristics of the teaching-learning process is the human interaction that occurs between students and a caring, sensitive, skilled teacher.

That same care, sensitivity, and skill must come into play when teachers determine report card grades. The summary of learning that appears on a report card should not come as a surprise to the student, teacher, or parents. It should simply confirm the trend in achievement that a student has demonstrated over time. Surprises tend only to occur when the trend in a student's achievement is over-ridden by faulty methods used to compute a final grade. *Talk About Assessment* will steer you away from those pitfalls and allow you to report achievement with confidence.

Assessment Q & A

Question

What do I do about the student who merely wants to pass and doesn't care about excellence?

Answer

Lack of motivation to produce quality work may be the result of boredom, poor self-esteem, the absence of role models at home, or other factors. Teachers can increase the motivation of students by

- setting clear, relevant, and achievable goals for learning
- assigning engaging and authentic tasks
- providing frequent oral feedback while students are working
- demonstrating through their words and actions that they believe in the capacity of all students to be successful

Remember that you are not alone in your efforts. Parents are also concerned when students seem unmotivated, so make parental contact a priority. Of course, there will always be some students who choose to do minimal work. Don't blame yourself. Teachers do not fail students, but some students choose to fail themselves!

A Note on the Big Ideas

As you work your way through *Talk About Assessment*, you will notice each of the four sections of this resource opens with several Big Ideas. You will also find one Big Idea appearing at the start of each chapter. None of the Big Ideas resides in a single chapter, however. Together, the eight Big Ideas serve as threads for the entire resource. They link concept with practice at every turn and help you to connect planning, teaching, and learning with assessment.

SOME KEY ASSESSMENT TERMS

A glossary of the bold-face terms that appear throughout this resource is provided on page 437. However, some of these terms are defined by provincial or local documents in idiosyncratic ways. For example, the term *evaluation* is defined quite differently in various provinces. Similarly, the definition of *diagnostic assessment* varies widely as one travels across the country. Although there are no absolute definitions for any of these terms, in *Talk About Assessment* the following definitions will be used.

Figure 1-1: Some Key Assessment Terms	
Assessment	gathering data about student knowledge and/or skills, either through informal methods, such as observation, or formal methods, such as testing
Assessment *for* learning	assessment designed primarily to promote learning. Early drafts, first tries, and practice assignments are all examples of assessment for learning
Assessment *of* learning	assessment designed primarily to determine student achievement at a given point in time. Report card grades should be comprised of data from assessments of learning
Evaluation	making judgements about student-demonstrated knowledge and/or skills
Grading	summarizing assessment data for reporting purposes in the form of a letter or numerical grade
Diagnostic assessment	assessment to determine appropriate starting points for instruction
Formative assessment	assessment that occurs data during the learning process, and provides feedback to both students and teachers to help improve learning
Summative assessment	assessment that occurs at the end of a significant period of learning and summarizes student achievement of that learning

Assessment? Evaluation? Grading? What's the Difference?

Some of the terms listed in Figure 1-1—specifically *assessment, evaluation,* and *grading*—cause more confusion than others. It is important to distinguish these terms from one another.

Grading

The term *grading* is used less frequently in Canada than in the United States. In Canada, the term *mark* is used more frequently. Unfortunately, it can be confusing when "mark" is used to refer both to the scores assigned to individual pieces of student work *and* to the overall score on a report card. For example, you might say, "Damian earned a mark of 18/25 on the quiz," but also, "I have to enter my report card marks tonight."

Ken O'Connor (2002) urges Canadian educators to use *grading* to refer exclusively to the summary score on a report card. In this sense, the grade is recognized as the summary of a set of marks that explains where the student stands with respect to a set of achievement standards. And, while report card grades assume more importance for students and parents as time goes on, O'Connor cautions that "…grading is not essential to teaching and learning." (p. 17)

Assessment and Evaluation

If grading has little to do with teaching and learning, what roles do *assessment* and *evaluation* play? Before this question can be answered, you must understand that, although related, assessment and evaluation are two distinct processes.

Imagine that you are a skating coach heading off to the arena early one Saturday morning. One of your skaters, Sarah, runs through her new two-minute routine from start to finish. At the end of her performance, she skates over and asks, "How did I do, coach?" You hold up a card that says 4.5. Sarah looks puzzled. "What's that supposed to mean?" she asks. "You're my coach, not a judge. Give me some feedback! Talk to me!"

Can you see Sarah's point? She is asking to be *assessed*. She needs *feedback* in words, not a score. She needs specific information about what she did well, what she did poorly, and what to change. She requires this information in order to improve her performance.

Assessment is feedback and its primary purpose is to promote learning for students (Wiggins, 1998). *Evaluation*, on the other hand, is the process of judging work against a standard. It should only occur once the practising and coaching for a particular performance is over. In a skating competition, the judge's mandate is to simply pass judgement, not help Sarah improve her performance. As Sarah's coach, your mandate is to help Sarah improve her skills.

Teachers, of course, are called on to both assess (provide feedback) and evaluate (pass judgement), but sometimes it is hard to differentiate between the two. At times, they are fused into a single process.

However, once the distinction between assessment and evaluation is understood, the role each plays in teaching and learning becomes much clearer. *Assessment* plays an essential role in helping students learn and improve their work. *Evaluation* informs students about the quality of a given task or piece of work, relative to a known standard.

The simplest prescription for improving education must be dollops of feedback.

John Hattie, 1992

Assessment *for* learning and assessment *of* learning

Educators are now using the terms *assessment for learning* and *assessment of learning* to differentiate between the coaching and judging functions just described. Assessment *for* learning encompasses both diagnostic (initial) and formative assessment; it is assessment that occurs during the instructional process and is primarily intended to help students improve their learning. Assessment *of* learning includes all summative assessment; it occurs when a teacher deems it necessary to determine the extent of a student's achievement in relation to an established standard. Figure 1-2 compares the purposes and characteristics of the two types of assessment.

Figure 1-2: Comparing Assessment *for* Learning and Assessment *of* Learning	
Assessment *for* Learning	**Assessment *of* Learning**
• Designed to assist teachers and students by checking learning to decide what to do next	• Designed to provide information to parents, school, and board level administration, as well as students
• Used in conferencing	• Presented in a periodic report
• Uses detailed, specific, descriptive feedback in words, not scores	• Summarizes information with numbers or letter grades
• Focuses on improvement of student's previous best	• Compares student achievement with established standards

SOURCE: ADAPTED FROM RUTH SUTTON, 2001

ASSESSING YOUR OWN ASSESSMENT PRACTICE

As you work your way through *Talk About Assessment*, you will learn about assessment strategies and tools that can be adapted for your own classroom. Before you begin that journey, take a few moments to assess the quality of your current practice.

First, gather or list all of the assessment strategies, tasks, and tools that you are currently using for a specific class that you teach. You can refer to this bundle as your "assessment toolkit" for that class. If you work as a member of a grade team, complete this process collaboratively.

▲ **If you work as part of a grade team, you can work collaboratively to assess your current practice.**

Above all else, assessment must improve student learning. Too often, though, students focus on getting the highest marks, and learning assumes secondary importance.

These are the criteria that you will apply to your current assessment toolkit:

1. Does my assessment toolkit promote student learning?
2. Is my assessment toolkit responsive to individual students' needs?
3. Do I use data from my assessment toolkit to adjust instruction for individual students and for the whole class?
4. Do the elements of my assessment toolkit that I use for reporting include a sufficient sample of learning?
5. Are all components in my assessment toolkit valid measures of what I intend to assess?
6. Are all components in my assessment toolkit reliable measures of what I intend to assess?
7. Is my assessment toolkit for this class manageable for me in terms of my workload?

1. Does my assessment toolkit promote student learning?

Above all else, assessment must improve student learning. Too often, though, students focus on getting the highest marks, and learning assumes secondary importance.

Consider the following example in which Mr. Jordan, an intermediate core program teacher, decided to make a few small yet profound changes to his method of marking tests in his mathematics class. He had become disillusioned by the continued poor performance of many of his students and decided that he needed to find a way to turn tests into opportunities for learning, rather than mere audits of his students' lack of understanding. The changes Mr. Jordan made to his test routine are found in Figure 1-3.

Figure 1-3: Using Tests to Identify Misunderstandings in Mathematics

1. Students get an outline of what they need to study.
2. Students work with a partner or small group on practice questions and discuss any difficulties they are having.
3. Students write the test.
4. Teacher marks the test using checkmarks to indicate work that is correct and circling errors with a pencil. No numerical marks appear on the test.
5. Teacher returns tests; students focus on the circled errors and correct them. They may work on their own, with a partner, or in a small group.
6. Once students have made as many corrections as possible, teacher meets individually and shows the student the mark he or she achieved on the test.

(continued)

▲ **This post-test chat involved clarifying a concept by orally probing the student's misunderstanding.**

7. If the test is formative, students may submit their corrected test and have their mark upgraded. If the test is summative, the original mark stands.

8. Teacher analyzes the data from the tests, identifying questions that most students had trouble with, those that some students had trouble with, and those that individual students had trouble with.

9. Teacher plans further whole-class, small-group, or individual instruction on the basis of this analysis.

Two years after implementing this strategy, Mr. Jordan no longer hears his students say, "Oh well. Failed another math test! On to the next unit. I know I'm useless in math!" Instead, the students see the tests as opportunities to confirm what they know and as red flags to identify what they do not yet understand. They also know that Mr. Jordan will take the time to address their misunderstandings before moving on.

2. Is my assessment toolkit responsive to individual students' needs?

To identify the strengths and needs of all students, assessment must be flexible. Flexibility is important throughout the year, but especially so when you are conducting initial or diagnostic assessment with students at the start of a new school year, as you will see in Casey's story.

CASE STUDY 1 | The Fastest Car

Casey walked into Ms. Ross's classroom on the first day of school, his head hung low. His headphones suggested he didn't want to speak or be spoken to. When Ms. Ross asked the class to take out their notebooks, Casey did so reluctantly.

Ms. Ross asked the students to close their eyes and visualize themselves 20 years into the future. "Imagine that you are doing exactly what you want to do, in the place where you dream about living," she told them. "Now write what you see."

As she walked around the room, she came to Casey's desk. He had written nothing. Ms. Ross asked him to remove his headphones and inquired what he had seen with his eyes closed. "N-n-nuthin'," he replied. Ms. Ross quickly realized that Casey had a serious stammer. Later, she checked his student record and read that he was learning disabled, with serious difficulties in both reading and writing.

During the first week of that term, Casey was reluctant to write anything or to speak publicly. However, during the quiet reading periods that took place for 15 minutes after the lunch break, Casey would eagerly retrieve a car magazine from his backpack and devour each article. Ms. Ross saw that he read every article from start to finish, and wasn't merely looking at the glossy photographs. One afternoon, as Ms. Ross walked by his desk, Casey said, "Ms. Ross? See this car? It's the fastest production car ever built." No stammer evident when Casey's an expert in the subject matter!

After a brief chat about the performance of the car, Ms. Ross said to Casey, "Why don't you write a report about this car, tracing its history from prototype to this year's model?" The expression on Casey's face quickly told her that this was the best assignment he had ever been given.

Over the next few days, Casey worked on his report, beginning with a rough draft, and eventually producing a word-processed report, printed on paper that featured a background screen of the car itself. One afternoon, he explained to Mr. Ross the technology behind trapping images on a page—a skill that she had never even attempted.

From the moment Casey completed this piece of work, which was of exceptional quality, his demeanour in class changed completely. He held his head higher and began to offer answers to questions. He also started to interact and joke with his peers.

Had Ms. Ross assessed Casey's writing skills *prior* to directing him to produce the report, the conclusions she may have drawn would have been inaccurate. Only after she gave Casey the opportunity to write about his favourite topic was she able to perceive his strengths. Ms. Ross also created an atmosphere of trust: Casey was now engaged in her class, he trusted her and, most importantly, he felt more confidence in his abilities as a student. Ms. Ross could now begin challenging him to produce quality work on topics that were not as interesting to him, and she also could expect him to produce better work on his next report. The flexibility she demonstrated towards Casey enabled him to be successful and promoted further learning.

As the school year progressed, Casey began to take a leadership role in group activities that involved problem-solving and showed great insights when asked to predict the surprise endings to short stories that were read aloud to the class. Ultimately, he produced a remarkable short story of his own.

This case study also reveals the essence of assessment *for* learning. The purpose of Ms. Ross's assessment was to engage Casey in the teaching-learning process. She wasn't concerned about marks at this time; nor was she concerned that Casey appeared unwilling or unable to complete the same tasks as the other students in the class. Rather than rushing to collect the first score to enter in her mark book for Casey, she concentrated on gaining his trust. She found out what he was passionate about, then gave him the opportunity to demonstrate the best that he could do.

3. Do I use data from my assessment toolkit to adjust instruction for individual students, and for the whole class?

Instruction must always be adjusted according to the assessment data gathered. The following examples illustrate two simple ways this can be done. The first case involves reading the data horizontally; that is, examining the data gathered for one student. It is late September and records indicate that Mario is struggling.

Instruction must always be adjusted according to the assessment data gathered.

Regardless of whether Mario is required to write, speak, or perform, he is consistently having difficulty. Mario's teacher realizes she needs to investigate the possible causes of his problems: Is there information in his student record to indicate specific learning deficits? Are there issues at home that may be affecting his work? Whatever the reason(s), the assessment data represent a red flag and demand further investigation into the source of the difficulty and what interventions to use.

Figure 1-4: Mario's Assessment Data									
Student	Goals Letter	Oral Introduction	Descriptive Paragraph	Reading Log	Poetry Reading	Test	Film Review	Story Draft	Poetry Response
	4/9	6/9	7/9	10/9	12/9	14/9	17/9	20/9	24/9
Andrea	Lev 4	Lev 3+	Lev 4	Lev 4	Lev 3	6/10	Lev 3+	Lev 4-	Lev 4
Chen	Lev 3+	Lev 3+	Lev 3	Lev 4-	Lev 3	5/10	Lev 4	Lev 3	Lev 3
Mario	Lev <1	Lev 1	Lev <1	Lev 1	Lev 1	3/10	Lev <1	Lev 1	<Lev 1
Sophie	Lev 2+	Lev 3	Lev 3	Lev 3+	Lev 3	5/10	Lev 4-	Lev 4-	Lev 4
Vlad	Lev 2	Lev 3-	Lev 3	Lev 2	Lev 2	4/10	Lev 3	Lev 3	Lev.3

Figure 1-5: September 14 Assessment Data									
Student	**Goals Letter**	**Oral Introduction**	**Descriptive Paragraph**	**Reading Log**	**Poetry Reading**	**Test**	**Film Review**	**Story Draft**	**Poetry Response**
	4/9	6/9	7/9	10/9	12/9	14/9	17/9	20/9	24/9
Andrea	Lev 4	Lev 3+	Lev 4	Lev 4	Lev 3	6/10	Lev 3+	Lev 4-	Lev 4
Chen	Lev 3+	Lev 3+	Lev 3	Lev 4-	Lev 3	5/10	Lev 4	Lev 3	Lev 3
Mario	Lev <1	Lev 1	Lev <1	Lev 1	Lev 1	3/10	Lev <1	Lev 1	<Lev 1
Sophie	Lev 2+	Lev 3	Lev 3	Lev 3+	Lev 3	5/10	Lev 4-	Lev 4-	Lev 4
Vlad	Lev 2	Lev 3-	Lev 3	Lev 2	Lev 2	4/10	Lev 3	Lev 3	Lev.3

The second case involves reading assessment data vertically, that is to say, examining the data for the whole class on a specific assessment task.

The highlighted data in Figure 1-5 shows that none of the students performed well on the September 14th test. The teacher needs to investigate why most students were not successful at this task. Perhaps it was as simple as a fire alarm interrupting the class. On the other hand, if the teacher thought that the majority of students were well-prepared for the task when it is obvious they were not, then it is quite possible that the instruction leading up to the assessment was not effective. Two things need to occur in response to the data:

- The material must be taught over, possibly with a new instructional approach.
- If the teacher had planned to include the data from this assessment in students' report card grade calculation, she should delete this data from her records. It is probably invalid.

The case study that follows further illustrates how to use assessment *for* learning to make instructional decisions.

It is always a challenge—for both student and teacher—when a child arrives part-way through the school year. In Evan's case, he had to make many adjustments. His position in a large and busy family and his quiet personality meant he often got overlooked. Mrs. Singh immediately recognized that Evan had some distinct and special needs. Using a variety of assessment tools, she was able to gather the data and evidence she needed to determine how to adjust her program to meet his needs. By not centring him out, she gently allowed him to find his place and develop the confidence to interact with his peers and participate in class discussions. Providing the one-on-one interaction with a reading buddy

CASE STUDY 2 | Evan Finds His Voice

Evan moved from a rural setting to his new Grade 2 class in late September. He had a shy demeanour and did not actively engage with his classmates. Mrs. Singh, his teacher, used a variety of assessment strategies to track her students' progress in reading, writing, spelling, and oral language. By mid-October, she had
- gathered anecdotal records
- observed her students carefully as they worked and interacted with one another
- held an individual reading and writing conference with each student

As Mrs. Singh suspected, Evan's reading, writing, and oral language skills were all below grade level. He did not contribute to class discussions and, when spoken to, tended to answer in one-word responses or simple sentences. He selected books with simple text or repeated patterns, and often chose to read the same books over and over. He did not have many reading and decoding strategies and was uncomfortable in one-on-one reading situations.

Mrs. Singh reviewed her assessment data for reading and determined there were a variety of reading levels in her class. She decided to add guided reading to her reading program to better accommodate the needs of all her students. She was able to place Evan in a small group with three students who were all reading at the same level. This allowed the opportunity for the three students to build their confidence as readers and for Mrs. Singh to teach specific reading and decoding strategies appropriate to the students' needs.

Mrs. Singh's use of the teacher-librarian and the resource teacher twice weekly for the guided reading portion of the lesson allowed three of her four groups to have instruction while the fourth group worked independently. Because the groups were rotated between the teachers, Mrs. Singh was able to work with each group regularly and to assess their progress through observation and direct interaction.

Evan was also paired with a reading buddy from a Grade 5 class. The older student was kind and gentle, and had good reading skills and a great sense of humour. He and Evan met twice a week to enjoy reading from a variety of genres. They kept a record of the material they read and used a Reading Reflection sheet to encourage self-reflection and a positive attitude about reading.

Mrs. Singh was fortunate to have a parent volunteer who could work with Evan twice a week. To help build Evan's confidence as a reader and improve his oral language and speaking skills, Mrs. Singh decided to have the parent read stories with Evan and have him practise retelling them.

As mid-term interviews approached, Mrs. Singh reviewed her assessment data for Evan. Her anecdotal records noted that he was still reading and writing below grade level but had moved up a level in his guided reading. Her observations confirmed that he was more confident and comfortable interacting with fellow students and teachers. He participated more willingly in class discussions and was beginning to use more complex sentences in his responses. An initial reluctance to interact with others (teacher, parent volunteer, and reading buddy) was gone and he enthusiastically welcomed the opportunity to work with them.

and a parent volunteer helped build his confidence as a learner and his ability to interact with others. Evan's confidence and abilities continued to grow and when a new student arrived in January, it was Evan who volunteered to take the new student under his wing.

4. Do the elements of my assessment toolkit that I use for reporting include a sufficient sample of learning?

There are two issues for teachers to consider when they sample students' learning. First, they must ensure they gather an appropriate balance of *write*, *do*, and *say* assessments. If assessment is to provide all students with sufficient opportunities to demonstrate what they have learned and the skills they have acquired, then your assessment repertoire must include tasks that require students to say and do, as well as to write.

Teachers of students in Grades 4 to 8 tend to favour assigning written work and gathering assessment data by entering marks in their mark book and making anecdotal notes about each student's strengths and areas of need.

On the other hand, teachers of Kindergarten to Grade 3 students make extensive use of observation as an assessment strategy, whereby they observe groups of students, or individual students, and record their observations using a variety of assessment tools. These teachers also recognize the importance of conferencing with individual students, sometimes to discuss work in progress, or to talk about a student's successes and challenges.

All three modes—write, do, say—and the corresponding assessment strategies used by the teacher—mark, observe, listen—are necessary and legitimate at *all* grades and in *all* subject domains. Which mode to use, and when, depends not on the age of the students, but on the nature of the learning to be assessed. All students, from Kindergarten to Grade 12, need opportunities to demonstrate their learning through all three modes.

Second, there is a principle in assessment theory known as the *triangulation of data* that requires teachers to draw assessment data from three different sources in order to maximize the reliability of the conclusions they reach. To apply this principle in the classroom, it is recommended that for any given learning target (e.g., problem-solving in math or expository writing) teachers have at least three pieces of assessment data from which to derive a grade for reporting. The pieces should be gathered at different points during the term, but should not include first tries or early attempts.

The triangulation of data requires teachers to draw assessment data from three different sources in order to maximize the reliability of the conclusions they reach.

Unfortunately, the first reporting period in the year often occurs too early to enable teachers to gather three polished pieces. For this reason, the "three-pieces principle" is a rule of thumb. If reporting timelines preclude the gathering of a valid sample, you may wish to indicate this fact in the anecdotal comments on the report card.

5. Are all of the components in my assessment toolkit valid measures of what I intend to assess?

Validity addresses the match between the learning you wish to assess and the assessment strategy and tool you use to assess that learning. I once worked with a teacher who had just spent a lesson familiarizing her students with the microscope and had taught them how to focus on a prepared slide. She showed me the assessment task she planned to use the next day, before assigning students their first science investigation.

The task involved a diagram of a microscope and a randomized word list for the controls on the microscope. Students were to label the diagram correctly. When I asked her what she intended to assess, she replied, "Whether or not my students can focus the microscope."

▲ **Focusing a microscope: writing about it isn't the same as doing it.**

I asked her, "Isn't it possible that a student could label the diagram perfectly, yet not be able to focus the microscope at all?"

"Yes," she replied. "But what do you suggest?"

"I think you know," I said.

"You mean I have to ask the students to focus their own microscope, and then I have to walk around and look through each one, assessing how well they have demonstrated the skill?"

"Exactly," I replied. "The assessment you have designed is a test of *knowledge*, yet according to what you've told me, you want to assess a *skill*. The paper-and-pencil task would be a valid way to assess knowledge about the focus controls, but if your purpose is to assess the skill of focusing, then a performance assessment is required."

6. Are all of the components in my assessment toolkit reliable measures of what I intend to assess?

Reliability involves the measure of consistency of results obtained when different assessors administer the same assessment at different times to students with similar characteristics. Reliability is a crucial variable in test design and administration, especially if the stakes are high and important decisions regarding students will be made on the basis of assessment data. For these reasons, standardized tests include a strict set of administrative procedures governing time allotted for completing the test, instructions to students, and methods of scoring.

In classroom assessment, there is not as much need to be as concerned about standardizing the conditions under which an assessment task takes place. Nevertheless, reliability is an extremely important criterion to bear in mind when designing your own assessments, as the following situation makes clear.

Ms. Davis and Mrs. Martin both teach Grade 4 Language Arts. They have planned much of their program collaboratively, including the resources they are using and the major assessments they will assign their students. They have both spent several lessons teaching their students a variety of comprehension strategies to use when reading an unfamiliar passage of text. In discussions, they have also noted how remarkably similar the achievement results of their respective classes seem to be.

Both teachers decide to use the same summative task to end the unit: they have their students complete a series of comprehension questions on the same reading passage. When they compare the results, however, they are surprised to find that Mrs. Martin's students have been far more successful.

"What happened?" asks Ms. Davis, incredulously. "I'm so disappointed!"

To solve the mystery, they compare notes about how they administered the summative task and eventually realize that Mrs. Martin permitted her students to use dictionaries to help them understand unfamiliar words in the passage, while Ms. Davis had not. Therefore, any comparisons that the teachers make between the results achieved by their two classes will be *unreliable* because of this significant difference in the testing conditions.

7. Is my assessment toolkit for this class manageable for me in terms of workload?

In assessment practice, just as in student work, quantity is rarely, if ever, representative of quality. You need strategies for marking and record-keeping that are efficient for you, as well as effective in helping your students learn. Most teachers wonder whether all the marking they do makes a significant difference in the quality of work their students produce, and if they really need to formally mark every piece of work their students complete in order to arrive at a valid report card grade. In fact, it is quite possible to mark less while, at the same time, actually improving the quality of student work. The hardest step is the first one: you must critically examine your current practice and remain open to new approaches.

The most important concept related to manageability—becoming more efficient and effective in assessment practices—is sampling. Teachers teach far more and students learn and produce far more than can ever be assessed summatively and reported on. Therefore, it is crucial to identify a *critical sample* of work for grading and reporting purposes. To use a sports analogy, a critical sample comprises the *games*, not the *practices*. The practice work helps students improve their learning by receiving feedback from the teacher and peers. It does not need to be scored.

> *In assessment practice, just as in student work, quantity is rarely, if ever, representative of quality.*

Summary

This chapter introduced eight Big Ideas that provide the foundation for *Talk About Assessment*.

1. Assessment serves different purposes at different times.
2. Assessment must be planned and purposeful.
3. Assessment and instruction are inseparable because effective assessment informs learning.
4. Assessment must inform students what they have done well, what they have done poorly, and what they need to do to improve.
5. Assessment is a collaborative process.
6. Performance standards are an essential component of effective assessment.
7. Assessment must be balanced and flexible in order to improve learning for all students.
8. Grading and reporting student achievement is a caring, sensitive process that requires teachers' professional judgement.

- This chapter also defined some key assessment terms and singled out the terms *assessment, evaluation, grading, assessment for learning,* and *assessment of learning* for further discussion.
- Finally, the chapter helped you examine and check your current assessment toolkit for quality, effectiveness, and efficiency.

Applying My Learning

Use *Tool 1.1: How Does My Current Assessment Toolkit Shape Up?* (page 288) to assess your assessment toolkit for your class.

1.1, Chapter 1 Review

How Does My Current Assessment Toolkit Shape Up?	
Criterion	**Maintain / Modify / Change Practice**
1. Does my assessment toolkit promote student learning?	
2. Is my assessment toolkit responsive to individual student needs?	
3. Do I use data from my assessment toolkit to adjust instruction for individual students and for the whole class?	
4. Do the elements of my assessment toolkit that I use for reporting include a sufficient sample of learning?	
5. Are all of the components in my assessment toolkit valid measures of what I intend to assess?	
6. Are all of the components in my assessment toolkit reliable measures of what I intend to assess?	
7. Is my assessment toolkit for this class manageable for me in terms of workload?	

288 *Tool 1.1*   Copyright © 2007 by Nelson, a division of Thomson Canada Ltd.

TOOL 1.1

How Does My Current Assessment Toolkit Shape Up? p. 288

Chapter 2

DIFFERENT PURPOSES FOR ASSESSING STUDENT WORK

BIG IDEA 1 Assessment serves different purposes at different times: it may be used to find out what students already know and can do; it may be used to help students improve their learning; or it may be used to let students and their parents know how much they have learned within a prescribed period of time.

ASSESSMENT MYTHS AND REALITIES

It was the first day of a new term. Ms. Kara, a Grade 8 teacher, was introducing her students to her classroom routines and expectations. She described how she approached assessment and evaluation by highlighting the following points on an overhead transparency:

- You begin the year with 100 percent overall and full marks for each assignment.
- As you complete each assignment, marks are deducted for errors and your overall grade is lowered.
- You will find this approach far more motivating than a "reward" model.

Ms. Kara asked if there were any questions. The room grew quiet, then one student spoke up. "Miss," he asked, "Does this mean if I don't hand anything in, I'll get 100 percent?"

The student's question forces us to consider whether our students regard assessment and evaluation as a series of rewards and punishments, having little to do with teaching and learning. Every teacher will agree that the primary purpose of assessment is to improve student learning. Many students, however, see assessment as maintaining or accumulating as many points as possible. The teacher's role becomes that of accountant—maintaining records of daily credits and debits. Unfortunately, parents and guardians often embrace this approach by being less concerned with their child's learning and more concerned with marks and test scores.

The primary purpose of assessment is to improve student learning.

Is there anything you can do to counter this trend? There is, but putting assessment back on the rails leading to improved student learning can be challenging. (Consider that Ms. Kara's story that opens this chapter is a real-life example—part of an approach to evaluation in science recommended at a faculty of education!) The first step is to be clear about

- the real purpose for assessing student learning, and
- your role in that purpose—a role that is not, primarily, that of an accountant.

Assessment Is a Human Process

Assessment, as Ruth Sutton observes, is about communication:

> *It is worth noting, right from the start, that assessment is a human process, conducted by and with human beings, and subject inevitably to the frailties of human judgement. However crisp and objective we might try to make it, and however neatly quantifiable may be our "results," assessment is closer to an art than a science. It is, after all, an exercise in human communication. (Sutton, 1992)*

Note the number of times the word *human* is used in this quotation. Effective teaching and learning is a uniquely human endeavour. Ask a group of adults to identify one significant learning from their school years, and most will struggle to answer the question. Rephrase the question as, "Who was the best teacher you had in school?" and watch the responses flow. People remember for a lifetime the teachers with whom they identified on a human level.

Effective teaching and learning is a uniquely human endeavour.

▲ **Assessment is "an exercise in human communication."**

Question

When students come into my class in September, they're all at different levels. How do I deal with this?

Answer

The first order of business is assessing students' prior knowledge and skill levels so that you can make appropriate instructional decisions. This involves conducting a wide variety of initial or diagnostic assessment activities. (See Assessment for Learning: Diagnostic Assessment, page 33.)

Assessment is more than maintaining records of daily credits and debits.

So why are educators, often at the expense of the human dimension, preoccupied with crispness and objectivity in assessment?

Accountability, consistency, reliability—these have become the buzzwords of assessment. These variables are extremely important when developing rigorous external tests, such as those adopted by most states and provinces across the United States and Canada. If valid comparisons are to be made about students from different jurisdictions, then reliability in the test instruments is essential.

However, in day-to-day classroom assessment, reliability is *not* the most important variable. If it were, we could maximize reliability by removing the teacher from the equation, replacing existing forms of assessment with multiple-choice items, running the scoring sheets through a scanner, and using a computer to generate the overall scores.

Reliability would soar, but at what price?

The teacher's role is not that of accountant, and assessment is more than maintaining records of daily credits and debits.

Many years ago, I taught in a small residential school for adolescents with severe learning disabilities. Among my students was Trevor, a bright young man from northern Ontario. All of the students in my class required individualized programs specific to their needs. I yearned, however, to read and explore one piece of literature together so that we could all talk about it and share ideas. The George Orwell classic, *Animal Farm*, seemed the right choice because of its Grade 6 reading level and themes appropriate for all ages.

Since none of my students was an independent reader, I began by reading the first two chapters, embellishing the text with appropriate animal noises and actions. I stopped at a suspenseful spot and said, "Right, now each one of you is going to become a character on the farm. Each day, I'll read part of a chapter and stop at a crucial point. Your task is to continue the chapter, from your own point of view as Napoleon, Boxer—whomever you have chosen to be. Your residence counsellors will scribe for you if you need them to."

Within a few days, each of the boys was writing first-person narrative in his journal, taking up the action from where I had stopped. A week or so into this process, Trevor's counsellor, Andy, came to see me before school and said, "Damian, I need to talk to you. It's about Trevor."

"Trevor?" I said, surprised. "What has Trevor done?"

"It's not a behaviour problem," Andy assured me. "It's just that for the past three nights, there's been a knock at my door, somewhere between midnight and three a.m. It's Trevor. He can't sleep because he wants me to read to the end of the chapter to see if his prediction about what is going to happen to him is correct!"

Although Trevor had come to the school functionally illiterate, he was now so determined to learn to read and write that his counsellor was complaining of being woken up in the middle of the night to help him decode the words on the page!

Drama, I discovered, was another way to encourage greater self-esteem among students like Trevor. It allowed these students to explore ideas that were not so accessible through reading. One week I taught the boys some basic mime routines, such as pushing against a wall and climbing a ladder. During the first lesson, I realized that none of the students was watching me. It took only a few seconds to figure out why: all eyes were on Trevor as he inched his way along an imaginary ledge. Trevor was such a natural mime that I invited him to teach the next day's class. After some gentle persuasion, Trevor agreed. The next day, he needed only a few minutes of preparation before he was running the show and doing a fine job. The impact on Trevor's self-esteem was huge and long-lasting.

What do these two anecdotes about Trevor have to do with assessment? They highlight the important relationship between needy students and a teacher searching for ways to promote successful learning. At the residential school office, Trevor's student record took up the better part of a file drawer, and contained countless assessments documenting in precise detail his deficits—a litany of what he could not do. Sadly, his file was not unique. Over time, the teachers in that school began to realize that significant success would require uncovering each student's strengths and working through them to address their needs—in short, the human side of assessment.

> ## Tips for Teaching
>
> Have you ever heard of the word *assidering*? Probably not—it's a made-up word. As Grant Wiggins (1993) observes, the word *assess* comes from the Latin, *assidere*, meaning "to sit with." Taking the time to sit beside students at every possible opportunity may be the best way to provide them with the feedback they need to improve their learning.

▲ **"Assidering:" Sitting with students to help them improve.**

Accumulating Points versus Learning

Two different conceptualizations of assessing student leaning have just been outlined:

- a process that encourages students to accumulate as many points in as short a time as possible
  OR
- a process that promotes learning

Few teachers have just the first purpose in mind. Yet reporting deadlines and school structures often conspire against your intended purpose for assessment: to promote learning. You may begin a new term committed to using assessment to further student learning, only to find yourself abandoning that purpose to generate sufficient marks for the first report card grade. This resource is intended to help you

- use assessment information to promote learning and
- use assessment data to record students' progress toward specific targets and performance levels.

Note the words *assessment information* and *assessment data*. This difference provides a clue for proceeding on this journey together. Students require information about the quality of their work in order to improve their performance. This information tells students

- what they have done well
- what they are struggling with
- what they need to do to improve

Teachers gather all kinds of information about students' performance by observing, listening, and reading the work that students produce. Effective assessors select from this mass of information details to communicate to students, either verbally or in writing. This is assessment *information*.

Report cards, on the other hand, require only a summary of this information in the form of achievement *data*. These data are used to inform parents and guardians how well their child is performing, relative to a set of known standards. They may be expressed as numerical scores, letter grades, rubric levels, or a combination of these. For the most part, data are merely numbers—a form of shorthand.

Students require information about the quality of their work in order to improve their performance.

Many Purposes for Assessing Student Learning

Of course, the purpose of assessment is not either to improve student learning *or* to gather assessment data. Clearly, assessment has many different purposes. When I pose the question, "Why do we assess students' learning?" at the beginning of a workshop, teachers typically respond with answers such as the following:

- to make decisions about how best to instruct students
- to inform students, parents, and other adults about what has been learned and what still needs to be learned
- to inform students, parents, and other adults about the quality of what has been learned; that is, to answer the question, "Is it 'good enough'?"
- to inform students, parents, and other adults about how much growth has occurred
- to make promotion decisions with respect to the next grade, the next level of education, or graduation
- to select students for placement in specific programs
- to motivate students to work harder.

All of these purposes are sound, important, and defensible. However, problems arise when there is no clarity around the purpose of a specific assessment and, as a consequence, students are unclear about the purpose for the assessment.

Coach, Judge, or Both?

When determining the purpose for a specific assessment, you need to ask yourself: is the primary purpose for assigning a task to provide students with an opportunity to practise new skills or for students to demonstrate how well they have mastered this skill? In the first instance, the teacher needs to assume the role of coach; in the second instance, he or she needs to assume the role of judge.

Teachers are called on to both coach and judge, but recent research has indicated conclusively that when teachers combine these two functions, students make much smaller learning gains than when the functions are separated. The Assessment Reform Group at King's College in London, England, has confirmed that when students receive feedback alone, they make greater gains in learning than students who receive both feedback and a score (Butler, 1988).

Figure 2-1: Coaching and Judging Functions—Fused and Separated

▲ Coaching and judging functions fused: Smaller learning gains

▲ Coaching and judging functions separated: Great learning gains

It is common practice in intermediate and senior grades for work to be returned with numerous comments and suggestions for improvement (feedback), as well as a numerical score or mark (judgement). How do most students respond to this confusion? Ironically, it is usually only the highest-performing students who take the time to read all the feedback from their teacher *and* look at their mark. The poorest performing students may skip all the comments and go directly to the last page to see what mark they received.

Although marks can actually limit learning by drawing students' attention away from feedback for improvement, students typically demand marks. Maybe you have already experienced the frustration of offering a student detailed feedback on an assignment only to find yourself derailed with a terse, "Yeah, but what *mark* did I get?" At a recent workshop, one teacher said to me, "I agree completely with what you're saying. But unless I put a mark on everything, students won't do the work."

Sometimes I ask teachers if they have ever tried leaving marks off student work. Many have not. I ask how they would respond if a new player joined the soccer team and announced, "Don't expect me to attend practice—I just show up at the games." Once the laughter subsides, they usually say they would tell the player, "No practice, no play."

In the context of the classroom, early drafts of work may be considered "practice" time for students. This work deserves both written and one-on-one feedback to help the student improve. Only the "game" work, however, receives a score. When teachers use this approach, they often find that students, regardless of grade level, perceive the advantages of all the free coaching and practice runs provided during class time, and start to take the feedback as seriously as marks or similar rewards.

To sum up, each assessment task must be approached according to its specific purpose. If the purpose is summative, that is, to summarize learning after a significant period of instruction, then focusing on marks may be appropriate. If, on the other hand, the primary purpose for the assessment is to improve student learning, then, instead of a score, provide information to students about what they have done well, what they are struggling with, and what they need to do to improve.

In the next section, you will have the opportunity to explore how the two phases of assessment *for* learning—diagnostic/initial assessment and formative assessment—can promote student learning.

ASSESSMENT FOR LEARNING: DIAGNOSTIC ASSESSMENT

Initial or **diagnostic assessment** marks the starting point of each student's learning journey.

That starting point involves a complex interplay of elements, including prior knowledge and skills, attitudes, and personal experiences. Each of these elements needs to be considered during an initial assessment, especially one that occurs at the start of a new school year. This section explores a number of initial assessment strategies that reflect the impact of attitudes and personal experience on the quality of information to be gathered about students' current levels of understanding and current skills. Throughout this section, the terms *initial* or *diagnostic* assessment are used to refer to the assessments that occur at the beginning of a new school year, or at the beginning of a new unit or topic of study, before instruction begins.

A Note of Caution

One of the pitfalls of diagnostic assessment is the affective impact it can have on students. For example, teachers may mistakenly assume that it is more important to identify what students do *not* know and are *not* able to do, than what they *do* know and *are* able to do. They may assume that only by uncovering learning deficits will they know how to proceed with appropriate instruction. This may work well with students who are secure and highly motivated, have supportive adults at home, and possess the necessary resources to help them learn. But diagnostic assessment used primarily as a process to determine learning deficits can prove intimidating and discouraging for those students who know they aren't successful at school. For these students, assessing for learning gaps will only confirm how incompetent they are.

One important factor influencing the initial or diagnostic assessment is students' attitudes about a subject, which are shaped by previous experiences with that subject. These experiences can generate motivation,

> **Big Idea Recap**
>
> Assessment *for* learning is assessment designed primarily to promote students' learning. Assessment *of* learning is assessment designed to determine how much learning has occurred after a period of instruction.

Video Clip 1:

Gr. 7/8 Mathematics— Using Assessment for Different Purposes
14:11 minutes

positive attitudes, and even excitement. They can also foster anxiety, fear, and embarrassment. Students who are anxious about their ability to learn or who already dislike a particular subject will likely struggle without some sort of intervention.

Students' prior experiences with learning may also be influenced by environmental or cultural experiences at home. For example, students whose family members are avid campers may have viewed more animal habitats than students who live in the city. This doesn't necessarily mean that the camper will be more motivated than the city dweller to learn about science, but those prior experiences may influence a student's motivation.

STORIES FROM THREE CURRICULUM AREAS

This section will consider how prior knowledge and skills, attitudes, and previous experiences all come into play during initial assessments in three curriculum areas: mathematics, science and English.

Diagnostic Assessment: Mathematics Example

When researching the Thomson-Nelson K–8 mathematics resource, the development team interviewed scores of teachers across Canada. One tool requested by many teachers was a definitive diagnostic test for each grade that would enable them to quickly identify students' weaknesses in mathematics at the beginning of the school year. To meet this need, the resource provides a *Getting Started* lesson to introduce each unit and to serve as an initial assessment opportunity. The *Getting Started* lesson was designed to

- engage students
- activate their prior knowledge about the topic (what they have learned previously, can remember, or know intuitively)
- enable the teacher to observe, listen, and record each student's strengths and areas of need

The significant characteristic of the *Getting Started* lesson is that it is not a rigorous diagnostic test. Why was this model chosen? Clearly, teachers need to discover as early as possible what procedural skills and conceptual understanding students have. But in our haste to gather this information, we sometimes compromise both the validity and the reliability of our assessment. If students experience anxiety as a result of having to face a battery of diagnostic tests during the first few days of a new term, then the information gathered may not accurately represent what they know and are able to do.

Alternatively, a teacher using the *Getting Started* lesson at the beginning of a unit might say to his students: We are going to spend the first day getting to know each other's strengths and needs. I'm going to ask you to talk to me, to write some things, and to show me what you can do. I just need to see how much you already know and can do so that I can plan my lessons better. So, let's get started.

Figure 2-2 illustrates a *Getting Started* lesson for grade 3. Notice how this instructional approach utilizes students working in pairs as well as teacher-led discussion. Moreover, the context for the lesson is familiar. The intent is to engage students, put them at ease, and build confidence, thereby discovering what they know and can do in terms of addition and subtraction.

Whenever I use testing to assess the strengths and needs of students in September, they clam up or get so nervous, they can't do anything!

A SPECIAL EDUCATION TEACHER

Figure 2-2: "Getting Started" lesson

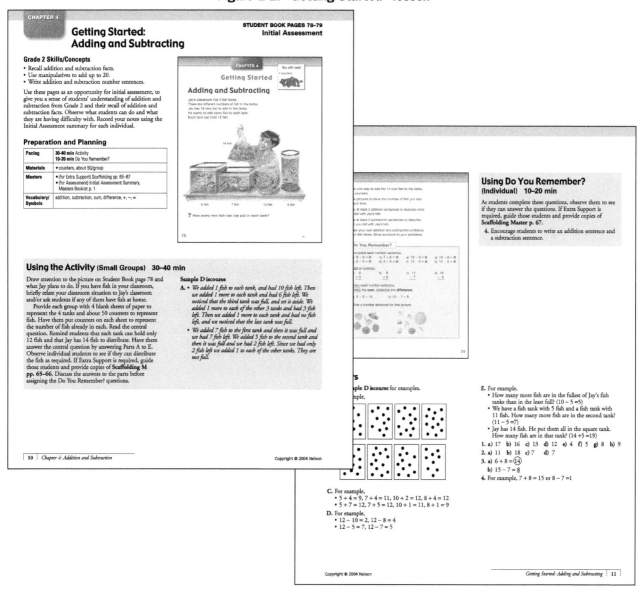

Information gathered early in the term about each student's strengths and needs, as well as information gathered at the start of a new unit or strand, may be recorded anecdotally on a tool such as the *Initial Assessment Summary*.

Figure 2-3: Initial Assessment Summary

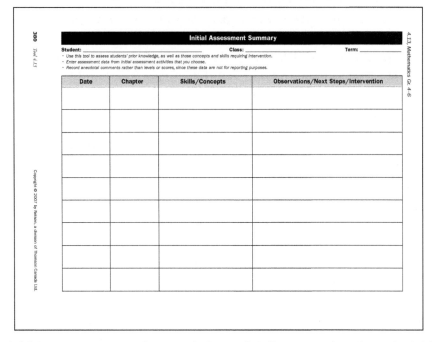

▲ **Initial assessment may be recorded anecdotally on a tool such as the Initial Assessment Summary**

The *Getting Started* activities include opportunities for students to talk about their current understanding and to demonstrate their current skills, as well as opportunities to write. This is essential, since many students are unable demonstrate what they know and can do if the initial assessment only requires them to write.

When conducting an initial assessment, it is wise to avoid jumping to conclusions about students' misconceptions and skill deficits. This can lead to oversimplifying the precise nature of students' misconceptions, or the reasons why students make certain errors. The following case study illustrates in detail the problem with oversimplification.

It illustrates two important purposes for initial or diagnostic assessment: to find out students' current skills and conceptual understanding with respect to a new topic, and to activate student's prior knowledge. Remember, initial assessment is strictly assessment for learning. In other words, it plays no part in determining report card grades.

| CASE STUDY 1 | **Allan Tackles Fractions** |

Allan is about to be introduced to decimal fractions. Ms. Lee, his teacher, doesn't expect her Grade 4 students to have much prior knowledge of this topic because they have never worked with decimals before. During a brainstorming session, Ms. Lee discovers that her students have seen decimals in the context of dollars and cents but they don't know the term *decimal point* so she writes the term on the board.

She asks her students about terms such as *tenth* and *hundredth* and finds that they are familiar with them, but only in the context of ordinals (e.g., someone is 10th in line). Ms. Lee realizes this could be an issue since fractions provide a different context for using this terminology. She discusses this difference with her students. Then she begins teaching the unit.

A few days later, Ms. Lee notices that Allan is struggling when comparing decimals. She sits with Allan and uses a picture to show him that 0.2 of a square takes up much more space than 0.02 of a square. Allan agrees and Ms. Lee moves on to the next student.

When she checks Allan's work at the end of the class, she discovers that he has shown 0.03 as greater than 0.3. Both Allan and Ms. Lee are frustrated. She is puzzled about Allan's lack of understanding, especially after she had modelled problems for him using pictures and he appeared to understand. Allan has previously been successful in math, yet this new concept is eluding him.

Finally, days later during a conversation with his teacher, Allan finally says in frustration, "But 0.03 has more digits than 0.3 so it must be bigger!" All along, Allan's experience with evaluating the size of whole numbers had been interfering with his ability to evaluate the size of decimal numbers. Despite the fact that Allan's previous teachers had carefully taught place value while having him compare whole numbers, he had figured out that he could also count digits when determining the relative value of decimals. Allan needs to learn that while this strategy works fine in some cases, it does not work in all cases. He has over-generalized a rule and must learn about the exceptions to that rule.

Initial assessment information assists teachers both in overall planning and in customizing instruction to meet individual needs. We know students are more successful when they can relate new learning to something they already know. We also know that students are more motivated when they are able to connect new learning to something familiar in their personal lives. The two purposes of initial assessment go hand in hand and illustrate how assessment and instruction work together to improve learning.

Diagnostic Assessment through Problem Solving

Another way to activate and assess prior knowledge is to involve students in an investigation or problem-solving experience related to a new topic of study. Open-ended tasks are the most effective since they provide for a range of student performance, enabling the teacher to assess each individual's current level of knowledge and skill. An open-ended task is characterized by the following conditions:

- It requires more than the recall of facts and skills.
- It is instructive to both the student and the teacher.
- It can be solved in more than one way or allows for more than one correct answer.

To design such tasks, it is first necessary to anticipate the prior knowledge students may bring to the task. Perhaps you are about to begin a unit on addition of fractions with your class. You think your students know some simple fraction terminology and notation. You are wondering whether any students have experience adding fractions or are able to use a strategy to approximate a procedure for adding fractions. An open-ended task will engage students and get them excited about the topic while also providing you with information about their prior knowledge.

For example, you could ask students to colour a picture on a 10 x 10 grid and then describe their pictures using numbers. As students work, ask questions to probe for more knowledge:

- "Who can use fractions to tell about their picture?"
- "How would you write the fraction you just named?"
- "Who can tell an addition story about their picture? Who can do it using fractions?"

After students have completed the task, collect samples of their work, prepare a summary of the collective class knowledge, and prepare anecdotal notes about individual students' successes and difficulties.

Using a Journal to Uncover Experiences

To uncover students' attitudes toward and prior experiences with fractions, you might ask them to respond to appropriate prompts in a journal. Simple prompts such as the following work best:

- "What do you know about fractions?"
- "Where have you seen fractions?"
- "What you would like to know about fractions?"

Students' journal responses, combined with the work completed on the 10 x 10 grid, will provide a rich bank of initial assessment information about prior knowledge and skills, attitudes, and experiences. There isn't anything complicated about these activities. They are intended simply to get students thinking about the new topic to be learned, and to provide you with information about their strengths and areas of need.

Diagnostic Assessment: Science Example

There is no single best strategy for assessing prior knowledge and understanding. However, it is important to activate students' knowledge and understanding before assessing it. In active learning situations, students also stimulate one another's thinking. As teacher, you may be able to gather a rich bank of initial assessment information in a relatively short period of time.

A commonly used prior-knowledge assessment tool is a KWL chart. (See Figure 2-4.)

KWL stands for **K**now, **W**ant to Learn, and **L**earned. In the **K** section of the chart, students contribute ideas they already know about the topic. In the **W** section, they anticipate and record items to be learned and also share their interests about the topic. The **L** section, completed at the end of the unit of study, is where students record their new learning and answers to questions they posed in the W section.

Creating KWL charts as part of the initial assessment phase of the learning cycle is motivating to students and provides a window for assessing the collective prior knowledge of the class. They can be created in cooperative groups using chart paper and markers. In primary classrooms, the teacher can take on the role of recorder.

Video Clip 2:

*Gr. 3/4 Science—
Co-operative Group
Learning and
Assessment*
09:31 minutes

Tips for Teaching

Activating prior knowledge is akin to priming a pump. The word *activate* suggests that students are actively involved with the content being assessed. It also implies that students will be *doing*, not merely reading and writing. Finally, as the assessor, you will be watching and listening, not simply marking.

Figure 2-4: Sample KWL Chart for a Grade 2 Science Class

What We **K**now	What We **W**ant To Know
· Spiders are different colours.	· Which spiders are poisonous?
· Spiders are different sizes.	· How do spiders make webs?
· Spiders live outside.	· How do spiders eat?
· Spiders are poisonous.	
· Spiders have 8 legs.	
· Spiders are scary.	

What We Learned

· Only a few spiders are poisonous to humans like the Black Widow and the Brown Recluse.

· Spiders eat by sucking up the liquid in the body of the prey.

· Spider silk is a liquid that hardens when it is pulled out of the spinnerets.

· Different spiders make different kinds of webs.

The teacher reviewing the chart shown in Figure 2-4 can see that students bring some knowledge about spiders to the lesson, as well as some misconceptions (spiders have eight legs, spiders are poisonous), and certain attitudes (spiders are scary). Through further probing, the teacher will undoubtedly reveal that students' prior knowledge is based on the experiences they have had with this content.

Other graphic organizers such as mind maps, word webs, and Venn diagrams may be used in similar ways. The choice of organizer will depend on the topic and the age level of the students being assessed.

The Importance of Probing Questions

Research by cognitive psychologists tells us that understanding students' prior knowledge is critical to the process of effective teaching and learning (Graves, 1983; Inhelder & Piaget; 1958; Dewey, 1938; Vygotsky, 1986). However, it is also true that students' prior knowledge may be incomplete or based on a misconception. Asking probing questions is an effective strategy for uncovering misconceptions. This holds true during the initial assessment phase of learning, as well as throughout the learning cycle.

Teachers often ask if it is acceptable to prompt students during an assessment. Some teachers are concerned that intervening during assessment may impact the validity of the assessment data. While this may be true when conducting summative assessments, probing for information during initial assessment is not only acceptable but necessary.

Often students have knowledge about a topic that they have tucked away and not used for some time. Jogging a student's memory with carefully chosen questions not only enables you to include this information in your assessment summary, but also prepares the learner to readily associate new information with previously learned material. Returning briefly to the topic of fractions, probing questions about students' prior experiences could be:

■ What about the clock? Does it use fractions?
■ What about when you play the piano? Does this involve fractions?
■ Do you hear any fraction words when you play sports?

Information gathered through probing questions can provide the teacher with vital insights about the instruction that individual students require to promote understanding.

Diagnostic Assessment: Language Arts/English Example

Initial assessment in language arts is less concerned with established content than with the skills students are expected to acquire on a grade-by-grade basis. The skills associated with language arts strands—reading, writing, listening, speaking—are essential to student success in all school subjects, as well as in the world beyond school. For this reason, initial assessment in language arts class assumes critical importance.

Perhaps the best advice for the teacher when conducting initial assessment in language arts is the following: *Talk less and listen more.* Students should spend the first few days of a term writing about whatever they choose, reading aloud whatever they choose (to you and their peers) and talking about whatever interests them. By providing many opportunities for your students to demonstrate expressive and receptive literacy skills using materials and contexts that are familiar to them, you are far more likely to gather valid assessment information than if you present them with challenging and unfamiliar tasks.

If this approach sounds unstructured and informal, it is! However, the goal is to create an atmosphere of trust in the classroom, not one of intimidation. As students begin to feel comfortable with what you are asking them to do, patterns will begin to emerge. Those who are highly skilled will be easy to identify as will those who are struggling. Take note of those students who experience difficulty with these unstructured opportunities so that you can plan further, in-depth diagnostic assessment.

> ### Tips for Teaching
>
> Ensure that you have multiple sources of evidence, gathered on different occasions, and ideally involving different modes (write, do, say) before drawing conclusions about an individual's level of understanding or skill.

 CASE STUDY 2 | **Getting Through to Carlos**

Mr. Martell, a Grade 6 teacher, loves the first days of a new school year, even though he finds the adjustment to the rigours of teaching leaves him very tired at the end of the day. But he is always fascinated by the new students that he meets. He relishes the time spent getting to know them.

He particularly enjoys his language arts class and the opportunity to discover all of the varied interests of his students. Far from feeling rushed to assign the first piece of writing, Mr. Martell encourages his students to tell him what they most like to read or to write about. By letting his students decide on the content at the beginning of the year, Mr. Martell has found that he is able to gather much more valid information about his students' reading, writing, and speaking skills.

One year, however, Mr. Martell couldn't get through to one boy, Carlos. By the end of the first week of school, Carlos had yet to open his mouth or produce any written work. On Monday of the second week, Mr. Martell came to class wearing the colours of West Ham United, his favourite soccer team in England, his birthplace. They had just been promoted to the premier league after languishing in the lower division for several years. And the previous Saturday, they had beaten none other than Manchester United!

Carlos ambled into class late and shuffled to his desk. When he saw his teacher's shirt, he sniffed. "Just lucky," he said, loud enough for Mr. Martell to hear.

Other than responding to his name during attendance each day, these were the first words that Carlos had spoken since the beginning of the year. Each language arts class began with ten minutes of quiet reading and Mr. Martell seized the opportunity to go over and speak with Carlos.

continued

"How do you know about West Ham United, Carlos?" he asked.

"I know everything about soccer, everywhere," replied Carlos.

"I bet you don't know what the West Ham United theme song is," challenged Mr. Martell.

"I'm Forever Blowing Bubbles," said Carlos.

"Wow! So, who's your team, Carlos?"

"Benfica," said Carlos.

"Bet you've never heard of a player named Eusebio," challenged Mr. Martell.

"'Course I have," replied Carlos. "My dad has a book about him."

"Have you read it?" asked Mr. Martell.

"I tried, but it's got some big words."

"Bring it in tomorrow and I'll help you with it," he said.

Carlos did bring his dad's book on Eusebio the next day. Over the next two weeks, Mr. Martell spent time teaching him word-attack strategies to facilitate his reading. Given his passion for soccer, Carlos was highly motivated to read this text, despite the fact that he found it challenging.

Tips for Teaching

Engaging the student, activating prior knowledge and skills, building trust, and improving self-esteem—these are the essentials when conducting initial assessment with students, especially with reluctant and struggling students.

The Importance of Anecdotal Records

To be useful to teachers for planning purposes, initial assessment information should be anecdotal in nature. While initial assessment may include some skills-based activities, truly useful information will include details about the quality of work and prior knowledge observed, as well as things *not* observed that you expected to see. Because the information gathered during initial assessment serves only to inform instruction (or possibly to communicate a specific concern to a parent or to support staff), numerical scores, letter grades, and achievement levels have no place in this type of record-keeping.

While assessing, teachers use a variety of recording devices including sticky notes, clipboards, and index cards. However, at the end of an initial assessment session, it is helpful to consolidate all the information gathered so that you can see where the class is at a glance, and highlight specific concerns involving individual students. (See Figure 2-5.) Such consolidation of assessment information will make it easier as you begin planning for instruction, as the following example shows.

As an introduction to a unit on fractions, students in Mrs. Wilson's grade 3 class were asked to use pattern blocks to create a picture showing what they knew about the fractions 1/2, 1/3, and 1/6.

When the students had completed their pictures, Mrs. Wilson asked the students at each table to talk about their picture with their classmates. As the students talked, she moved from table to table, observing, listening, and asking probing questions such as

- Could you tell the group about your picture?
- How did you show 1/2, 1/3, and 1/4?
- What can you tell us about the different sizes of the fractions?
- Where do you use fractions at home or at school or in your neighbourhood?

Mrs. Wilson's summary of this initial assessment appears in Figure 2-5.

\multicolumn{5}{c}{**Figure 2-5: Summary of Initial Assessment**}
Student Name	**Content Knowledge/ Skills**	**Attitudes**	**Experiences**	**Notes**
Adam	· identifies simple fractions, knows 2 halves make a whole, writes simple fractions (1/2, 1/4) correctly	· is a little nervous about sharing ideas · thinks fractions are confusing	· takes piano lessons · recognizes that we use fractions when telling time	· needs to build confidence— ask him to share some of his music understanding with the class
Megan	· could orally use simple fractions to tell about her picture but could not record · seemed confused about which is more: 1/4, 2/4	· was very engaged in the drawing aspect of the task · happy to share her ideas	· knew the word "quarter" from working with money, but doesn't seem to see its connection to fractions	· will need to have early concepts of comparing simple fractions reinforced before using pattern blocks

If the research has shown conclusively that feedback in words, not scores, is the single most powerful strategy we have for improving learning, do we have any choice but to find ways to integrate this practice into our teaching on a regular basis?

Video Clip 3:

Gr. 5/6 Science— Communicating Performance Standards to Students
12:39 minutes

ASSESSMENT FOR LEARNING: FORMATIVE ASSESSMENT

The second phase of assessing *for* learning is formative assessment -- assessment that is ongoing throughout the term. We have already seen that feedback is a critical characteristic of assessment for learning (Black & Wiliam, 1998). There are two significant variables if such feedback is going to maximize student learning:

- quality of the feedback
- how soon students receive feedback following completion of a task

These variables call into question the practice of returning marked work days or even weeks after it has been completed. Are there strategies that you can integrate into existing classroom routines to provide students with immediate feedback? The following case study presents an easy-to-implement language arts strategy that does just that.

| CASE STUDY 3 | **Rethinking Her Approach** |

Ms. Fortier had been teaching Grade 7 for several years in Vancouver suburb when she felt the need for a change and moved to a downtown school. In her previous school, she had come to rely on a formula for teaching language arts classes that involved teaching a lesson, assigning a written piece of work for the next day, collecting it, marking it, and returning it to students.

The first day in her new school, Ms. Fortier taught a lesson. There were a number of behavioural disruptions during the class, but she finished the lesson and assigned the evening's work. The following day, only two students turned in the completed work.

So she tried again—with the same result— the next day.

"All these students are going to fail!" Ms. Fortier told herself anxiously. She re-examined her carefully planned program and the texts that she had given so much thought to selecting. Then

and there, she decided it was time for a change.

After chatting with colleagues who had taught at the school for several years, Ms. Fortier decided to move her writing program from students' homes into her classroom. At least twice each week, she ran Writers' Workshop. This involved no formal, whole-class instruction. Instead, she worked with individuals or small groups of students to help them improve their writing.

At the beginning of class, students went directly to the filing cabinet and retrieved their portfolios. Students could work alone or with the writing partner they had been assigned for that month. They worked on different pieces, depending on individual pacing. There was a set of required pieces for the portfolio, as well as a specified number of self-selected pieces.

During the Writers' Workshop, Ms. Fortier held five-minute conferences with eight students who had been told two days before that

continued

they would be meeting with her. She focused on each student's strengths and areas of need, and made suggestions for improvement. Her record-keeping was purely anecdotal. She used a simple exercise book—one page for each student. (See Figure 2-6.)

If a student needed more than five minutes of her time, or if someone who had not been booked for a conference required help on that day, that student would "take a number" and wait for Ms. Fortier to finish her scheduled conferences.

By the time she was ready to complete the first set of report cards, Ms. Fortier had met with every student three times and had compiled a rich bank of anecdotal assessment data. This helped enormously with her report writing, and gave her lots of information to share on Parents' Night.

Figure 2-6: Ms. Fortier's Anecdotal Assessment Data

Name: Chris Lee
Year: 2005

Date	Focus	Strengths	Needs	Next Steps
September 20	Biography	- lots of detail - very honest	- run-ons - spelling a problem	- mini-lesson with Chris and others with same need
October 11	Short story (1st draft)	- shows imagination! - lots of material!	- run-ons and fragments - spelling	- peer-assessment with Alex

Teachers with large classes may find that conferencing with small groups of students is more manageable than one-on-one conferencing. In fact, learning can actually increase when a conference involves the teacher and several students talking about their work. Many struggling students fail not because they cannot do the work, but because they do not do the work. Ms. Fortier's strategy helped her students structure their time so that many of them completed assignments for the first time in their lives, allowing them to leave behind the cycle of failure that may have characterized their school experiences. It provided each student with immediate, anecdotal feedback and also identified early on any students who were having difficulty.

Tips for Teaching

To minimize interruptions and maximize the effectiveness of one-on-one conferencing, the rest of your class must be engaged in quiet work. Clear guidelines for behaviour during conferencing can be developed jointly with students and posted in the classroom.

If assessment for learning is going to improve student achievement, teachers need carefully planned opportunities to provide feedback to their students.

If assessment *for* learning is going to improve student achievement, teachers need carefully planned opportunities to provide feedback to their students. In addition to conferences, the following strategies are also effective:

- If all or most students in a class are having difficulty with a specific task, examine a sample of student work on the overhead projector.
- Spend time as a class analyzing anchor papers. An anchor paper is a sample of student work that represents a specified level of achievement, such as Level 3 on a four-point scale. Anchors help students and teachers develop shared understanding about the performance indicators associated with specific levels of achievement.
- If a group of students is struggling with a particular concept or procedure, you may wish to teach a mini-lesson to this group while the rest of the class completes other work.

Assessment *for* Learning: Am I Already Doing It?

Video Clip 1:

Grade 7/8 Mathematics—Using Assessment for Different Purposes
14:11 minutes

Often teachers leave a staff development session feeling that they should change everything they are doing when, in fact, much of their current practice is working well. However, it is useful to take an inventory of one's practice from time to time.

In the following checklist, notice the key word *routinely*. Each of the practices referred to in these questions needs to be a routine part of any classroom regimen. Take a few moments to reflect on the following questions, then read the discussion of the importance of each strategy that follows.

Implementing Assessment for Learning in Your Classroom
1. Do I routinely share learning goals with my students so they know where we are heading?
2. Do I routinely communicate to students the standards they are aiming for before they begin work on a task?
3. Do I routinely have students self- and peer assess their work in ways that improve their learning?
4. Does my questioning technique include all students and promote increased understanding?
5. Do I routinely provide individual feedback to students that informs them how to improve?
6. Do I routinely provide opportunities for students to make use of this feedback to improve specific pieces of work?

1. Do I routinely share learning goals with my students so they know where we are heading?

How many times have you been asked by a student, "Why are we doing this?" or "What do I need to know this for?" Students ask these questions when they don't know the destination of their learning. If, on the other hand, you plan your program by using "backward design"—beginning with an essential question and a culminating performance task that will provide evidence of students' learning—then you and your students are much more likely to work together in a focused, meaningful way. (See Chapters 13 and 14 to learn about the backward design model.)

To help students stay focused, provide them with one, two, or, at most, three overarching goals that will let them see where they are headed. For example, the planning template in Figure 2-7 identifies the big ideas and essential skills of a Grade 2 Science unit, and describes a culminating task for the unit. The teacher communicates these elements to students at the beginning of the unit, so they know where they are headed and can see the purpose of each day's work.

Figure 2-7: Template 3: Unit Culminating Assessment Task Plan

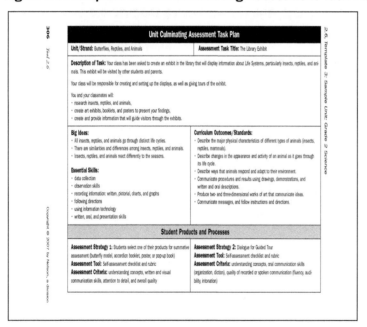

Template 3: Sample Unit Culminating Assessment Task Plan, p. 306

Video Clip 3:

Gr. 5/6 Science— Communicating Performance Standards to Students
12:39 minutes

2. Do I routinely communicate to students the standards they are aiming for before they begin work on a task?

Students deserve to know your standard for quality before they begin a task. They need to know what elements of a given task are important, and how you will assess the quality of each element. Checklists, rubrics, and exemplars are the tools we use to clarify standards for our students. The following case study shows how one class assembled the criteria for a rubric together.

Students deserve to know your standard for quality before they begin a task.

Mrs. Wearn's Grade 3 class had been studying Growth and Change in Plants. The students gathered data on the kinds of trees growing in the park next to the school. They graphed this data and compared their findings. As a class, they planted an amaryllis bulb and observed and recorded its growth. They investigated what plants need in order to grow and the effect on plant growth when those needs aren't provided for.

As a culminating task, Mrs. Wearn had each student plant a vegetable or flower seed, care for it, observe and record its growth, and make a final report. The curriculum outcomes that she wanted to assess were as follows:

- Design and conduct a hands-on inquiry into seed germination or plant growth.
- Record relevant observations, findings, and measurements, using written language, drawings, charts, and graphs (e.g., produce a series of drawings to show a plant at different stages of development).
- Communicate ideas and information for specific purposes and to specific audiences.
- Use visual material to reinforce a message.

Together, Mrs. Wearn and her students developed a rubric that would be used to assess their work. Here is part of their conversation.

"After we plant our seed, we are going to need to keep track of its growth," said Mrs. Wearn. "What are some ways we might do that?"

"You could draw pictures to show how your plant changes as it grows," said Ahmed.

"I'm going to make a graph like we did for the amaryllis to show how much it grows," Becky interjected.

"Those are two excellent ways to keep a record," said Mrs. Wearn. "Perhaps we should include both ways in our record-keeping part of the report. What else do we need to consider? What about telling our group what we learned? How should we do that?"

"Use your best talking voice," offered Matty.

"That's right. What kinds of things will you say and do?"

"You need to tell about how the plant grew and changed using the pictures and graphs," said Anna.

"Excellent. Anything else?"

"You need to remember to say everything in order so everyone understands what we learned," she added.

"Those are all very good ideas so let's make a list of the criteria we will include in our rubric."

Mrs. Wearn wrote on chart paper:
- Gathering information—pictures and graph
- Presenting information
- Supporting information with data

Under Mrs. Wearn's guidance, students were able to make decisions about what criteria would be assessed and what a good report would look like.

TOOL 3.20

*Rubric for "Plants"
(Culminating Task:
Grade 3), p. 361*

Rubric for "Plants" Culminating Task: Grade 3				
Criteria	**Level 1**	**Level 2**	**Level 3**	**Level 4**
Inquiry Question	· has difficulty posing an inquiry question	· needs some help to pose an inquiry question	· independently poses an inquiry question	· poses a thoughtful inquiry question
Gathering Data/ Record Keeping	· has difficulty gathering, recording, and organizing data	· needs some help to gather, record, and organize data	· independently gathers, records, and organizes data	· gathers, records, and organizes data effectively
Communication	· has difficulty organizing ideas and presenting information	· needs some help to present information so it is clear and organized	· independently presents information	· presents information clearly and precisely
	· ideas are incomplete or unclear	· ideas are simple but are in order	· ideas are clear and make sense	· ideas are well-expressed and are interesting
Information Supported with Data	· has difficulty using data collected to support ideas presented	· needs some help to use data collected to support ideas presented	· independently uses data collected to support ideas presented	· effectively uses data collected to support ideas presented so they are clear and informative

3. Do I routinely have students self- and peer assess their work in ways that improve their learning?

Recently, I visited a language arts class where students were delivering brief oral book reports to the whole class. Each student's report was between one and two minutes in length. After a dozen reports, many of the youngsters put their heads down on their desks and dozed off. Upon hearing the words, "I would strongly recommend this book to anyone," all heads would jerk up in response to the end of the report. At this point, students were asked to assign the report a score out of 10.

Later, the teacher and I met to debrief the lesson and talk about how we could change her approach. We discussed the following alternatives:

Video Clip 3:

Gr. 5/6 Science—Communicating Performance Standards to Students
12:39 minutes

- Divide the class into three groups so that each student presents his or her report to only nine students instead of 29. This reduces students' anxiety level and cuts the time required to hear from all students by two-thirds. Circulate from group to group to monitor and assess the presentations.
- Provide a checklist and discuss it with students before they prepare their reports.
- During each presentation, the other students must listen and observe carefully, referring to the checklist as a guide. Afterwards, they provide feedback to the speaker by stating
  - what the speaker did well
  - what the speaker struggled with
  - what the speaker should do next time to improve

The teacher commented on how much more engaged the students might be using this approach to peer assessment, instead of assigning a score out of 10 to every one of their classmates.

4. Does my questioning technique include all students and promote increased understanding?

From a pedagogical point of view, the most appropriate purpose for asking questions aloud in class is to check whether everyone understands what they are being taught. However, it is almost impossible to check that everyone understands a particular concept without questioning each student individually. What happens when a teacher poses questions to the whole class?

Typically, only a few students respond. They tend to fall into two groups: keen students who know the answer and assertive students who enjoy attention and feedback from the teacher and their peers. Far too many students in large classes remain uninvolved in the oral question-and-answer sessions that are an integral part of most lessons.

Here are some suggestions for improving your oral questioning technique so that it allows you to assess the level of understanding of all your students.

Tips for Improving Oral Questioning Practice

- Find alternatives to asking questions of the whole class. Your attention needs to be directed toward those students who do not have the answer. Use a Think-Pair-Share strategy (Kagan, 1990) to ensure that all students are engaged in thinking: *Yesterday, we learned why the air temperature is higher in the summer months and lower in the winter months. In your notebook, jot down the reasons for this, without looking at your notes. Then turn to your partner and compare your answers. In two minutes, I shall ask for responses.* You can use this strategy either at the beginning of a lesson to activate prior knowledge or as a check for understanding after teaching new material.

- Try not to always be the "quarterback" at the front of the class. Hand the responsibility for talking over to the students. For example, start the lesson with the following: *Take a moment to jot down a question you have about what we learned in science yesterday. Then work with a partner and take turns asking each other your question. See if you can answer your partner's question! In five minutes, I'll ask for volunteers to share their questions with the class.* Yes, the volume in your classroom will increase, but on-task noise is good!

- Conduct frequent checks for understanding of the whole class when you are teaching new material: *We have been talking about the difference between perimeter and area. If you have a clear understanding of this difference, thumbs up. If you sort of understand this difference, but need some clarification, thumbs horizontal. If you don't understand this difference, thumbs down. Show me your thumbs.* As a follow-up, convene a small study group of the students who showed you their thumbs down or horizontal and work with them until they understand the concept.

- While students are working, move around the room and ask individual students a key question for understanding. On any given day, ask only a sample of the students in your class. Keep a simple log to ensure that you monitor every student's understanding on a regular basis over the course of a term.

- Build in regular, one-on-one conferences with individual students to check their understanding of key concepts. These may be very brief—one minute or less. This strategy will ensure that there are no "invisible" students in your class.

The key to learning is identifying students' misconceptions and helping them to arrive at correct conceptions.

Video Clip 1:

Gr. 7/8 Mathematics— Using Assessment for Different Purposes
14:11 minutes

5. Do I routinely provide individual feedback to students that informs them how to improve?

Black and Wiliam (1998) have determined conclusively that feedback in the form of words—what the student did well, did poorly, and needs to do to improve—is one of the best strategies for improving student learning. Moreover, the sooner this feedback follows the completion of a task, the more effective it is in improving students' work. These conclusions should lead all of us in the field of education to promise the following:

> *I must schedule time to meet with each of my students regularly, one-on-one, however briefly, to monitor their understanding and to provide specific anecdotal feedback about their work.*

Nothing in any curriculum document is as important as this decision, which you alone have the power to make. Do not hesitate to schedule Writers' or Readers' Workshops, or Sustained Silent Reading time. Schedule whatever you need into your long-range instructional plan so that you will have regular opportunities to meet individually with students to provide them with this vital feedback.

6. Do I routinely provide opportunities for students to make use of this feedback to improve specific pieces of work?

Picture a coach working with a young gymnast. Imagine the athlete completing a vault and hearing her coach tell her what she did well and what she needs to change to improve the vault. And then try to imagine the coach *not* saying, "Okay. Now let's see you try that vault again." In the world of sports, when coaches work with athletes, they observe their performance, provide them with feedback, then automatically tell their athletes to repeat their performance to see if the feedback has been incorporated.

In classrooms, do teachers automatically require students to repeat a task or revise a piece of work, incorporating the feedback they have been provided with? Too often, the feedback is, "Too bad you didn't do very well, but we have to move on. There's lots to cover." Yet, without the opportunity to improve their work, the feedback students receive is fruitless.

Summary

- The question, "Why do we assess student learning?" examined the many purposes for assessment.

- Teachers are under pressure to assess for instructional purposes and to gather scores and marks. (This resource can help you assess for both purposes.)

- There are many approaches to initial or diagnostic assessment that can be used in mathematics, science, and English/language arts.

- Initial or diagnostic assessment activates students' prior knowledge, understanding, and experience and helps teachers and students focus instruction and learning on specific areas of need.

- It is essential to pay careful attention to students' attitudes, and the prior experiences that have shaped those attitudes when conducting initial assessment.

- Simple strategies for conducting assessment *for* learning can be used on a daily basis in the classroom.

Applying My Learning

Using Tool 1.2: *Implementing Assessment for Learning in My Classroom* (page 289), examine your current practice. Your responses will likely affirm many of the strategies you are using at present, but you may also discover some areas where you may wish to make changes to better respond to the needs of your students. After you have finished checking off your responses, describe on this chart or in another notebook what you plan to do to include this strategy in your repertoire.

1.2, Chapter 2 Review

Implementing Assessment *for* Learning in My Classroom

Use the chart below to examine your current practice. Your responses will likely affirm many of the strategies you are presently using, but you may also discover some areas where you may wish to try different approaches to better meet the needs of your students.

After you have finished checking off your responses, describe on this chart or in a journal what you plan to do to include this strategy in your repertoire.

R = Rarely   S = Sometimes   C = Consistently

Do I?	R ✓	S ✓	C ✓	Notes
1. Do I share learning goals with my students so they know where we are heading?				
2. Do I communicate to students the standards they are aiming for **before** they begin work on a task?				
3. Do I have students self- and peer assess their work in ways that improve their learning?				
4. Does my questioning technique include **all** students and promote increased understanding?				
5. Do I provide individual feedback to students that informs them how to improve?				
6. Do I provide opportunities for students to make use of this feedback to improve specific pieces of work?				

Tool 1.2 **289**

TOOL 1.2

Implementing Assessment for Learning in My Classroom, p. 289

ADAPTING ASSESSMENT FOR STUDENTS WITH SPECIAL NEEDS AND SECOND LANGUAGE LEARNERS

 BIG IDEA 3 Assessment must be balanced, including oral, performance, and written tasks, and be flexible in order to improve learning for all students.

CHALLENGES OF ADAPTING ASSESSMENTS

Students with special needs, and those whose first language is neither English nor French, face particular challenges when required to complete assessment tasks. For this reason, it is often necessary to adapt your assessment approach for these students.

When adapting a task, how can you ensure that the assessment information gathered is both **valid** and **reliable**? Generally, it is important to

- minimize any disadvantages students may experience as a result of their exceptionality
- encourage students to persevere at a task, while ensuring that they are not deceived about their present level of achievement
- maximize students' opportunity for success
- avoid invalidating the assessment results by over-compensating for the students' special need

Adapting assessments for students with special needs is not always an easy process, especially when conducting assessment of learning—assessment that will be used for grading. One of the most important factors to consider is bias.

Sources of Bias

In an effort to be fair to students with special needs, we may inadvertently introduce bias into our assessments. Typically, the bias derives from one of two sources:

1. A lot of support is provided during the assessment, but the assessment data is reported without reference to the support given.
2. The student is unable to demonstrate a particular learning target, so the task is modified significantly, but the achievement is reported in terms of the original learning target.

The following illustration sheds light on these two sources of bias.

Emily, a bright Grade 3 student, has been identified as having a communication exceptionality that severely limits her ability to express her ideas in writing. During the first term, the teaching assistant in Emily's class scribes for Emily whenever the teacher assigns written work.

When Emily's parents receive her first report card, they are surprised to see that Emily has an "A" in the Writing strand. There is no mention in the anecdotal comment about the accomodations that were made to her program. Clearly, the grade is misleading, and serves only to confuse both Emily and her parents. While Emily's ideas may be original, thoughtful, and creative, it is essential to record the amount of support she received in order to be able to commit her ideas to paper.

In the second term, the teaching assistant is no longer in Emily's class so her teacher allows Emily to present her ideas orally in one-on-one conference situations as a substitute for the writing assignments. Once again, Emily's parents are surprised by the report card since there is no indication that Emily has not completed the requirements associated with the Writing strand. Again, the information from the assessment is misleading. It suggests to Emily and her parents that she has achieved a particular achievement target when, in fact, she has not.

The message to be derived from this example is simple: communication of assessment information must be perfectly clear to students and their parents and guardians in terms of what has been achieved and how much support was provided to enable the students to achieve a given learning target.

> ### Tips for Teaching
>
> Your own eyes and ears are your most important assessment tools! Trust them to help you identify students who need special consideration. The information you gather through observation will be invaluable, both to identify needy students and to plan to meet their needs. Your observations will also augment your written assessments when it is time to conduct them.

DIAGNOSTIC ASSESSMENT FOR STUDENTS WITH SPECIAL NEEDS

Try to record your observations of students with special needs during the first few days and weeks of a new term. The set of observations that you record for each student will not only make it much easier to adjust instruction to meet the needs of each individual, but it will also help you adapt both assessment for learning and assessment of learning tasks.

Figure 3-1 provides a model for observing students in three areas:

- responses to instructional materials and tasks
- responses to others in the class
- responses to environmental variables

Figure 3-1: Classroom Observation of a Student with Special Needs

TOOL 1.3

Classroom Observation of a Student with Special Needs, p. 290

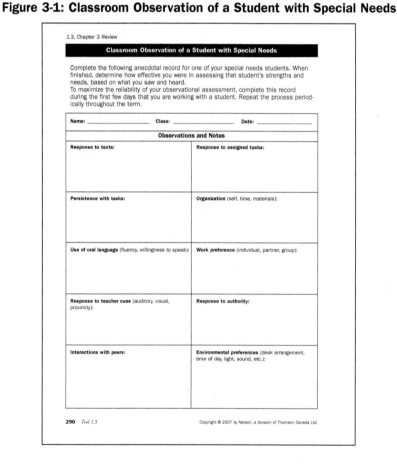

Adapting Specific Tasks for Students with Special Needs

Assessment involves determining what an individual knows and can do. However, unless a student can accomplish a task to some degree, you will not be able to get the information you require. The biggest challenge involved in assessing students with special needs is balancing your specific assessment demands with the amount of support, or **scaffolding**, that you provide to help students succeed on a given task. Scaffolding refers to the supports provided to increase the likelihood that a student will succeed at a task.

CASE STUDY 1 | **Scaffolding Jeremy's Learning**

Jeremy is in Grade 3. He has been identified as learning disabled with significant deficits in language processing, expressive language, and mathematical computation. His teacher, Mr. Kandil, has just taught a lesson about adding and subtracting tens and has assigned the class several questions to help them practise what they have just learned and demonstrate their understanding. One of the more challenging questions reads: *Alex's class received 90 pins altogether from Nova Scotia and Alberta. They have 50 more Nova Scotia pins than Alberta pins. How many Alberta pins do they have? Show your work.*

Mr. Kandil expects that Jeremy will have great difficulty with this problem because it requires students to both process the language of a word problem and make the necessary computations symbolically. Nevertheless, he decides to let Jeremy attempt the problem. The solution Jeremy provides is 90 – 50 = 40.

Jeremy's faulty solution tells Mr. Kandil that Jeremy has not understood the nature of the question and that he has focused on the number 50 as the number to be added or subtracted. Mr. Kandil pulls out the base ten rods and asks Jeremy to count out 9 rods to represent the 9 tens. With the rods, Mr. Kandil uses a guess-and-test strategy with Jeremy, writing out the number sentence for each guess. Jeremy realizes that he needs 5 more rods than Mr. Kandil. With each combination that Jeremy writes as a number sentence, Mr. Kandil asks Jeremy if he has 5 more rods than he has.

Jeremy begins to demonstrate understanding, and Mr. Kandil decides he is ready to

return to the original problem using the base tens as a model. Mr. Kandil has Jeremy write down the number sentences so that he can see the connection between what he is modelling and how the model is represented symbolically.

Mr. Kandil has Jeremy use manipulatives to help him solve the problem and uses the guess-and-test strategy as scaffolding. Mr. Kandil's assessment of Jeremy's learning up to this point has been assessment *for* learning. As long as his assessment purpose remains formative, then it is appropriate to use as much or as little scaffolding as necessary.

Figure 3-2: Addition-and-Subtraction Example from *Nelson Mathematics*

Name: _____   Date: _____

STUDENT BOOK PAGE 83

8. Alex's class received 90 pins altogether from Nova Scotia and Alberta. They have 50 more Nova Scotia pins than Alberta pins. How many Alberta pins do they have?

To find the number of Alberta pins, do the following.

• For which province are there more pins? _____

• Use an organized list to guess and test.

Try 5 Alberta pins for a first guess.

Keep guessing as many times as you need until you have found the number of Alberta pins that meet both conditions.

Guess	Number of pins altogether	Number of Alberta pins	Number of Nova Scotia pins	Does it work?
1	90	5		
2	90			
3	90			
4	90			

Students truly understand a concept when they are able to apply it to solve a new and unfamiliar problem without prompting or other kinds of support.

Scaffolding is always intended to be temporary. More scaffolding may be required early in the learning process as students construct knowledge and understanding and skills. But just as scaffolding is gradually taken down as the construction of a building proceeds, so can scaffolding gradually be removed as students progress.

Students truly understand a concept when they are able to apply it to solve a new and unfamiliar problem without prompting or other kinds of support.

When Mr. Kandil wants to assess Jeremy's understanding of the concept and procedures involved in adding and subtracting tens—in other words, when he is conducting assessment *of* learning—he may avoid the use of scaffolding. Only then will Mr. Kandil be able to draw valid conclusions about Jeremy's learning. If the results of the assessment indicate that Jeremy is unable to complete a set of specified tasks successfully, then both Jeremy and his parents need to know this information.

Jeremy's case study highlights the need for clarity in three areas:

- What is the learning target?
- What is the student's success in achieving this target?
- What support has been provided to enable the student to achieve the target?

Assessment Q & A

Question

How do I know what my students are capable of doing if I always have to provide support to them?

Answer

When students are learning new concepts and acquiring new skills, lots of support or scaffolding must be provided. As the child becomes more proficient, you can gradually remove the scaffolding. During this stage of learning, assessment is not judgmental—in other words, do not judge the student's knowledge or skill against a standard. Rather, simply coach the student toward proficiency.

Once the student has had time to practice and you have provided plenty of feedback, assessment of learning can occur. At this point, it is important to find out how proficient the student is without support. If the student is unsuccessful, provide scaffolding once again, or perhaps try reteaching the concept using a different instructional approach. At this stage of learning, the goal is for the student to demonstrate the desired concept or skill without support.

As a rule of thumb, when assessing *for* learning, provide as much support as necessary to promote learning; when conducting assessment *of* learning, find out what the student knows or is able to do with minimal or no support from you. This does not preclude providing accommodations for students with special needs. You can provide additional time on a task, or allow the student to demonstrate learning without scaffolding through a different mode (for example, orally instead of in writing).

Ways to Adapt Assessment Tasks

There are three possible levels of intervention to be considered when using an assessment task with students who have special needs or are second language learners: accommodation, modification, and substitution.

Accommodating the Student

Accommodation involves using the same assessment task used with other students while accommodating the needs of the special student by providing supports such as more time, visual aids, or a different environment in which to complete the task. The demands of the task, as well as the achievement target to be assessed, remain the same.

Modifying the Task

Modification involves changing the assessment task in some way to increase the likelihood that the student will succeed. The task itself is made less challenging for the student. For example, if the assessment is an open-ended problem-solving task, scaffolding may be provided that directs the student through the steps in the problem-solving process. While such scaffolding may enable the student to complete the task, the addition of the scaffolding changes the achievement target. No longer is the student's ability to apply the problem-solving model independently being assessed. Such modifications must be noted and reported if the task is to be used as part of the student's assessment *of* learning.

> **Tips for Teaching**
>
> Be sure to consult your provincial and local policy documents for specific interpretations of the terms *accommodation, modification,* and *substitution.*

Levels of intervention: accommodation, modification, and substitution.

▲ **An open-ended or problem-solving task can be modified through scaffolding that directs a student through the appropriate steps.**

Substituting the Task

Substitution involves replacing a given task with one more appropriate for the student with special needs. For example, suppose that you plan to have your Grade 5 social studies students deliver brief oral presentations to their classmates about early civilizations. This task is designed to provide assessment information about two learning outcomes:

- show how innovations made by various early civilizations have influenced the modern world (understanding)
- speak clearly when making presentations (skill)

Linh has recently arrived from China. She studied English in China but is reluctant to speak in front of the class. Substitution for this task could involve replacing the oral report with a written one, or Linh could be permitted to present her material in a one-on-one situation at the end of class.

Both substitutions would only enable you to assess Linh on the first outcome, not the second. However, you could replace the second outcome with the following one: communicate information, explain a variety of ideas and follow the teacher's instructions.

Elements of an Assessment Task that May be Adapted

The next step is to determine which aspects of an assessment task may be accommodated, modified, or substituted for students with special needs, or second language learners.

Adapting the Mode

Mode is the means by which a student demonstrates learning, such as writing, doing, or speaking. The mode of an assessment task may be adapted to suit an individual or group of students. For example, if a student has deficits in written communication, then it is acceptable to adapt the mode by allowing the student to demonstrate learning through oral communication.

The only exception to this type of adaptation would be if a learning target specifies a writing skill. For example, if students are to demonstrate they can organize and develop ideas using paragraphs, then it is not possible to assess this particular student at this point in time. No one—neither the student nor the parents and guardians—would benefit from being told the student has demonstrated this skill.

Adapting the Strategy and Tool

Strategy refers to the task students complete, such as participating in a debate, conducting research, or writing a paragraph. The strategy can be adapted or substituted to suit an individual or group of students. For example, Linh's teacher (see example above) can substitute either a written report or a one-on-one session for a class oral presentation.

Tool refers to the instrument used to record assessment information, such as a checklist, rubric, or scoring guide. When the strategy has been adapted or substituted, the tool should also be adapted. The rubric developed for the class presentation could still be used to assess Linh's performance, but only those criteria that deal with the student's understanding can be checked. The criteria addressing presentation skills must be omitted.

Figure 3-3: Partial Rubric for Oral Presentations				
Criteria	**Level 1**	**Level 2**	**Level 3**	**Level 4**
Understanding (include when assessing Linh's performance)	· ideas and arguments reflect limited knowledge of topic	· ideas and arguments reflect some knowledge of topic	· ideas and arguments reflect solid knowledge of topic	· ideas and arguments reflect sophisticated knowledge of topic
Communication (omit when assessing Linh's performance)	· speech lacks fluency, expressiveness, and/or audibility	· speaks with some fluency, some expression, and is audible some of the time	· speaks fluently, expressively, and audibly	· speaks fluently, expressively, and audibly in ways that are highly effective

Adapting the Constraints

Constraints are the limits imposed on an assessment task. These include

- time constraints (e.g., "You have 60 minutes to complete this task.")
- materials/resource constraints (e.g., "You may not use calculators for this task.")
- level of independence (e.g., "You may work with a partner.")

The constraints of an assessment task may be adapted to suit an individual or group of students. Many students with learning disabilities are at a disadvantage because of the time constraints imposed on assessment tasks. Allow these students to take the time they need to complete the task successfully by, for example, providing an alternative setting supervised by a teaching assistant. Second language learners could be permitted to use an English/first language dictionary in order to reduce their language disadvantage.

Many students with learning disabilities are at a disadvantage because of the time constraints imposed on assessment tasks.

CASE STUDY 2 | Kam's Book of Newts

Kam is eight years old, and a student in Mr. Land's Grade 2/3 class. He has recently been identified as learning disabled. He struggles with reading and writing and sees himself as "not good at that stuff."

Kam receives extra help in language arts through resource withdrawal, but Mr. Land wants Kam to be included in the class's writing program. He believes that all students can improve their writing skills if they have lots of opportunities to write, and that a community of writers fosters positive energy. Kam struggles to write narratives but has a keen interest in anything creepy or crawly.

Mr. Land provides time each day for his students to engage in the writing process. This includes

- self-selection of a topic
- development of ideas
- conferences with the teacher
- revision and editing
- publishing of polished work

Mr. Land has gathered a small group of students who require extra support and benefit from having the writing process modelled for them. For example, they are learning how to use a graphic organizer to gather information in point form and develop those ideas into

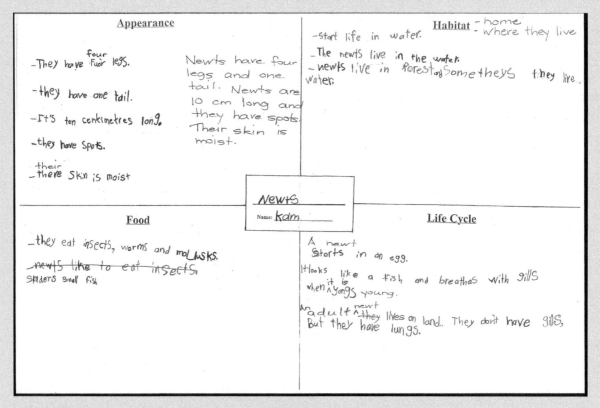

Appearance

-They have four legs.

-they have one tail.

-It's ten centimetres long.

-they have spots.

-there their skin is moist

Newts have four legs and one tail. Newts are 10 cm long and they have spots. Their skin is moist.

Habitat – home – where they live

-Start life in water.

-The newts live in the water.

-newts live in forest and some theys they live water.

Newts

Name: Kam

Food

-they eat insects, worms and molusks.

-newts like to eat insects.

spiders small fish

Life Cycle

A newt starts in an egg.

It looks like a fish and breathes with gills when it is yongs young.

An adult newt they lives on land. But they have don't have gills, lungs.

▲ **Mr. Land showed Kam how to use this graphic organizer to record his research information and support his sentence-writing.**

continued

sentences. The goal is to publish their ideas in a book.

Mr. Land showed Kam how to use this graphic organizer to record his research information and support his sentence-writing.

Kam is able to gather information from simple text and, with assistance from the resource teacher, more complex text. He struggles to create sentences, but once he is shown some strategies (e.g., combining the heading, "where they live" with the jot notes to make a sentence), he is able to plan a book about newts. He benefits as well from a conference with Mr. Land on turning simple sentences into more complex ones.

Mr. Land also encourages Kam to use the text and a word bank to check his spelling. Kam was not familiar with this process, but once he saw how little effort it took to copy words from the text, he applied the strategy.

Mr. Land used three criteria to assess the students' work:

- quality and communication of ideas and information
- use of conventions
- use of sources to check spelling

As he assessed Kam's work, Mr. Land noted that although Kam required assistance to organize and communicate his ideas and to apply expected conventions of spelling and punctuation, the finished product met the outcomes. Rather than penalize Kam for his lack of writing skills, Mr. Land accommodated his needs by providing assistance. His goal was to continue to provide Kam with appropriate tools and strategies so he could work more independently as time progressed.

As Kam experienced success in writing a book about newts, he also began to see himself as a writer. Using the strategies provided, his writing skills improved and he started planning his next book-on bats!

Adapting the Marking

Finally, the **marking** of an assessment task may be adapted to suit an individual or group of students. This entails using your professional judgement when examining student work and deciding to what extent an individual's exceptionality may have interfered with his or her performance. For example, consider the situation of Kam, described in Case Study 2.

A Note of Caution

While it is often necessary to adapt your assessment approach for students with special needs and second language learners in the ways described above, it is equally important to follow through with appropriate grading and reporting so that achievement information communicated to parents and guardians is clear, valid, and reliable. (See Chapter 15 for more details about this issue.)

Summary

- The goal of adapting assessment for students with special needs and second language learners is to obtain accurate information about achievement while controlling for the learning deficits that may interfere with a student's performance.

- Clarity of communication to parents and guardians about what students can and cannot achieve is essential.

- Observational assessment yields critical information that helps teachers adapt instruction and further assessment.

- Scaffolding refers to the supports that may be provided to help students complete a learning task. When scaffolding is provided for an assessment *of* learning task, caution should be exercised to ensure that achievement data are not distorted.

- There are three levels of intervention when adapting assessment to suit students with special needs and second language learners: accommodation, modification, and substitution. These terms may differ according to provincial and/or local policy.

Applying My Learning

Focus on one of your own students with special needs and complete Tool 1.3: *Classroom Observation of a Student with Special Needs* (page 290). Once you have completed this task, determine how effective you were in assessing that student's strengths and needs, based on what you saw and heard.

TOOL 1.3

Classroom Observation of a Student with Special Needs, p. 290

1.3, Chapter 3 Review

Classroom Observation of a Student with Special Needs

Complete the following anecdotal record for one of your special needs students. When finished, determine how effective you were in assessing that student's strengths and needs, based on what you saw and heard.

To maximize the reliability of your observational assessment, complete this record during the first few days that you are working with a student. Repeat the process periodically throughout the term.

Name: _____   Class: _____   Date: _____

Observations and Notes

Response to texts:	**Response to assigned tasks:**
Persistence with tasks:	**Organization** (self, time, materials):
Use of oral language (fluency, willingness to speak):	**Work preference** (individual, partner, group):
Response to teacher cues (auditory, visual, proximity):	**Response to authority:**
Interactions with peers:	**Environmental preferences** (desk arrangement, time of day, light, sound, etc.):

The following text appears on the poster in the image:

Dichotomous Key for the Dogs of...

1a. If the dog is a solid color, go to 2.
1b. If the dog is not a solid color, then go to 4.
2a. If the dog is black, it is a Newfoundland.
2b. If the dog is not black, go to 3.
3a. If the dog has a brown body and black face, it is a pug.
3b. If the dog has a brown body and only black on nose, it is a cocker spaniel.
4a. If the dog is black, white, brown, has long ears, it is a basset hound.
4b. If the dog has no brown, go to 5.
5a. If the dog is spotted, it is a dalmatian.
5b. If the dog has all white legs and black ears, it is a S...

BIG IDEAS
in Section 2

1. Assessment serves different purposes at different times: it may be used to find out what students already know and can do; it may be used to help students improve their learning; or it may be used to let students and their parents know how much they have learned within a prescribed period of time.

3. Assessment must be balanced, including oral, performance, and written tasks, and be flexible in order to improve learning for all students.

4. Assessment and instruction are inseparable because effective assessment informs learning.

5. For assessment to be helpful to students, it must inform them in words, not numerical scores or letter grades, what they have done well, what they have done poorly, and what they need to do next in order to improve.

6. Assessment is a collaborative process that is most effective when it involve self-, peer, and teacher assessment.

7. Performance standards are an essential component of effective assessmen

Section 2

My Assessment Toolkit

Section 2 of this resource introduces the nitty-gritty of assessment—issues that you, the teacher, confront daily.

Chapter 4 addresses the question of standards—what they are, why we need them, and how to use them.

Chapter 5 deals with the "who" of assessment. What are the do's and don'ts of self- and peer assessment? Can very young children reliably assess their own work or the work of their peers? This chapter also examines a controversial area—assessment in co-operative group learning situations.

Chapter 6 addresses the need for a balanced approach to assessment. *Balance* means ensuring that your assessment toolkit requires students to show and talk about their learning, as well as write about it.

Chapters 7, 8, and 9 deal with performance assessment, oral assessment, and written assessment respectively. Chapter 10 shows you how to integrate all three assessment modes successfully in your classroom. Chapter 11 discusses the use of student portfolios and shows why this strategy is effective for connecting teaching, learning, and assessment.

Chapter 12 provides guidelines for the selection and creation of assessment tools to complement a balanced set of assessment strategies. This chapter helps you navigate the contentious waters of rubric assessment and reviews the use of more conventional tools such as running records, rating scales, and checklists.

Chapter 4

STANDARDS

 BIG IDEA 7 Performance standards are an essential component of effective assessment.

Ask people on the street what they think the word *standard* means and you will hear many responses. A standard could be

- the best example of something ("the standard of excellence in the auto industry")
- the level of performance you must reach ("Olympic standard")
- average ("standard hotel room")
- a flag carried at the front of an army
- what you expect everyone to be able to do ("You must meet the minimum standards of literacy.")
- something people should be striving toward for the good of all ("raising standards")

The Collins Gage Dictionary defines *standard* as "a level of quality or measurement."

Today's educators refer to the following standards in education:

- **Curriculum/content standards** are descriptions of what students are expected to learn, including knowledge, skills, and values, beliefs, and attitudes.
- **Performance standards** are descriptions of prescribed levels of performance on a task or series of tasks.

CURRICULUM/CONTENT STANDARDS: WHAT DO STUDENTS NEED TO LEARN?

There are many terms used to refer to the knowledge, skills, values, and attitudes that students are expected to acquire as a result of the teaching and learning process: *learning outcomes, expectations, learning targets, content standards*. Whatever the term used, curriculum or content standards answer the question, "What should be taught?" They are designed to maximize the overlap of the three circles shown in Figure 4-1.

Figure 4-1: Intended Curriculum, Taught Curriculum, Learned Curriculum

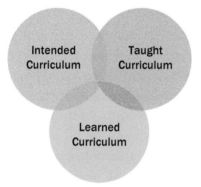

The *intended curriculum* refers to the mandated provincial, state, or local curriculum that describes what students are expected to learn. The *taught curriculum* refers to what teachers actually deliver in the classroom. The *learned curriculum* refers to what students learn as measured by a variety of assessments. Ideally, these three are the same as shown by the three overlapping circles in Figure 4-2.

The learned curriculum refers to what students learn as measured by a variety of assessments.

Figure 4-2: Intended, Taught, and Learned Curriculum

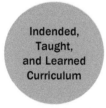

▲ **100 percent overlap of intended, taught, and learned curriculum**

Fragmentation of Teaching, Learning, and Assessment

The past decade has seen a trend in North America toward a much more prescriptive curriculum, a trend reflected in the specific learning outcomes that detail what students are expected to learn on a year-by-year basis. One of the dangers of a highly prescriptive, standards-driven curriculum is that teaching, learning, and assessment can become fragmented. In jurisdictions where curriculum documents resemble shopping lists of outcomes, teaching can become micromanaged and assessment reduced to checking off the outcomes as they are "covered."

Moreover, teaching that is governed by countless specific outcomes ignores what is known about the developmental nature of learning.

Recent advances in technology, such as hand-held computing devices, also threaten to promote micromanagement of teaching and assessment. It is very tempting to enter a class list of names into such a device, along with a list of learning outcomes, and then "assess on the fly" by recording an achievement level for each student on each outcome.

The negative implications of such an approach—for students and teacher—can be profound. Students suffer when they are deprived of the rich engagement that comes from working on complex, meaningful tasks. Instead, they face too many small, isolated exercises matched to one or two specific learning outcomes. Teachers suffer because they are overwhelmed with record-keeping. Consider, for example, a Grade 7 Ontario teacher with responsibility for teaching mathematics, science and technology, language arts, and social studies. If there are 30 students in the class, this teacher would be responsible for managing 10 890 pieces of assessment data—even if there were only one assessment per learning outcome for each student!

The Whole Versus the Sum of Its Parts

Aside from the logistics, there are other issues at stake. Enslavement to learning outcomes runs contrary to what is known about learning. True learning—in the sense of true understanding—involves more than demonstrating isolated bits of knowledge or skill at a given moment in the classroom. True learning is a *gestalt*. That is to say, when students truly understand a significant concept or master a set of skills, the "whole" of that learning is more than the sum of its parts.

Consider, for example, the skills and knowledge associated with effective oral communication. One curriculum document states that by the end of Grade 5, students will

- use vocabulary learned in other subject areas in a variety of contexts
- use appropriate words and structures in discussions or classroom presentations
- identify appropriate uses for slang and colloquial language
- use complex syntactical structures (e.g., principal and subordinate clauses)
- use tone of voice, gestures, and other non-verbal cues to help clarify meaning when describing events, telling stories, reading aloud, making presentations, stating opinions, etc.
- speak clearly when making presentations

While these specific outcomes describe some of the essential skills associated with oral communication, truly effective oral communication involves more than a checkmark beside each individual skill. When students have truly mastered oral communication, they can integrate these skills and adapt them easily to a variety of tasks. In other words, they can generalize their learning to new situations. One of the dangers of micromanaging teaching and assessment is that it can obscure this essential requirement of learning: that students be able to apply their learning in unfamiliar situations.

An essential requirement of learning is that students be able to apply their learning in unfamiliar situations.

Applying Learning to New Situations

In mathematics, a lesson often begins with a sample problem illustrating a new procedure. After being taught how to complete the procedure, students work through a series of problems similar to the ones shown in the teaching example. Based on their responses to the problems, the teacher will determine whether the students have understood the new learning.

Video Clip 1:

Gr. 7/8 Mathematics— Using Assessment for Different Purposes
14:11 minutes

▲ **The ability to estimate in real-life situations indicates true understanding of the skill of estimation.**

As an example, estimation is a skill students are taught and use frequently in math class. But what if you showed a child $20 and asked him to estimate whether you had enough money to pay for the groceries in your cart? Only those students who truly understand the skill of estimation will have no trouble moving from the classroom context to real life. Unless students demonstrate that they can adapt and apply new learning in situations that are not identical to the example provided in the lesson, there is no evidence of true understanding, only evidence that they can follow a script. Well-designed culminating performance tasks provide students with opportunities to synthesize a number of skills and concepts they have learned during a unit or a term, but also require them to apply their learning in a new or innovative way.

Similarly, planning units of study around rich assessment tasks ensures that teaching and learning remains focused on significant and enduring concepts and skills, rather than on numerous outcomes. In my workshops, I help teachers understand how to teach to outcomes and expectations, but also how to focus their assessment on students' performance on meaningful tasks. (This process is described in detail in Chapters 13 and 14.)

PERFORMANCE STANDARDS: HOW GOOD IS "GOOD ENOUGH"?

A true standard ... points to and describes a specific and desirable level or degree of exemplary performance—a worthwhile target irrespective of whether most people can or cannot meet it at the moment.

GRANT WIGGINS, 1998

Performance standards are publicly known, agreed-upon statements about the quality of student work and achievement. Prior to the 1980s, educators relied most often on what are known as *norm-referenced standards* to measure student achievement. How well one student was doing was determined by comparing him or her to a known group of students. This known group could be the rest of the class, all the students in the grade, or a representative sample of students in the same province or from across the country. In each case, the standard against which student achievement was measured was the performance of a selected group of students.

In a norm-referenced model, the actual standard of quality may vary, depending on the sample of students. "A" quality work for a Grade 7 student in one year may be superior or inferior to "A" quality work from the previous or succeeding year. (See Chapter 15 for a detailed discussion of grading.)

Most provinces and states now advocate that *criterion-referenced standards* be used to measure achievement on classroom assessments. This involves measuring student performance against pre-determined indicators (criteria) that describe one or more levels of quality. In a criterion-referenced model, the standard is known and remains relatively constant—"relatively" because the agreed-upon standard may periodically be adjusted up or down, depending on students' success in meeting a given standard.

Most provinces have also established criterion-referenced standards as part of their large-scale assessment initiatives. Some provinces, such as Ontario, have identified a provincial standard—Level 3 on a four-point scale—for both provincial and classroom assessments.

Comparing Norm- and Criterion-Referenced Assessment

There is an important difference between these two approaches to assessment. With norm-referenced assessment, the range of student achievement is distributed across a full range of possible scores. A few students will achieve a perfect score, a few will achieve very low scores, and the majority will be somewhere between these two extremes. (See Figure 4-3.) Norm-referenced assessment emphasizes the gap, or *range*, between high- and low-achieving students.

Figure 4-3: Range of Student Achievement in a Norm-Referenced Approach

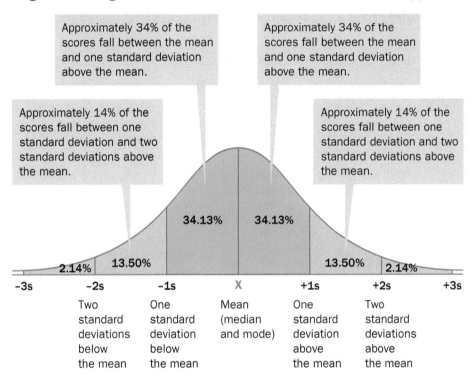

Approximately 34% of the scores fall between the mean and one standard deviation above the mean.

Approximately 34% of the scores fall between the mean and one standard deviation above the mean.

Approximately 14% of the scores fall between one standard deviation and two standard deviations above the mean.

Approximately 14% of the scores fall between one standard deviation and two standard deviations above the mean.

| 2.14% | 13.50% | 34.13% | 34.13% | 13.50% | 2.14% |

| −3s | −2s | −1s | X | +1s | +2s | +3s |

| | Two standard deviations below the mean | One standard deviation below the mean | Mean (median and mode) | One standard deviation above the mean | Two standard deviations above the mean | |

With criterion-referenced assessment, it is expected that most students will reach the standard because it represents the level of achievement that students must meet if they are to be successful in the next grade, or once they leave school. Teachers need to do everything in their power to help all students achieve the standard by the end of the term or school year. In short, criterion-referenced assessment aims to close the gap or range between high- and low-achieving students. Consequently, one of the benefits of criterion-referenced assessment is that it can help to eliminate competition and may, in fact, foster cooperation among students. Rather than competing for the few "As" that will be awarded, all students are encouraged to strive for success.

With criterion-referenced assessment, it is expected that most students will reach the standard because it represents the level of achievement that students must meet if they are to be successful in the next grade, or once they leave school.

Video Clip 3:

*Gr. 5/6 Science—
Communicating
Performance Standards
to Students*
12:39 minutes

*Most students can hit the
target if they can see it
clearly and if it stays still.*

RICK STIGGINS

Using Performance Standards in the Classroom

Provincially developed performance standards are often broad and generic, since they must suit a wide range of schools and communities. Responsibility for developing classroom-ready assessment tools based on these standards, such as checklists and rubrics, typically falls to writing teams at the local or school level (see Chapter 12). Classroom teachers can use these tools to help students improve their learning.

Teachers are primarily responsible for ensuring that students know the standards for quality work. They are also responsible for using these standards on a day-to-day basis to help students improve their work. Teachers' responsibilities concerning performance standards may be seen in terms of before, during, and after teaching, as shown in Figure 4-4.

Figure 4-4: Teacher Responsibilities for Performance Standards

Before Teaching	During Teaching	After Teaching
• understand and internalize what the standards look like • create and/or locate appropriate assessment tools (checklists, rubrics) based on the mandated standards • ensure that students and parents and guardians are familiar with the tools (e.g., post rubrics on the bulletin board; provide students with copies of rubrics; send rubrics home) • collect samples of student work anchored to the standards from previous classes (students require examples of work at different levels to see what it looks like)	• use the tools (rubrics, checklists, exemplars) to provide regular feedback to students in individual or small-group conferences • teach students the skills required to use these tools for self-assessment and for peer assessment (students need to be able to assess their own work, and the work of their peers, without constantly relying on the teacher)	• use the tools to help make professional judgements about students' achievement • engage in periodic moderation (group marking with other teachers using work samples, rubrics, and exemplars) to ensure collective agreement about the standards • refer to standards when communicating with students and parents and guardians about achievement

Figure 4.5 illustrates how Ms. Cole uses a rubric for Communication of Mathematics Understanding to assess her Grade 3 students' responses to a three-part question dealing with measurement. Prior to students beginning their work, Ms. Cole explains the rubric to her students so they are clear about the criteria for effective communication. Depending on her assessment purpose, Ms. Cole may use this same rubric to determine her students' skills at the beginning of a unit of study, to provide feedback to help them improve their work, or to help determine their report card grades for this strand.

Figure 4-5: Assessment of Communication in Mathematics

TOOL 4.21

Rubric for Communication,
p. 389

Communication Rubric—Mathematics

Expressive Communication: (Speaking, Writing, and Representation)

Name: _____   Date: _____

- This is a generic assessment tool. Not all criteria are necessarily appropriate to a given task.
- This scale should be used to assess the degree to which students are able to communicate about their understanding of concepts, procedures, and problem-solving strategies. Use only those criteria that are appropriate to a given task.
- Level 1 represents a limited performance but one in which the student has engaged with the prescribed task to some extent. Some students will perform below Level 1.

Criteria	Level 1	Level 2	Level 3	Level 4
Explanation and Justification of Mathematical Concepts, Procedures, and Problem Solving	provides **limited or inaccurate** explanations/justifications that **lack clarity** or **logical thought**, using **minimal** words, pictures, symbols, and/or numbers	provides **partial** explanations/ justifications that exhibit **some clarity** and **logical thought**, using **simple** words, pictures, symbols, and/or numbers	provides **complete, clear,** and **logical** explanations/ justifications, using **appropriate** words, pictures, symbols, and/or numbers	provides **thorough, clear,** and **insightful** explanations/ justifications, using a range of words, pictures, symbols, and/or numbers
Organization of Material (written, spoken, or drawn)	organization is **limited** and **seriously impedes** communication	**some** organization is evident	organization is **effective** and **supports** communication	organization is **highly effective** and **aids** communication
Use of Mathematical Vocabulary	uses very **little** mathematical vocabulary, and vocabulary used **lacks clarity and precision**	uses **some** mathematical vocabulary with **some degree of clarity and precision**	uses mathematical vocabulary with **considerable clarity and precision**	uses a **broad range** of mathematical vocabulary to communicate clearly and **precisely**
Use of Mathematical Representations (graphs, charts, diagrams)	uses representations that exhibit **limited clarity** and **accuracy** and are **ineffective** in communicating	uses representations that exhibit **some clarity** and **accuracy**	uses representations that are **clear** and **accurately** communicate information	uses representations that are **clear, precise,** and **effective** in communicating
Use of Mathematical Conventions (units, symbols, labels)	**few** conventions are used correctly	**some** conventions are used correctly	**most** conventions are used correctly	**almost all** conventions are used correctly

Tool 4.21   **389**

4.21, Mathematics Gr. 4–6

---

88 | *Nelson Assessment: Mathematics 3*

Name: STUDENT SAMPLE   Date: ____   Focus on Communication

Explaining Relationships

1. Explain each relationship.

a) A millimetre is shorter than a metre.
   Show how you know. Use words, numbers, and/or pictures.

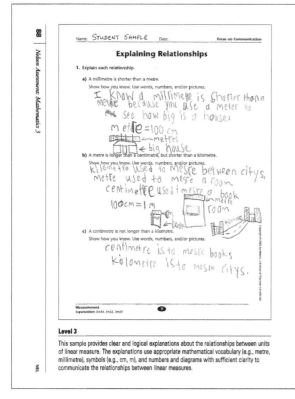

b) A metre is longer than a centimetre, but shorter than a kilometre.
   Show how you know. Use words, numbers, and/or pictures.

c) A centimetre is not longer than a kilometre.
   Show how you know. Use words, numbers, and/or pictures.

Measurement
Expectations: 3m34, 3m33, 3m39

Level 3

This sample provides clear and logical explanations about the relationships between units of linear measure. The explanations use appropriate mathematical vocabulary (e.g., metre, millimetre), symbols (e.g., cm, m), and numbers and diagrams with sufficient clarity to communicate the relationships between linear measures.

NEL

NEL

Name: STUDENT SAMPLE   Date: ____   Focus on Communication

Explaining Relationships

1. Explain each relationship.

a) A millimetre is shorter than a metre.
   Show how you know. Use words, numbers, and/or pictures.

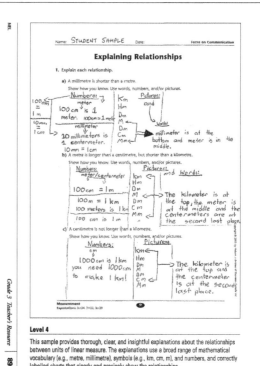

b) A metre is longer than a centimetre, but shorter than a kilometre.
   Show how you know. Use words, numbers, and/or pictures.

c) A centimetre is not longer than a kilometre.
   Show how you know. Use words, numbers, and/or pictures.

Measurement
Expectations: 3m34, 3m33, 3m39

Level 4

This sample provides thorough, clear, and insightful explanations about the relationships between units of linear measure. The explanations use a broad range of mathematical vocabulary (e.g., metre, millimetre), symbols (e.g., km, cm, m), and numbers, and correctly labelled charts that clearly and precisely show the relationships.

Grade 3 Teacher's Resource | 89

Assessment Q & A

Question

What about large-scale testing? What is its true purpose? Sometimes I feel as though I'm being pulled in opposite directions between my own assessment issues and the demands of large-scale testing.

Answer

Large-scale testing is not designed primarily to improve student learning. Its purpose is to provide data about how well a school system is performing to

- provincial or state governments
- school board or district officials
- school administrators
- parents and guardians

The quality of performance is usually measured against content standards, performance standards, and past performance. Not surprisingly, the increase in large-scale testing has accompanied the introduction of standards-based education across the western world. Content standards prescribe what we expect students to know and be able to do at the end of each grade and large-scale testing measures how successful we have been in equipping students with this learning.

Large-Scale Test Design

With few exceptions, large-scale testing involves only paper-and-pencil assessment. This is a drawback, because written assessment must always be balanced with performance and oral assessments in order for the assessment data to be valid. The reliance of large-scale testing on paper-and-pencil formats can be especially harmful to students with special needs, despite the accommodations provided for them.

Many large-scale testing programs reflect the belief that teaching and learning is about presenting students with numerous facts to memorize. It follows, therefore, that students who are successful at these tests are able to access the correct facts and slot them into a series of prompts.

Problems with Large-Scale Testing Programs

Large-scale testing is sometimes seen as an intrusion on the teacher's daily routines and program. In an ideal world, there would be a perfect match between the curriculum represented by the standards, the tests used to measure achievement of the standards, and day-to-day teaching and learning. If such a match were ever achieved, large-scale testing might become more popular. However, many teachers feel that large-scale testing represents only a narrow band of the curriculum. If they "teach to the test," it is only because testing attracts so much attention from educators, parents and guardians, and the media.

Benefits of Large-Scale Testing Programs

Before conclusions can be reached about student achievement, data must be gathered from three different sources at three different times. (See page 20.) Data from standardized testing may comprise a key portion of this data. Other sources of data might include your own classroom-based assessments and provincial assessments. By carefully examining and analyzing data from three different sources, you and your principal can determine whether a consistent picture of students' strengths and needs emerges, or whether there are significant discrepancies. It should be noted, of course, that individual student data from provincial tests may not be available to teachers. Regardless, comparisons of class data derived from three sources will provide plenty of material for analysis.

Issues Concerning Performance Standards

Recently, a teacher asked me, "What if the standard for Level 4 [the highest level] keeps getting pushed higher by the most able students in our school so that increasing numbers of our students are not able to reach that standard?" The question reflects a misunderstanding of criterion-referenced assessment. Student performance will not keep pushing the standard higher. The standard for Level 4 performance can only be raised when those responsible for standard-setting conclude that the standard is too low and needs to be raised.

Once a province has established a set of performance standards, local school district support staff, principals, and teachers spend time making those standards explicit by

- gathering samples of student performances calibrated to those standards, which become the local anchors and exemplars
- discussing what these standards look like for a wide variety of assessment tasks and producing tools such as rubrics that serve as more specific descriptions of these standards
- sharing these assessment tools with other teachers, students, parents and guardians so that, over time, everyone begins to internalize the standards for quality work

In Chapter 9, you can read how teachers collaborate in a moderation or group-marking session to consolidate their expectations regarding work quality. Chapter 12 contains information about rubrics and checklists.

These activities help to consolidate everyone's understanding as to what the performance standards look like as expressed in actual student work. True, there will be some students whose work not only meets but surpasses the highest level on a performance scale. You might say that such work "exceeds the standard." If many students exceed the standard, this would indicate that the standard needed to be re-examined.

Standard defined as "the best example of something" should not be confused with the definition of standard that is "what you expect everyone to be able to perform." For example, the current standard of performance for a marathon run is 2 hours and 4 minutes—meaning this is the current best-in-the-world time. Only one runner in the world has achieved this standard. But the standard to qualify for the Boston Marathon in the Open Men's division is 3 hours and 10 minutes. While challenging, this standard is still within reach for most male recreational runners between the ages of 22 and 30.

Performance standards for assessment tasks should be comparable to the second definition—that is, they should represent a challenging yet achievable level of performance for most students. (See Chapter 3 for information about adapting assessment for students with special needs and second language learners.)

How do challenging performance standards affect students who are not identified as having special needs, yet who constantly fall far short of the standards? In these situations, the professional judgement of caring and sensitive teachers is essential, especially in the current climate that is so focused on accountability.

Returning to our analogy, if you are a recreational runner who has completed a local 10K race and you decide that you would like to run your first marathon, what would you set as your finishing time goal? Would it be the qualifying time to run the Boston Marathon? Of course not. You would set a challenging yet realistic goal, given that you are a novice marathon runner.

When working with struggling students, teachers sometimes make the mistake of presenting them with the "Boston Marathon qualifying time" as the expected performance standard for a piece of work before they have "run their first marathon." Teachers who tend to do this should consider Mr. Diaz's approach, shown in the following case study.

CASE STUDY 1 | One Step at a Time

Mr. Diaz has reviewed the writing outcomes for his Grade 2 students and has been drawing materials from the Ministry of Education website to help him plan his program. He decides to assign his students the task of writing a short narrative. Since this task is one of the Ministry's **exemplars**, both a rubric and a set of anchors linked to each of the four achievement levels are available to help him assess the task.

Mr. Diaz spends several lessons reading short narratives with the children and helping them understand the elements of a story. He then brainstorms with the class the criteria that should appear on a rubric for assessing their own stories. That night, he uses this list of criteria, as well as the Ministry's rubric to develop a simple student-friendly rubric. (See Figure 4-6.)

The next day, Mr. Diaz shares the rubric with the children to help them understand what he expects in terms of quality, explaining that the very best narratives sound like the descriptors in the Level 4 column.

As students begin to work, Mr. Diaz quickly realizes that Jessica is having great difficulty. She

continued

Figure 4-6: Teacher/Peer Rubric: Grade 2 Narrative

TOOL 3.8

p. 348

Criteria	Level 1	Level 2	Level 3	Level 4
A Good Story (Reasoning)	• You need to add more events that will make your story more interesting. For example …	• Some parts are interesting but some parts are not. For example …	• Your story has many interesting events.	• What a great story!
Sounds Real (Communication)	• You need to read your story and make changes that will make it sound like a real story. For example …	• Some parts sound like a real story but some parts do not. For example …	• Your story almost sounds like a real story.	• Your story sounds just like a real story.
Organized (Organization)	• You need to read your story and make changes that will make it easy for the reader to follow. For example …	• Some parts are easy to follow but some parts are confusing. For example …	• Your story is easy to follow.	• Your story is very well organized.
No Mistakes (Conventions)	• You need to read your story and correct the errors that make it difficult to understand. For example …	• You need to read your story and correct the errors that make some parts difficult to understand. For example …	• You need to do a final check and correct the small errors in your story.	• Your story has no errors.

348 · Tool 3.8

3.8, Language Arts K to 3

appears to have little understanding of what he has taught about narrative elements. She also has some serious deficits in her writing skills.

Clearly, the Level 4 indicators in Mr. Diaz's rubric would prove challenging to Jessica and trying to meet them could potentially discourage her. At this point in the term, Level 1 represents an appropriate goal for Jessica to strive toward and should be Mr. Diaz's expectations regarding the standards he would like Jessica to achieve. Once she has had some initial success by meeting these standards, he will help her strive toward the same standard as her peers.

Figure 4-7: Jessica's Attempt at Narrative

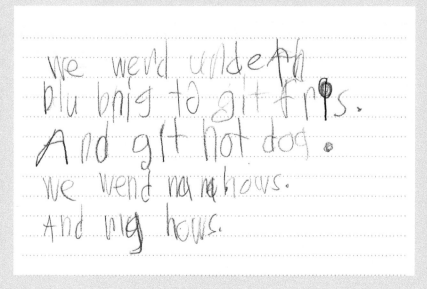

Mr. Diaz used his professional judgement to mediate between the provincial performance standards established for Grade 2 writing and his classroom reality as represented by students like Jessica. This case study illustrates that standards must be very carefully applied to students with learning difficulties. While all students can be successful, many of them need to be shown small, achievable steps to get started.

Summary

- Curriculum or content standards are descriptions of what students are expected to learn, including knowledge, skills, and values, beliefs, and attitudes.
- Performance standards are descriptions of prescribed levels of performance on a task or series of tasks.
- Teachers need to ensure that curriculum documents do not undermine the quality of what is taught by presenting learning in a piecemeal fashion. True learning reflects a *gestalt*—in other words, the whole is greater than the sum of the parts.
- Criterion-referenced assessment is replacing norm-referenced assessment as the standard for classroom assessment practice. This means that student work is assessed against known standards for quality as reflected in tools such as checklists, rubrics, and exemplars.
- Standards need to be agreed to by teaching teams and communicated to students and their parents and guardians so that everyone can work toward the common goal of improving students' learning.
- Teachers need to exercise their professional judgement when assessing student work against standards to ensure that all students are motivated to improve their work and no students are discouraged by standards they perceive as unachievable.

Applying My Learning

Use Tool 1.4: *Assessing My Current Use of Performance Standards* to reflect on your current understanding and use of performance standards. Focus on one subject area at a time. In the middle column, rate your current practice, and in the right column, note steps you might take to improve your practice. As always, undertake this kind of work with your colleagues, not on your own.

1.4, Chapter 4 Review

Assessing My Current Use of Performance Standards

R = Rarely   S = Sometimes   C = Consistently

Self-Assessment Questions	Current Practice			Maintain / Modify / Change Practice
	R ✓	S ✓	C ✓	
Before teaching:				
1. Do I understand our local/provincial performance standards? (That is, do I have an overall sense of what Level 4 represents as opposed to Level 3, and so on?)				
2. Have I created and/or located appropriate assessment tools (rubrics, checklists, etc.) based on the mandated standards?				
3. Have I taken steps to ensure that students and parents become familiar with these tools? (For example, have I posted rubrics on the bulletin board, provided students with copies of rubrics, sent rubrics home for parents to see, and so on?)				
4. Am I collecting samples and maintaining collections of student work from previous classes that are anchored to the standards?				
5. Do I negotiate assessment criteria with my students?				
During teaching:				
6. Do I use the tools—rubrics, checklists, exemplars—to provide regular feedback to students?				
7. Do I teach students the skills required to use these tools for self- and peer assessment?				
After teaching:				
8. Do I use these tools to help make professional judgments about students' achievement?				
9. Do I engage in periodic moderation (group marking with other teachers, using work samples, rubrics, and exemplars) to ensure a collective agreement about our performance standards?				
10. Do I refer to these standards when communicating with students and parents about achievement?				

Tool 1.4   **291**

TOOL 1.4

Assessing My Current Use of Performance Standards, p. 291

Chapter 5

WHO'S THE ASSESSOR? TEACHER, PEER, AND SELF-ASSESSMENT

>
> **BIG IDEA 6**
> Assessment is a collaborative process that is most effective when it involves self-, peer, and teacher assessment.

COLLABORATING WITH STUDENTS IN THE ASSESSMENT PROCESS

...self-assessment by pupils, far from being a luxury, is in fact an essential component of formative assessment.

BLACK AND WILIAM, 1998

Assessment is not something that is "done" to students; it is a process of collaborative communication in which information about learning flows between teacher and student. This two-way exchange of information is at the heart of assessment for learning. If assessment *for* learning (see Chapter 1, page 13) is to improve the quality of students' work, then students must also be involved in their own assessment.

Teachers play a key role in coaching their students to be competent assessors. Students need to

- know and understand how their teacher defines quality work
- know the expectations with respect to quality work and performance
- be trained in the use of assessment tools such as checklists and rubrics
- be coached in assessment process skills such as conferencing, self-assessment, and peer assessment
- be constantly reminded, especially as they progress toward intermediate grades, that the purpose of completing work is to improve their learning, not to accumulate as many points as possible in as short a time as possible

If you have already embraced the idea of students being involved in their own assessment, you may have heard parents and other adults remark that, "Surely assessment is the job of the teacher, not the students." Such comments are sometimes made when parents are upset about what they perceive to be unfair grading of their child's work by a peer, or because they do not understand the purpose of peer assessment. To prevent this from happening, follow this important guideline when including students in the assessment process: *Do not ask students to assign marks, either to their own work or to the work of their peers.* Marking is part of evaluation (judgement) of student work and it is the responsibility of the teacher. Instead, train students to use anecdotal assessment when doing peer and self-assessment. Provide them with frequent opportunities to practise these skills to help them learn deeper and better.

Marking is part of evaluation (judgement) of student work and it is the responsibility of the teacher.

How Students Benefit from Being Involved in Assessment

Students benefit in the following ways when they participate in the assessment process:

Video Clip 7:

Gr. 2 Language Arts— Using Portfolios to Improve Self- and Peer-assessment
07:55 minutes

- They come to understand the standards for quality when they have to apply these standards themselves (peer and self-assessment).
- They learn to be less dependent on the teacher for feedback about the quality of their own work and, as result, are better able to independently monitor the quality of their own work (peer and self-assessment).
- They develop metacognitive skills so they are more able to adjust what they are doing to improve the quality of their work (peer and self-assessment).
- They develop and refine their capacity for critical thinking (peer and self-assessment).

NEL

Who's the Assessor? Teacher, Peer, and Self-Assessment **83**

- They broaden their own learning when they see how their peers approach a given task (peer assessment).
- They practise and hone their communication and social skills when they are required to provide useful and meaningful feedback to others (peer assessment).

I am often asked, "How frequently should my students be involved in self- and peer assessment?" The answer is more a matter of purpose than frequency. The question teachers should ask is, "What is my purpose when I ask students to assess their own work, or the work of their peers?" Decisions about who should assess a given task—teacher, self, peers, or a combination of these people—are best made with that question in mind. That said, there are certain points in the teaching/learning process when peer and self-assessment are most effective:

Peer assessment should be routine practice when students are working on early drafts of written material.

- Peer assessment should be routine practice, when students are working on early drafts of written material, as long as they
  - know what to look for in a partner's work,
  - use an assessment tool such as a checklist to focus their comments, and
  - are required only to provide anecdotal comments, not scores
    Approached this way, peer assessment can be extremely effective in improving the quality of work before you view it.

- Self-assessment should be routine practice in subjects such as mathematics where students typically complete practice questions following the teaching of a new concept or procedure. Students can check their solutions against those provided in a solutions manual or at the back of the textbook to determine whether they've "got it" or need to review the new learning and complete more practice work. Do not record scores from these exercises—the purpose of such work is just practice. At a later date, there may be a test or assignment that you can score and count toward students' grades.

COLLABORATION IN ACTION: TWO CASE STUDIES

The following case studies illustrate how to use a combination of teacher, peer, and self-assessment to accomplish different assessment purposes. Ms. Calvert incorporates teacher, peer, and self-assessment at different stages of a writing task to improve the work of her students in language arts. Mr. Fleming moves from an entirely teacher-driven assessment approach to one that emphasizes collaborative communication in his mathematics classroom.

| CASE STUDY 1 | Ms. Calvert's Language Arts Class |

For some time, Ms. Calvert has been feeling that she is doing too much marking of her students' written work. Every time she assigns a task, however small, she feels compelled to collect it and take it home to mark. She raised this concern with the literacy consultant in her district. As a result of their discussion, Ms. Calvert began to share assessment responsibilities with her students.

Today, Ms. Calvert is teaching a lesson on how to improve the sensory impact of writing. She begins by showing students pairs of sentences such as the following:

Sentence Type 1: Marco walked up to the house.

Sentence Type 2: His heart pounding with each step, Marco inched toward the cobweb-covered door of the crumbling mansion.

Ms. Calvert asks her students to discuss with their writing partners what makes the second sentence in each pair more effective than the first. After a few minutes, students share their observations. Based on their responses, she writes on the board a set of guidelines about writing descriptive sentences that appeal to the senses:

Writing Effective Descriptive Sentences

- Vary the syntax. Don't always begin with the subject.

Example: "His heart pounding, Marco..."

- Vary the sentence length. Short sentences create suspense.

- Use, but don't overuse, modifiers to provide sensory details. Example: "crumbling"

- Use concrete, specific nouns instead of generic ones.

Example: "mansion" instead of "house"

Next, Ms. Calvert provides students with five Type 1 sentences. Working alone, students are to rewrite them as Type 2 sentences. After fifteen minutes, Ms. Calvert instructs her students to do the following:

1. Read your sentences carefully and critically to ensure they are correct and that they meet the requirements listed on the board (self-assessment).

2. Ask your writing partner to give you feedback by indicating on each sentence
   - what makes it effective in appealing to one or more senses
   - what weakens its effectiveness
   - one suggestion for how to improve the sentence (peer assessment)

3. Have a brief, one-on-one writing conference with your writing partner during which you each take turns explaining your feedback (peer assessment).

Ms. Calvert monitors her students' progress on this peer assessment task. Once

continued

NEL

Who's the Assessor? Teacher, Peer, and Self-Assessment **85**

they have had sufficient time to complete it, she tells her students to revise their sentences, incorporating the feedback they received from their writing partners. The result of this activity will be polished sentences that can be submitted to her (teacher-assessment).

Depending on her assessment purpose and at what point in the term this task occurs, Ms. Calvert's assessment may be purely anecdotal (similar to the student assessment), or it may include a letter grade or level.

How is Ms. Calvert's new approach to assessment effective?

- In Step 1, students look critically at their own work, checking their sentences against the guidelines on the board. This is an essential but often overlooked step. Too often, teachers assess work that students have not even taken the time to read over. As a result, teachers spend a great deal of time correcting careless errors.

- In Step 2, students engage in thought-provoking peer assessment. They critically examine the quality of their partner's work and provide useful anecdotal feedback. Notice, there is *no* requirement that students score each other's work. Numerical scores are not relevant to this process. At this stage, students need information that directs them how to improve the quality of their work based on the assessment guidelines.

- In Step 3, students practise both interpersonal and communication skills as they provide feedback to their partners. Sometimes peers disagree or one peer will want more feedback. This part of the process can help both partners clarify their thinking and understanding about quality descriptive writing.

- Finally, in Step 4, Ms. Calvert collects her students' polished work so that she may conduct her own assessment. The quality of work Ms. Calvert receives is much improved compared to the work she might have received had she collected it without using the step-by-step assessment process.

Too often, teachers assess work that students have not even taken the time to read over. As a result, teachers spend a great deal of time correcting careless errors.

CASE STUDY 2 | Mr. Fleming's Mathematics Class

Mr. Fleming had taught junior-level mathematics in a consistent—some would say traditional—way for the past ten years. Until a year ago, Mr. Fleming believed that assessment meant measuring what his students had learned. He assumed that assessment was entirely the responsibility of the teacher. In recent years, Mr. Fleming became increasingly frustrated and disappointed with his students' poor achievement. These were his concerns:

- despite his best teaching efforts, many students did not understand the math concepts.
- although he assigned homework on a daily basis, many students failed to complete it.
- he was constantly overwhelmed by the marking he felt compelled to do, yet he knew it had little impact on student learning.
- he was invariably disappointed by the poor performance of many students on the bi-weekly tests.

Last year, Mr. Fleming had the opportunity to visit a neighbouring school known for teaching excellence in mathematics. Mr. Fleming spent the day observing one teacher and her students and chatting with her about her success. As a result of this visit and subsequent communication with his colleague, Mr. Fleming implemented the following new strategies in his class.

1. He constantly checks for understanding to see whether the whole class, as well as individual students, are with him as he teaches a new concept or procedure (teacher-assessment). These checks include
- "show me your thumbs"
- oral questioning of individual students
- one-on-one conferencing
  (See Case Study 3, p. 44.)

2. After Mr. Fleming has checked for understanding, he assigns practice questions from the text. Students check their own solutions. If they are mostly correct, they move on. If not, they work with a partner to improve their understanding (self- and peer assessment).

3. Mr. Fleming builds into every lesson the opportunity for students to talk with their peers to consolidate understanding by listening and responding to each other as they make sense of new learning (peer assessment). For example, as part of a lesson on adding four-digit whole numbers (figure 5-1), Mr. Fleming might instruct

Figure 5-1: Lesson on Adding Whole Numbers

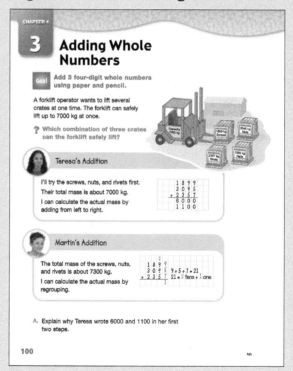

continued

NEL

Who's the Assessor? Teacher, Peer, and Self-Assessment **87**

students to discuss the following questions in pairs:

- How did their estimates help Teresa and Martin?
- Would you choose to add from left to right like Teresa, or to regroup like Martin? Why?

Discussing these questions allows students to talk about their solutions, and not simply write them in their notebooks. As students talk, they are consolidating their understanding. While this results in a noisy classroom, there is "good noise" (the chatter of students sharing their learning) and "bad noise" (off-task chatter).

4. Mr. Fleming's students know that when math class begins, they must have last night's homework open on their desks (teacher-assessment). Mr. Fleming has them work on a brain-teaser written on the board while he spot checks the homework of 8 to 10 students to see if they have completed the assigned work Mr. Fleming's only concern during these checks is whether or not the homework has been completed, not whether it is correct. He uses a sampling system to ensure that he checks each student's homework four times in each reporting period and to determine the "Homework Completion" level for the report card. His sampling method is very simple:

Figure 5-2: Homework Completion		
Number of Checks	Times Complete	Rating
4	4	E (Excellent)
4	3	G (Good)
4	2	S (Satisfactory)
4	1	N (Needs Improvement)

In the past year, Mr. Fleming has noticed a big improvement in his students' attitudes, especially those students who had been struggling. Long before they have to write a unit test, his students know that Mr. Fleming will check their level of understanding and address any misconceptions they may have.

Mr. Fleming realized he had been teaching curriculum rather than teaching kids. He had been driven more by pressure to cover the outcomes than by a commitment to learning for all. If the purpose of teaching is to "uncover understanding" (Wiggins, 1998), then Mr. Fleming knew he had left that purpose behind.

As a footnote, a fellow teacher noticed an increased noise level coming from Mr. Fleming's class. When he dropped in to see why, he discovered a positive and math-focused buzz—the sound of students engaged and talking excitedly about what they were learning.

These two case studies illustrate the power of collaboration in the assessment process. Ms. Calvert realized that if she involved her students in peer and self-assessment, she could save herself a lot of marking while, at the same time, significantly improve the quality of the student work that she did mark. After introducing a feedback loop into his mathematics, Mr. Fleming was better able to monitor his students' understanding and respond immediately to those who were having difficulty, rather than waiting for poor test results to indicate this. He also discovered that by integrating peer and self-assessment into his daily routines, he could deepen mathematical understanding while lessening his marking load!

CAN YOUNG CHILDREN PEER AND SELF-ASSESS?

Recently, a Grade 2 teacher asked if I thought five- and six-year-olds could peer and self-assess reliably. I replied with a question of my own: "Do you think it's important for young children to be engaged in peer and self-assessment?"

"Absolutely!" she said without hesitation.

"So perhaps," I continued, "we should be less concerned with reliability than we are with providing young children with lots of opportunities to practice peer and self-assessment."

"I understand what you're saying," she said. "Reliability is about consistency. But before we can expect children to demonstrate consistency, they need lots of practice."

I smiled. "Exactly. Reliability is vital when we are talking about assessment of learning—assessment that is going to be used for reporting student achievement. But self- and peer assessment by students in all grades should be limited to assessment for learning—assessment that helps them improve their work."

"OK, here's another question," she said. "What should peer and self-assessment look like in the early grades?"

"Descriptive feedback," I said, "such as 'This is what you did well' and 'This is what you could do to make it better.' Children should not be assigning marks and numerical scores to their own work or the work of their peers."

"Of course," she said. "That's my job."

"They'll also learn more about assessment and become more critical thinkers if they have to provide descriptive feedback instead of a score, I explained."

This discussion illustrates two important themes:

- Assessment to promote learning must take the form of descriptive feedback.
- Students of all ages benefit from engaging in peer and self-assessment; however, assessment for reporting purposes is the responsibility of the teacher.

Children in Grades 1 and 2 are capable of learning how to peer and self-assess if their teachers model these skills and provide simple tools such as those shown in Figures 5-3 and 5-4.

The happy and sad faces coupled with words such as *yes, sometimes,* and *no,* in Figure 5-3, help young children understand the concept of assessment through their prior knowledge and experience of these emotions. However, associating assessment with happiness should gradually

While students of all ages benefit from peer and self-assessment, assessment for reporting purposes is the responsibility of the teacher.

NEL

Who's the Assessor? Teacher, Peer, and Self-Assessment **89**

Figure 5-3: Me as a Speaker

Self-Assessment Checklist: Me as a Speaker			

Name: _____ Date: _____

Grade: _____

This self-assessment is read to and discussed with students initially. Students use the form independently over time.

Self-Assessment—Speaking Behaviours	No ☹	Sometimes 🙂	Yes 😊
I look at the person I'm speaking to.			
I speak clearly.			
I speak loudly enough, but not too loud.			
I try to stay on the same topic.			
I know how to take a speaking turn.			
I let the person know when I am finished speaking.			
I interrupt by using the "GAG" strategy.*			

* **G**et the person's attention
Apologize for interrupting
Give the reason for interrupting

Figure 5-4: How We Worked Together

How We Worked Together			

Name: _____ Date: _____

Who is in our group:

_____

_____

_____

_____

Circle the answer that tells about your group.

We got our work done.	No	Some of it	Most of it	Completely
We took turns talking.	No	Some of the time	Most of the time	All of the time
We shared the work.	No	Some of the time	Most of the time	All of the time
We helped each other.	No	Some of the time	Most of the time	All of the time
We encouraged each other.	No	Some of the time	Most of the time	All of the time
We were polite to each other.	No	Some of the time	Most of the time	All of the time
We feel good about our work.	No	Some of it	Most of it	All of it

▲ **These tools provide appropriate self- and peer assessment opportunities for students in the early grades. Students are required to think about a specific behaviour, then reflect on the frequency with which they themselves did this, or the frequency with which their peers demonstrated this skill.**

TOOL 3.11

Self-Assessment Checklist: Me As a Speaker, p. 352

TOOL 3.23

How We Worked Together, p. 364

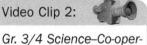

Video Clip 2:

Gr. 3/4 Science–Co-operative Group Learning and Assessment
09:31 minutes

give way to a clearer notion of assessment as a process that is concerned with the quality of students' work. As soon as possible, children should be exposed to the idea that assessment information describes how well they have demonstrated a specific skill, and not how happy they are.

ASSESSMENT AND EVALUATION IN CO-OPERATIVE GROUP SITUATIONS

Teachers at all grade levels recognize the benefits of co-operative work situations to facilitate the learning of certain outcomes and to foster interpersonal skills. If co-operative group strategies comprise a significant portion of your instructional time, it is reasonable to expect that a proportional amount of your assessment *of* learning data will be gathered while students are working co-operatively. Often, for example, teachers assign students to work with a partner or in small groups when completing major performance tasks such as research projects, open-ended inquiries, design and technology projects, or oral presentations.

Group Grades and Individual Accountability in Co-operative Group Situations

Unfortunately, assessment data gathered from a group of students working co-operatively may lack reliability. When students are working in a group, it becomes more difficult to assess the skills each student has mastered or the concepts each student understands. The work of other students may seriously distort individual assessment. If a given assessment task is summative (and may, therefore, comprise a portion of that student's report card grade), the assessment must be reliable in order to be fair.

How then do you assess individual achievement on group tasks? The eight guidelines that follow are derived from the world of work. For example, at a Ford plant, many employees work together to produce a new car (a final product), yet no attempt is made to evaluate each line worker's contribution. The product is evaluated as a whole and receives a group grade. On the other hand, each employee is evaluated individually according to his or her performance on the production line—the process component. Employees receive different "marks" according to individual performance.

In the classroom, this real-world approach to evaluation looks like this:

1. Ensure fair and appropriate grouping of students for summative tasks. Grouping students according to ability can have a significant impact on the quality of learning that occurs: high-achieving students grouped together typically produce work of superior quality; low-achieving students should only be grouped together if the teacher is going to monitor them closely. Heterogeneous groupings may be the most beneficial for all students, provided that the teacher monitors them frequently.

2. Clearly indicate timelines and due dates for the process components, as well as the final products, to impress upon students the need to be responsible to the group. Frequent process checks will ensure that everyone in the group is pulling his or her weight.

3. Assign a group mark to any product that the group is responsible for, such as a model, or an oral or visual presentation.

4. Assign an individual mark to each student for a work log or journal used to record learning during the process.

5. Assess each student individually for work habits demonstrated during the process.

Follow these eight guidelines to ensure both group and individual accountability in co-operative group situations.

NEL

Who's the Assessor? Teacher, Peer, and Self-Assessment **91**

6. Provide opportunities for students to assess their own work and the work of their peers. Provide time to deliver feedback to their peers about the quality of their finished products. In both cases, students should assess but not score each other's work.

7. Ensure that each student has fully understood the essential learning associated with the task by including in your assessment data a brief written or oral defense as a check. Depending on the age of your students, this may take various forms (i.e., a short written test or a series of critical questions). If you decide to ask a series of questions, use a clipboard and move from group to group while students are working. Ask each student one of these critical questions to ensure that all students in the group understand. Your assessment data may become part of each student's process mark.

8. All marks, scores, or levels for all components of the task are assigned by the teacher, not the students.

To see how these eight guidelines can be applied in a Grade 7 science class, consider the following culminating task.

Task: Design a Solar-Heated Swimming Pool

Problem

As the world's population increases and our standard of living rises, we use more energy. But many of our sources of energy, for example, oil and gas, are not renewable. Using oil or gas heaters to warm a swimming pool is a waste of energy.

Design Brief

Design and build a controllable device that uses only solar energy to heat the water for a model swimming pool to 25°C.

Assessment

■ Guideline 3: The teacher may assign either one overall mark or a series of marks to the whole group for the following components:
  – development of a plan
  – testing and recording of results
  – model of the swimming pool, oral presentation of model, and results

■ Guideline 4: The teacher may assign either one overall mark or two separate marks to each student for the following components:
  – written report
  – technical drawing of the model

■ Guideline 5: The teacher may assess each student on the safe use of materials and tools.

■ Guideline 6: Students may be asked to complete a self-assessment (see Figure 5-5) and/or a group-assessment checklist either during the project or at its conclusion to help them reflect on the quality of their own work and the work of their colleagues. Groups may also assess the work of other groups. This could include providing feedback about the quality of their models, their oral presentations, or both these components.

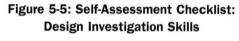

Figure 5-5: Self-Assessment Checklist: Design Investigation Skills

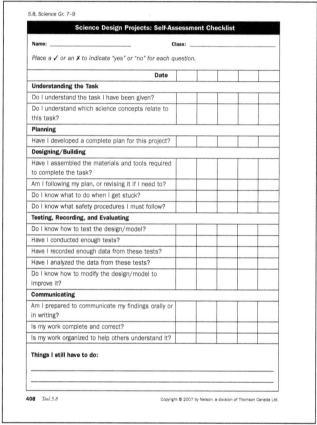

TOOL 5.8

Self-Assessment Checklist for Science Design Projects, p. 408

■ Guideline 7: The teacher observes, listens, and asks each student a key question for understanding while students work on their designs and models. The teacher records the quality of responses on a sheet attached to a clipboard. Sample key questions for the swimming pool task might include the following:

– *Does your model demonstrate passive solar heating, active solar heating, or the greenhouse effect? How do you know?*

– *How does your device guard against the danger of electric shock?*

– *Once the pool has been heated to 25°C, what are some energy-efficient ways to maintain that temperature?*

NEL

Who's the Assessor? Teacher, Peer, and Self-Assessment **93**

Note that not all assessments are intended to be conducted this way. This illustration identifies all of the possible ways in which this co-operative task could be assessed, and identifies appropriate practices. A teacher would select only some of these assessment components. Remember, efficient and effective assessment involves sampling student performance, not assessing everything all of the time.

Peer and Self-Assessment in Co-operative Group Situations

One important reason for students to work in co-operative groups is to give them a taste of real-world situations where working with others is the norm. Co-operative group tasks provide students with opportunities to practise both the social and work skills necessary for collaborating with their peers. When students assess their own contributions to the group or assess the contributions of peers, they understand better what quality work and performance looks like and, as a result, increase the objectivity of their assessments.

Peer and self-assessment must focus on indicators of performance, not on marks. This means that peer assessment requires students to provide their group colleagues with feedback, while self-assessment requires objective reflection on their own performance. The most important principle to keep in mind when students peer and self-assess in co-operative groups context is: *Train students in the skills of self and peer anecdotal assessment and provide them with frequent opportunities to practice these skills. Do not require students to assign marks—that is the teacher's responsibility.*

Summary

- Peer and self-assessment help students internalize the standards for quality work.
- Through being involved in the assessment process, students develop the capacity to be objective about the quality of their own work.
- When students are taught how to peer and self-assess, the quality of work they submit for marking improves.
- Effective and routine use of peer and self-assessment can significantly reduce the amount of marking for teachers.
- Very young children can learn how to peer and self-assess.
- The following guidelines ensure best practices for assessing group work:

1. Ensure fair and appropriate grouping of students for summative tasks.
2. Clearly indicate timelines and due dates for the process components, as well as the final products, to impress upon students the need to be responsible to the group.
3. Assign a group mark to any product that the group is responsible for, such as a model, or an oral/visual presentation.
4. Assign an individual mark to each student for a work log or journal used to record learning during the process.
5. Assess each student individually for work habits demonstrated during the process.
6. Provide opportunities for students to assess their own work and the work of their peers.
7. Ensure that each student has fully understood the essential learning associated with the task by including a brief written or oral defense as a check.
8. All marks, scores or levels for all components of the task are assigned by the teacher, not the students.

Applying My Learning

Working with a colleague, choose either Ms. Calvert's Language Arts Class or Mr. Fleming's Mathematics Class. Review the case study together and then use the following questions to guide a discussion about possible applications of Ms. Calvert or Mr. Fleming's strategies in your own classrooms:

Case Study Discussion Questions

- What features of Ms. Calvert or Mr. Fleming's approach intrigued you the most? Why?
- Which of the strategies—teaching, assessment, or both—used by Ms. Calvert or Mr. Fleming do you want to try in your own classroom?
- Which of the strategies used by Ms. Calvert or Mr. Fleming would you not consider using? Why not?
- What resources and supports would you need from colleagues and/or your principal in order to implement approaches such as those used by Ms. Calvert or Mr. Fleming?

Chapter 6

CLASSROOM ASSESSMENT STRATEGIES

BIG IDEA 3 Assessment must be balanced, including oral, performance, and written tasks, and be flexible in order to improve learning for all students.

ASSESSING A BROAD RANGE OF KNOWLEDGE AND SKILLS

Classroom assessment has come a long way since the days of "teach, test, hope-for-the-best." We now know that not only do students learn in different ways, but they also need to demonstrate their learning in different ways. Moreover, not all learning can be adequately assessed through written assessments alone. Students require opportunities to write, do, and say in order to demonstrate what they have learned. Teachers respond to each of these types of assessment by marking, observing, and listening, respectively.

Why should students have opportunities to demonstrate their learning in different ways? Because no single test assesses all kinds of knowledge and skill. How would you react, for example, if the Ministry of Transportation dispensed with the driving demonstration portion of the drivers' test and simply required candidates to achieve 85 percent or better on the multiple-choice test? Although the multiple-choice test that new drivers take is an excellent measure of what they know, it is not intended to assess their driving skill, nor does it provide a sufficient sample of all of the learning targets essential to safe driving. In the same way, while written tests can be valid assessments of what students know, they are often inadequate measures of students' skills or their ability to apply what they have learned to real-life problems.

Before you read how to assess in different ways, review the following terms. (See also Chapter 3, pages 60–63.)

The heart of accuracy in classroom assessment revolves around matching different kinds of achievement targets... to the appropriate assessment method.
Rick Stiggins et al., 2004

The Assessment Mode

As discussed in Chapter 3, the assessment **mode** refers to how students demonstrate their learning—write, do, say, or a combination of all three. It is essential to use all three modes when designing a unit's assessment plan for the following reasons:

- Different learning outcomes require different assessment modes. For example, consider the following Grade 3 Science and Technology outcomes:
  - identify the major parts of plants and describe their basic functions
  - design and conduct a hands-on inquiry into seed germination or plant growth
  - ask questions about and identify some needs of plants, and explore possible answers to these questions
- While the first outcome might be assessed through a written task, assessing the second demands a performance task, and the third would be best assessed by listening to students talk to one another and to their teacher.
- Not all students are able to demonstrate their learning most effectively through writing. Faulty conclusions could be drawn about the learning of students with writing deficits if they are assessed only by written work.

The Assessment Strategy

An assessment **strategy** refers to the specific task chosen for students to engage in. A debate, a quiz, a mind map, and a design project are all assessment **strategies**. Choosing a strategy should depend on the type of learning to be assessed. Often, the curriculum outcomes can provide important clues for selecting the most appropriate assessment strategy, as the following examples show.

Grade 7 Language Arts Example

- Listen and respond constructively to alternative ideas or viewpoints (valid assessment strategy: classroom discussion, debate, or one-on-one conference).
- Use a variety of sentence types (statements, exclamations, questions, commands) appropriately and effectively (valid assessment strategy: writing a short story or one-act play).

Grade 4 Mathematics

- Draw items using a wide variety of SI units of length (valid assessment strategy: drawing).
- Investigate measures of circumference using concrete materials (valid assessment strategy: inquiry).
- Explain the rules used in calculating the perimeter and area of rectangles and squares (valid assessment strategy: journal entry, letter, or one-on-one conference).

It is critical to use a wide variety of assessment strategies drawn from all three modes—write, do and say—in order to gather sufficient assessment data about students' learning. This concept of a balanced approach to gathering assessment data is equally important, whether the purpose is assessment *for* learning or assessment *of* learning.

When assessing *for* learning, all three modes and a variety of strategies should be used to

- obtain an accurate picture of students' strengths and needs
- make the best decisions about future instruction

The goal is to obtain an accurate picture of a student's current level of understanding and skills, which will lead to appropriate instructional decisions. This may involve relying on more than the written mode.

When conducting assessment *of* learning, all three modes and a variety of strategies should be used to

- obtain an accurate picture of students' strengths and needs
- compile a valid, reliable sample of their achievement at this point in time for reporting purposes

To gather sufficient assessment data, use a wide variety of assessment strategies drawn from all three modes—write, do, and say.

If the written mode is relied on too heavily at this stage, there may be the risk of drawing inaccurate conclusions about what the student has learned at the end of a period of instruction.

The Assessment Tool

An assessment **tool** is the instrument that is created or selected to record assessment data in order to

- provide feedback to the student
- help teachers make instructional decisions
- compile data for reporting.

Assessment tools include checklists, rubrics, running records, and rating scales.

Checklists, rubrics, running records, and rating scales are all assessment tools. The type of tool used is usually determined by the assessment strategy to which it corresponds. For example, if students are working on a hands-on performance task in mathematics, you might use a checklist with a clipboard.

On the other hand, if you are assessing children's books created by your students, you might use a rubric that you distributed before they began working. (See Figure 6-1.) The same tool can be used to guide students as they work (assessment *for* learning) and help you mark their polished work (assessment *of* learning). (See Chapter 12: Selecting and Developing Quality Assessment Tools.)

Video Clip 9:

Planning a Common Assessment Task and Team Marking
09:37 minutes

Figure 6-1: Rubric for Producing a Children's Book

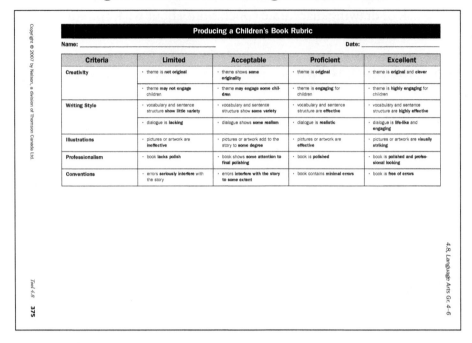

SELECTING APPROPRIATE CLASSROOM ASSESSMENT STRATEGIES

Teachers face several challenges as they select assessment strategies:

- What type of strategy should I use and when?
- How frequently should I use each strategy?
- How do I assess student learning when students are performing or speaking, as opposed to writing?
- Should I use the same strategy with all students?

How Do I Choose a Strategy?

*Choose an assessment
strategy after carefully
examining the curriculum
outcomes to be assessed.*

Stiggins et al. (2004) speak about the need to ensure an appropriate target-method match when selecting or creating assessment strategies. In other words, teachers should choose an assessment strategy after carefully examining the curriculum outcomes to be assessed. It is critical that you are certain about precisely what you intend to assess.

Compare these two conversations between two Grade 6 teachers planning a social studies unit.

Conversation 1

Sam: Marcia, what would be some good activities to include in this unit?

Marcia: My students really enjoyed creating scrapbooks about the First Nations last year. It was a good activity because even students with weak writing skills could do well. They found photographs and created drawings to put in their scrapbook.

Sam: And my students had fun building dioramas of the Huron villages. That was a great project for the tactile learners I had in my class.

Conversation 2

Marcia: So the first thing we need to do is look at the Big Ideas for this unit. (Marcia reads aloud from the curriculum document.)

Students will

- identify ways in which the environment moulded Canadian Aboriginal cultures
- demonstrate an understanding of the social, political, and economic issues facing Aboriginal peoples in Canada today

Sam: How can we assess those things? They sound kind of vague to me.

Marcia: Well, let's think. Students could research the effects of the environment on early Aboriginal peoples. Then they could choose one of several ways to demonstrate their learning.

Sam: Like what?

Marcia: They could build a model, like a diorama, that showed the impact of the environment, or they could create a role-play showing the human side of things.

Sam: Okay, I see what you mean. But what should we assess? Maybe if we look more carefully at the curriculum outcomes, we'll get some ideas.

In the first conversation, the planning focus was on identifying activities that would be fun for students to do. Sam and Marcia are also trying to accommodate the variety of learning styles and intelligences demonstrated by their students. But without first identifying the learning they intend to assess, and then agreeing on the assessment criteria, they risk awarding high marks to visually appealing scrapbooks and dioramas that actually reveal little or no understanding.

In the second conversation, Sam and Marcia begin with the learning targets—the Big Ideas they want students to understand by the end of the unit. Then they identify assessment tasks matched to these Big Ideas. Their next step is to examine the curriculum in more depth to help them identify the assessment criteria they will use to determine students' depth of understanding following completion of the tasks. These criteria will include

- depth of specific conceptual understanding to be demonstrated
- quality of research skills to be demonstrated (see Chapter 13 for more information about strategy selection)

How Often Should I Use Each Strategy?

The frequency with which a particular assessment strategy is used also depends on the learning outcomes being assessed, as well as the purpose for the assessment. For example, one-on-one or small-group conferencing with students should be used routinely throughout the year. On the other hand, because conferencing is a time-consuming strategy, it must be integrated with other classroom routines in an efficient manner.

Strategies must be used often enough to ensure that students become proficient in the skills to be demonstrated. For example, if a teacher plans to use an open-ended mathematics investigation to gather assessment of learning data at the end of a unit, students must have had previous opportunities throughout the unit to practice the skills required by this task. Without such practice, students cannot be expected to perform successfully.

How Do I Assess Performance or Speaking?

Video Clip 8:

Gr. 3 Mathematics— One-on-One Student Interviews
05:59 minutes

There is no doubt that performance and oral assessment present logistical challenges that are not part of assessing written work. They require

- pre-planning to ensure that other students are meaningfully engaged while the teacher assesses individual students or groups of students
- a well-designed assessment tool that allows for observation "on the fly"

In Chapters 7 and 8, we will examine a number of highly effective strategies for performance and oral assessment.

Should I Use the Same Strategy for All Students?

The short answer is no. Students require a flexible approach to assessment if they are to demonstrate their learning successfully. However, many teachers struggle with the idea of giving students a choice about how they will demonstrate their learning. Often I hear the question, "How can I assess their work fairly if they're all producing different things?" Once again, the solution is to start with the learning target to be assessed.

In the Grade 6 social studies example on page 101, once Sam and Marcia were clear about the learning they needed to assess, they were able to see that students could demonstrate this learning in a variety of ways. Their next step would be to determine the assessment criteria, regardless of what task their students choose to complete. In other words, they will design one rubric that will serve to assess the variety of products their students produce.

The table in Figure 6-2 will help you match assessment strategies to learning targets.

> **Tips for Teaching**
>
> Note that *understanding* is a common assessment target. *Understanding By Design* (Wiggins and McTighe, 1998) will provide you with a thorough discussion of the various facets of student understanding that need to be assessed.

Figure 6-2: Examining My Current Assessment Practice for Balance

Assessment Mode and Strategy	Purpose for Assessment	Assessment Tool
Oral Communication Conference Informal discussion Oral questioning	Provide feedback on work Assess skills (e.g., reading) Assess depth of understanding	Anecdotal record/Rubric
Performance Assessments Skills demonstration	Assess level of performance of skills	Checklist/Rubric/Rating scale
Design project Inquiry/investigation Media product Simulation	Assess application of knowledge and skills Assess depth of understanding	Checklist/Rubric
Presentation Role-play	Assess understanding and communications skills	
Written Assessments **Quizzes/Tests** · selected response · short answer · extended response	Assess knowledge Assess knowledge and understanding	Scoring guide Scoring guide Marking scheme
Graphic Organizers · mind map · word web	Assess depth of understanding Assess depth of understanding	Rubric
Extended Writing · article · brochure · report · review	Assess depth of understanding	Rubric/Checklist
· journal · portfolio	Assess understanding and communication skills Assess metacognition	

Summary

This chapter has clarified some of the terminology that is used to describe assessment practices:

- **Mode** refers to how students will demonstrate their learning—through written work, oral communication, or a performance task. A balanced approach to assessment draws from all three modes to ensure that teachers gather valid and reliable information about what students know and are able to do.
- **Strategy** refers to the specific task students are asked to do to demonstrate their learning. An investigation, a written report, and an oral presentation are examples of strategies.
- **Tool** refers to the instrument used to record assessment information. A rubric, a checklist, and an anecdotal record are examples of tools.

In Chapters 7 to 11, we will explore in detail a wide range of assessment strategies associated with the three modes—write, do, and say—and see how they match your varied assessment purposes. In Chapter 12, you will learn about selecting and developing high quality assessment tools to match these strategies.

Applying My Learning

Using Tool 1.6: *How Balanced is My Assessment Toolkit?* (page 293, see also Figure 6-2), examine either a major unit of study or your program overview for one subject to determine whether you are currently balancing your assessment modes. The *Purpose for Assessment* column will help you make adjustments as you review your current set of strategies.

TOOL 1.6

How Balanced is My Assessment Toolkit?, p. 293

1.6, Chapter 6 Review

How Balanced Is My Assessment Toolkit?

Assessment Mode and Strategy	Assessment Purpose	Assessment Tool
Oral Communication Conference Informal discussion Oral questioning/defence Structured talk with peer	provide feedback on work assess skills (e.g., reading) assess depth of understanding assess depth of understanding	Anecdotal record
Performance Assessments Skills demonstration	assess level of performance of skills	Checklist/rubric/rating scale
Design project Inquiry/investigation Media product Simulation	assess application of knowledge and skills assess understanding	Checklist/rubric
Presentation Role-play	assess understanding and communication skills	Checklist/rubric
Written Assessments **Quizzes/Tests** Selected response Short answer Extended response	assess knowledge assess knowledge assess knowledge and understanding	Scoring guide Scoring guide Marking scheme
Graphic Organizers Mind map Word web	assess understanding assess understanding	Rubric Rubric
Extended Writing Article Brochure Report Review	assess depth of understanding assess communication skills	Rubric/checklist
Journal Portfolio	assess metacognition	Rubric/checklist

Tool 1.6 **293**

Chapter 7

PERFORMANCE ASSESSMENT

> **BIG IDEA 3** Assessment must be balanced including oral, performance, and written tasks, and be flexible in order to improve learning for all students.

DESCRIBING A PERFORMANCE TASK

Performance assessment has long been a feature of music and physical education classes. As the name suggests, performance assessment requires students to perform a skill, or a set of skills, rather than write about what they have learned.

However, performance assessment is not always that straightforward. The language arts teacher, for example, might ask, "What about when students produce a piece of creative writing? I could consider it a performance assessment because they are performing writing skills, correct?" I would argue that creative writing is not performance assessment. The following definition helps explain why:

> *Performance assessment is any assessment in which the teacher's role is to observe while students perform. (Stiggins, 2004)*

A creative writing assignment would not be considered a performance assessment because the teacher does not observe students, for assessment purposes, while they write. On the other hand, staging a talk show would be considered an example of a performance assessment.

▲ **After writing about her chosen character in a language arts class, this student rises to perform in-character. Only the second phase of this activity comprises the performance assessment.**

When teaching science, many teachers say they are continuously using performance assessment because their students engage in hands-on lab experiments. However, after closer investigation, it often emerges that students' lab skills are assessed through a written report, in which case a performance assessment has not occurred. Performance assessment in a science classroom requires teachers to

- determine the skills they plan to assess
- develop a rubric or checklist for assessment purposes
- observe students while they are performing the experiment
- record their observations on the rubric or checklist

Addressing Performance Task Challenges

True performance assessment is messy, time-consuming, and labour-intensive, but it is usually highly engaging and great fun for students and teachers alike. The following guidelines will help you manage the logistical challenges. It is not possible to assess all students during one performance task. Rather, the goal is to sample students' performances. To do this,

- observe only a small group of students on any given day
- spend a brief period of time observing and recording your assessment for each student
- observe each student several times in order to build up a body of observational evidence

Observations made early in the school year can be used to provide feedback to students to help them improve a specific set of skills (assessment *for* learning). Observations made toward the end of the school year can be used to report on students' skills (assessment *of* learning). It is important to ensure that there are a sufficient number of observations on which to base assessment *of* learning conclusions. While recognizing there are time limitations, as a general rule, try to make at least three observations about a given set of skills for reporting purposes.

Authentic Assessment

Authentic assessment is a subset of performance assessment. It is an assessment task that mimics real-world experiences by assigning students real-life roles and engaging them in contexts as similar as possible to those encountered in the world beyond the classroom. For example, the following authentic assessment task could be used as the culminating task in a math unit on volume and measurement:

> ### Tips for Teaching
>
> **Observing Performance**
> To help you achieve your target number of observations, ask yourself the following questions:
> - How many students can I observe in one session?
> - Should I inform the students of the assessment? (Note: Informing students they are being assessed may compromise reliability if it causes atypical student performance.)
> - Have I clarified my behavioural expectations for students not being assessed?
> - Have I prepared or selected an easy-to-use assessment tool?
> - How will I provide feedback to students?

You work in the packaging department of the D & B Chocolate Company. Your job is to design and construct a closed container that will hold the largest volume of D & B candies for shipping, using the materials provided. You will present your design and report to the company executives, and include all important data and formulae. (Adapted from Wiggins, "Standards, Not Standardization", 1993)

One of the great benefits of authentic assessment tasks is that they make academic subjects such as math more relevant and more engaging, especially for those students who find textbook-driven math difficult to understand. By their very nature, authentic assessment tasks show how theories and concepts are applied in the real world.

DESIGNING RICH PERFORMANCE TASKS

Performance assessment can be as straightforward as assessing a simple skill demonstration such as focusing a microscope or dribbling a basketball. However, a rich performance task is differentiated by a number of characteristics, including

- the range of curriculum outcomes it addresses
- the depth of assessment data it yields
- the amount of classroom time it requires

This section explores seven essential design considerations for creating rich performance assessment tasks:

1. Rich performance tasks provide evidence of essential learning.
2. Rich performance tasks demand innovation and creativity on the part of the student.
3. Rich performance tasks present students with an engaging challenge that requires persistence to complete.
4. Rich performance tasks engage students in problem-solving and decision-making.
5. Rich performance tasks are appropriate to all students and a range of student abilities.
6. Rich performance tasks provide for individual accountability when the task involves cooperative work.
7. The assessment criteria for rich performance tasks should reflect the essential learning of the unit and be communicated to students before they begin work.

> **Tips for Teaching**
>
> Since rich performance assessment tasks are created during the overall program planning process, refer to Chapter 13, which describes the entire planning process.

1. Rich performance tasks should provide evidence of essential learning.

Wiggins and McTighe (1998) describe three levels of relative importance when referring to curriculum outcomes. These levels are illustrated in Figure 7-1.

Figure 7-1: Establishing Curricular Priorities

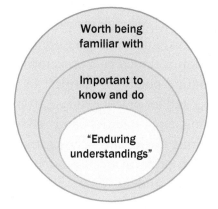

While a rich performance task may address all three levels, it *must* provide evidence of students' enduring understanding in one or more subject areas.

A rich performance task must provide evidence of students' enduring understanding.

Consider the following outcomes from a Grade 4 science curriculum:

- Describe how rotary motion in one system is transferred to rotary motion in another.
- Describe how gears operate in one plane (e.g., spur gears, idle gears) and in two planes (e.g., crown, bevel, or worm gears).

A key question remains: *Why do we need pulleys and gears in the first place?* While it may be important that students be able to describe how spur gears operate in one plane and crown gears operate in two planes, students also need to understand *why* pulleys and gears are necessary.

The enduring understanding for this unit is: *Through the transfer of force, pulleys and gears make work easier.* By the end of the unit, the teacher must assess the extent to which all students have acquired this understanding. A rich performance task would enable students to demonstrate their understanding, while also providing evidence that they have learned the difference between spur and crown gears.

2. Rich performance tasks demand innovation and creativity on the part of the student.

When teaching emphasizes memorization of facts and students are not required to apply their learning, students may end up knowing a lot but understanding little. Think of the basketball coach who drills young players endlessly until they have perfected lay-ups, but then puzzles over the players' lack of skill when playing another team. Demonstrating an isolated skill on cue in the school gym provides no guarantee that players will be able to execute this skill under pressure in a real game.

A classroom situation is similar to a basketball game. When students are presented with routine questions identical to the questions used to introduce new learning and for practice, they can't provide proof that they understand this learning. Such questions only allow students to demonstrate that they can mimic the learning demonstrated by the teacher.

When designing rich performance assessment tasks, it is important to devise tasks that require students to

- demonstrate the skills and knowledge they have acquired during a unit of study by applying them to previously unseen problems
- make thoughtful, purposeful decisions about which concepts to apply and which procedures to use to enable them to solve the problem

Consider the following example for a Grade 3 math unit. Students have been learning about area and grids, including how to measure using square units and how to solve problems using models. To provide evidence that they have understood the concepts and procedures, the teacher assigns the following rich performance task.

Task: Design a Dream Bedroom

Design a dream bedroom. Your model will be a floor plan drawn to scale, complete with all furniture you wish to include. You may wish to consider including some of the following:

- computer table
- chairs
- bookshelf
- desk
- couch
- bedside tables

Submit a written description of your dream bedroom, explaining why you included each piece. As you work, consider how to design a bedroom that

- is well-planned
- has enough, but not too much space
- makes good use of space

Throughout the course of the unit, students have learned and practised all of the necessary concepts and procedures required to complete this task. Now they must make thoughtful decisions about which concepts to apply and which procedures to use—and in what order—to design this bedroom. In other words, they must demonstrate innovation and creativity.

3. Rich performance tasks present students with an engaging challenge that requires persistence to complete.

It is a myth that students do not like to work hard. Most students are quite happy to undertake challenging work and to spend a significant amount of time on a task, provided they see the work as both relevant and engaging. Science can provide some of the most absorbing learning, especially if it includes hands-on tasks that help students understand how scientific theories connect to the real world.

Consider these tasks in which students synthesize and apply what they have learned in a Grade 7 unit about heat energy. Since both tasks address the same essential learning outcomes, students are instructed to choose whichever task most interests them:

▲ **Science can provide some of the most absorbing learning, especially if it includes hands-on tasks.**

Task 1: Design a Device that Delays Heat Transfer

Problem Situation

We use appliances to cook food and to keep it cool. Ovens, refrigerators, and similar devices will not waste nearly as much energy if they are designed to prevent heat transfer to or from the outside.

Design Brief

Design and build a container that will keep a cold pop can as cool as possible from breakfast until lunchtime.

> ### Task 2: Design an Environment to Protect Plants
> #### Problem Situation
> Every year, more people in Canada discover the advantages of growing their own plants for food or for beauty. But because the growing season in Canada is short, many plants die prematurely when frost strikes early.
> #### Design Brief
> Design and build a model of a greenhouse or other environment that would allow a plant to grow when outdoor temperatures are low. The environment must also resist overheating to prevent plants from dying as a result of too much heat.

To complete either of these tasks, students must spend a considerable amount of time in both the design and building stages. They will encounter unforeseen problems along the way and will have to persevere in order to succeed. However, the fact that these tasks are relevant, are rooted in real-world challenges, and require students to "do" science and technology will encourage most students to persist through to their successful completion.

4. Rich performance tasks engage students in problem-solving and decision-making.

In each of the tasks described above, problem-solving and decision-making skills provide the foundation for the learning that students are required to demonstrate. Just as solving problems and making decisions distinguishes mundane tasks from complex ones in the real world, rich performance tasks demand that students display these skills in a way that simple tasks do not.

A rich performance task requires students to follow these problem-solving steps:

1. Understand the problem—what does the task require me to do?
2. Make a plan—what strategies and procedures will I use to complete the task?
3. Carry out the plan—how do I use and monitor these strategies and procedures?
4. Look back—how successful have I been in completing the task?
5. Communicate—how will I report my findings and/or share my solution with others?

While students work on a rich performance task, you and your students should assess their progress together. Too often, assessment takes place after the task has been completed and is limited to the finished

Just as solving problems and making decisions distinguishes mundane tasks from complex ones in the real world, rich performance tasks demand that students display these skills in a way that simple tasks do not.

product. Yet much of the learning is demonstrated by students while they are working on the task. Teachers can assess problem-solving and decision-making skills by observing students, asking probing questions, and recording observations on a checklist or rubric as students work on the task. (See assessment tools in Part 2 for a range of checklists and rubrics.)

5. Rich performance tasks are appropriate to all students and a range of student abilities.

All students are capable of completing rich assessment tasks, regardless of ability, gender, or grade level. However, depending on these variables, the degree of scaffolding needed for individuals or groups of students will vary. (See Chapter 3.) An open-ended task is more challenging for students since it includes little scaffolding and demands that students make more decisions than a task that includes a lot of scaffolding.

Figure 7-2: Student Response to Design a Dream Bedroom Task

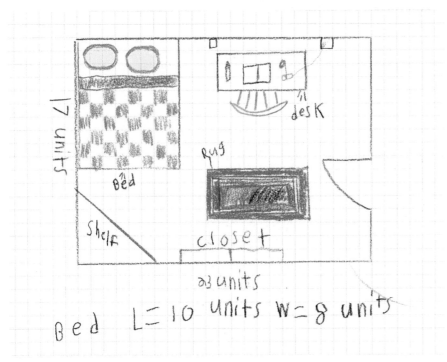

To illustrate, consider the "Design a Dream Bedroom" task described on page 110. For some students, the task could be left open-ended. However, other students may benefit from scaffolding, such as the following, that guides them through the problem-solving process:

1. **Understand the problem**

- What do you know about area and perimeter?
- What furniture is appropriate for a bedroom?
- How can you make the furniture in proportion to the size of the bedroom?

2. **Make a Plan**

- Use chart grid paper to show the area of the bedroom.
- Use square tiles to represent the area of your furniture.

3. **Carry Out the Plan**

- Draw the shape of your bedroom on the grid paper.
- Create the pieces of furniture and place them on the floor plan.

4. **Look Back**

- Is there enough room to move around the bedroom?
- Are the pieces of furniture in proportion to the size of the room?

5. **Communicate**

- Explain why you think your design is a good one.
- Describe the furniture you chose to include and tell why you did so.

Further scaffolding could be provided by presenting students with a checklist:

	Yes	No
Did you make your floor plan of the bedroom an appropriate size?	❏	❏
Did you make the furniture an appropriate size for the room?	❏	❏
Did you allow for enough space to move around in the room?	❏	❏
Did you show enough detail?	❏	❏
Did you explain your thinking?	❏	❏
Did you use math language?	❏	❏

All students deserve the challenge and engagement that rich performance tasks provide. Because of the myths that prevail about the limitations of students with special needs, however, rich performance tasks are often reserved for students who are considered gifted or highly able. Chapter 10 illustrates how all students are able to complete such tasks, and can benefit from the learning and assessment opportunities that characterize these rich performance tasks.

6. Rich performance tasks provide for individual accountability when the task involves cooperative work.

Students are assigned to work in cooperative groups because such groupings replicate real-life working conditions. Moreover, if groups work well, members can produce something that is greater than the sum of its parts. Unfortunately, the data gathered during group assessment can often be of poor quality. (See Chapter 5.) Some students may receive credit for work they did not complete, while other students may receive less credit than they deserve.

To help you avoid such problems, refer to the guidelines on pages 91–92 of this resource. They will ensure that your assessment data are valid and that no student's mark is adversely affected by the work that other students do or do not complete.

When students are in co-operative groups, it is essential to ensure that no student's mark is adversely affected by work that other students do not complete.

7. The assessment criteria for rich performance tasks should reflect the essential learning and be communicated to students before they begin work.

Criteria refer to the attributes of a rich performance task that will be assessed. They inform students which aspects of the task require the bulk of their attention. Identifying the assessment criteria is an essential step in task design. Once identified, the criteria must also be communicated to students before they begin work on the task.

Refer again to the tasks on pages 111–112. Because both tasks address the same set of learning outcomes, and because each task requires students to design and build a device or a model, you can use a generic set of assessment criteria for both tasks. However, each task also requires its own set of specific design criteria. For each criterion, "I" indicates "individual assessment" and "G" indicates "group assessment."

Identifying the assessment criteria is an essential step in task design. Once identified, the criteria must also be communicated to students before they begin work on the task.

Process Criteria (Tasks 1 and 2)

- Understanding of problem (I)
- Development of a safe plan (G)
- Choice and safe use of materials, tools, and equipment (I)
- Testing and recording results (G)
- Evaluation of model (G)

Communication Criteria (Tasks 1 and 2)

- Clarity and effectiveness of presentation (G)
- Written report (I)
- Technical drawing of model (I)

Product Design Criteria (G)

Task 1: Design a Device that Delays Heat Transfer

- Container must fit inside a standard lunch box.
- Pop can should contain 355mL and be at refrigerator temperature at beginning of experiment.

Task 2: Design an Environment to Protect Plants

- Environment must support at least one plant.
- To avoid energy waste, only energy from the sun can be used.
- Temperature in the environment should remain constant. It should not drop below 10°C, even if outside temperatures are lower than 10°C. It should not rise above 30°C, even in bright sunshine on a warm day.

Culminating Tasks

Rich performance tasks, in the form of culminating tasks, can bring closure to a unit of study by presenting students with the opportunity to synthesize and apply their learning.

Rich performance tasks, in the form of culminating tasks, can often bring closure to a unit of study by presenting students with the opportunity to synthesize and apply their learning. Seen this way, a rich performance task becomes the destination that students are traveling toward. (See Chapter 13 for a detailed explanation of program planning, including the use of culminating tasks.)

At the beginning of a unit, both you and your students will benefit from knowing what the culminating task will be, since it can provide

- a goal that everyone is working toward
- a rationale for the various concepts and skills that will be taught en route to the culminating task

You will also be less likely to encounter the "Why do-we-have-to-learn-this-stuff?" questions that can derail instruction.

Summary

- Performance assessment requires students to demonstrate their learning by doing. During a performance task, the assessor observes and records the quality of the performance.
- A subset of performance assessment is authentic assessment, which resembles as closely as possible a real-world task. Hence, authentic assessment tasks usually require students to assume roles. These tasks often bring out the best in terms of student performance because they are engaging and relevant to real life.
- Seven guidelines for designing rich performance tasks help ensure quality assessment.

Applying My Learning

Choose a performance task that you have designed or a task that you have selected from a resource. Review the seven guidelines for designing rich performance tasks (see pages 109–116) and use Tool 1.7: *Evaluating the Quality of a Performance Task* to

- examine and evaluate the quality of that task
- improve the task where it is deficient.

1.7, Chapter 7 Review

Evaluating the Quality of a Performance Task		
Quality Criterion	**Evaluation of Task*** (✓) or (✗)	**Maintain / Modify / Change**
Task provides evidence of essential learning		
Task demands innovation and creativity on the part of the student		
Task presents students with an engaging challenge that requires persistence to complete		
Task engages students in problem solving and decision making		
Task is appropriate for all students		
If task involves co-operative groups, there is provision for individual accountability		
Assessment criteria for task reflects the essential learning		
Assessment criteria are communicated in student-friendly language before students begin work		

TOOL 1.7

Evaluating the Quality of a Performance Task, p. 294

Chapter 8

ASSESSMENT THROUGH ORAL COMMUNICATION

BIG IDEA 6 Assessment is a collaborative process that is most effective when it involves, self-, peer, and teacher assessment.

Talk enhances the development of literacy. It is not a subject, but rather a condition of learning in all subjects.

DAVID BOOTH, 1991

▲ **Talk—a condition of learning**

Sampling the informal talk that occurs between and among students is a key step in determining their level of understanding.

Talk is a "condition of learning" (Booth, 1991) rather than a product of it. For this reason, it is not usually considered an appropriate target for assessment. In many instances, though, talk can provide rich evidence of students' learning. Consider the child who consistently performs poorly on written work and never raises a hand to answer questions. When asked to discuss a problem with a partner, however, this student is full of ideas and insights. Isn't the substance of this talk equally valid evidence of this student's learning?

Although talk need not be assessed all the time (that would be impossible), sampling the informal talk that occurs between and among students is a key step in determining their level of understanding.

LITERACY CONTEXTS

Students need to talk in order to learn. Talk helps children

- question new learning
- decide what they do and do not understand
- clarify their thinking
- clarify their peers' thinking
- challenge ideas in order to consolidate understanding
- try out their interpretations on the world around them

In short, talk is often the vehicle for learning. To help us appreciate David Booth's contention that "talk is a condition of learning in all subjects," consider the six literacy contexts presented in Figure 8-1.

Figure 8-1: Literacy Contexts: Purpose, Focus, and Audience						
Literacy Context	**Personal Literacy**	**Information Literacy**	**Media Literacy**	**Social Literacy**	**Technical Literacy**	**Cultural Literacy**
Purpose	• using language to understand self	• using language to learn about the world	• using language to interpret media messages	• using language to work with others	• using language to explain and find solutions	• using language to appreciate culture
Focus of Learning	• exploring thoughts, feelings, and experiences to discover and understand what and how they think and who they are	• accessing, recording, analyzing, synthesizing, and communicating information	• creating, interpreting, and critically examining messages in media texts	• encouraging, supporting, and working with others	• investigating and explaining technical works in a problem-solving context	• interpreting, responding to, and creating literary texts reflecting our literary heritage
Focus of Instruction/ Assessment	• Reading • Writing • Speaking • Listening • Viewing • Representing	• Reading • Writing • Speaking • Listening • Viewing • Representing	• Reading • Writing • Speaking • Listening • Viewing • Representing	• Reading • Writing • Speaking • Listening • Viewing • Representing	• Reading • Writing • Speaking • Listening • Viewing • Representing	• Reading • Writing • Speaking • Listening • Viewing • Representing
Audience	• Self	• Self • Peers • Teacher • Other adults	• Self • Peers • Teacher • Other adults	• Peers	• Self • Peers • Teacher • Other adults	• Self • Peers • Teacher • Other adults

SOURCE: NELSON LANGUAGE ARTS, GRADES 1–6

Although it could be argued that all six contexts exist in all subjects, it is certainly true that every school subject involves at least two contexts. In mathematics, for example, students use

- information literacy when using a computer
- social literacy when solving a problem with their peers
- technical literacy when using the language specific to mathematics

Notice also that the six modes of language—reading, writing, speaking, listening, viewing, and representing—apply equally to each of the literacy contexts. From an assessment standpoint, this means that assessment in each of these modes should occur at different times throughout the year, in all subject areas.

This chapter examines the kinds of assessment strategies that allow students to demonstrate their speaking and listening skills, and matches these strategies with appropriate tools to gather assessment data. (See also Chapter 12.)

TALK

Talk is a generic term encompassing the many informal interactions that occur during an instructional period. It can involve two peers, a small group, or the whole class, and may also include the teacher. Because talk is informal and exploratory, it can reveal a great deal about students' conceptual understanding, as well as their ability to think on their feet. These elements are the "content" of talk; assessment of these elements will reveal students' knowledge and understanding of a particular subject.

CASE STUDY 1

Using Conversation to Assess Understanding

Rachel and her Grade 3 classmates are learning about patterns. Their teacher, Mr. Stern, has asked the students to bring from home an object with a repeated pattern so he can formally assess their understanding about repeated patterns. As Mr. Stern and the students consider the items brought from home, the following conversation ensues:

Mr. Stern: What have you brought, Rachel?

Rachel: I've brought a towel that has a pattern on it.

Rose: What kind of pattern is it, Rachel?

Rachel: A rectangle pattern.

Mr. Stern: Rachel, can you use the word *attribute* to describe the pattern on your towel for us?

Rachel: Okay. I'll try. One attribute is ... uh ... I guess I'm not sure.

Mr. Stern: Rose, can you help Rachel? Can you

continued

use the word *attribute* to help describe the pattern on Rachel's towel?

Rose: I think so. One attribute is shape. There are three shapes that repeat on the pattern—sun, cloud, and rain.

Rachel: Oh, now I remember! Colour is another attribute. Yellow and white.

Mr. Stern: So besides shape and colour, are there any other attributes to the pattern on Rachel's towel?

Rose: Number, like there are three shapes.

Mr. Stern is able to use this conversation to assess Rachel and Rose's conceptual understanding of attribute as it relates to patterns.

At first, Rachel is tentative in her grasp of the concept, but, with Mr. Stern's supporting questions and Rose's deeper understanding, Rachel is able to consolidate her understanding. Using the generic rubric for depth of understanding of concepts (see Figure 8-3), Mr. Stern might assess her current understanding as Level 2. Depending on when it occurs in the term, this one brief assessment event is likely to be assessment for learning that helps Rachel improve her learning. As a reporting period approaches, Mr. Stern will use the same rubric to conduct assessment of learning by assessing Rachel's level of understanding at that point in the year.

Figure 8-3: Partial Rubric for Conceptual Understanding				
Criterion	Level 1	Level 2	Level 3	Level 4
Depth of Understanding	· demonstrates only a superficial understanding of concept(s), i.e., restates what was taught but with inaccuracies	· demonstrates a growing but still incomplete understanding of concept(s), i.e., provides incomplete explanation of thinking	· demonstrates grade-appropriate understanding of concept(s), i.e., provides appropriate and complete explanation of thinking	· demonstrates in-depth understanding of concept(s), i.e., provides clear, complete, and logical explanation that may go beyond what was taught

▲ **The more students practise oral skills, the more confident they become, and the more you can focus on the content of their communication.**

Students benefit from daily opportunities to practise their speaking and listening skills so that they perform better when assessed.

IMPROVING ORAL SKILLS

In language arts or English classes, teachers are generally not as concerned with the subject content of talk as they are with speaking and listening skills such as clarity and fluency of speech, range of vocabulary, correctness of grammar, and so on. (Although vocabulary is considered an aspect of content, the ability to select and use a broad range of vocabulary is a skill.) Students benefit from daily opportunities to practise their speaking and listening skills so that they perform better when assessed.

Some teachers choose to incorporate talk into the context of a lesson. For example, you could ask students to orally present their work before they have completed it and have students provide on-the-spot oral feedback. This strategy builds both oral skill and confidence.

When incorporated into your classroom routine, games such as the following also provide good strategies for developing oral fluency and increasing students' self-confidence.

Just a Minute!

Just a Minute! is based on the BBC 4 radio show of the same name. This game works best with students in Grades 4 to 8, but can be adapted to suit students in earlier grades.

Directions

Create teams of four players. Use a rotating schedule so that all teams get to play an equal number of games over the course of a school term. You may wish to create a league that runs throughout the term.

Prepare a list of simple and fun topics to use, such as

- weekends without parents
- my best shopping spree
- bugs I love
- joys of email

Have each player on each team chose a number from 1 to 4. Flip a coin to decide which team goes first, and read aloud the following simple rules. (You will act as timekeeper and moderator. Note that the one-minute time limit can be shortened for students in early grades.)

Rules

1. Each player on each team will speak for one minute on a topic assigned by me.

2. I will start my stopwatch as soon as I've assigned the topic.

3. The speaker must not hesitate, repeat important words, or go off-topic.

4. While a player is speaking, the opposing team's players must listen carefully for hesitation, repetition, or off-topic talk.

5. If you hear a player of the opposing team hesitate, repeat, or speak off-topic, rap loudly on your desk and call out, "hesitation," "repetition," or "off-topic."

6. I will stop the watch and rule on whether or not the interruption is legitimate.

7. If I rule the interruption legitimate, then the player who called out the interruption will continue speaking on the same topic for the remainder of the minute.

8. The object of the game is to get as many points as possible:

   - 1 point for a legitimate interruption

   - 1 point deduction for an illegitimate interruption
     (The speaker did not hesitate, repeat, or go off-topic.)

   - 2 points if you are speaking when one minute is up

   - 5 points for speaking the entire minute without being interrupted

---

The Alphabet Illness Game

This game is most appropriate for students in the early grades.

Directions

Beginning with the following phrase, each student names an ailment that prevents him or her from attending school today: "I can't go to school today because I've got _____." The only rule is that the ailments must be in named in alphabetical order. For example, the first student might start with, "I can't go to school today because I've got allergies." The next student could say, "I can't come to school today because I've got allergies and a backache." The third student may say, "I can't go to school today because I've got allergies, a backache, and a cough." (You can choose to either make this a memory game or allow students to suggest an illness for their letter only.)

SOURCE: DAVID LAZEAR, SEVEN WAYS OF KNOWING-UNDERSTANDING MULTIPLE INTELLIGENCES (PALATINE, IL: SKYLIGHT PUBLISHING, 1991)

Class Discussion

Class discussion provides an opportunity for the informal exchange of ideas among you and your students.

Class discussion provides an opportunity for the informal exchange of ideas among you and your students. It is an essential classroom routine because it requires students to think about their learning. Although teachers tend to not assess informal discussion, some assessment evidence from these discussions should be gathered as many students demonstrate their deepest learning during these sessions.

It is important during discussions to differentiate between the content knowledge and the skills that students demonstrate. Figure 8-4, for example, illustrates a partial checklist that allows you to assess students' understanding of science concepts, as well as their oral language skills.

Figure 8-4: Partial Oral Language Checklist for Grade 7 Science	
Conceptual Understanding	**Speaking and Listening Skills**
· understands what conservation of fresh water means · can explain human impact on fresh water supply · is aware that water treatment is, itself, a source of pollution · knows that water molecules are polar: they attract other substances · can explain how water treatment works	· introduces own ideas appropriately · responds appropriately to ideas of others · extends ideas of others · speaks fluently · uses vocabulary appropriate to the discussion · uses body language to encourage others and emphasize own ideas

Students need numerous opportunities to practise their skills before assessment of learning takes place.

Students need numerous opportunities to practise their skills before assessment *of* learning takes place; that is, before the assessment of student performance for grading and reporting purposes. If you choose to assess a class discussion, follow these guidelines:

1. Tell students that you will be assessing the discussion. Some students thrive when they have an audience, while others are reluctant to speak in class. If a discussion is going to be assessed, all students need to know so the reluctant speakers will be encouraged to participate.

2. Give students the checklist or rubric that you will be using before you have the discussion. It should describe the speaking and listening skills you intend to target.

3. Moderate the discussion so that reluctant speakers have a chance to speak and no individual monopolizes the discussion.

4. Assess the discussion using your checklist or rubric.

5. Assess only a sample of students during any one session. You may assess another sample of students during the next session.

6. Aim to have at least three assessments of each student for assessment of learning (reporting) purposes.

Figure 8-5 illustrates a partial rubric for assessing class discussion. (See Part 2 for a range of assessment tools to use in informal speaking and listening situations.) The complete rubric for this tool can be found on page 376.

Figure 8-5 Partial Rubric for Speaking and Listening

TOOL 4.9

Informal Speaking and Listening Rubric, p. 376

Informal Speaking and Listening Rubric

Name: _____ Date: _____

Categories/Criteria	Level 1	Level 2	Level 3	Level 4
Thinking	· demonstrates **limited ability** to explore/express thoughts when speaking to others	· demonstrates **some ability** to explore/express thoughts when speaking to others (e.g., is beginning to reflect, analyze, hypothesize)	· **explores/expresses** own **thoughts** when speaking to others (e.g., reflects, analyzes, hypothesizes)	· **explores/expresses** **original/creative thoughts** when speaking to others (e.g., reflects, analyzes, hypothesizes)
	· demonstrates **limited ability** to build on the ideas of others	· demonstrates **some** ability to build on the ideas of others	· **builds** on the ideas of others when speaking	· **integrates and extends** the ideas of others when speaking
Communication	· expresses ideas, opinions, feelings with **limited clarity** when speaking to others in terms of: · fluency · volume · speed · intonation · inflection	· expresses ideas, opinions, feelings with **partial clarity** when speaking to others in terms of: · fluency · volume · speed · intonation · inflection	· expresses ideas, opinions, feelings **clearly** when speaking to others in terms of: · fluency · volume · speed · intonation · inflection	· expresses ideas, opinions, feelings **clearly and in an engaging manner** when speaking to others in terms of: · fluency · volume · speed · intonation · inflection
	· uses a **limited** vocabulary	· **attempts to use** new vocabulary	· uses new vocabulary **effectively**	· **explores** new vocabulary **successfully**
	· has **difficulty** maintaining appropriate eye contact when speaking	· maintains eye contact **some of** the time when speaking	· maintains **appropriate** eye contact when speaking	· **establishes and maintains** eye contact when speaking
	· makes **limited** use of gestures when speaking	· makes **some** use of gestures when speaking	· uses gestures **effectively** when speaking	· uses gestures **naturally and effectively** when speaking
Active Listening	· demonstrates **limited ability** to listen to others' ideas, opinions, points of view	· listens **some of the time** to others' ideas, opinions, points of view	· listens **attentively** to others' ideas, opinions, points of view	· listens attentively and **respectfully** to others' ideas, opinions, points of view
	· challenges others' ideas, opinions, points of view **may be inappropriate**	· **attempts to challenge** others' ideas, opinions, points of view appropriately	· challenges others' ideas, opinions, points of view **appropriately**	· challenges others' ideas, opinions, points of view **appropriately and constructively**
	· asks **few** questions	· **attempts to** ask appropriate questions	· asks **appropriate** questions	· asks **insightful** questions
	· has **difficulty** demonstrating appropriate posture and body language when listening to others	· demonstrates appropriate posture and body language **some of the time** when listening to others	· demonstrates **appropriate** posture and body language when listening to others	· **encourages** speaker through appropriate use of posture and body language

376
Tool 4.9
4.9, *Language Arts Gr. 4–6*
Copyright © 2007 by Nelson, a division of Thomson Canada Ltd.

Oral Question-and-Answer

Asking students questions during class is a standard teaching tool. Oral questioning may be used to

■ assess students' prior knowledge and experience when beginning a new topic or introducing a new concept

■ monitor students' ongoing level of understanding while a new topic or concept is being taught (This tells you when to slow down, rephrase, or clarify new material that is proving difficult for students to understand.)

■ engage students more fully with new material by asking questions that help them connect new learning to their own experience

■ consolidate what has been taught before moving on to new material.

Video Clip 1:

Gr. 7/8 Mathematics— Using Assessment for Different Purposes 14:11 minutes

As with other oral assessment, whether to assess student performance during a question-and-answer session should be decided ahead of time. Not every session needs to be assessed and, in fact, assessment in this context should be the exception rather than the rule. That said, assessment information of this kind is important because many students are able to demonstrate their understanding orally but may have difficulty demonstrating it in writing. One way to stay responsive to evidence of learning obtained through oral questioning is to keep a simple assessment tool, such as a notebook or a clipboard, ready and available for recording anecdotal data. (See Figure 8.6.)

Figure 8-6: Anecdotal Recording

Andrea			
Date	Strengths	Needs	Next Steps
October 14	demonstrated sophisticated understanding of poem, "If I Could Fly," during Q & A by showing empathy for narrator and connecting to her personal experience		

Some students will always raise a hand whenever a question-and-answer session begins. Others seem to never raise their hand, either to answer or to ask a question. It is important, therefore, to continually monitor the participation rate of all students.

Figure 8-7: Scatter Plot

| CASE STUDY 2 | **Response to Poetry** |

When exploring short forms of writing, an excellent alternative to the typical question-and-answer session in a language arts class is the Personal Response model. Mrs. Chin's Grade 6 class is exploring a poem using this approach:

Mrs. Chin: Today, we're going to use Response to Poetry to read and talk about a poem called "The Question." First of all, I want you to move your desks very quietly into a circle so that we can all see and hear one another.

You all did that very well! Now, let's review how we do Response to Poetry.

Patti, would you start us off?

Patti: First, we read the poem together. Then we think about it quietly for a few minutes. Then … I forget what's next.

Mrs. Chin: Roberto, can you help us out? What comes after thinking quietly to ourselves about the poem?

Roberto: Uh, then we start going round the circle and everyone takes a turn to say what they think the poem is about.

Mrs. Chin: That's right. And if you're not sure, you may say, "Pass." You may only pass once, though, okay?

Tan: Then, when we've gone all around the circle, we start over again?

Mrs. Chin: That's right, Tan. But what do we say the second time around?

Tan: We say how a line in the poem reminds us of something that's happened to us, or to someone we know.

Mrs. Chin: Well done, Tan. So, let's begin by reading the poem together…

The Response to Poetry model is an excellent opportunity for assessing students' oral language skills. It has many advantages over a conventional question-and-answer approach:

- All students participate.
- The structure provides scaffolding so that reluctant students do not feel nervous responding.
- By going around the circle, students' level of understanding builds in a cumulative fashion.
- The circle encourages students to listen to and extend the contributions of their peers.

Conferencing

A conference is an informal discussion focussed on a single piece or a portfolio of student work. A conference may involve just the student and the teacher; it may occur between two students; or it may be a three-way discussion involving the student, a parent or guardian, and the teacher.

Conferencing is the best way to provide students with the feedback that is essential to both assessment *for* and *of* learning. For a conference to be effective in improving learning, there should be clear focus, such as a specific skill the students need to improve. Teachers who are experienced conference practitioners train students how to prepare for a conference.

Video Clip 6:

A Three-Way Reporting Conference (Teacher/ Student/Parent) 06:45 minutes

Mrs. Amaro was teaching her students how to improve their study skills. She asked them to write a journal entry entitled, "How I Study for a Test." During Writers' Workshop, Mrs. Amaro spent a few minutes conferencing with Anya. First she read Anya's journal entry:

Mrs. Amaro then began her conference as follows:

Mrs. Amaro: Anya, I want you to read this to me, please.

Anya: Do I have to?

Mrs. Amaro: I'd like you to read it to me so that I can help you improve your writing. If you read it aloud, I'll bet that you'll be able to hear for yourself how to improve your journal entry.

Anya: Okay. (Anya reads her entry aloud.) I think it's fine.

Mrs. Amaro: Well, there are plenty of good points in your entry, but there are a few things we need to work on. What is this word? (Mrs. Amaro points to *snakes*.)

Anya: Snack—you know, something to eat.

Mrs. Amaro: Oh, right. (Mrs. Amaro writes the words *snake* and *snack*). Anya, would you read these two words for me?

Anya: Snack, snack…Oh, I see. I wrote *snake* instead of *snack*.

Mrs. Amaro: Do you remember what makes the vowel sound *a* long, as in *snake*, instead of a short sound as in *snack*?

Anya: Yes, the letter *e* after *k*.

Mrs. Amaro: Well done, Anya. Now, I really think we should work on using periods correctly. I want you to read these two phrases. (Mrs. Amaro points to "When I have a test coming up" and "Until I can remember it of by heart.") Are they complete sentences?

How I Study for a Test
When I have a test coming up. I normally leave it to the last minute. I hope I can stop that habit so I can be successful in my life.
Then I take out my books and read my notes over and over. Until I can remember it of by heart. Some times I can't remember all the notes because it's to long. I put it in to my own words or in to little words. After I get someone in the house. To give me the question and I give the answer. After I get a snakes and read it one more time. Than go to sleep because sleep it relaxes you for the test.

Anya: What do you mean?

Mrs. Amaro: Does each phrase express a complete thought, or do they need other phrases to help you understand them?

Anya: Well, I guess you need all of it.

Mrs. Amaro: Could you explain, using the actual words from your entry?

Anya: At the start, you need to hear, "When I have a test coming up. I normally leave it to the last minute."

Mrs. Amaro: Right. So maybe a period isn't needed?

Anya: You have to have something there, don't you?

Mrs. Amaro: Yes, but what should you use instead of a period?

Anya: A comma?

Mrs. Amaro: Well done. Now, let's see if you're able to find other places where you've used periods incorrectly. Read over your entry again and see if you can spot the same problem.

continued

Notice some of the things that Mrs. Amaro did and did not do in this conference with Anya:

- She did not overwhelm Anya by pointing out all of the problems with the piece all at once.
- She focused Anya's attention on the most serious problem first—the use of periods—and worked with her to see if she had the necessary understanding to correct her own work.

After several minutes, Mrs. Amaro ended her conference with Anya. The next time they meet, Mrs. Amaro may first check that Anya has consolidated her understanding of period use, and then move on to another focus such as nouns and their corresponding pronoun referents. She will use the same anecdotal recording tool to document Anya's progress as a result of conferencing.

Anecdotal Recording

Anya			
Date	Strengths	Needs	Next Steps
November 23	· diction · word-processing	· use of complete sentences and periods · noun/pronoun referents	· check for mastery of period use · work on nouns and their pronoun referents

In-Class Interviews

Many students will reveal far more about what they do and do not understand in a subject area if they have opportunities to talk to you—one-on-one—on a regular basis. The in-class interview is more formal than the conference. Rather than focusing on samples of student work, you can use this time to assess student understanding by asking a series of probing questions. Many teachers like to schedule in-class interviews as a reporting period approaches since the interview can generate essential evidence of each student's level of understanding at that point in time.

You are probably wondering how you are going to find the time to interview every one of your students. Clearly, lack of time and large class sizes make scheduling interviews a challenge. However, the assessment evidence that can be gathered during one-on-one interviews is so rich that it is important to find the time within the instructional cycle. By using a structured approach such as the one outlined below you can be sure that

- students having difficulty are identified early
- no students slip through the cracks
- every student has several opportunities for one-on-one contact before the first report card goes home

Video Clip 8:

Gr. 3 Mathematics— One-on-One Student Interviews 05:59 minutes

Ms. Olsen had just completed a *patterns* unit with her Grade 1 class and wanted to assess each student's understanding of the concepts they had been taught. She planned to interview each student using in-class time while other students worked on other activities.

Interview: Sorting and Patterning	
Interview Questions/Prompts	**Student Responses/Observations**
D = Directions Q = Questions P = Prompts	
D Place 30 to 40 pattern blocks or attribute blocks in front of the student.	
Q What can you tell me about these blocks?	*They are different colours.*
P Is there anything else you can tell me?	*Some are square.*
D Have the student choose a sorting rule and sort the blocks using the rule.	*Selects all the squares.*
Q What is your sorting rule?	*They are all orange.*
D Point to a block that the student did not include in the group.	
Q Why did you not put this block into your group?	*It isn't orange.*
D Have the student choose a different sorting rule and sort the remaining blocks.	*Selects all the yellow hexagons.*
Q What is your sorting rule for this group?	*They are yellow.*
Q How is this group different from the other group?	*They're yellow.*
P Is there another way you can tell how they are different?	*They aren't orange.*
Q How is this group similar to the other group?	*I don't know. They're not the same.*
P Can you think about something besides colour?	*You mean the shapes? These are squares and I can't remember what the others are called.*
D Describes objects using attributes such as size, colour, shape.	*Identified attribute of colour.*
D Sorts a group with like attributes.	*With confidence.*
D Expresses a reasonable sorting rule for the group of objects.	*Used colour.*
D Explains a non-example using attributes and/or sorting rule.	*Yes.*
D Contrasts groups using attributes.	*Prompting helped her provide more detail.*
D Compares groups using attributes.	*Needs more opportunities to compare attributes.*

continued

Her goal was to record each student's responses and then take a minute or two to assess the appropriate curriculum outcomes. She would use the information at report card time. Her plan looked like this:

- Create a recording sheet that spells out the tasks and specific questions for students, related to the appropriate learning outcomes.
- List any prompting questions to be used if necessary.
- Provide space for observations and student responses.

Ms. Olsen began with Lucy. As she completed the tasks, Lucy demonstrated that she was capable of sorting, identifying, and creating a pattern. Ms. Olsen noted that Lucy would need more opportunities to use appropriate math vocabulary. Ms. Olsen also noticed that Lucy focused her sorting and patterning on colour. Since Grade 1 students are required to identify patterns using a variety of attributes—colour, shape, or size—Ms. Olsen wrote that Lucy should be encouraged to explore other attributes to broaden her conceptual understanding. She asked prompting questions to support Lucy, and recorded that she would need more opportunities to gain confidence and ability. Ms. Olsen's interview notes are shown in the table on the previous page.

Ms. Olsen gained a great deal of insight from her interview with Lucy. She was able to witness first-hand what Lucy knew and could do. Ms. Olsen also gained valuable information about the concepts and skills she needed to revisit as she planned her future math instruction.

Managing In-Class Interviews

Here are some suggested tips on how to build one-on-one interviews into your classroom routine.

1. Establish specific times during the term when you will conduct interviews. Scheduling interviews in the days leading up to a reporting period will generate essential evidence for this purpose.
2. Set up a schedule so that you interview five to eight students during each session.
3. Inform the students who will be interviewed the day before so they will be prepared.
4. Create a large poster that clearly describes your behavioural expectations for the rest of the class during interview time and review it on each "Interview Day."
5. Assign the rest of the class engaging, quiet work to minimize interruptions.
6. Time each interview to last no longer than five minutes. If a particular student needs more time, he or she may return once the other students scheduled for that day have had their interviews.
8. Use a student interview form to keep track of each interview.
9. Refer to your interview notes when talking to parents and guardians.

Assessment Q&A

Question

How can I find the time to hold one-on-one conferences with 30 students and get the rest of the class to behave while I'm holding the conferences?

Answer

Teachers who use one-on-one conferencing most effectively schedule this time into their instructional routine. They and their students know when the conferences will occur. Spend time early in the year talking to students about your behavioural expectations during conferencing time. When conferencing, use non-verbal cues to keep the rest of the class on task, and ensure that they have engaging and meaningful work to do.

Zach's teacher, Mr. McLean, had provided his class with an extensive list of social studies topics to choose from. Zach had chosen to research medieval weapons and warfare. He spent two weeks working on his project, scouring the library stacks, surfing the Internet, and even asking his parents to take him to the local university to interview a professor who specializes in the time period. As presentation day approached, Zach prepared a set of cue cards to assist him as he talked about the slides in his audio-visual presentation.

As he was about to begin his presentation, Zach was so nervous that he was trembling. Mr. McLean reassured Zach that he had done an excellent job on his research, and that his material was so good, he had nothing to worry about.

Zach began to speak. He stood rigid, staring fixedly at his cue cards, and read them in a barely audible mumble. Despite Mr. McLean's suggestions to speak up, he continued in the same quiet monotone until he had read all of his cards. Then, still without looking up, he asked, "Are there any questions?"

From an assessment standpoint, the assessment data gathered from Zach's presentation are of little value. Yes, the data show that, at this point in time, Zach is not able to deliver an effective oral presentation. But that is all that can be concluded from his presentation! Prior to the presentation, however, Mr. McLean had already assessed Zach's research skills. Zach demonstrated excellence in this area, reflected in the library, Internet, and interview research he had completed. But to assess the quality of Zach's understanding about medieval weapons and warfare resulting from his research, Mr. McLean will have to either

• examine his written work and his presentation slides and/or
• have a one-on-one conference with Zach to ask him about what he has learned

Mr. McLean can also help Zach become more proficient in his presentation skills. For example, Zach could prepare for his class presentations by presenting an informal presentation to Mr. McLean alone. Subsequently, Zach could be asked to present his material to a very small group of classmates, preferably classmates he feels comfortable with. In this way, Mr. McLean would be scaffolding the performance in order to build Zach's self-confidence.

Class Presentations

When students are unnerved by speaking in front of their teacher and peers, the quality of that assessment data is compromised and will be of questionable validity.

Oral presentations often serve as the culminating product of research- and inquiry-based projects. Self-confident, able students who enjoy performing in front of the teacher and their peers may see such presentations as an opportunity to shine. On the other hand, shy, nervous students, second-language learners, and those who struggle with the process components of the project may dread such a moment. This range of affective responses to the presentation experience can lead to serious problems with both the validity and reliability of the assessment data gathered during these presentations.

When students present, your goal is to assess the quality of the information they have gathered as well as the quality of their communication skills. When students are unnerved by speaking in front of their teacher and peers, the quality of that assessment data is compromised and will be of questionalble validity. Validity refers to the degree to which an assessment actually provides data about the learning being assessed. (See Chapter 1, page 21.)

Furthermore, if a student is unnerved at the prospect of presenting material in front of the class, a very different picture of his or her performance will emerge compared to a situation in which he or she presents the material to the teacher alone. Reliability refers to the extent to which the assessment data gathered about a student regarding a specified learning target would remain consistent if the assessment were administered by a different assessor, or in a different context. (See Chapter 1, page 22.)

> *Reliability refers to the extent to which the assessment data gathered about a student regarding a specified learning target would remain consistent if the assessment were administered by a different assessor, or in a different context.*

Managing Class Presentations

Have you ever overheard students chatting on their way to class, anticipating two days of class presentations: "Hey, two whole days when we don't have to do any work! Let's hear it for Mr. Andrews!" There are ways to prevent your precious instructional time from being swallowed up by 30 or more back-to-back student presentations. The following simple tips will help you save class time, engage all students during peer presentations, and improve learning:

Video Clip 3:

Gr. 5/6 Science—Communicating Performance Standards to Students
12:39 minutes

1. Divide the class into groups where students can support each other during the preparation phase by providing feedback to each other. For example, divide a class of 30 students into three smaller groups.
2. Communicate your standards for a quality presentation by providing students with an oral presentation rubric. Then, model for students an ineffective presentation to illustrate how *not* to present: mumble, avoid eye contact, read woodenly from a script, and so forth. Instruct students to work in pairs and assess the elements of your presentation based on the rubric. Working from their observations and the rubric, list the criteria for an effective presentation. Then deliver the improved presentation, ensuring the standard you set is achievable for all your students.
3. Have each individual or group present only to their own smaller group, not to the entire class. Depending on the size of the classroom, groups may present concurrently or you may need to make arrangements to use more than one location.

4. Group members are responsible for providing feedback. Provide them with a rubric and anecdotoal form such as the ones shown in Figure 8-8 and Figure 8-9. (These forms may be found on pages 377–378 of this resource.)

5. Move from group to group during the presentations, monitoring on-task behaviour while assessing the quality of the presentations. You do not need to observe each presentation in its entirety; sampling is an essential feature of efficient assessment practice.

Figure 8-8: Partial Presentation and Speech Rubric

Copyright © 2007 by Nelson, a division of Thomson Canada Ltd.

Presentation and Speech Rubric

Name: _____   Date: _____

- This rubric is appropriate to assess a variety of oral presentations.
- Use only those criteria that are appropriate for a given assessment task, at a given time.
- Focus on the indicators when conducting assessment for learning; focus on the indicators and performance levels when conducting assessment of learning.

Categories/Criteria	Level 1	Level 2	Level 3	Level 4
Content	· ideas are derived from another source or cliché OR · material lacks depth and may include many inaccuracies	· ideas show some original thinking OR · material shows some depth but may include inaccuracies	· ideas are creative and original OR · material is well researched and accurate	· ideas are creative, original, and sophisticated OR · material is thoroughly researched and accurate
	· responses to questions are hesitant or unclear and may not be appropriate	· responses to questions are somewhat clear and generally appropriate	· responses to questions are clear and appropriate	· responses to questions are clear, appropriate, and insightful
Organization	· opening lacks clarity	· opening attempts to introduce topic	· opening clearly introduces topic	· opening is engaging, original, and clearly introduces topic
	· ideas are presented with significant lapses in logic	· ideas are presented with some lapses in logic	· ideas are presented in a logical sequence	· ideas are presented logically and in an original way

Figure 8-9: Peer Feedback Form

4.11, Language Arts Gr. 4–6

Peer Assessment Checklist: Oral Report

Assessor: _____   Class: _____

	Yes	No
Content		
1. The presentation included sufficient details.		
2. The material presented was interesting to listen to.		
Communication		
3. The speaker's voice was loud enough to hear easily.		
4. The speaker's voice was clear so that I could understand easily.		
5. The speaker delivered the presentation at an appropriate speed.		
6. The speaker made eye contact with the audience.		
7. The speaker used gestures to help make points clear.		
Organization		
8. The presentation had a clear beginning that caught my interest.		
9. The presentation had a clear conclusion.		
10. The speaker connected the ideas so that I could follow easily.		

What you did well:

_____
_____
_____

What you did not do well:

_____
_____
_____

Next time, I suggest that you

_____
_____
_____

378 *Tool 4.11*   Copyright © 2007 by Nelson, a division of Thomson Canada Ltd.

Summary

- Talk is a vehicle for learning.
- Talk is an essential medium through which students reveal their depth of understanding, as well as their misconceptions.
- It is important for students to have frequent opportunities for informal speaking and listening, some of which will be assessed.
- Class discussions may be used to assess both students' content knowledge as well as their communications skills. Teachers must decide which of these domains is the focus for their assessment.
- Oral question-and-answer should be used strategically and should, over time, include all students.
- Personal response to text is an excellent though under-used strategy for engaging all students in oral communication.
- Conferencing and interviews provide excellent assessment opportunities, but teachers need to ensure their purpose is clear and they have a reliable means for recording information.
- Class presentations tend to benefit some students and seriously disadvantage others. Careful planning needs to occur prior to presentations if valid assessment information is to be derived from them.

Applying My Learning

Work with your grade team or other colleagues to discuss and analyze your current use of the following oral strategies:

Talk	Personal Response to Text
Games	Conferencing
Class Discussions	In-Class Interviews
Oral Question-and-Answer	Class Presentations

Consider:

- the clarity of what you intend to assess. Use your provincial or local curriculum documents to match learning outcomes/expectations to each strategy.
- the purpose for assessing student performance. For example, do you use the strategy when assessing for learning, when assessing of learning, or when assessing for a combination of both? In some cases, you may indicate that you do not assess students' performance.
- how to record assessment information for each strategy
  This includes the tool you use (checklist, rubric, anecdotal record, and so forth), as well the frequency of the assessment.

ASSESSMENT THROUGH WRITING

> **BIG IDEA 5** For assessment to be helpful to students, it must inform them in words, not numerical scores or letter grades, what they have done well, what they have done poorly, and what they need to do next in order to improve.

ASSESSMENT STRATEGIES FOR WRITING

This chapter on written assessment intentionally follows the chapters on performance and oral assessment. All too often, teachers use writing as the default option of the three assessment modes (write, do, say) and ask students to write about what they have learned.

▲ **Writing is not easy for all students.**

Although students must learn to express themselves in writing, writing assessments may lack validity and reliability for students who lack skill in this mode of communication. Carey, for example, may know and understand a lot about science but, due to his difficulties with written language, is unable to communicate his learning through this mode. If Carey's teacher does not provide him with opportunities to demonstrate his science knowledge and understanding by saying and doing, flawed conclusions may be drawn about Carey's learning. When planning assessment, ensure a balance of modes and strategies. Without a balance between write, do, and say, skilled writers will always have an advantage over those students with writing skill deficits.

Figure 9-1 identifies some of the ways in which students may demonstrate their learning in written form. Note how certain written forms are more or less suited to specific learning targets or purposes.

Figure 9-1: Sample of Written Assessments		
Strategy	**Purpose for Assessment**	**Assessment Tool**
Written Assessments **Quizzes/Tests** · selected response · short answer · extended response	Assess knowledge Assess knowledge and understanding	Scoring guide Scoring guide Marking scheme
Graphic Organizers · mind map · word web	Assess depth of understanding	Rubric
Extended Writing · article · brochure · report · review	Assess depth of understanding	Rubric/Checklist
· journal · portfolio	Assess understanding and communication skills Assess metacognition	

Deciding whether to use a test, graphic organizer, or extended piece of writing should be made while considering your overall assessment plan for a unit of study.

Deciding whether to use a test, graphic organizer, or extended piece of writing should be made while considering your overall assessment plan for a unit of study.

Tests and Quizzes

A test or quiz is an appropriate assessment strategy if you want to assess what students know or understand. Quizzes may be thought of as frequent, low-stakes checks to determine whether students are acquiring important facts and terminology in a specific subject. They are well-suited for assessing students' knowledge about a given topic. Think of quizzes as practices—they are not the "game." (See page 32.) As such, quiz results should not count toward the assessment of learning data used for grading and reporting.

A test, on the other hand, is more substantial than a quiz and includes a variety of question types: selected response items such as multiple-choice, matching, and fill-in-the-blank questions as well as short-answer and extended-response items where students answer questions in complete sentence and/or paragraph form. Consequently, a test may be used to assess whether students understand concepts and ideas, as

Graphic organizers minimize the amount of text students have to write but reveal evidence of both understanding and misconceptions.

opposed to simply knowing them, since the extended responses provide students with opportunities to explain their thinking in detail.

Students usually ask before a test, "Does this count?" Of course, every assessment should *count*, insofar as it counts toward helping students improve their learning. But students want to know whether the results from a particular test will be factored into their report card grade. Section 4 of this resource provides detailed information about what should and should not count toward a grade. Some tests, like quizzes, may be used for practice only, while others may comprise a portion of a student's grade.

Graphic Organizers

Students who have difficulty writing may use graphic organizers to express ideas and demonstrate conceptual understanding. Graphic organizers such as word webs, Venn diagrams, and mind maps minimize the amount of text students have to write but reveal evidence of both understanding and misconceptions.

Figure 9-2: A Sample of Graphic Organizers

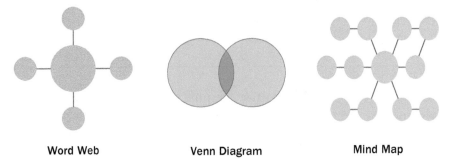

Word Web   Venn Diagram   Mind Map

Conferencing with students individually to ask them to explain their thinking after they have completed a graphic organizer is an excellent way to assess depth of understanding. This kind of "in-the-moment" assessment typically yields much more and richer information than can ever be obtained by simply collecting and marking students' graphic organizers. The words and pictures on the page are not nearly as important as the thinking that led to them. A one-to-one conference is the only way to tap into the student's thinking to reveal the source of a misconception or, alternatively, the source of a powerful insight. In this case, the process is more important than the product.

The assessment of graphic organizers is not about a score or grade. Rather, it is about working with individual students—especially those struggling to understand new learning. Record anecdotal observations using a simple tool such as a notebook, using a two-page spread for each student. You can organize your observations in a chart labelled "Strengths, Weaknesses, and Next Steps."

CASE STUDY 1 | **Anatoly's Venn Diagram**

Mrs. Graham's students had already used Venn diagrams successfully in math and science. She decided to have them use Venn diagrams in their language arts class to compare their experiences with those described in a book they had just finished reading.

Mrs. Graham began by drawing a Venn diagram on the board. Next, she outlined the two things the students would compare as a class:

• the ideas in the book *Crazy Cranberries*
• a recent class trip to a cranberry marsh

Through careful questioning, Mrs. Graham elicited from her students the similarities and differences, which she recorded on the Venn diagram. Next, Mrs. Graham directed the students to choose a book that they had read and liked. She asked them to repeat the activity, using a Venn diagram to compare their chosen book to the people, places, and events in their lives.

Mrs. Graham decided to interview her students so that they could explain their thinking and consolidate their understanding. The anecdotal notes she recorded would be valuable for reporting purposes and planning future instruction. Her findings would also help her accommodate students with individual needs and provide appropriate student groupings.

Anatoly chose the book *Snow Day*. He wrote the title on one side of the Venn diagram and began to retell the story in the space below. Mrs. Graham noticed what he was doing and sat down beside him. The following conversation took place.

Mrs. Graham: I see you have chosen *Snow Day* as your book.

Anatoly: Yes, I like this book.

Mrs. Graham: What are some of the things you liked in the book?

Anatoly: I liked when they built the snow fort and when they got a day off school.

Mrs. Graham: Hey, great retelling! Can you write down the things they did on their snow day in point form?

Anatoly: I don't have to use sentences?

Mrs. Graham: No, just get your ideas down right now.

(Anatoly records "build a snow fort.")

Mrs. Graham: How can you remember what else the kids in the book did?

Anatoly: Can I look in the book?

Mrs. Graham: That's a good idea.

(Mrs. Graham leaves Anatoly to work. Later, Anatoly requests her help. He has written a few ideas on his page.)

Mrs. Graham: Looks like you found some of the things the children did on their snow day. What's your next step?

Anatoly: Write down the things I do when we have a snow day.

Mrs. Graham: That's good. Do you remember what we do with this part in the centre where the circles overlap?

Anatoly: I think that's for things that are the same.

Mrs. Graham: Excellent.

(Anatoly records a few more ideas. When Mrs. Graham comes back, she notices that he has not written anything in the centre part of the

continued

Venn diagram.)

Mrs. Graham: I see the middle part of your Venn diagram is empty.

Anatoly: I don't know what goes there.

Mrs. Graham: Well, let's look at what you have recorded and see if there are things the kids did in the book that are the same things you do on a snow day. You like to build snow forts and so did the kids in the book. That's something that is similar so if you write it in the middle part of the diagram, it will be in both circles.

(Anatoly looks unsure. Mrs. Graham takes a red pencil and traces one circle. She uses a blue pencil to trace the other. She points to the centre part and asks Anatoly which circle the middle part belongs to.)

Anatoly: Oh, now I get it! The middle is part of both circles, so if I write "snow fort" in there, it will be in both circles. And hockey too. I play hockey. That can go in the middle.

Mrs. Graham: OK. How about some things that are similar but not necessarily about what you do on a snow day. Is the person telling the story a boy or a girl?

Anatoly: Right. I think it's a boy telling the story, so can I put that in the middle because we are both boys?

Mrs. Graham: Good work. Try and think of a few more things and I'll be back.

Mrs. Graham realized that although he could sort objects using a Venn diagram, Anatoly did not transfer all his understanding to the specific language arts context. Sitting beside Anatoly to walk and talk him through the application not only supported him in completing the task, but also provided Mrs. Graham with insight into his strengths and weaknesses. Once Anatoly had finished the task, he was able to share what he had done with a group of students with increased confidence.

Figure 9-3: Anatoly's Completed Venn Diagram

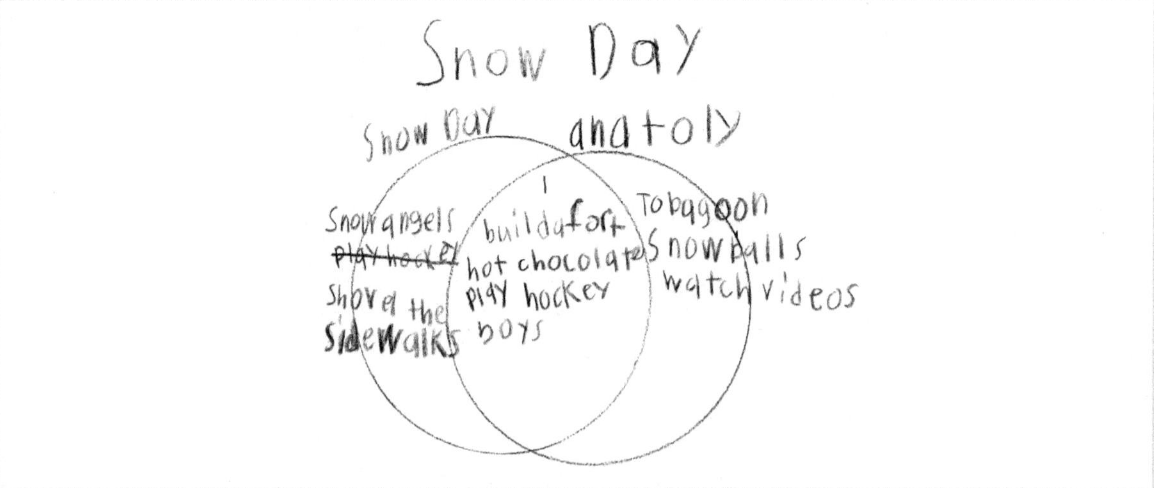

Extended Writing

Extended writing includes all forms of prose that students produce to demonstrate their knowledge and understanding in a subject area such as social science, as well as all forms of creative writing assigned in English or language arts classes.

▲ **Writing helps students reflect on their learning.**

Students need to write daily to

- help them reflect on their learning
- connect new learning to prior knowledge and experience
- explore what they do and do not understand about new learning
- consolidate their learning

Too often, extended writing is viewed only as written assignments—the formal pieces of written work handed to the teacher for marking.

There are several problems with this limited view of extended writing, especially in the intermediate grades:

- Students expect all their assignments to be marked, so, to avoid an unbearable marking load, teachers don't assign a lot of writing.
- When teachers do assign writing, there can be a long wait between students completing the assignment and receiving the marked piece. The opportunity for meaningful assessment *for* learning is lost. Students may not remember much of what they wrote, and almost certainly will not be motivated to improve the piece based on teacher feedback.
- Finally, students become even more convinced that the only purpose for writing is to accumulate marks.

The Vital Role of Personal Writing

Students should be encouraged to develop a writing habit, just as they need to develop a reading habit.

Instead of a marks-driven approach to writing, students should be encouraged to develop a writing habit, just as they need to develop a reading habit. They should write something personally meaningful every day, without expecting to hand it in to be marked. It could be a written journal or a secure online blog—a place to record significant, personally memorable thoughts, feelings, or observations about themselves, school, friends, learning, or problems they are facing. I encountered a powerful example of a personal writing strategy many years ago while visiting a school in the Niagara region of Ontario.

CASE STUDY 2 | Send Me a Letter

Mr. Beckett taught students in an inner-city school. Each September, he faced a new group of boys and girls who had been let down by the system too many times. Although Mr. Beckett had seen and heard it all before, he remained undaunted. "Perhaps more than anything else," he explained, "these kids want someone to talk to, someone who's interested in what they have to say."

That's why, on the first Friday of a new school year, Mr. Beckett would invite each of his students to write him a letter. "Sure, some of them ask, 'Who are you kidding? Me, write a letter to you! Which planet is this guy from?' So I never force the issue," he recounted.

Typically, some students wouldn't write to Mr. Beckett on the first Friday. But when they saw him handing their classmates a personal, sealed letter the following Monday, and realized they weren't going to get one, most students wrote to Mr. Beckett the following Friday. Within a couple of weeks, usually all the students were participating.

Mr. Beckett's letter-writing strategy took a lot of work on his part. Each weekend, he made time to respond to every letter he received. But Mr. Beckett felt it was time well spent. Because the writing was authentic—it

had a real purpose and a real audience—the quality of the students' writing improved dramatically from week to week. Mr. Beckett did not formally mark the work or circle any errors. Because the students wanted to communicate with Mr. Beckett, they were intrinsically motivated to improve the quality of their writing. He did request that students write to him every week and, on occasion, Mr. Beckett had to remind a student that he was owed a letter.

There is another interesting side to this story. I discovered Mr. Beckett and his letter writing while visiting his school one day. He described this approach to me before I visited his class. As I sat in his classroom that morning, Mr. Beckett came over to me with a file folder in his hands and said, "Here, Damian. You might like to look at these."

In the folder was a set of his students' letters. Just as I began to read them, a young woman got up from her desk, and walked indignantly over to Mr. Beckett. "Sir," she said, "you're not allowed to let anyone else read those letters. They're personal—between us and you."

Of course, Mr. Beckett realized his mistake, immediately retrieved the folder from my grasp, and apologized to his students for his error.

Should the letters written by Mr. Beckett's students be assessed? If so, how? Mr. Beckett didn't need to "mark" the letters in the conventional sense because his students were sufficiently motivated by the task to improve the quality of their writing themselves. He was able to record anecdotally how each student was improving his or her writing skills, based on the evidence present in their letter writing. Mr. Beckett's assessment, therefore, consisted of

- an anecdotal record, documenting each student's improvement in writing skill
- a record of whether each student had written the required number of letters

Student Journals

Although journals are often favoured by teachers, they are not as popular with students. The reason: "Journals are boring!" or "I've got nothing to say," and so on. The problem is often one of timing and lack of context. Many teachers ask students to write in their journals first thing in the morning or at the beginning of a class. No surprise, then, when students respond by complaining, "I don't know what to write … I've got nothing to say."

Asking students to write in their journals at the end of the class or day can stimulate plenty of thoughtful writing. Providing simple prompts can stimulate plenty of thoughtful writing. Handled this way, journal writing is appropriate for all subject areas. Consider the following case study in the context of science:

Asking students to write in their journals at the end of the class or day can stimulate plenty of thoughtful writing.

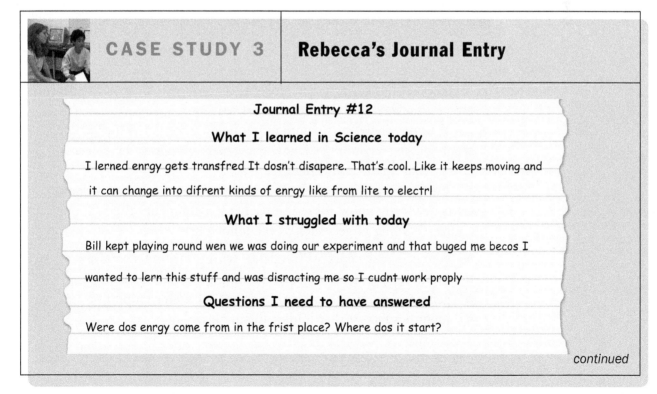

CASE STUDY 3 | **Rebecca's Journal Entry**

Journal Entry #12

What I learned in Science today

I lerned enrgy gets transfred It dosn't disapere. That's cool. Like it keeps moving and it can change into difrent kinds of enrgy like from lite to electrl

What I struggled with today

Bill kept playing round wen we was doing our experiment and that buged me becos I wanted to lern this stuff and was disracting me so I cudnt work proply

Questions I need to have answered

Were dos enrgy come from in the frist place? Where dos it start?

continued

Mr. Gold uses three simple prompts to encourage thinking and deepen understanding in his Grade 3 science class. Consider the following brief journal entry that Rebecca completed one day at the end of an experiment dealing with light and sound energy:

By using the same three prompts on a regular basis, Mr. Gold has trained his students to become deeply reflective thinkers. This approach is **metacognition** at its best. Rebecca and her classmates see their journals as a friendly, willing learning partner. They feel free to tell their journal anything about how their learning in science is progressing. As you can see, although brief, Rebecca's journal entry demonstrates her

- growing conceptual understanding
- difficulties in dealing with the learning environment
- awareness of what she needs to learn next to deepen her understanding of the concept of energy

▲ **A journal can be a friendly, willing learning partner.**

Mr. Gold also uses his students' journals to focus discussion when conducting one-on-one conferences—something he does on a regular basis to help assess their ongoing learning.

What criteria should be used when assessing journal entries such as Rebecca's? The criteria associated with the conventions of written assignments—sentence structure, spelling, and grammar—are clearly inappropriate for the journal entries written by Mr. Gold's students. Before you can choose more appropriate criteria, you must first clarify the learning target associated with science journal writing.

Your provincial curriculum might include outcomes such as "demonstrate an understanding of how movement is caused by forces and by energy that is stored and then released."

But to assess whether Grade 3 students truly *understand* science concepts or merely know some science facts, assessment criteria should also address learning targets such as the following:

- connects new concepts in science with prior understanding
- monitors own level of understanding on a daily basis
- generates questions to clarify conceptual understanding
- identifies factors that inhibit further learning

With these assessment criteria, Mr. Gold is able to use the journal entry to assess the depth of Rebecca's science thinking and understanding.

ASSESSING WRITING: CLARIFYING THE LEARNING TARGET

Clarity of learning targets is essential to identifying appropriate assessment criteria for any writing task. Too often, whatever the task, the teacher assesses every aspect of writing. Students tend to become discouraged and overwhelmed by all their apparent errors. When assessing writing, the general rule of thumb is *the focus of your assessment should match the focus of your instruction.*

For example, if the focus for instruction has been improving the organization of expository paragraphs, then paragraph organization should be the sole criterion for assessment. Any errors students make in spelling and grammar can be dealt with at another time with other pieces of writing. This is why anecdotal records tracking each student's strengths and deficits are so valuable. By focusing instruction and assessment on one aspect of writing at a time, deficits can be noted and effectively addressed.

By focusing instruction and assessment on one aspect of writing at a time, deficits can be noted and effectively addressed.

Different Targets for Different Writing Purposes

Write Traits, a research-based writing program, identifies six traits for focusing instruction and assessment:

- voice
- ideas
- organization
- conventions
- word choice
- sentence fluency

For each trait, the resource provides a teacher rubric and corresponding student rubric that identify descriptors of quality. (A sampling of The *Write Traits* rubrics are included in this resource on pages 369–372.)

The *Write Traits* assessment rubrics are designed to suit a variety of writing purposes: persuading, entertaining, informing, and so forth. You may prefer to teach writing by focusing specifically on a given purpose and using a separate rubric to assess each purpose. Figure 9-5 illustrates some of the genres associated with the three purposes for writing.

> ### Tips for Teaching
>
> Have you been using a separate rubric for each writing task? Did you find yourself overwhelmed? Since rubrics are supposed to help students, parents, and teachers agree on the standards for quality work, changing the target for each task will only overload you and frustrate students and parents.
>
> An alternative is to use generic rubrics matched to the purpose for student writing—expository, creative, and personal writing. A generic rubric can also be used to assess the writing process. See Sections 4 and 5 in Part 2 for these rubrics.

Figure 9-5: Partial List of Genres		
Expository Writing	**Creative Writing**	**Personal Writing**
· paragraph	· story	· diary
· report	· poem	· journal
· article	· song	· log
· essay		· reflection

This approach to writing can simplify assessment since rubrics are designed for each of the three purposes, eliminating the danger of "rubric overload." (You will find rubrics designed for specific writing purposes in sections 4 and 5 of Part 2 of this resource.)

From Learning Targets to Assessment Criteria

Everett Kline uses a wonderful workshop activity to illustrate why so many teachers set narrow and often inappropriate criteria for student writing tasks. His intent is to illustrate the need to differentiate between the different purposes we have in mind when we assign writing tasks.

EK: I want each of you to think about the best piece of writing you've read in the past month. It may be a novel, an article, or a poem. It may be a published work, or something a student wrote. Okay? Everyone has a text in mind?

Now, I want you to jot down exactly what qualities made that piece of writing so great.

All right. Let's hear from each of you. What made your chosen text so memorable? Who'd like to start?"

Participants:
  "It made me cry!"
  "I loved the ending!"
  "It took me to a place far away."
  "It made me think."
  "I loved the heroine!"
  ....

EK: What? Did no one marvel at the sentence structure? Wasn't anyone moved by the writer's use of prepositions? Did none of you rave about the quality of the subject–verb agreement?"

(All the participants laugh.)

EK: Now take a look at this set of criteria for assessing student writing and tell me what you think of them, in light of the discussion we've just had.

(Kline then flashes this slide on the screen.)

Figure 9-6: Five Criteria for Assessing Writing

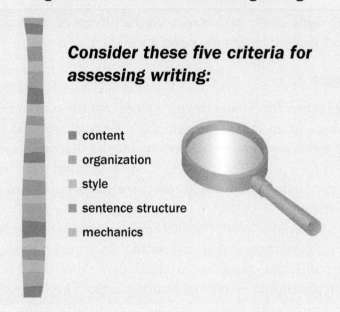

Consider these five criteria for assessing writing:

- content
- organization
- style
- sentence structure
- mechanics

There is a lot of fidgeting and chatter in the room before one of the participants says, "I see your point, but those criteria are important, aren't they?"

EK: Yes, they are important. But do they capture the qualities that each of you identified when I asked you what made your favourite piece so wonderful? The point I wish to make is that the criteria we typically use to assess student writing ignore those very qualities that distinguish excellent writing—writing that moves us—from writing that is simply "correct."

When discussing their favourite pieces of writing, the participants in Kline's workshop all focused on the *impact* the piece had made on them (Wiggins, 1998). Unfortunately, impact is often omitted from assessment criteria for student writing. This illustration shows the importance of using appropriate assessment criteria for written work; it is one of the most important aspects of assessment design. (See Chapter 12, for more details about the selection and development of high-quality assessment tools.)

INCREASING THE QUALITY OF WRITTEN ASSESSMENTS

What other tools and processes are required to ensure quality assessment of written work? **Exemplars** and **anchor** papers are essential assessment tools for students and teachers, and moderation is an essential assessment and professional learning activity for teachers. (See Glossary for definitions of these terms.)

Exemplars may be established locally and teachers in a single school can benefit significantly by engaging in the process of moderation. (See Holding a Moderation Session, pages 150–151.)

Exemplars

An **exemplar** provides students with a model for the standard of quality expected on a given task. The exemplar reflects the specific indicators associated with a superior level of performance on that task. For example, an exemplar for a piece of work assessed on a four-point scale, with 4 representing the highest level, would reflect the characteristics of a Level 4 student response.

Students should always be shown several exemplars representing the full range of performance that falls within the superior level.

Students should always be shown several exemplars representing the full range of performance that falls within the superior level. Without several very different exemplars, students may think that Level 4 performance represents an exceedingly narrow range. They may respond by trying to imitate the single exemplar, an approach that does not encourage creativity.

Anchor Papers

Anchor papers are samples of student work that reflect each of the levels of performance expected for a given task. They may be selected from a set of student responses from a previous year, or they may be selected by a team of markers from current-year responses, prior to a moderation session. They are used to help teachers increase the reliability of their assessment of a task. Unlike exemplars, which reflect only the highest or expected level of performance, anchors may be selected for all four levels on a four-point scale.

▲ **Moderation enables teachers to reach consensus on the standards for quality work.**

Moderation

Moderation brings together a group of teachers who teach the same grade to assess a specific assignment. Their goal is to reach an agreement about the levels or scores assigned to a set of student responses. The process is called *moderation* because it tries to eliminate any extreme scores that individuals may assign in favour of a moderated score that represents the consensus of the group. When moderating a set of student papers, teachers rely on the following tools:

- a clear statement of the assigned task
- a rubric or other scoring tool that includes the assessment criteria and performance indicators used to define quality
- exemplars, if students were provided with them before the task
- anchors reflecting each of the performance levels identified on the rubric or scoring tool

Moderation brings together a group of teachers who teach the same grade to assess a specific assignment.

Video Clip 9:

Planning a Common Assessment Task and Team Marking
9:37 minutes

Mrs. Kennedy and her Grade 8 team colleagues assigned their social studies classes the following task:

- A proposal has been made to construct a Big Box store in your community. The proposed site will cause the destruction of a beautiful forest that is home to numerous species of birds and other wildlife. Write an editorial for your local newspaper opposing this project.

The teachers instructed their students to find editorials in the local newspapers and bring them to class the next day. The lesson for that day had two goals:

- Have students identify criteria that will be used to assess the editorials they will write.
- Select several exemplars from the newspaper editorials to reflect the standards for quality work required on this task.

Mrs. Kennedy and the other Grade 8 teachers met at the end of the day to share the lists of criteria that each of their classes had generated, to develop a rubric for the task, and to select three or four exemplars from the newspaper editorials that their students had brought to class that day. Their consolidated set of assessment criteria appears in Figure 9-7. (Note that the students who developed this list used simpler words, but the intent of the criteria remains the same.)

Figure 9-7: Criteria for Assessing an Editorial

Criteria for Assessing an Editorial
Clarity of opinion
Persuasiveness
Diction
Conventions

Mrs. Kennedy and her colleagues drafted a four-level rubric to share with their students along with the three exemplars selected from the student-gathered editorials. (See Chapter 12 for guidelines on developing rubrics.) Over the next few days, they provided their students with plenty of class time to:

- work on their own editorials
- benefit from teacher and peer feedback about their rough drafts
- produce polished versions of their editorials

The teachers then collected the editorials. Working independently at first, they each selected from their own students' work one or two potential anchors for each of the four levels on the rubric. The teachers then met for a collective marking or moderation session during which they used the following guidelines:

Moderation

1. Review the rubric and the two exemplars that students were given to ensure you all understand the demands of the task and the standards for quality.

2. Share and discuss the potential anchors each teacher has selected and collectively choose two anchors to represent each level on the rubric.

3. Divide the editorials from all classes so that each teacher assesses student work from all classes.

4. Each teacher assesses ten editorials holistically, sorting them into five groups (from Level 4 to Below Level 1). (Note: Teachers with no previous moderation experience should begin by sorting editorials into three groups (High, Low, Unsatisfactory), then sort the High group into Levels 4 and 3, and the

continued

Low group into Levels 2 and 1.)

5. Pause at this point and check the assessments of your colleagues by reviewing each others' piles to determine whether all of you are in agreement. This is easily facilitated if each teacher moves one seat down to check their neighbour's piles.

6. Discuss as a group any challenging editorial that did not seem to fall easily into any one level or caused significant disagreement about its assigned level.

7. Continue assessing the remaining editorials. Repeat Steps 5 and 6 as often as necessary.

The process of moderation described in this case study is an excellent way for teachers to

- increase their understanding of criterion-referenced assessment
- improve their assessment skills
- improve the reliability of the achievement scores they assign to a set of student responses

Moderation is one of the most effective ways of providing teachers with professional development in assessment because it engages them directly in their craft. Yes, the process takes time and requires the teachers involved to negotiate a common time when they are able to meet. For these reasons, moderation may only occur once or twice each year. However, the importance of moderation in helping you improve your own assessment literacy cannot be over-emphasized.

Moderation is one of the most effective ways of providing teachers with professional development in assessment because it engages them directly in their craft.

MANAGING THE MARKING LOAD

▲ **Marking should significantly improve the quality of work but should not consume all your time.**

Talk About Assessment emphasizes the distinction between the coaching (assessment *for* learning) and judging (assessment *of* learning) functions of assessment (see p. 13). How does this essential distinction apply to typical marking practice? To answer this question, first ask yourself: *Does the time I spend marking student work make a significant difference in the quality of work produced?*

How did you answer? No? Not really? I'm not sure? Perhaps some of you answered yes. In that case, I will ask another question:

How do you know it makes a significant difference?

If you have the data to demonstrate that the time you spend marking does in fact improve the quality of your students' work, then skip the rest of this chapter! If not, read on.

In my experience, marking ineffectively is common and marking effectively is rare. The following three practices appear to be the most prevalent. They are also the least effective in helping students to improve:

- marking everything students produce
- marking each piece on every criterion, all of the time
- making corrections for students

Let's examine the many problems inherent in each of these practices.

Marking Everything Students Produce

When teachers use the term *marking*, they usually mean collecting student work and spending a considerable amount of time circling and correcting errors, making comments, and assigning a letter grade or numerical score to each piece. Too often, the work teachers spend hours marking was produced by students in the blink of an eye. Moreover, many students submit work without completing even the most cursory self-assessment to check for quality and correctness. For all of these reasons, time spent marking this kind of work is usually time wasted.

Teachers who differentiate between *practice work and polished work* collect and mark only polished work. Before collecting work, teachers must insist that it be thoroughly self-assessed and possibly peer assessed using a detailed checklist to ensure that it is high quality—at least in the eyes of the author and possibly a classmate.

Marking everything students produce might also mean marking an entire piece of student work for style and conventions rather than just the first page. Clearly, the entire piece of work must be read in order to assess content, but such assessment is holistic and, therefore, relatively quick and easy to complete. On the other hand, since the marking of conventions such as spelling and grammar is so time-consuming, and

Teachers who differentiate between practice work *and* polished work *collect and mark only polished work.*

given that most students will continue to make the same errors throughout the paper, why continue to mark conventions beyond the first page?

Marking Each Piece on Every Criterion

Marking is supposed to help students improve their learning and the quality of their work. So think about this question: *Does returning an assignment covered in red ink accomplish that goal, or does it merely frustrate and defeat the student?* Most students are not motivated to improve when they are bombarded with a litany of their errors and numerous suggested changes.

I have already suggested that when assessing writing, what is assessed should match what was taught. (See page 145.) If the focus for a series of creative writing lessons is creating believable characters, then the focus for assessment should be character descriptions, not spelling and grammar, as well. If, on the other hand, students are creating publicity posters for an upcoming school event, then correct spelling and grammar are essential and should be a major focus for assessment.

In a balanced writing program, all of the important elements of writing will be addressed over the course of a term or a year. The key to improvement for students and manageability for you is not trying to do it all at once. Focus is key: your teaching needs to be focused; students' work needs to be focused; assessment needs to be focused; and improvement efforts need to be focused.

Simply put: Don't mark everything for everything, all of the time.

Focus is key: your teaching needs to be focused; students' work needs to be focused; assessment needs to be focused; and improvement efforts need to be focused.

Making Corrections for Students

During workshops, once people are feeling comfortable, I often ask, *"Okay, time for the truth. Hands up if you actually correct the errors on your students' written work?"* Most teachers are honest and admit that they do. I then like to follow up by asking, "Who's trying to improve their writing: you or your students?"

Marking is successful when it motivates students to think for themselves. If teachers make all the corrections, then they have done all the thinking for their students. Furthermore, they have wasted hours of precious time engaged in an activity that discourages, rather than promotes, further learning.

Marking is successful when it motivates students to think for themselves.

The purpose of marking is to draw students' attention to aspects of their work that are incorrect or need improvement. This can be done by circling portions of their work and using question marks or abbreviations to denote the nature of certain errors such as *sp.* to denote spelling errors or *awk.* to denote awkward syntax. Use of such marking shorthand is commonplace, effective, and efficient, but going the next step and making the corrections is counterproductive.

So let's summarize.

Figure 9-8: Effective Use of Marking Time

If time is wasted by ...	It follows that time can be saved by ...
· marking everything students produce · marking everything, for everything, all of the time · making corrections for students	· providing clear targets and marking only quality work · teaching the skills of, and having students use, self-assessment before submitting work for marking · focusing marking on what was taught · circling but not correcting errors

Summary

■ Written assessments fall into three major categories: tests and quizzes, graphic organizers, and extended writing.

■ Tests and quizzes are excellent strategies for determining what students know and understand. However, not all students perform well in testing situations; a fact to consider when forming conclusions about the assessment evidence gathered from written tests.

■ Graphic organizers may enable students who struggle with written responses to demonstrate visually their level of understanding. Asking students to explain the material they have presented in a graphic organizer can provide valuable insights into their learning.

■ Extended writing is an essential strategy for assessing many kinds of learning; yet it is often limited to formal written assignments that take time to mark, thereby denying students the immediate feedback that is crucial for learning. Encourage students to write daily, using personal formats such as letters and journals. Quickly scan such writing samples during class time and provide immediate feedback.

■ Students must understand the purpose for writing and know the criteria for assessment before they begin writing.

■ Exemplars go hand in hand with rubrics to help students understand what quality writing looks like.

■ You can significantly improve the reliability of your assessments, as well as your assessment skills by collaborating with colleagues in moderation sessions. Anchors assist in this process.

Applying My Learning

Review the section Increasing the Quality of Written Assessments (pages 148-151), including the case study "Holding a Moderation Session." Arrange with your grade team or other colleagues to hold a moderation session. During and after the session, be sure to reflect on what worked well, as well as any problems you encountered so that you can refine your practice for the next session.

Chapter 10

ASSESSMENT AS INQUIRY

> **BIG IDEA 3** Assessment must be balanced, including oral, performance, and written tasks, and be flexible in order to improve learning for all students.

THE INTU MODEL

Educators agree that the ability to design and conduct an independent research project is an essential skill for today's graduates. Independent research projects also let classroom teachers

- combine a number of content standards in one assignment
- encourage students to apply their learning in an integrated way

The INTU model equips students with a set of essential research and communication skills, while providing rich opportunities for teacher, peer, and self-assessment.

This chapter examines the INTU model. INTU stands for "I need to understand…," a term coined by Carl Bereiter and Marlene Scardamalia (1996). The INTU model equips students with a set of essential research and communication skills, while providing rich opportunities for teacher, peer, and self-assessment

There are four phases to the INTU model. Students begin by formulating their own research question—their INTU. Then they seek an answer to their question by researching it extensively, using books, magazines, journals, newspapers, film and television, the Internet and other electronic resources, and/or one-on-one interviews with peers and adults (if appropriate). Next, they organize their information, acknowledging differing points of view or conflicting arguments, and prepare and deliver a professional presentation on their findings to the class. The final phase involves self, peer, and teacher assessment of their work.

Curriculum Outcomes Addressed by INTU

INTU-based projects combine assessment with instruction in ways that promote learning across a vast array of learning targets and disciplines. One strength of the INTU model is that it addresses many curriculum outcomes spanning several core subject areas—a clear advantage at a time when teachers are expected to cover so many outcomes.

The table in Figure 10-1 is a sampling of the more than 40 curriculum outcomes that students demonstrate as they work through their INTU projects. For the sake of simplicity, the table focuses on students in Grade 8; however, the INTU model is suitable for students from Grade 3 to college level.

One strength of the INTU model is that it addresses many curriculum outcomes spanning several core subject areas.

Figure 10-1: A Sampling of Curriculum Outcomes Addressed Through INTU Projects	
Subject	**Curriculum Outcome Examples**
English	• Locate explicit information and ideas in texts to use in developing opinions and interpretations. • Use a variety of organizational techniques to present ideas and supporting details logically and coherently. • Investigate potential topics by formulating questions, identifying information needs, and developing research plans to gather data. • Locate and summarize information from print and electronic sources. • Group and label information and ideas; evaluate the relevance, accuracy, and completeness of the information and ideas; and discard irrelevant material. • Make constructive suggestions to peers. • Plan and make oral presentations to a small group or the class. • Analyze their own and others' oral presentations to identify strengths and weaknesses.
Science	• Select and integrate information from various sources, including electronic and print resources, community resources, and personally collected data, to answer the question chosen. • Gather, organize, and record information using a format that is appropriate to the investigation.
Social Science	• Demonstrate an ability to collect, organize, and synthesize information from a variety of sources. • Select and use appropriate methods and technology to communicate the results of inquiries and present a variety of viewpoints on issues. • Develop and use appropriate questions to define a topic, problem, or issue, and use these questions to focus an inquiry. • Locate and use effectively materials from primary sources (e.g., field research, surveys, interviews) and secondary sources (media, CD-ROMs, Internet) to research an issue. • Demonstrate an ability to distinguish among opinion, argument, and fact in research sources. • Describe biases in information and identify what types of information are relevant to particular inquiries.
Technology	• Share information using media tools and a variety of technologies. • Use a variety of software applications, such as word processing, to document projects from conception to completion.

What does the INTU model look like when implemented in the classroom? To help you explore the four phases of the model, you will read about Anna and Freddie, two students who have IEPs (individual education plans) that address their communication exceptionality. You will track their progress as they conduct research into pit bull terriers, a topic they have chosen to pursue.

Phase 1: Formulating an INTU Question

Students need to discover that good research begins with a clear, focused question. When I worked as a school librarian, students would confront me daily with questions like: "Mr. Cooper, do you have any information about black holes, Afghanistan, the Olympics, mad cow disease, …?"

My reply was always, "Of course I have information about black holes, Afghanistan, the Olympics, mad cow disease, and so on. But before we talk any further, I want you to go back to your classroom and write down a specific question about your topic that you want to answer."

Students need to discover that good research begins with a clear, focused question.

▲ **Gathering whatever information is available is not a good plan.**

When students begin their research with a vague topic, they often find themselves overwhelmed with information. As a result, they tend to plunge in by summarizing whatever they find. There is no directed research happening—students are merely gathering and assembling whatever information is most readily available.

When students are explicitly taught how to formulate a meaningful question, they undertake purposeful, directed research. In order to answer the question, they must make numerous decisions about the relevance, quality, bias, and objectivity of the information they find. To illustrate, contrast the following topics with their corresponding INTUs:

Figure 10-2: Vague Topics Compared with INTU Questions	
Topic	**INTU**
Testing Consumer Products on Animals	I need to understand both sides of the debate about whether it is right to test consumer products on animals.
Video Gaming	I need to understand whether video gaming is helpful or harmful to learning for teenagers.
Downloading Music	I need to understand the arguments made by consumers, record companies, and artists for and against downloading music.

When Anna and Freddie asked Ms. Chen, their teacher, if they could research pit bull terriers, she agreed and then helped them to formulate their INTU. She started by asking, "What is about pit bulls that interests you two?"

"I want to find out why they attack people," Anna replied.

"OK," said Ms. Chen. "But are all pit bulls dangerous?"

"No way!" Freddie interjected. "My neighbour has one and it's never attacked anyone." Ms. Chen then asked Anna and Freddie why they thought pit bulls were often in the news recently.

"Because more people across Canada want them banned?" Anna suggested.

"Freddie," asked Ms. Chen, "how do you think your neighbour would feel if pit bulls were banned?"

"He'd fight it!"

"So it seems that we have two sides to this issue," Ms. Chen said to the two students.

"Does that mean we have to look at both sides?" Anna asked.

"Yes, it does," said Ms. Chen. "So what might your INTU be?"

"How about: 'I need to understand why some people want to ban pit bull terriers while other people don't,'" Anna offered.

"Freddie, what do you think?" asked Ms. Chen.

"I like that," said Freddie, nodding his head.

Phase 2: Formulating a Research Plan

Once students have a well-written INTU, they learn how to break it down into research categories and then how to develop a key research question for each category. Figure 10-3 shows a useful template for helping students with this step. You can see how Anna and Freddie moved from their INTU to research categories, and then, with support from Ms. Chen, developed a series of key research questions.

Once students have a well-written INTU, they learn how to break it down into research categories and then how to develop a key research question for each category.

Figure 10-3: Research Categories and Key Research Questions

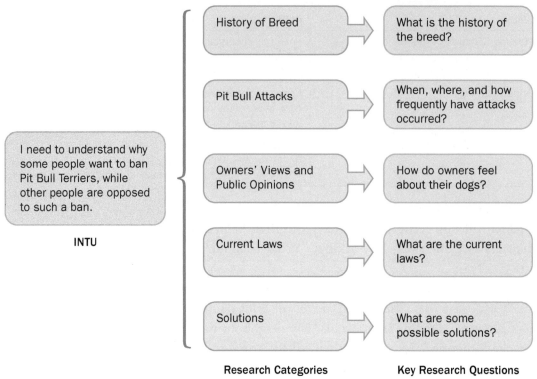

Research Categories

Key Research Questions

Phase 3: Locating, Recording, Examining, and Organizing the Information

Students know by this stage of their education that it is not especially hard to find information. Owing to advances in information technology, the greater research challenge currently facing students is sifting and sorting through the vast amount of information in print and electronic media. For this reason, it is important to approach the information accessing and organization elements of an INTU with care.

One source of confusion for students is the way that the Internet has blurred the distinction between primary and secondary resources. When students use a search engine, there is no in-built quality control filter. A Google search, for example, will produce both legitimate resources as well as personal web sites replete with bias and errors. Consequently, it is important to exercise extreme care and caution when encouraging students to use the Internet as an information source.

Despite the Internet's appeal, students may benefit from being directed to locate information from several other sources before going to digital sources. For example, Ms. Chen provided the following guidelines to ensure that her students learned how to access a variety of information sources, including the Internet.

▲ **Armed with better research questions, students can be directed to locate information in print resources before going to the Internet.**

Figure 10-4: Student Guidelines for Locating and Gathering Information

1. You must draw information for your INTU from the following sources:

   • at least four print sources—books, newspapers, magazines, brochures

   • a student-developed public opinion survey administered to a sample of peer and adults (sample size to be negotiated with your teacher)

   • at least four Internet sources

2. You will receive an orientation to these sources from the school librarian before beginning your project.

3. All of your sources must be recorded on the Note-Taking Sheets provided by your teacher.

As Ms. Chen's students located and accumulated large amounts of information, Ms. Chen moved from group to group, listening and observing. She was able to assess for learning by providing feedback, reminding students of the importance of their key research questions in focusing their research and, ultimately, in answering their INTU. She also scheduled brief conferences with each research group to check on their progress and identify potential problems as they continued to work.

The following conversation illustrates the depth of thinking that occurred as Anna and Freddie examined the information they were collecting:

Freddie: Anna, look at this web site! One hundred and twelve pit bull owners and not one attack!

Anna: Yes, but that's a web site for pit bull owners. They might not tell you about attacks, even if they know they happened.

Freddie: So does that mean we can't use this site?

Anna: Let's ask. (Anna calls to Ms. Chen.) Miss, can you help us? We don't know whether we can use a site when it only tells one side.

Ms. Chen: What do you both think? Have you found many sites that present different sides of the debate?

Anna: I guess not. Maybe we can use sites like this, but I think we have to explain that it only shows one side of the issue.

Freddie: I just found this article on the CBC web site and ... hey, it gives both sides! It also shows which places have decided to make laws about pit bulls.

Ms. Chen: Sounds good, Freddie. So what's the word we use when someone only presents one side of an argument?

Anna: Biased!

Ms. Chen: Well done, Anna. You can use these sources, but you need to make sure that you explain in your presentation when one of your sources appears to be biased.

To be effective, assessment must occur throughout the INTU project.

To be effective, assessment must occur throughout the INTU project. Students learn about bias, objectivity, and reliability of information as they and you (or another assessor) work through the research process. Your role, as a roving facilitator, is to

- answer students' questions by posing more questions
- ask students to explain and justify their decisions
- cause students to rethink their direction and consider alternatives

This is the point where Ms. Chen noted which students were beginning to understand that research is a complex process and which students still tended to believe everything they read. Students in the second group required further support before they would be able to recognize bias. Ms. Chen used a research skills rubric for teacher- and self-assessment. (See Figure 10-5. The complete version of this rubric appears on page 411.)

Figure 10-5: Partial Research Skills Rubric

TOOL 5.11

Research Skills Rubric,
p. 411

Categories/Criteria	Level 1	Level 2	Level 3	Level 4
Use of Resources	has **difficulty** formulating a research question and tries to use a **single** strategy for locating and selecting information	formulates a **tentative** research question and uses a **limited range** of strategies for locating and selecting information	formulates a **clear** research question and uses **several** strategies for locating and selecting information	formulates an **insightful** research question and uses a **full range** of strategies for locating and selecting information
	accesses information from **only one** resource	is able to access information from **more than one** resource	is able to access information from a **variety** of resources (print, electronic, human)	is able to access information from a **full range** of resources (print, electronic, human)
Quality of Information	has **difficulty** distinguishing between fact and opinion	collects information which represents a **single** point of view	collects information which represents **different** points of view	collects information which represents **all relevant** points of view
	has **difficulty** locating information that is related to the issue, concept, or topic	locates **some** information that is related to the issue, concept, or topic and some that is not	locates information that is clearly related to the issue, concept, or topic	locates information that reflects a **sophisticated understanding** of the issue, concept, or topic
Recording Information	**copies** main ideas from resources	**summarizes some** main ideas from resources in own words	**summarizes** main ideas from resources in own words	**integrates** main ideas from resources with own ideas on the topic
	only acknowledges sources **when prompted**	**attempts to** acknowledge sources correctly	**acknowledges** sources correctly	routinely acknowledges all sources
	has **difficulty** recording and organizing information	uses a **limited number** of strategies to record and organize information with some success	uses **strategies** to record and organize information	uses a **range of strategies** to record and organize information effectively
Use of Information	shows **little evidence** of having formulated own ideas/opinions	**attempts to** combine research with own ideas/opinions	**combines** research with own ideas/opinions	**combines** research with own ideas/opinions in a **fluent and**

Telling students what level they are operating at is not an effective use of this rubric. Instead, Ms. Chen helped her students use this rubric effectively by pointing out the indicators that described what they were currently doing and what they needed to do to enhance their skills. Ascribing a performance level only occurred once the research process was over and she was ready to assign students a summary grade to indicate their level of achievement.

As we saw in Chapter 2, assessment *for* learning focuses on

- what the student is doing well
- what the student is struggling with
- what the student needs to do to improve

Assessment *of* learning, however

- occurs once the task has been completed
- indicates to the student his/her current level of achievement, relative to a known standard

Phase 4: Preparing, Sharing, and Assessing Our Research

The INTU model is extremely rich in terms of the range of essential skills that can be taught and assessed. Preparing, self-assessing, and delivering oral presentations are among these essential skills.

Ms. Chen decided to introduce the presentation skills section of the INTU-based project by delivering a dreadful presentation herself and inviting her students to critique everything that was wrong with it. Ms. Chen's presentation not only provoked laughter, but it also generated a

---

Tips for Teaching

How can technically savvy students be prevented from getting carried away by the sound and animation possibilities of new technology? As always, your role is to keep students' attention focused on what is important, as opposed to what seems the most fun. For example, one way to keep students focused is to have them complete a basic set of presentation slides, corresponding to each of their key research questions, before allowing them to add any special effects.

rich class discussion about what an exemplary presentation should look like.

The widespread availability and use of presentation software has added another layer of complexity to classroom presentations. A technically sophisticated presentation will not compensate for a student's deficient oral communication skills, but without skillful teacher intervention, many students believe it will.

As in each INTU phase, assessment for learning occurs *while* students prepare their presentations. This could take the form of making comments and asking questions as you move from group to group. You could even have students do a trial run-through of their entire presentation, either for you or for a small group of critical friends. Students can receive feedback and fine-tune their presentation before formally presenting to the class and invited guests.

INTU presentations can occur in a number of ways, depending on the time available and the number of students. In a small class, such as Anna and Freddie's class, the teacher may opt to have groups present their work to the whole class, with every student being responsible for providing feedback on the quality of each presentation.

In a large class, this approach may consume too much class time. Instead, split the class into three groups. Each research group or pair can then present to about eight to ten peers, and each student is responsible for providing feedback for only one-third of the presentations. (See Chapter 8, pages 132–133, for more information on this strategy as well as Video Clip 3.)

During the presentations, you can move from group to group to ensure that everything is running smoothly. Since you will have already assessed each research group or pair while students worked on their INTU, and since each group's slide presentation and written report will be submitted for teacher assessment, it is not necessary for you to hear each group's presentation in its entirety.

Planning for effective peer assessment is crucial if students are to provide meaningful feedback to their classmates. This feedback should be anecdotal only; it is not appropriate for students to assign marks to the work presented by their peers; such marks are typically unreliable and serve no useful purpose. (See Chapter 5, for more information on peer assessment.) Instead, equipped with the same rubric that outlines the criteria for oral presentations (see page 377 for this rubric), as well as the Peer Assessment Checklist on p. 378, students can

- observe, listen, and ask questions during each presentation
- take several moments to reflect on the presentation

- provide immediate, face-to-face feedback to presenters (what they did well and what they struggled with)
- offer constructive suggestions for how to improve the presentation

The INTU model for student-directed research is highly effective because it promotes rich thinking and learning, while enabling teachers to integrate assessment with instruction. It is a model that is popular with students because it is engaging and self-directed; it is popular with teachers because it addresses a vast array of essential skills across all core subject areas. It also can be used with students across a wide range of abilities, including students like Anna and Freddie.

The INTU model for student-directed research is highly effective because it promotes rich thinking and learning, while enabling teachers to integrate assessment with instruction.

Summary

- The INTU model integrates performance assessment, oral assessment, and written assessment through student-directed research projects.
- The INTU model includes four phases:
  - Phase 1—formulating an INTU (I need to understand ...) question
  - Phase 2—formulating a research plan
  - Phase 3—locating, recording, examining, and organizing the information gathered through the research phase
  - Phase 4—preparing the presentation, sharing it with peers, and assessing the quality of the project
- The INTU model can be mastered by students of all ability levels, including those identified with special needs.

Applying My Learning

Share the INTU model with your colleagues and your school administration to determine whether there is sufficient interest and support in your school to try this approach. Use the *Talk About Assessment* web site to pose any questions you might have for the author as you embark on this project.

Chapter 11

PORTFOLIO ASSESSMENT

 BIG IDEA 4 Assessment and instruction are inseparable because effective assessment informs learning.

When we give students a chance to share their knowledge with each other and with us, they learn and we learn. Celebrating our accomplishments by sharing our work with others is part of the process of learning.

DAVIES, 2000

Portfolios are sometimes considered "add-ons" that require too much time to implement and assess. However, student portfolios can actually help you organize many elements of instruction and assessment in a way that promotes more student engagement and self-reflection. In short, asking your students to use portfolios is an excellent strategy for connecting teaching, learning, and assessment. Portfolios are also one of the most effective ways to make assessment a collaborative process. Teachers who have the most success with portfolios have integrated them fully into their instructional routines.

HOW SHOULD A PORTFOLIO WORK?

Ideally, a portfolio is much more than a container for storing student work. It should be a window on learning that enables you and your students' parents to see inside the learning process. As such, the portfolio provides a focus for student-teacher conferencing, as well as a focal point for discussions on Parents' Night.

The portfolio is also about self-discovery and self-directed learning. It provides

- a focus for learning activities and teacher-student conferencing
- a place to gather evidence of essential learning

A major purpose for using portfolios is to foster student metacognition. That is, portfolios teach students how to monitor, think about, and then improve the quality of their own work and in the process, become less dependent on the teacher's assessment of their work.

Portfolios teach students how to monitor, think about, and then improve the quality of their own work.

Types of Portfolios

There are different types of portfolios:

- The *working portfolio* travels from grade to grade and contains samples of a student's work in a given subject area.
- The *showcase portfolio* is used to demonstrate best work in much the way an artist collects best pieces for showing at galleries or to prospective employers.
- The *assessment portfolio* is an ongoing record of a student's achievement of learning goals.

The assessment portfolio serves a vital role in assessment *for* learning. For some teachers, the portfolio becomes the focus of the student's work. It contains a broad array of materials, including inventories, written pieces, certificates, photographs, and assignments, as well as personal artifacts that are as individual as the students in the class.

USING PORTFOLIOS IN THE CLASSROOM

Students need to develop a sense of ownership around their portfolios. As the school year progresses, it is important for them to view their portfolios as a reflection of their improved learning and achievements. It is therefore important for you and your students to view the portfolio as an integral part of everything that happens during the year.

Video Clip 7:

Gr. 2 Language Arts— Using Portfolios to Improve Self- and Peer- Assessment
07:55 minutes

Effective portfolio programs integrate learning with assessment by providing a regular time for students to work on their portfolios. For example, teachers may designate a Portfolio Day each week when students work on required or self-selected tasks. Students come to expect that on Portfolio Day there will be no direct teaching. Instead, they will work on materials in their portfolio and you will spend the time conferencing with a number of students about their portfolios. Each student knows ahead of time when it is his or her day to meet with you, and prepares for the conference accordingly.

What Goes into the Portfolio?

Some teachers in junior and intermediate grades like to differentiate between two sections in a student's portfolio: a public section and a personal section. The public section is open to you, the teacher, and possibly to peers and parents. These items may be assessed and discussed during a conference. The personal section is for the student's own use. Generally speaking, no one but the student sees the contents of this section.

▲ Students have some discretion about what they choose to put in their portfolios, but there are some required elements that provide evidence of essential learning.

All portfolios should contain a combination of required and optional elements:

- Required elements include specific pieces of work that you have designated in order to provide evidence of essential learning. In language arts, these might include a required number of writing samples demonstrating students' skills in both expository and creative writing. In mathematics, such elements might include solutions to key word problems, tests that identify what a student has mastered, or letters to a relative explaining key concepts and how each one connects to the world outside of school.

- Optional elements are items that the student has decided to include as evidence of a particular strength or interest, or possibly as evidence of an area requiring some improvement.

Section 2

My Assessment Toolkit

Each portfolio piece—whether required or optional—should have a reflection strip attached to it. The reflection strip (see Figure 11-1) is a critical element of the portfolio process. It requires students to indicate why they selected a particular piece and what it demonstrates about their learning. (For more about the reflection strip, see Ms. Wright's Integrated Portfolio Program on page 172).

Figure 11-1: Reflection Strip

Reflection Strip
Complete and attach this Reflection Strip to each item you choose to include in your portfolio.
Name: _____ **Date:** _____
This piece of work shows: ☐ how I have improved an earlier draft ☐ something important that I learned ☐ something I need to work on ☐ something I need help with ☐ something I am proud of ☐ what I do outside of school ☐ how well I have learned something
1. I choose to include this item because:
2. How does this item demonstrate the thing(s) I've checked above?
3. Other important things about me that this item shows:

TOOL 5.16

Reflection Strip for Portfolio Entries, p.416

The Reflection Strip requires students to indicate why they selected a particular piece for their portfolio and what it demonstrates about their learning.

The portfolio may also contain non-print materials, such as CD-ROMs or videotapes showing artifacts, photographs, or other items that are personally meaningful to the student.

NEL

Portfolio Assessment **169**

ASSESSING THE PORTFOLIO

The portfolio's greatest strength is that it is an ever-changing window on each student's learning. For this reason, it is an excellent focus for providing feedback to students about what they are doing well and what they need to improve.

There are several ways in which the portfolio may be assessed, as well as a number of people who need to be involved in the assessment.

Diagnostic Assessment (assessment *for* learning)

TOOL 5.10

Assessing Prior Knowledge: Diagnostic Assessment p. 410

Including information from diagnostic assessments in a student's portfolio gives both teacher and student baseline information from which to measure growth in achievement. Figure 11-2 illustrates a simple diagnostic assessment tool that may be included in a science portfolio. It records how students' understanding of key concepts develops from the beginning of a unit through to its conclusion.

Figure 11-2: Sample Science Portfolio Assessment Tool

Getting Started

1. You have no difficulty identifying your friend and yourself. But imagine how different the world would look if you could magnify your eyes the way microscopes do. Imagine you could zoom right down to your friend's cells.

   a) Could you tell the difference between a cell from your arm and a cell from your friend's arm?
   b) What if you could see a cell from a fish's fin and a cell from your arm - could you tell which was which?
   c) And if you could see a cell in a lettuce leaf, could you tell it apart from your arm?

2. Just as a network of roads carries people and goods throughout a city, so a network of blood vessels, thousands of kilometres long, carries a living fluid throughout your body. The driving force is your heart, beating continuously over 40 million times a year, whether you are asleep or awake.

   a) Why do you need this system?
   b) What does it mean to say that blood is a living fluid?

3. Plants are an essential part of the circle of food and energy that connects all life on Earth. Plants make food, and you need that food either directly or indirectly, to stay alive. To make that food plants need water. But water flows downhill.

   a) How does water get from the ground up to the tip of the tallest trees?
   b) Is there any similarity between this movement and the movement of blood from your heart to your head?

Diagnostic Assessment Master 2: Accessing Prior Knowledge

Read the three Getting Started sections. You will probably have some ideas already about how to answer the questions, but as you work through this unit, you will learn much more. Write the best answers you can right now in the second column. Before the end of the unit, write your revised answers in the third column.

Question	My Answers at the Beginning of the Unit	My Revised Answers Near the End of the Unit
1. (a)	I think cells from my arm and my friends would look the same.	
(b)	I think I could tell the difference from my arm cell and a fish cell.	
(c)	I'm sure a lettuce cell would be different from my arm cell.	
2. (a)	Blood is what keeps us alive.	
(b)	Blood is a living fluid means blood keeps us alive.	
(c)		
3. (a)	Trees such water up from their roots.	
(b)	No. Blood gets pumped by the heart and trees don't have a heart.	
(c)		

Write any additional questions in your notebook.

▲ **Notice that this student has some initial understanding about cells, but also has some significant misconceptions. At the end of the unit, the student will return to this sheet and complete the second column to reflect his increased understanding.**

Formative Assessment (assessment *for* learning)

Formative assessment of the portfolio occurs through conferencing between the student and teacher. During a conference, you might ask the student about

- specific items in the portfolio
- why certain items were selected for inclusion
- the kind of information the student has noted on the reflection slips
- what a specific item shows about his or her learning

The student, peers, parents, and the teacher may all be involved in aspects of formative assessment. (Portfolio assessment tools may be found in Section 5 of Part 2.)

Summative Assessment (assessment *of* learning)

You may wish to include assessment data from students' portfolios as part of your overall report card grade. As noted earlier, the required elements in a portfolio may include polished pieces of work that you have identified as evidence of essential learning. The marks assigned to these pieces may comprise a significant part of your assessment of learning data.

Assessment data from students' portfolios can form part of an overall report card grade.

Assessment Q & A

Question

On Portfolio Day, I often run across homework and projects that I know have been completed with lots of adult help. What can I do about this situation?

Answer

As a general rule, homework should

- reinforce what has been learned in school
- provide students with additional practice to consolidate their learning

Homework should not require parents and guardians to assume the role of the teacher; instead, the parent's role should merely be to support the child's learning. This will decrease the likelihood that parents are completing homework for the child.

When it comes to projects and major assignments, requiring students to complete the bulk of the work during class time is usually a good solution. During a major project, there should be frequent progress checks when students must show you the work they have done to date. These checks will enable you to identify inappropriate parent involvement long before the work is to be completed.

Distributing a project assignment sheet to students that includes a note to parents emphasizing the need for students to work independently will also help. If the problem persists, a phone call or face-to-face meeting with the parent will be necessary.

Note the term *polished pieces*. An individual student's portfolio may contain several pieces of work related to the same assignment, including initial brainstorming, tentative first draft, second draft that includes revisions based on peer and teacher, feedback, and polished version.

Only the mark assigned to the polished piece would be included as part of the student's report card grade. All of the other pieces represent the student's evolving learning.

A variety of tools to help you implement a portfolio program in your classroom is available in Section 5 of Part 2. These tools include checklists and rubrics, as well as reflection strips.

CASE STUDY 1 — Ms. Wright's Integrated Portfolio Program

Ms. Wright has been using portfolios in her Grade 5 class for several years. She has found them well-suited to the integrated curriculum approach that she favours. The portfolios speak volumes about the richness and complexity of her students' learning. They contain works-in-progress, including scribbles, first tries, sketches, notes, and reflections.

Portfolios help Ms. Wright to accomplish a wide range of tasks:

- Her students use the portfolio to organize their work at all stages, from vague ideas to works in progress to polished, ready-to-publish pieces.
- Ms. Wright uses the portfolio as a focus for one-on-one student conferences that occur every week in her classroom.
- As a reporting period approaches, Ms. Wright asks her students to ensure that their portfolios contain all the required elements. She uses these as evidence of essential learning to help determine their grades.
- At Ms. Wright's school, student-led parent-teacher conferences occur after report cards have gone home. Each student uses the portfolio as the focus for this conference, choosing samples to demonstrate to their

parents both their achievements to date, as well as what they are struggling with.

Ms. Wright knows that if portfolios are to improve student learning, they must become an integral part of her classroom routines. To accomplish this goal, Ms. Wright uses a four-step approach: collect, select, reflect, and inspect.

Step 1: Collect

Students *collect* samples of their work in language arts, math, and social studies to place in their portfolios. Their collections include written work, CD-ROMs containing word-processed pieces, photographs and other images they may have downloaded or created, and presentation slides they are working on. Each student's portfolio includes required elements that comprise evidence of essential learning, as well as self-selected optional elements.

Step 2: Select

Ms. Wright instructs her students to *select* work from their portfolios at different times for a variety of purposes. Prior to

- *one-on-one conferences*, she asks students to select a piece of work they need help with.
- a *peer-assessment conference*, Ms. Wright asks her students to select a piece of work that requires peer input.

continued

- *student-led parent-teacher conferences*, she asks students to select the pieces that best illustrate their achievements.

Step 3: Reflect

The *reflect* step is one of the most important aspects of an effective portfolio program. In this step, students attach a reflection strip to every piece they select for each of the purposes described in Step 2. Students use these strips to comment on the reasons they have selected these pieces to include in their portfolios. For example, during a one-on-one conference with Ms. Wright, Khan uses the reflection strip to prompt himself as he explains to Ms. Wright how his later draft is a significant improvement on an early draft. (See Figure 11-4.)

The reflect step places the onus on the student, not the teacher, to assess the quality of the work. Although the teacher may affirm the student's self-assessment or point out additional aspects of the work that need attention, it is the student who is responsible for initiating the assessment. In order to do this, students must

- know the target for quality work
- have an assessment tool such as a rubric or checklist, and perhaps an exemplar, to guide their assessment
- compare the quality of work with the indicators contained in the tools

Figure 11-3: Khan's Letter

1210 Park Crescent
Saskatoon

January 15, 2007

Dear Grandpa,

Our winter break was awesome. We have had cold and snowy weather for weeks now, so I couldn't wait for a couple of weeks off to skate and play hockey on the pond near our house. Yoshi always sleeps in when there's no school so I woke him up every morning so we could eat breakfast quick and go play. Most days, we picked up my friend Aaron on the way to the pond because he's a real good hockey player. Way better than me and Yoshi.

Anyways on Friday when we finished playing, mom said we could come in and have hot chocolate and donuts and I ate three! Then we played Nintendo on Aaron's computer for 2 hours. After that, we watched Narnia on DVD and Aaron's mom made us popcorn. I saw the movie when it first came out but the DVD had more stuff on it, like outtakes. I love those.

So as you can see the winter break was great and I'm not real happy about going back to school next week. Give my love to Grandma and please come visit this summer.

Love from Khan

Figure 11-4: Khan's Reflection Strip

Reflection Strip

*Complete and attach this Reflection Strip to each item **you** choose to include in your portfolio.*

NAME _Khan_   DATE _Feb 4_

This piece of work shows:

☑ how I have improved an earlier draft
☐ something important that I learned
☐ something I need to work on
☐ something I need help with
☐ something I am proud of
☐ what I do outside of school
☐ how well I have learned something

1. I choose to include this item because:
   This polished draft of my letter to grandpa has lots of detail and looks like a real letter.

2. How does this item demonstrate the thing(s) I've checked above?
   My first letter was boring because it had no interesting details. Also, it didn't look like a letter

3. Other important things about me that this item shows:

continued

The "Reflect" step ensures that the portfolio becomes a powerful process for teaching students how to assess their own work objectively.

Step 4: Inspect

Steps 1, 2, and 3 are ongoing activities that occur throughout the term. They are all student responsibilities. Step 4 is the teacher's job, and is the point when the assessment shifts from assessment *for* learning to assessment *of* learning. Ms. Wright *inspects* the evidence of essential learning in each student's portfolio. The mark that she assigns to each required piece will contribute significantly to the report card grade that each student receives.

This case study illustrates how portfolios can be used as a medium through which you communicate with your students about their progress and achievement, as well as the focus for students to communicate with their parents about their learning. The next case study illustrates yet another way to use portfolios—this time, with younger children.

CASE STUDY 2 | # Portfolios for Mr. Ang's Students

Mr. Ang knew he was an organized and effective teacher, but he wanted to create a community of learners who would take more ownership of their learning. He decided to introduce portfolios as a means of featuring important evidence of learning. Mr. Ang sensed that portfolios would also be a powerful way to communicate students' learning during parent interviews. Students could present their own work during a conference they would run themselves.

Mr. Ang discussed how to use portfolios effectively with Ms. Wright, his colleague. (See Case Study 1.) Although Mr. Ang teaches Grade 2, he decided to follow Ms. Wright's four-step approach. Mr. Ang spoke to his principal about his plan and used the outline shown in the figure on page 175 to explain his goals.

The portfolios included pieces of work from all subjects. Mr. Ang took photos of work too

▲ **In Mr. Ang's class, students' portfolios comprised pieces of work from all subject areas.**

large to include and had the students provide descriptions of those pieces of work. Each portfolio piece included a student reflection that described:

continued

Mr. Ang's Goals	Mr. Ang's Plan
1. Shift from teacher-centred assessment to more student self-assessment/reflection.	1. Introduce the use of portfolios to students and parents.
2. Enable students to gain information about themselves as learners.	2. Introduce regular one-on-one conferencing.
3. Enable students to take more responsibility for their learning.	3. Set aside time for students to work on their portfolios.
4. Promote student-led conferences using the portfolios.	4. Provide guidelines and model on how to use the portfolios in student-led conferences.

• why they had chosen it
• what was notable about it
• their own assessment of the piece

Mr. Ang modelled and then provided students with many opportunities to self-assess.

As the time for parent interviews approached, Mr. Ang scheduled three or four student-parent conferences each day after school. Before the conferences began, Mr. Ang indicated to parents that he would be available after each conference to talk to them and answer any questions.

Mr. Ang gave the students guidelines to prepare them for their conference. Each student would select, present, and discuss

• a favourite piece of writing
• a piece of science work
• a piece from their portfolio of which they were especially proud

In addition, they would be required to

• teach their parent how to play a math game that had helped them consolidate a concept
• read their parent a favourite book they had reviewed and share their review

Mr. Ang provided time for the students to work in pairs to practise their student-parent conferences. He wanted them to be comfortable and confident about how they would present their learning. Mr. Ang monitored their progress, answered any questions, and gave encouragement.

The conferences were a huge hit with both the parents and the students. The students felt empowered by their portfolios and by leading the conferences. The parents told Mr. Ang they now had a clear picture of their child's strengths and areas of need. They also loved having their child (and not the teacher) present their accomplishments.

Video Clip 6:

A Three-Way Reporting Conference (Teacher/Student/Parent)
06:45 minutes

Summary

- The portfolio is much more than an assessment strategy. It is an ongoing part of a learning program that integrates assessment with instruction.
- When implemented effectively, a portfolio is a window on a student's learning.
- Effective portfolio programs involve a four-step process: collect, select, reflect, and inspect. Students, teachers, and parents may be involved in all four phases.
- The portfolio is a highly effective strategy for teaching students how to become effective assessors of their own work. For this to occur, they must be held responsible for selecting many of the pieces that go into their portfolio, and for explaining why they have selected these pieces.
- Portfolios should encompass the various purposes for which teachers conduct assessment at different times during a term, including
  - diagnostic assessment to determine students' strengths and needs
  - formative assessment to provide feedback while students are learning
  - summative assessment after a significant period of instruction

Applying My Learning

With colleagues, examine current portfolio use in your school and explore ways to learn more about this powerful process. Consider assembling a Portfolio Team to reflect on and implement best practices. Your team could fulfill one or more of the following functions:

- Research how portfolios are currently used by teachers in your school.
- Research the latest professional literature on portfolios and make it available to colleagues.
- Meet on a regular basis to share best practices with team members in order to refine portfolio practices in your school.

You could begin by conducting the survey provided on page 177: *Examining Portfolio Use in My School* at a staff meeting.

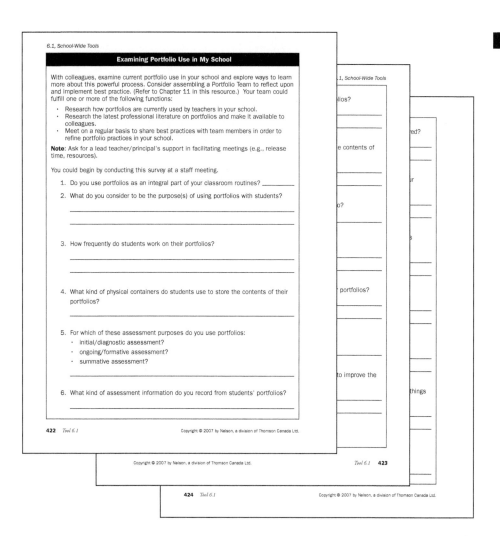

6.1, School-Wide Tools

Examining Portfolio Use in My School

With colleagues, examine current portfolio use in your school and explore ways to learn more about this powerful process. Consider assembling a Portfolio Team to reflect upon and implement best practice. (Refer to Chapter 11 in this resource.) Your team could fulfill one or more of the following functions:

- Research how portfolios are currently used by teachers in your school.
- Research the latest professional literature on portfolios and make it available to colleagues.
- Meet on a regular basis to share best practices with team members in order to refine portfolio practices in your school.

Note: Ask for a lead teacher/principal's support in facilitating meetings (e.g., release time, resources).

You could begin by conducting this survey at a staff meeting.

1. Do you use portfolios as an integral part of your classroom routines? _____

2. What do you consider to be the purpose(s) of using portfolios with students?

_____

_____

3. How frequently do students work on their portfolios?

_____

_____

4. What kind of physical containers do students use to store the contents of their portfolios?

_____

5. For which of these assessment purposes do you use portfolios:
   - initial/diagnostic assessment?
   - ongoing/formative assessment?
   - summative assessment?

_____

6. What kind of assessment information do you record from students' portfolios?

_____

422   *Tool 6.1*   Copyright © 2007 by Nelson, a division of Thomson Canada Ltd.

Copyright © 2007 by Nelson, a division of Thomson Canada Ltd.   *Tool 6.1*   **423**

424   *Tool 6.1*   Copyright © 2007 by Nelson, a division of Thomson Canada Ltd.

TOOL 6.1

Examining Portfolio Use in My School, pp. 422–424

Chapter 12

SELECTING AND DEVELOPING QUALITY ASSESSMENT TOOLS

 BIG IDEA 1 Assessment serves different purposes at different times: it may be used to find out what students already know and can do; it may be used to help students improve their learning; or it may be used to let students and their parents know how much they have learned within a prescribed period of time.

ASSESSMENT TOOL BASICS

Assessment **tools** are used to record data about student performance. They include checklists, running records, rubrics, marking schemes, and rating scales.

Here are some of the challenges teachers often report about the selection of assessment tools:

1. Where do I find the best classroom assessment tools?
2. How do I judge the quality of assessment tools?
3. Do I need different kinds of tools for different purposes?
4. How many different tools do I need?

Talk About Assessment answers the first question by including a wide variety of assessment tools organized by division and subject area in Part 2 of this book. This chapter will help you answer the three remaining questions and help you decide what assessment tools to use in your classroom.

Many assessment tools currently available miss the mark when it comes to quality. In my experience, teachers and students benefit the most from using a relatively small number of high-quality tools, each one matched to a particular assessment purpose.

Figure 12-1 lists the most common assessment tools, their purposes, and some of their strengths and limitations. Many of these tools may be used for diagnostic, formative, and summative purposes. (See Chapter 2.)

Figure 12-1: Assessment Tools, Purposes, Strengths, and Weaknesses

Assessment Tool	Purpose	Strengths (+) and Weaknesses (−)
Anecdotal record—ongoing written observations about students' progress, collected over time	• tracks growth in specific skills by highlighting areas of strength and need	+ useful for providing detailed information to students and parents − time-consuming
Anchors—student work samples that correspond to the performance levels set out in a rubric **Exemplars**—samples within the anchor set that represent the expected standard of quality	• when used in conjunction with a rubric, helps teachers and students see what a set of performance standards look like in practice	+ provides teachers and students with models of quality work − can limit student creativity if used inappropriately or if only one sample is provided for each performance level
Checklist—a list of specific skills to be demonstrated during a performance task or attributes required in a product	• used for self-, peer-, or teacher-assessment; determines whether a specific performance or product contains all of the required elements	+ makes expectations clear to students; effective and reliable for self- and peer-assessment − informs students about deficits but not how to improve
Developmental continuum—a detailed chart that identifies typical stages of skill acquisition and the observable indicators associated with each stage	• used in core skill areas such as reading and writing to assess students' current skill levels and plan instruction that will move them to the next stage	+ helps teachers design instruction based on assessment through observation; provides parents with precise information about their child's strengths and needs − sometimes used inappropriately for grading purposes
Frequency scale—a scale used to measure how frequently a desired behaviour or attribute occurs	• used to inform students how frequently they demonstrate a required behaviour or exhibit a desired attribute	+ efficiently assesses behaviours and learning skills − inappropriate if quality rather than quantity is the variable to be assessed
Rating scale—a scale that assigns a numerical value to one or more assessment criteria	• used to inform students of the extent to which they met a required criterion	+ efficiently matches a score to a desired criterion − does not inform students how to improve
Rubric—a set of criteria and performance indicators arranged according to expected levels of performance	• communicates to teachers, students, and parents what is expected in a given performance or product before it occurs; is also used to assess the quality of the performance or product once it has been completed	+ clarifies for teachers, students, and parents what quality work looks like − poorly written rubrics may focus on quantity as opposed to quality − can limit the range of student performance if poorly written
Running record—a form of anecdotal record most often used to record reading performance	• records specific reading errors to determine a student's reading level and identify skills needing remediation	+ useful to inform instructional decisions − requires one-on-one assessment
Scoring guide—a precise explanation of how marks are awarded for specific questions on a test or for specific performance indicators on a product	• used to increase the reliability of marking; may also be used to clarify expectations for students	+ fosters discussion among teachers about their expectations for quality work − can narrow the possible range of student responses

ENSURING THE QUALITY OF ASSESSMENT TOOLS

There are five basic quality checks that you may find helpful when selecting or designing assessment tools for different situations:

1. Does the assessment tool match the assessment purpose?
2. Does the assessment tool match the assessment strategy?
3. Does the assessment tool provide valid and reliable information about student performance?
4. Does the assessment tool provide students with feedback?
5. Have I kept the number of assessment tools manageable?

1. Does the Assessment Tool Match the Assessment Purpose?

As we saw in Chapter 2, there are many different purposes for assessing student performance. These include

- determining areas of strength and need in order to plan instruction
- providing feedback to students on early tries or first drafts to help them improve
- summarizing what students have learned at the end of a unit or term.

Assessment tools may serve one or more of these purposes. For example, the Initial Assessment Summary, shown in Figure 12-2, is intended only for consolidating information about a student's strengths and needs early in a school year. On the other hand, the Problem-Solving Rubric, shown in Figure 12-3, may be used for initial, formative, and summative assessment throughout the year. (Note: Full-page versions of the tools shown in this chapter may be found in Part 2.)

TOOL 4.13

Initial Assessment Summary, p. 380

Figure 12-2: Initial Assessment Summary

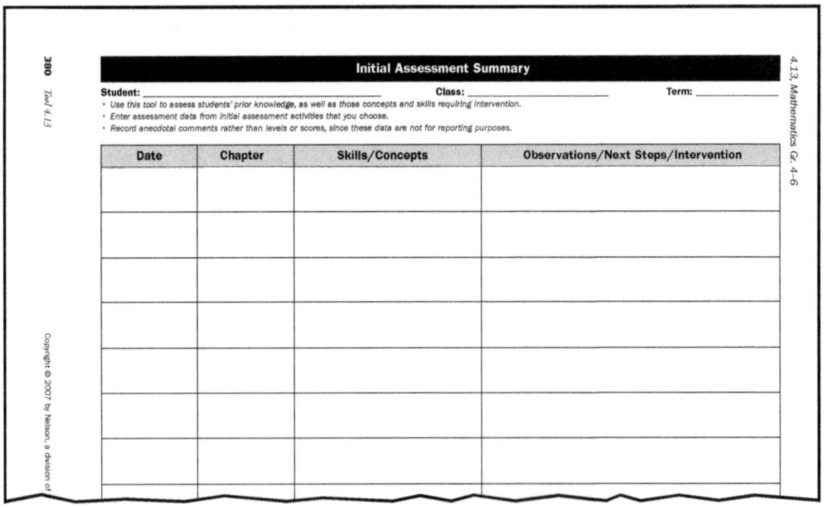

380 *Tool 4.13*

Initial Assessment Summary

Student: ______ **Class:** ______ **Term:** ______

- *Use this tool to assess students' prior knowledge, as well as those concepts and skills requiring intervention.*
- *Enter assessment data from initial assessment activities that you choose.*
- *Record anecdotal comments rather than levels or scores, since these data are not for reporting purposes.*

Date	Chapter	Skills/Concepts	Observations/Next Steps/Intervention

4.13, Mathematics Gr. 4–6

Copyright © 2007 by Nelson, a division of

Figure 12-3: Problem-Solving Rubric

Problem-Solving Rubric

Name: _____ Date: _____

Criteria	Level 1	Level 2	Level 3	Level 4
Think: Understand the Problem	· shows **limited** understanding of the problem (e.g., is unable to identify sufficient information or to restate problem)	· shows **some** understanding of the problem (e.g., is able to identify some of the relevant information but may have difficulty restating problem)	· shows **complete** understanding of the problem (e.g., is able to identify relevant information and to restate problem)	· Shows **thorough** understanding of the problem (e.g., is able to differentiate between relevant and irrelevant information and is able to rephrase problem)
Plan: Make a Plan	· shows **little or no evidence** of a plan	· shows **some** evidence of a plan	· shows evidence of an **appropriate** plan	· shows evidence of a **thorough** plan
Do: Carry Out the Plan	· uses a strategy and **attempts to** solve problem but **does not arrive at a solution**	· carries out the plan **to some extent**, using a strategy, and develops a **partial and/or incorrect solution**	· carries out the plan **effectively** by using an **appropriate strategy** and **solving the problem**	· shows **flexibility** and **insight** when carrying out the plan by **trying and adapting**, when necessary, one or more strategies **to solve the problem**
	· shows **little evidence** of revising plan when necessary	· shows **some** evidence of revising plan when necessary	· shows **strong** evidence of revising plan if necessary	· revises plan in **insightful ways**, if necessary
	· use of procedures includes **major errors and/or omissions**	· use of procedures includes **several errors and/or omissions**	· use of procedures is mostly correct, but there may be a **few minor errors and/or omissions**	· use of procedures includes **almost no errors or omissions**
Review: Look Back	· has **difficulty** identifying either errors or omissions in the plan or in the attempted solution	· shows **some ability to check** the plan and attempted solution for errors and/or omissions	· **checks** the plan and solution for procedural errors and omissions	· **thoroughly reviews** the plan and solution for effectiveness of strategies chosen and for procedural errors and omissions
	· draws **faulty** conclusions based on **insufficient** evidence	· draws **partial** conclusions based on **some** evidence	· draws **appropriate** conclusions based on **sufficient** evidence	· draws **thoughtful** conclusions based on **all available** evidence

The basic requirement for any assessment tool intended to provide feedback to students is that it communicate information in words, not merely in scores. Most rubrics include both score points or levels and performance indicators. If the assessment purpose is diagnostic or formative, then the focus should be on the indicators; if the purpose is summative, then the score or level will also be of concern. The Problem-Solving Rubric shown in Figure 12-3 is an example of a tool that could be used for any one of these purposes.

As a teacher, I took several years to realize that there was often an inverse relationship between the time a student spent on a piece of work and the time I had to spend marking it! We can avoid this problem by providing students with a checklist such as the one shown is Figure 12-4 and requiring them to self and/or peer assess their work. Such tools must be designed to focus students' attention on specific aspects of the work to be assigned.

> **Tips for Teaching**
>
> Some studies have indicated that providing students with both anecdotal feedback and a score does little to improve learning. (Butler, 1988.)

Figure 12-4: Self-Assessment—My Writing Ideas

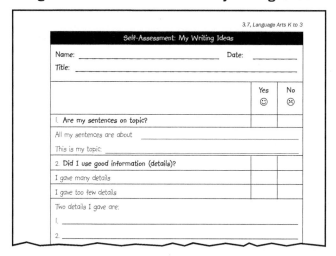

Video Clip 3:

Gr. 5/6 Science—
Communicating
Performance Standards
to Students
12:39 minutes

2. Does the Assessment Tool Match the Assessment Strategy?

Your assessment tool must be easy to use and enable you to record whatever information the assessment strategy is intended to provide. For example, if your students are conducting a science investigation, then an appropriate tool to record your observations might be a checklist attached to a clipboard. As students conduct the investigation, you can move around the classroom, observing a sample of students, and asking questions to probe their understanding. (See Figure 12-5.)

Figure 12-5: Teacher Checklist for Science Performance Standards Inquiry

TOOL 5.7

Teacher Checklist for Science Performance Skills, p. 407

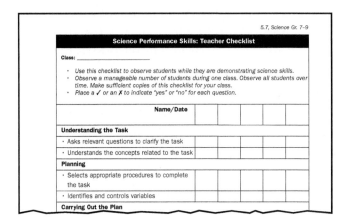

If you are conducting one-on-one reading assessments with young children, a running record is an appropriate tool for capturing anecdotal information. (See Figure 12-6.)

Figure 12-6: Running Record

TOOL 3.2

Running Record, p. 341

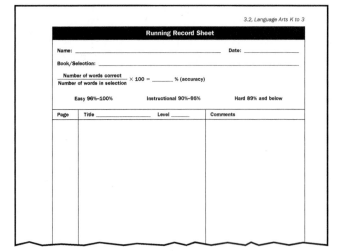

3. Does the Assessment Tool Provide Valid and Reliable Information About Student Performance?

A valid assessment tool (see page 21) measures or gathers information about student performance on precisely those learning targets you intend to assess. If you intend to assess creativity in writing, for example, then the checklist, rubric, or other tool that you use must describe the indicators of creativity you expect students to demonstrate. (See Figure 12-7.) For examples of rubrics that include creativity as a criterion, see Sections 4 and 5 in Part 2.

Figure 12-7: Indicators of Creativity				
	Level 1	**Level 2**	**Level 3**	**Level 4**
Creativity	· ideas are very simple, derivative, and reflect little imaginative thought	· ideas are simple, but reflect some original and imaginative thought	· ideas are complex, and reflect original and imaginative thoughts	· ideas are sophisticated and reflect original and highly imaginative thoughts

A reliable assessment tool (see page 22) will minimize the possible sources of measurement error that could cause two teachers to assess similar student work quite differently. By working with your colleagues to select or develop assessment tools, you can increase the reliability of your assessment since you will have a shared understanding of the targets you intend to assess.

The reliability of rubrics can be improved by paying careful attention to the performance indicators. Compare the poorly worded indicators in Figure 12-8 with the indicators shown in Figure 12-7 above. Vague and imprecise wording of indicators reduces the reliability of a rubric.

When you work with your colleagues, you increase the reliability of your assessment because you develop a shared understanding of the targets you intend to assess.

Figure 12-8: Poorly Worded Indicators of Creativity				
	Level 1	**Level 2**	**Level 3**	**Level 4**
Creativity	· ideas are not very creative	· ideas are somewhat creative	· ideas are creative	· ideas are very creative

4. Does the Assessment Tool Provide Students with Feedback?

If an assessment tool is intended to provide students with feedback to help them improve their performance, care must be taken to ensure that the language used is age-appropriate. Resources such as *Write Traits* include both a teacher and student version of each rubric to ensure that students understand precisely what they need to do to improve their work. (You can find these rubrics on pages 369–372).

For assessment tools to inform students effectively on how to improve their work, they must

- use language that is age- and grade-appropriate
- include performance indicators that clearly describe the attributes of quality work at several performance levels so that students can see what they need to do to improve
- encourage students to improve by identifying the attributes, not the deficits, of quality work

Figure 12-9: Sample "Limited Level" Indicators	
Example 1	**Example 2**
· Work reflects minimal indicators of quality · Errors interfere with the intended communication · Student has significant difficulty explaining concepts	· Work is messy · Work is full of careless errors · Student demonstrates little or no understanding of concepts

For struggling students, simply aiming to produce work that meets the minimal standard may be a significant challenge. Consider the sample "Limited Level" indicators shown in Figure 12-9.

Example 1 indicates that the student is producing work or is providing some explanation, albeit with significant errors or difficulties. The limited indicators serve as a goal for the student who previously may not have been completing work at all. Indicators such as these encourage a student to "get into the game" to improve his or her work. From this point, teachers can help the student move toward adequate performance.

In contrast, the indicators in Example 2 are negative in tone and potentially discouraging for the student. Furthermore, the Example 2 indicators include inferences by the assessor. The word *messy* is a relative term, subject to each person's own notions of what is messy or tidy. Similarly, unless you are standing over students as they complete the task, you can only make assumptions whether errors are the result of carelessness or lack of understanding. Assessment tools that encourage teachers to make inferences rather than observations can seriously compromise the reliability of classroom assessments. Indicators such as these discourage students from improving their work.

Video Clip 2:

Gr. 3/4 Science— Co-operative Group Learning and Assessment 09:31 minutes

5. Have I Kept the Number of Assessment Tools I Use Manageable?

One of the goals of this resource is to make assessment more manageable for teachers. Having a different tool to assess each piece of work or performance you assign is not going to help you achieve this goal! An assessment tool needs to be

- generic enough to gather assessment information about a given learning target
- specific enough to provide students with detailed feedback about how to improve their work or performance.

Figure 12-3 (see page 181) is an example of a flexible assessment tool. (See page 386 for a full-page version of this tool.) You could use this rubric every time you wish to assess the mathematics problem-solving skills of your students. In this respect, the rubric represents a generic set of skills. By using the same rubric all year, your students—and their parents—come to understand and internalize the standards for problem solving. During the term, you might assess students on only some of the five criteria, depending on which steps in the process you have been teaching. At the end of a unit or term, however, you may assess students' mastery of the entire problem-solving process.

Although the rubric is generic in the sense that it applies to all mathematical problem solving, the indicators at each level are specific enough to provide students with detailed feedback about what they need to do differently to improve their performance.

So, to return to the question, "Have I kept the number of assessment tools I use manageable?"—and using mathematics as an example—I suggest that teachers need only four generic rubrics, one each for

- problem solving
- understanding concepts
- applying procedures
- communicating learning

These four rubrics are available in Section 4 of Part 2 of this book. Clearly, you will need other tools, such as checklists and scoring guides to assess homework, tests, and so on, but these four generic rubrics enable you to assess the essential processes in mathematics.

Assessment tools must be generic enough to gather assessment information about a variety of learning targets. At the same time, they must be specific enough to provide students with detailed feedback about how to improve their performance on a specific task.

QUANTITATIVE VERSUS QUALITATIVE ASSESSMENT

Quantitative assessment counts the number of correct items or measures the worth of a product or performance by assigning it a score or percentage. **Qualitative** assessment describes the attributes of a product or performance according to indicators typically organized on a scale. So how do you know when to use a quantitative or qualitative tool? Let me share an anecdote before answering this question.

I will never forget attending a workshop with Spence Rogers at a time when I was teaching English in a secondary school. At one point, Rogers flashed this transparency up on the screen:

The Five Great Illusions of Achievement
1. Everything is worth 100 points!
2. All points are created equal!
3. If students don't perform successfully, take points off!
4. Fifty, sixty, or seventy points is good enough!
5. The more points you accumulate, the more achievement you have!
   (SOURCE: SPENCE ROGERS)

Reading that list confirmed something I'd had a hunch about since my first day of teaching:

My students were producing all these amazing ideas, arguments, stories, dramas, and debates. Yet for every one of these rich performances, I responded with the same, worn-out method of evaluation—a numerical fraction, usually with a denominator of either 50 or 100! Admittedly, I also spent countless hours writing detailed marginal notes and making innumerable corrections of the same set of errors. (See Managing the Marking Load on pages 151–154.) Still, most of my students headed straight for the mark on the last page.

Certain components of student work require quantitative marking, including

- knowledge of terms
- knowledge of formulas
- simple selected response test items

However, giving a numerical score to the most significant work that students produce is neither helpful nor informative for students. Complex performances such as investigations, debates, and design projects all need to be marked qualitatively. That is to say, for each of these rich performances, criteria for success (no more than four or five) must be identified. Then, for each criterion, a set of indicators must be developed that describe a range of performance on a "novice to expert" continuum. An example of such a tool is shown in Figure 12-10.

Figure 12-10: Oral Presentation Rubric				
Criteria	**Level 1**	**Level 2**	**Level 3**	**Level 4**
Subject Content	• content is inaccurate, and seriously lacking in completeness and interest	• content is partially accurate, but incomplete, and lacking in interest	• content is accurate, complete, and interesting	• content is insightful, thorough, and engaging
Use of Language	• language used lacks appropriateness to the purpose and audience	• some language used is appropriate to the purpose and audience	• language used is appropriate to the purpose and audience	• language is skillfully used to suit the purpose and audience
Voice	• delivery is stilted, is difficult to hear throughout, and there is minimal if any variation in tone or inflection	• delivery lacks fluency, is occasionally difficult to hear, and there is little variation in tone or inflection	• delivery is fluent, volume is appropriate, and intonation and inflection help maintain interest	• delivery is fluent, volume is appropriate, and intonation and inflection maintain a high degree of interest throughout
Handling Questions	• responses to questions are seriously limited and demonstrate little command of the subject	• responses to questions are hesitant and demonstrate uncertainty about the subject	• responses to questions are thoughtful and demonstrate a command of the subject	• responses to questions are insightful and demonstrate a strong command of the subject

USING RUBRICS EFFECTIVELY: DO'S AND DON'TS!

While the standards movement has its critics, one beneficial consequence has been the recognition that students have a right to know before they begin their work the performance criteria that will be used to assess that work. Through the introduction of tools such as rubrics, students today have a much clearer view of the target they are aiming for when they produce work or demonstrate a set of skills. Rubrics, though, are not popular with all teachers.

Mrs. Sandir, an intermediate-level teacher, recently said to me, "I can't deal with the subjectivity and inconsistency associated with these new approaches to assessment. I have to be able to count everything and express results in terms of hard numbers." Mrs. Sandir informed the group assembled in the workshop that she had tried to use rubrics with her students but had given up because she found them too subjective.

I cautioned Mrs. Sandir that a rubric, by its very design, is a qualitative tool. A rubric is useful because it promotes learning by informing students of the characteristics of quality work at several performance levels. Rubrics should be used to assess complex performance tasks that cannot be broken down into 50 or 100 equal parts.

Consider the partial rubric in Figure 12-11. Notice how the indicators for "Organization" describe the degree to which each criterion can be met. Note, too, that, although the indicators for "Argument" reflect the number of lapses, they also describe the extent to which these errors affect the report's ability to communicate an intended message; they do not simply quantify the number of errors made.

Figure 12-11: Partial Rubric for a Written Report				
Criteria	**Level 1**	**Level 2**	**Level 3**	**Level 4**
Argument	· **frequent lapses** in logic seriously weaken argument	· **some lapses** in logic, but not sufficient to seriously weaken argument	· logic of argument is **consistent**	· logic of argument is **consistent and sophisticated**
Conclusion	· conclusion is **ineffective**	· conclusion summarizes argument to **some extent**	· conclusion summarizes argument **effectively**	· conclusion summarizes and **extends** argument effectively
Organization	· overall organization is **limited**, i.e., significant flaws in introduction, body, and/or conclusion	· overall organization is **inconsistent**, i.e., some flaws in introduction, body, and/or conclusion	· overall organization is **effective**, i.e., effective transitions within and between introduction, body, and conclusion	· overall organization is **sophisticated**
Diction	· diction, tone, and/or level of language show a **limited sense** of purpose and audience	· diction, tone, and level of language show **some sense** of purpose and audience	· diction, tone, and level of language show a **clear sense** of purpose and audience	· diction, tone, and level of language are **skillfully adapted** to suit the purpose and audience
Conventions	· errors in language conventions **interfere with communication**	· **some** errors in language conventions, but not sufficient to interfere with communication	· language conventions are **used correctly**	· language conventions are used correctly **and for conscious effect**

Unfortunately, in some jurisdictions, teachers are being encouraged to use rubrics to assess everything! A rubric is a helpful tool only when assessing a complex performance involving a variety of skills. It is both unnecessary and inappropriate if the learning target is acquisition of simple information. For example, if students are going to memorize a series of safety rules before conducting their first laboratory investigation, then an appropriate assessment strategy would be a simple quiz. The scoring tool would be an answer key with students' achievement being recorded as a score out of 10.

Ironically, rubrics for complex tasks, which should include criteria such as depth of understanding or quality of argument, often include the least important attributes of the task: frequency of mechanical errors, number of resources used, or neatness of work. In other words, they include those criteria that may be easily quantified. Why? The answer lies in Mrs. Sandir's words. Unless she can count whatever variable she is assessing, she feels that her evaluation will be too subjective. Mrs. Sandir's fear of subjective assessment could result in a rubric like the one shown in Figure 12-12.

> *A rubric is a helpful tool only when assessing a complex performance involving a variety of skills. It is both unnecessary and inappropriate if the learning target is acquisition of simple information.*

Figure 12-12: Flawed Rubric for a Written Report				
Term Paper Rubric **Name:** Theresa				
Criteria	**Indicators**	**Weight**	**Points**	**Score**
Content	ideas reasoning quotes details addresses thesis	7	4	$7 \times 4 = \dfrac{28}{35}$
Organization	introduction thesis supporting statements transitions	6	5	$6 \times 5 = \dfrac{30}{30}$
Style	subject-verb agreement sentence errors verb tense sentence variety	5	3	$5 \times 3 = \dfrac{15}{25}$
Conventions	spelling punctuation capitalization	2	5	$2 \times 5 = \dfrac{10}{10}$
Total Score:				$\dfrac{83}{100}$

A teacher's role is similar to that of a coach. In the case of the teacher, she or he must note what a student does well, what the student has difficulty with, and what the student must do to improve.

It is important not to confuse subjectivity with professional judgement. One of the most important responsibilities of a teacher is to observe students as they learn and to provide feedback about

- what they are doing well,
- what they are having difficulty with,
- what steps they might take to improve.

In this respect, the teacher's role is similar to that of the coach observing an athlete. A coach would never attempt to quantify an athlete's performance during practice, yet many teachers fall into the trap of quantifying everything that students do. Successful coaching and teaching involves feedback.

A well-written rubric can provide a focus for such feedback. Poorly written rubrics, such as the partial one shown in Figure 12-13, can undermine learning. This rubric was given to students who were conducting research in the library, prior to starting work on a project.

Figure 12-13: Part of a Flalwed Research Process Rubric				
Criteria	Level 1	Level 2	Level 3	Level 4
Resources	· locates 1 resource	· locates 2 resources	· locates 3 resources	· locates 4 resources

I asked the teacher who distributed this rubric, "Isn't it possible that a student could return from the library with four resources, none of which is very helpful, yet another student could find one resource that was excellent?"

She replied, "The rubric doesn't lie."

"Well, the rubric is wrong!" I said, trying to control my sense of indignation.

Using Professional Judgement

A teacher's role when observing student performance is to exercise professional judgement in order to provide helpful feedback.

A teacher's role when observing student performance is to exercise professional judgement in order to provide helpful feedback. Quantity and frequency are variables often used to discriminate between levels of performance. Yet, when assessing a rich complex performance, quantity and frequency are the least important variables. They are, however, the easiest to measure and seem to provide teachers with the greatest degree of confidence when called on to justify their assessment data to students and parents.

Mrs. Sandir's concern about subjectivity may have simply been an expression of her discomfort in using professional judgement when observing students. Professional judgement requires teachers to use their skills of observation to assess performance against clear, known standards. Granted, professional judgement is less reliable than scoring a well-designed multiple-choice test. But no amount of multiple-choice questions will address all of the critical learning targets found in a rich curriculum.

Provided that students and teams of teachers discuss the rubrics they are using, they will all come to share a common understanding of what quality work looks like and will become confident in using the rubrics to assess.

Of course, even the best rubric is only words on a page. Students also need to see what a quality performance looks like. That is why students need anchors and exemplars to help them refine their performance. (See Chapter 9, page 148.) Anchors and exemplars—models of student work matched to levels of performance—can include written products and manufactured design projects, but they may also be videotapes of student performances.

For example, many years ago when teaching in a composite high school, I used a videotape of my senior academic English class as an *exemplar* of classroom behaviour for the students in my Grade 9 vocational English class. When their behaviour interfered with learning, I'd find a VCR and monitor, call a time-out and we'd watch what a productive classroom looked like. The video served as an exemplar of appropriate classroom behaviour.

In workshops, I often use Mrs. Sandir's issue with "the subjectivity and inconsistency associated with new assessment approaches" to introduce the distinction between learning that can be assessed quantitatively (e.g., spelling, simple procedures, terminology) and learning that, by virtue of its richness and complexity, requires qualitative description (e.g., problem solving, expository prose, debating skills). As a teacher, you need to consider which is more valid and fair: trying to explain to students the difference between an assignment or performance worth 68 percent and one worth 63 percent, or using a carefully constructed rubric that captures the critical attributes of the assignment (criteria) and describes the achievement on those attributes according to four levels of quality (indicators)?

Why "Less Is More"

The most important reason for using a rubric is that it clearly indicates to students what quality work looks like. No longer do students have to "guess what's in the teacher's head" to succeed at a given task. Now a well-constructed rubric informs them what a quality performance looks like before they begin to work. In this respect, a rubric moves the

Video Clip 9:

Gr. 3/4 Planning a Common Assessment Task and Team Marking
09:37 minutes

The most important reason for using a rubric is that it clearly indicates to students what quality work looks like.

standard for quality from the teacher to the students. It also allows groups of teachers who teach similar skills and knowledge to share a common understanding about the standards for quality work.

Poster-sized copies of rubrics should be displayed prominently in the classroom. It is critical that every student have a copy of the rubric to refer to and for their parents to examine so that, over the course of a term, everyone will gradually internalize both the criteria and indicators for quality performance.

When using rubrics, "less is more" or, more correctly, fewer is better. Why? Fewer rubrics makes it easier for students and teachers to internalize the standards. There is usually an optimum number of rubrics for a given domain—and an optimum amount of detail on each rubric—to ensure that learning targets are clear, specific, and manageable in number. Too many rubrics for students results in too many targets while too many rubrics for teachers leads to an unmanageable assessment load.

For example, one rubric in science class for assessing scientific investigations should suffice. Figure 12-14 illustrates part of such a rubric. The materials used and the degree of student autonomy may vary from one investigation to the next, but the same rubric can be used for most investigations. The teacher assesses only those criteria on the rubric that apply to a given investigation.

Figure 12-14: Partial Rubric for Skills and Procedures of a Scientific Inquiry				
	Level 1	**Level 2**	**Level 3**	**Level 4**
Questioning/ Hypothesizing	· has difficulty generating hypothesis	· generates a questionable hypothesis	· generates a valid hypothesis	· generates an insightful hypothesis
Planning	· identifies and controls few variables	· identifies and controls some major variables	· identifies and controls most major variables	· identifies and controls all major variables
Conducting/ Recording	· follows procedures in a limited way	· follows procedures with some competence	· competently follows procedures	· selects and follows appropriate procedures
Analyzing/ Interpreting	· provides limited analysis of data	· provides some analysis of data	· provides sufficient analysis of data	· provides rich analysis of data
Communicating	· errors interfere with communication	· some errors but not sufficient to interfere with communication	· minor errors	· few, if any, errors

Classifying Rubrics

Rubrics are often classified as being either *analytic* or *holistic*. Typically, an analytic rubric has several distinct criteria, each one accompanied by a distinct set of indicators. Figure 12-14 is an example of an analytic rubric.

A holistic rubric, on the other hand, contains a general set of indicators associated with each achievement level. These rubrics are often too vague and generic to be used to coach students toward excellent performance. (This is not their intended purpose.) For, example, the rubric shown in Figure 12-15 was designed for provincial assessment teams responsible for scoring large-scale mathematics assessments.

Figure 12-15: Partial Rubric Adapted from Grade 3 Mathematics Testing				
Categories/ Criteria	**Level 1**	**Level 2**	**Level 3**	**Level 4**
Problem Solving	• demonstrates a very limited understanding of problems by choosing and carrying out a few simple strategies that rarely lead to accurate solutions	• demonstrates a limited understanding of problems by choosing and carrying out some appropriate strategies that sometimes lead to accurate solutions	• demonstrates a general understanding of problems by consistently choosing and carrying out appropriate strategies that usually lead to accurate solutions	• demonstrates a thorough understanding of problems by choosing and carrying out innovative and appropriate strategies that almost always lead to accurate solutions

Teachers generally do not need separate analytic and holistic rubrics. It is preferable to have a rubric that can be used analytically when coaching students (assessing *for* learning), and holistically when conducting assessment *of* learning. Such multi-purpose rubrics strike a balance between being too vague or too detailed.

Figure 12-16 illustrates part of a rubric for assessing a formal speech. The indicators that the teacher observed during one student's first attempt have been circled. You could use this rubric during a one-on-one conference to point out to the student areas of strength and areas needing improvement. This would be using the rubric *analytically*. Because the feedback is formative, you would not need to summarize the assessment into an overall score.

Figure 12-16: Formative Assessment of a Formal Speech

Criteria	Level 1	Level 2	Level 3	Level 4
Communication of Ideas	• ideas are few, simple, and lack clarity	• ideas are clear and simple	• ideas are clear, original, and reflect some complexity	• ideas are clear, original, and sophisticated
	• audience is indifferent	• audience is occasionally engaged	• audience is engaged	• audience is moved
	• little evidence of adapting vocabulary to situation and audience	• vocabulary is usually appropriate to the situation	• vocabulary is appropriate to situation and audience	• vocabulary is skillfully selected to match situation and audience
	• responses to questions are insufficient	• responses to questions are brief and/or insufficient	• responses to questions are clear and complete	• responses to questions are thorough and insightful

Figure 12-17 illustrates the same rubric used much later in the term when the teacher needed to determine a summative score for the same performance. This time, the teacher looked at the pattern of observations and asked (while recognizing that the performance did not fall exclusively into one level): *What set of indicators best captures the overall level of performance at this time?*

This is using the same rubric *holistically*. In this case, the teacher uses professional judgement and determines that Level 3 represents the line of best fit for the student at this time.

Figure 12-17: Summative Assessment of a Formal Speech

Criteria	Level 1	Level 2	Level 3	Level 4
Communication of Ideas	• ideas are few, simple, and lack clarity	• ideas are clear and simple	• ideas are clear, original, and reflect some complexity	• ideas are clear, original, and sophisticated
	• audience is indifferent	• audience is occasionally engaged	• audience is engaged	• audience is moved
	• little evidence of adapting vocabulary to situation and audience	• vocabulary is usually appropriate to situation	• vocabulary is appropriate to situation and audience	• vocabulary is skillfully selected to match situation and audience
	• responses to questions are insufficient	• responses to questions are brief and/or insufficient	• responses to questions are clear and complete	• responses to questions are thorough and insightful
Most Consistent Level of Achievement: Level 3				

Developing a High-Quality Rubric

It is always preferable to collaborate with teaching partners or a grade team when developing assessment tools. The professional dialogue that characterizes cooperative work leads to a much deeper understanding of the standards you use to assess student work.

Collaboration, especially if you teach in a small school, is not always possible. If face-to-face collaboration is not possible, e-mail your ideas to colleagues for discussion or set up an online work group to develop your rubrics. Developing a rubric with colleagues is an excellent way to examine and discuss the standards for quality that you set for your students. As you work through the process of identifying criteria and developing the performance indicators at several levels, you will find yourself examining and questioning your own biases about student achievement.

Here are some guidelines to help you design your rubrics. The charts after each guideline illustrate an actual rubric under construction.

The Rubric-Development Toolkit

Before you begin this work, consult your local and provincial curriculum documents and review Chapter 4 on Standards in this resource. Then work through the following steps as a team.

1. Decide on the task or performance you wish to assess.
   (This example is written for a student-created children's book.)
2. If available, gather student samples from previous years
   For example, gather samples of student-created children's books from last year's class
3. Examine these samples and ask: What are the critical elements (criteria) we need to assess? Start by brainstorming all possible criteria. Then reduce the total number of criteria to between four and six essential elements of the task or performance. This is hard work and may lead to disagreements! But that's all part of the dialogue necessary to increase your understanding of assessment.

Criteria	Limited	Adequate	Proficient	Excellent
Creativity				
Writing style				
Illustrations				
Professionalism				
Conventions				

4. Look again at the samples of student work and ask: Based on these criteria, which samples represent a proficient level of achievement? Use these samples to help you begin writing performance indicators.

5. Choose one criterion and write a set of point-form performance indicators that describe Proficient for this criterion.

Criteria	Limited	Adequate	Proficient	Excellent
Creativity			· theme is **original** · theme is **engaging** for children	
Writing style				
Illustrations				
Professionalism				
Conventions				

6. Write the Proficient performance indicators for the rest of the criteria. Keep referring to the samples of student work to ensure you are capturing valid indicators of quality.

Criteria	Limited	Adequate	Proficient	Excellent
Creativity			· theme is **original** · theme is **engaging** for children	
Writing style			· diction and sentence structure are **effective** · dialogue is **realistic**	
Illustrations			· pictures or artwork are **effective**	
Professionalism			· book is **polished**	
Conventions			· book contains **minimal errors**	

7. Working from the Proficient Level, write the performance indicators for the Excellent, Limited and Adequate levels. (Note: It is critical to be clear about whether Limited represents the *minimal* level of acceptable work or *unacceptable work*. In the former case, you may expect many students to perform below the Limited level; in the latter case, Limited will represent the lowest level of performance you expect to see from any of your students. This issue is usually dictated by provincial or local standards. See page 184 for information about writing lowest-level indicators.

Criteria	Limited	Adequate	Proficient	Excellent
Creativity	• theme is **unoriginal** • theme **may not engage** children	• theme shows **some originality** • theme **may engage some children**	• theme is **original** • theme is **engaging** for children	• theme is **original** and **clever** • theme is **highly engaging** for children
Writing style	• vocabulary and sentence structure are **limited** • dialogue is **lacking**	• vocabulary and sentence structure show **some variety** • dialogue shows **some realism**	• vocabulary and sentence structure are **effective** • dialogue is **realistic**	• vocabulary and sentence structure are **highly effective** • dialogue is **life-like** and **engaging**
Illustrations	• pictures or artwork are **ineffective**	• pictures or artwork **add** to the story to **some degree**	• pictures or artwork are **effective**	• pictures or artwork are **visually striking**
Professionalism	• book **appears unfinished**	• book shows **some attention to detail**	• book shows **attention to detail**	• entire book is **polished** and **professional looking**
Conventions	• errors **seriously interfere** with the story	• errors **interfere** with the story to **some extent**	• book contains **minimal errors**	• book is **free of errors**

8. Take the time to review the completed draft of your rubric, ask the following questions, and revise the rubric as necessary:

a) Does the rubric represent an appropriate range of performance that we expect students to demonstrate on this performance or task? Revise any indicators that cause you to answer *No* to this question.

b) Does this rubric align with state or provincial performance standards, if these exist?
If not, revise the indicators as necessary.

c) As you read across the rubric, do the set of indicators for each criterion deal with the same features across all four levels?
If not, revise indicators that do not fit the set.

d) As you read across the set of indicators for each criterion, are the increments from level to level equal and appropriate for the grade level?
If not, revise indicators to achieve appropriate increments.

e) Does the rubric capture the essential qualities of the task or performance, or does it focus too much on those elements that are easy to measure?
If the latter, examine the rubric criteria and revise them.

f) Is it possible that a student could complete an excellent piece of work/demonstrate an excellent performance, yet receive a low level from this rubric?

If the answer is yes, revise the problem areas on the rubric.

g) Is it possible that a student could complete a poor piece of work/demonstrate a poor performance, yet receive a high level from this rubric?

If the answer is yes, revise the problem areas on the rubric.

9. Field-test the rubric with your students to validate it for quality before using it for assessment of learning purposes. Using the rubric for diagnostic or formative assessment is one way to accomplish this validation.

10. Share the polished rubric with other teachers, students, and parents to help everyone understand the standards of quality for the particular task or performance.

(ADAPTED FROM WIGGINS, 1998)

Summary

- An assessment tool is used to record information about student performance.
- Assessment tools must be designed or selected according to the purpose of the assessment, as well as the assessment strategy employed.
- Teachers have a responsibility to ensure that the assessment tools they use are of high quality.
- Some tools are intended to record quantitative assessment data, while others are intended to record qualitative information.
- Rubrics are qualitative tools and, as such, require a degree of professional judgement on the part of the assessor.
- Teachers need to discuss with their colleagues the type and number of rubrics they plan to use. This discussion will lead to decisions about using generic or task-specific rubrics, as well analytic or holistic rubrics.
- Teachers need to take great care when designing rubrics to ensure assessment quality.

Applying My Learning

Convene a group of colleagues—ideally a grade team—and develop a rubric to assess a major assessment task that you plan to assign your students. Use *The Rubric-Development Toolkit*, pages 195–198, to direct your work. If you are unable to work face-to-face with colleagues, establish an online work group to create your rubric.

2. Assessment must be planned and purposeful.

BIG
IDEAS
in Section 3

Program Planning with Assessment in Mind

Assessment planning is an integral part of overall program planning. If you wait until students have completed a major project or unit to make decisions about assessment, it is too late.

Chapter 13 introduces a backward design process and describes a set of planning templates that are reproduced in Part 2 of this resource, as well as on the CD-ROM.

In Chapter 14, you will read about teams of educators who have worked through the planning process and used the templates provided in this resource. Completed template samples are provided to help you replicate this process with your own team. Four sample units are provided in Part 2, as well as on the CD-ROM.

A Planning Model and Process

 BIG IDEA 2 Assessment must be planned and purposeful.

Planning your approach to assessment and evaluation is just as important as planning what you are going to teach. Why? Because assessment planning clarifies your goals for student learning. It identifies the evidence of achievement to prove that students have acquired the understanding and skills outlined in the curriculum. In the current climate, where accountability has become a major focus, there are three critical questions to ask:

1. What do we want each student to learn?
2. How will we know when each student has learned it?
3. How will we respond when a student experiences difficulty in learning?

DuFour, May 2004

The second question—How will we know when each student has learned it?—is the key assessment question.

BACKWARD DESIGN PLANNING

Backward design planning is becoming the preferred long-range planning method for teachers.

Backward design planning (Wiggins & McTighe, 1998) is becoming the preferred long-range planning method for teachers. It approaches planning by stating that if learning programs are to be effective for students, they must be designed with the final destination in mind. The teacher must be able to answer the question: By the end of the term, what critical things do I want my students to know and be able to do?

As an illustration of backward design planning, consider a typical driver's education class. Driving instructors begin planning their instruction by asking: What do we want each student to learn? The answer is: By the end of the course, the student drivers must have the knowledge, skills, and attitudes necessary to drive a car safely. Once driving instructors have identified the learning target, they ask a second question: How will we know when each student has learned it? The answer is the road test—the culminating performance—that all drivers must pass in order to get their license.

Along the way, student drivers must also pass a series of assessments to prepare for the road test, beginning with the written multiple-choice test. Each in-car lesson is a formative assessment that provides feedback to the student driver on his or her skills in preparation for the summative (culminating) assessment. Finally, the instructor plans the sequence of lessons that comprise the course, making sure that each lesson provides students with the opportunity to acquire knowledge and practise their skills. Both will be required to successfully complete the formative assessments and ultimately, to pass the culminating assessment.

Program planning in the classroom need not differ from a driver's education class. Teachers need clarity about

- the learning targets that will be set for students
- the formative and culminating assessments that will provide evidence that students have mastered these learning targets

Students need to be informed about

- the culminating assessments at the beginning of their learning so they have a clear sense of their learning destination
- why they are being asked to complete specific formative assessments along the way

Finally, the lessons must be designed so that they prepare students for both the formative and culminating assessments.

Planning Concerns

In workshops, I hear some common concerns about program planning, including

- I have no time to plan.
- The planning model looks good, but there's too much to do.
- I can't get my principal on board.
- The model talks about working with colleagues, but I teach in a very small school.
- I thought the new curriculum meant that teachers didn't have to do program planning.

Start small when you first begin to plan using backward design.

Making Time to Plan

Effective backward design planning does take time, but starting small can be a good way to begin. Start by focusing on only one unit. After you have learned the principles of the backward design model you can begin to transfer your new learning to other planning as time permits.

I often work with teams of teachers who have been freed from their teaching duties for a half day. In only one three-hour session, we are able to make a good start on a unit. The teams often brainstorm ways to complete the unit, such as communicating via a board intranet, getting together during prep time, or spending an hour after school. With a model to follow, these teams go on to gradually apply backward design planning to additional units throughout the year.

Using the Planning Model

Models exist to be modified, and the planning templates in this section require your input. Many teachers have made suggestions to bring them to their current configuration. You will no doubt see ways to modify them to suit your needs, so view both the model and templates as flexible. As well, although there are four planning templates, you may initially choose to use only one or two of them. In short, make the model your own.

As an alternative, you may wish to begin by developing one lesson. In that case, turn to Lesson Planning with the End in Mind (page 211).

Getting Administrative Support

The first person I usually meet when arriving at a school is the principal, and I have yet to meet one who has sent me away! My suggestions for improving learning and making assessment more manageable for teachers always draw a positive response from school administrators. Part of my role involves asking principals to help find the time and resources to enable teachers to meet, to learn, and to plan. Today's focus on professional learning communities (Eaker, Dufour, & Dufour, 2002) makes it easier to convince school administrators of the importance of this work. Convene a group of colleagues and go to your principal with a proposal to develop a long-range plan, or one unit, using the principles of backward design. Explain how your work can serve as a model for all teachers in your school to learn how to plan more effectively. It is unlikely that you will be turned down!

Working Collaboratively

While face-to-face planning with colleagues may be the most effective approach to program planning, teachers in small schools often have no choice but to work alone. The planning tools in this section can be used effectively by individual teachers. You may also be able to plan

To begin with the end in mind means to start with a clear understanding of your destination. It means to know where you're going so that you better understand where you are now so that the steps you take are always in the right direction.

Covey, 1990

colloboratively by making use of board e-mail or a board intranet. In this way, you can receive and provide helpful feedback to colleagues on draft units.

The Need for Planning

New teachers often question the need for program planning:

- I thought the ministry's new curriculum is intended to ensure consistency. Where's the consistency if we're all creating our own units?
- The new mathematics program my school has just purchased includes everything I need. Why would I continue to develop my own units?

Such questions concern me because I still believe, as I always have, that you, the teacher, are the key to learning. Teaching is a craft that requires practitioners to make thoughtful, intelligent decisions and choices before, during, and after each lesson. There is no such thing as a "teacher-proof curriculum." Program planning is a critical responsibility of all teachers, regardless of how prescriptive local or provincial curriculum guidelines may be.

Using the backward design approach to planning facilitates your understanding and management of curriculum outcomes by allowing you to focus on significant and meaningful assessment tasks. You should not try to assess every curriculum outcome. Many of these take care of themselves. In a driver's education class, for example, "the student places the key in the ignition" is an essential outcome because without mastering it, no further progress in driving can occur! Does that mean the examiner assesses this outcome? No, because it is a small part of the larger performance, which is driving the car. Likewise, in the classroom there are numerous curriculum outcomes that are essential to what the student is being asked to do but that do not need to be assessed.

A Planning Model

The four-step planning model presented in this section draws on the work of Grant Wiggins and Jay McTighe in *Understanding By Design* (1998). The overview in Figure 13-1 illustrates the templates recommended for use. These are available in Section 2 of Part 2 of this resource and on the accompanying CD-ROM. Included in Part 2 are several completed sample units that illustrate how you may use the templates to plan units for Grades K–8. In Chapter 14, you will read how a writing team created the Grade 7 integrated mathematics and science unit. Once you have read Chapter 14 and examined the sample units, you will have an

> ### Tips for Teaching
>
> Some teachers believe that standards and curriculum outcomes have "taken all the creativity and fun out of teaching." True, current curriculum documents do prescribe in greater detail than ever before what students are expected to learn. However, you still have plenty of flexibility in how you choose to teach and what resources you will use. This chapter provides you with the strategies and encouragement to focus on what is essential for students to know, understand, and be able to do.

excellent idea of what backward design planning looks and sounds like. View videoclip 4 on the DVD to see a planning team developing a unit.

At this point, take some time to examine the overview presented in Figure 13-1 and read the descriptions of the four templates that follow.

Template 1: Long-Range Assessment Plan

TOOL 2.1

Overview: The Program Planning Process, p. 298

Figure 13-1: The Program Planning Process—Overview

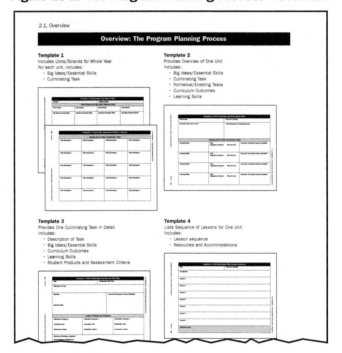

Figure 13-2: Template 1: Long-Range Assessment Plan

TOOL 2.2

Template 1: Long-Range Assessment Plan, pp. 299–300

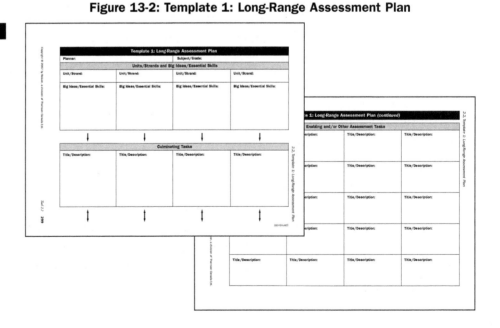

As its name suggests, Template 1: Long-Range Assessment Plan helps you to plan your entire program for the year. Choose whichever of the following approaches works best for you:

- Begin by completing a long-range assessment plan for each subject.
- Begin by designing the individual units first and complete the long-range assessment plan as the final step. (If you choose this option, go directly to Template 2: Unit Curriculum and Assessment Plan, page 301.)
- Begin by planning a single lesson. (If you choose this option, go directly to Lesson Planning with the End in Mind, pages 211–218.)

If you chose to complete Template 1 first, begin by identifying the units and strands that make up your program. (If you are working as a grade team, this can take place as a discussion between you and your colleagues.) Next, list the Big Ideas and Essential Skills for each unit. In many jurisdictions, these appear in curriculum guidelines. Examine them carefully to determine whether they are, in fact, broad and significant enough to be considered Big Ideas. Wiggins and McTighe provide an excellent treatment of how to determine if Big Ideas and Essential Skills are broad enough in their book, *Understanding By Design.* The purpose of identifying the Big Ideas and Essential Skills is to help you organize the curriculum outcomes, thereby allowing you and your students to focus on the critical learning—the learning targets that students should remember and retain long after they have left your class.

Big Ideas and Essential skills help you to focus on critical learning targets.

If you have to develop the Big Ideas and Essential Skills yourself, begin by asking: What must students know and be able to do at the end of each unit? Once you have identified the Big Ideas and Essential Skills for each unit, ask: How will I know that students have learned these? At this point, you and your team will discuss the culminating task that occurs at the end of each unit.

As you complete Template 1, identify each culminating task by its name or by a brief description of what students will be required to do. Next, your team must agree on the formative or enabling tasks that will prepare students for each of the culminating tasks. Keep in mind these points:

- Each set of assessment tasks should include an appropriate balance of written, performance, and oral tasks (i.e., *write, do, say*).
- Formative tasks are the building blocks that prepare students so they can succeed at the culminating task. For example, if the culminating task requires students to conduct research and make an oral presentation, then there must be formative tasks that allow students to practise these skills.

The term "enduring" refers to the big ideas, the important understandings that we want students to "get inside of" and retain after they've forgotten many of the details.
WIGGINS AND MCTIGHE, 1998

Template 2: Unit Curriculum and Assessment Plan

Figure 13-3: Template 2: Unit Curriculum and Assessment Plan

The backward design approach encourages us to think about a unit...in terms of the collected evidence needed to document and validate that the desired learning has been achieved...

WIGGINS AND McTIGHE, 1998

Template 2: Unit Curriculum and Assessment Plan

Unit/Strand:			Focus for Learning:
Big Ideas and Essential Skills:			Title/Description of Culminating Task:

Enabling and/or Other Assessment Tasks

Learning Habits:	Title: Diagnostic/Formative Write/Do/Say	Curriculum Outcomes/Content Standards:
Learning Habits:	Title: Diagnostic/Formative Write/Do/Say	Curriculum Outcomes/Content Standards:
Learning Habits:	Title: Diagnostic/Formative Write/Do/Say	Curriculum Outcomes/Content Standards:
Learning Habits:	Title: Diagnostic/Formative Write/Do/Say	Curriculum Outcomes/Content Standards:

Tips for Teaching

Depending on the structure of your curriculum documents, you may be able to enter numerical codes for the outcomes, rather than writing each one out.

Template 2: Unit Curriculum and Assessment Plan is the starting point for designing a single unit. You and your colleagues will use it to match curriculum outcomes to assessment tasks. In the spirit of backward design, you should complete this template starting with the Big Ideas and Essential Skills, then identify the culminating task for the unit, and describe the formative tasks last. Many teachers find listing the specific curriculum outcomes embedded in each assessment task (the far right column) the most tedious part of the process, so I always suggest leaving this step until the end.

Note that the left side of Template 2 has space for you to identify the learning habits addressed by each assessment task. Many districts now require that teachers gather and report data about achievement separately from data about learning habits. The latter typically include skills such as participation, cooperation, and initiative. Although no one disputes the importance of learning habits, data-gathering related to them often receives little attention. For this reason, learning habits are included on the planning templates.

The Culminating Task box suggests that you name this task and provide a brief description of what students will be required to do. (See Chapter 7 for a detailed discussion of how to design culminating tasks.) Note as well that each of the Enabling and/or Other Assessment Tasks boxes asks you to indicate whether the task is diagnostic or formative, and whether it requires students to write, do, or say. You may wish to review Chapters 2 and 6 for explanations about these design decisions.

Template 3: Culminating Assessment Task Plan

Figure 13-4: Template 3: Culminating Assessment Task Plan

Template 3: Unit Culminating Assessment Task Plan	
Unit:	Assessment Task Title:

Description of Task:

Big Ideas:	Curriculum Outcomes/Content Standards:
Essential Skills:	

Student Products and Processes

Assessment Strategy 1:	Assessment Strategy 2:	Assessment Strategy 3:
Assessment Tool:	Assessment Tool:	Assessment Tool:
Assessment Criteria:	Assessment Criteria:	Assessment Criteria:

Resources/Technology Integration:

Accommodations/Modifications:

(margin: 302 / Tool 2.4 / Copyright © 2007 by Nelson, a division of Thomson / 2.4, Template 3: Unit Culminating Assessment Task Plan)

Students who memorize facts or procedures without understanding often are not sure when or how to use what they know, and such learning is often quite fragile.

BRANSFORD, BROWN AND COCKING, 1999, QUOTED IN FLEWELLING, 2000

Template 3: Culminating Assessment Task Plan guides you in the design of the culminating task that you describe briefly on Template 2. There is plenty of room on Template 3 to list curriculum outcomes but again, you may prefer to do this as the final step. The template also provides space for you to describe up to three student products or processes. These are the components of the culminating task that you will assess.

Possible products include

■ written report
■ work log
■ scale model
■ oral presentation.

Processes might include

■ writing
■ problem-solving
■ research.

As you describe each product or process, identify the tool you will use to assess it. These might include a

■ rubric
■ checklist
■ anecdotal record.

For each product and process, you should also identify the criteria by which it will be assessed. For example, if you plan to use a rubric or a checklist to assess a written report, the criteria you intend to use to assess the report should appear on that tool. (See Chapter 12 for suggestions about identifying criteria.) If you list several learning habits beside the culminating task when completing Template 2, you could indicate in the Student Products and Processes section which specific learning habits will be assessed through each product or process.

There is room at the bottom of Template 3 for you to make notes about resources that you and your students might need to support the culminating task and opportunities to integrate information technology or other subject areas. This is also a place to make notes about accommodations and modifications that may be necessary to adapt the task for students with special needs. (See Chapter 3 for suggestions about adapting assessment for these students.)

Template 4: Instruction Plan/Lesson Sequence

Figure 13-5: Template 4: Instruction Plan/Lesson Sequence

TOOL 2.5

Template 4: Instruction Plan/Lesson Sequence, p. 303

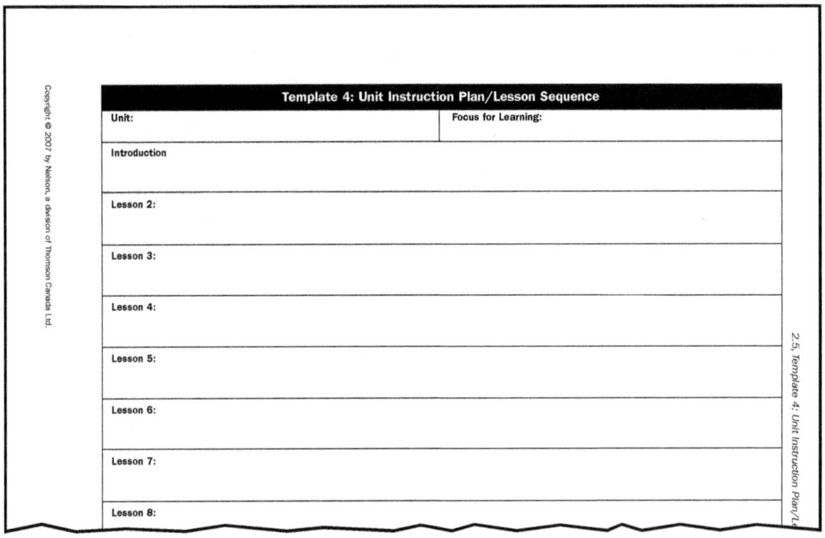
Copyright © 2007 by Nelson, a division of Thomson Canada Ltd.

Template 4: Unit Instruction Plan/Lesson Sequence	
Unit:	Focus for Learning:
Introduction	
Lesson 2:	
Lesson 3:	
Lesson 4:	
Lesson 5:	
Lesson 6:	
Lesson 7:	
Lesson 8:	

2.5, Template 4: Unit Instruction Plan/L

Teaching is a means to an end. Having a clear goal helps us as educators to focus our planning and guide purposeful action toward the intended results.

WIGGINS AND MCTIGHE, 1998

Template 4: Instruction Plan/Lesson Sequence helps you and your colleagues make decisions about the instructional strategies and sequence of lessons you will use to prepare students for the formative assessments and culminating task. As you discuss the lesson sequence, refer to your completed Templates 2, 3, and 4 to ensure that the lessons prepare students for the formative assessment tasks and build toward the culminating task. (The completed samples in Part 2 of this book show how this is achieved.) If you work in a grade team, you may find yourselves engaged in a lively debate about the pros and cons of including certain lessons and excluding others! This is professional learning at its best. I recently facilitated a writing team session in which, shortly after we began, the following dialogue occurred:

Richard: I hear what you're saying, Damian, but when I sit down to plan my lessons, I always ask myself, "What would be some fun activities for the kids to do?"

Damian: What do the rest of you think about that approach?

Leslie: I used to do that too. But it seems to me that the reason backward design is better is that it encourages teachers to ask questions like, "Why am I teaching this lesson? Does it connect to what my students must know and be able to do?" If a lesson doesn't clearly connect to important learning, then I may have to leave it out. Let's face it—our curriculum is too full anyway, so we can't spend time teaching stuff that isn't really important.

In Chapter 14, you will read how two grade teams worked through the planning process. The Grade 6 team uses Template 2; the Grade 7 team uses Templates 2, 3, and 4. Both teams face the same challenge—time! In some districts, principals fund writing teams to meet during the school year. However, many teams find their planning time limited to the last weeks of the summer vacation. Whichever is the case, quality program planning cannot be rushed. The mathematics-science unit described in Chapter 14 required four half days. However, most teachers find that once they master the process of program planning, it takes them less time.

If finding planning time is a major hurdle for you and your grade team, you can still follow the backward design process to develop a plan for a single lesson.

Lesson Planning with the End in Mind

As with a unit of study, a lesson is most effective when it has a specific purpose. The Ten-Step Lesson Plan (see Figure 13–6 on page 213) is an organizer that can help you ask and answer DuFour's three critical questions about learning. (See page 202.)

Setting a Learning Goal

Clarifying a lesson's learning goal is the critical first step in lesson planning. By asking what you want your students to know and be able to do by the end of this lesson, you are taking the first step to ensuring that class time will be well spent.

It is important to remember that a learning goal is not simply a statement of what students will be doing; put another way, what you want students to learn is not the same as how they will achieve that learning. Yet, in the rush to prepare lessons, it can often be tempting to think this way. Most teachers list in their daybooks what they plan to have students

The first step in lesson planning is to identify the lesson's learning goal.

work on during each lesson. But it is also important to ask the key question: Why are students completing this activity? This is why it is so important to first identify the learning goal.

Consider the following statements and decide which is the learning goal and which is the activity:

1. Students read *A Day in the Life of a Pioneer Child* and compare it to their own lives.
2. Students compare the life of a pioneer child with their own life and conclude which one is the harder life.

The first statement simply reminds the teacher of what to teach. It could be assessed by asking whether the students read the book and whether they compared it to their own lives. A simple "yes" in response to both questions provides no evidence that students have learned anything worthwhile!

The second statement is the learning goal. It identifies what students will have accomplished by the end of the lesson. To assess whether students have achieved the goal, the teacher must assess what conclusions the students arrived at in terms of whose life is harder: theirs or the pioneer child's.

Using Your Imagination

To plan effective lessons, try to imagine how your students will respond during the lesson, and make your instructional decisions accordingly. For example

- I need to *imagine* which students are going to have difficulty reading *A Day in the Life of a Pioneer Child*. Which students should complete the activity with a reading buddy or in a small group? What other teacher support can I provide so all students will understand the reading?
- I need to *imagine* which students are going to have difficulty reflecting on and drawing examples from their own lives to serve as a comparison to the life of a pioneer child. How can I facilitate self-reflection for these students?
- I need to *imagine* what conclusions students are going to make once they've compared *A Day in the Life of a Pioneer Child* to a day in their own lives. Will they conclude that their own lives are easier? What if the majority conclude their lives are more difficult? How do I manage this outcome?

By imagining how a lesson may actually unfold, you can make decisions about what to do when students have difficulties and prepare how to adapt your instruction as you teach.

The Ten-Step Lesson Plan

Typically, a Ten-Step Lesson Plan can be taught within an hour; however, it should be noted that more than one 40–60 minute time slot may be required to complete all ten steps. As well, depending on the nature and scope of the learning goal, some lessons may not involve all ten steps.

Figure 13-6: The Ten-Step Lesson Plan

1. Identify the learning goal.

2. Activate prior knowledge or experience (hook, engage personal experience).

3. Assess prior knowledge (diagnostic).

4. Present new learning.

5. Check for understanding.

6. Practise new learning and scaffold new learning.

7. Assess practice work (peer and self-assessment for learning).

8. Review and consolidate learning (tie back to learning goal).

9. Apply new learning to a new context.

10. Assess learning.

Video Clip 1:

Gr. 7/8 Mathematics– Using Assessment for Different Purposes
14:11 minutes

The following example shows how Kelly used the Ten-Step Lesson Plan to teach a Grade 7 mathematics lesson about stem-and-leaf plots.

1. Identify the learning goal.

Before the lesson begins, Kelly writes the learning goal on the board: *By the end of this lesson, you will be able to analyze a set of data using a stem-and-leaf plot.* She begins by drawing the students' attention to the board as she reads the goal aloud.

2. Activate prior knowledge or experience.

To "hook" students by personally engaging them in the activity, Kelly asks her students to think about a situation where they wanted to know specific information about a set of numbers. (For example, how much TV do I watch compared to others in the class?) Explain to students that they will organize data using a stem-and-leaf plot to help them see this type of information.

3. Assess prior knowledge.

Since this lesson builds on the previously taught concepts of mean, median, mode, and range, Kelly needs to check whether her students know these terms. She does this by asking them to write each term and a short explanation or example in their notebooks. As her students work, Kelly moves around the class to check that everyone is completing this task. After two minutes, she has them compare their explanations with a partner's and asks each pair of students to come to an agreement on the meaning for each term.

At this point, the noise level in the classroom begins to rise significantly, but Kelly simply moves around the room, checking that the discussion is on task. Kelly knows from experience that by keeping the allotted time quite short, students stay on track because there is a healthy element of competition to complete the task in the specified time.

Next, Kelly asks for four volunteers to come to the board to write either an explanation of one of the terms or to provide an example. She tells the rest of the class to quietly examine the work of their peers to see if they agree.

Once her volunteers are finished, Kelly thanks them, then turns to the class and says: "Let's begin with *mean*. Thumbs up if you agree with Alicia's explanation; thumbs down if you disagree; and thumbs horizontal if you're not sure. Now show Alicia your thumbs."

Most students display "thumbs up" but several students display "thumbs down." Kelly invites these students to ask Alicia for clarification of the term. Once Alicia has provided further explanation, Kelly asks these students if they are now clear about the definition of *mean*.

Kelly repeats the process for the remaining terms. Note how Kelly has accomplished three purposes with this simple strategy:

- She assesses the prior knowledge of all students (diagnostic assessment).
- She empowers students to take ownership for their own learning.
- She models and teaches self-assessment and peer assessment skills.

4. Present new learning.

Kelly is now ready to teach her students how to use a stem-and-leaf plot to analyze a set of data. She asks her students to tell her how many songs they have downloaded to their MP3 players. She records the following data on the board:

146	129	155	162	138	170	158	154
133	156	163	174	160	135	147	152
166	168	152	146	155	146		

Stem	Leaf
12	9
13	3 5 8
14	6 6 6 7
15	2 2 4 5 5 6 8
16	0 2 3 6 8
17	0 4

Kelly then begins to rearrange the data on the board as a stem-and-leaf plot. She completes the first row herself but then students quickly catch on and provide her with the data for rows 2 through 6.

5. Check for understanding.

Kelly now asks her students a series of questions to connect the data presented in the stem-and-leaf plot with previously taught concepts:

- Based on the data, how many downloads did the class make last month?
- What was the range of the number of downloads?
- What was the mode of the number of downloads made?
- What was the median of the number of downloads made?

6. Practise new learning and scaffold new learning.

This next step is a critical juncture in the lesson. Diagnostic assessments and achievement results to date have consistently identified three levels of mathematical ability in Kelly's classroom. Although Kelly uses a variety of heterogeneous groupings according to the subject she is teaching, she has found it most effective to group her students more homogeneously for math lessons.

She assigns ten minutes of practice work to all groups. Groups A and B will likely have sufficient understanding of stem-and-leaf plots to work ahead quickly with little or no teacher intervention. Kelly assigns them five practice questions to work on. They may work individually or with a partner.

Groups C and D will likely have a tentative understanding and should be able to work on some practice questions, but will probably need some support from Kelly. She assigns them two practice questions and tells them to use the "3-Before-Me" rule before raising their hand for her help. "3-Before-Me," which means students must try three sources of support before asking the teacher for help, is an excellent strategy to encourage resourcefulness. It reduces the likelihood of students simply not reading a question carefully, or asking for help before attempting to solve the problem themselves.

Kelly expects to work with Group E immediately. She will likely have to scaffold the new learning before these three students grasp how to analyze data using a stem-and-leaf plot. Once she's assigned work to Groups A through D, she sits down with Group E.

It is vital to the overall success of learning for all students that this practice portion of the lesson is brief. It is simply an opportunity for students to work with their peers to see if they have understood what has just been taught.

Far too often at this point in the lesson, teachers assign too much work that will require the rest of the class time to finish. Work that is not completed automatically becomes homework.

What is the wrong with this approach? At this point in the lesson, learning for many students is, at best, tentative and fragile. They are not ready to attempt ten or more questions on the new learning, and they certainly are not ready to work on these questions at home. A better alternative to this approach will be explained in Step 8.

7. Assess practice work.

As expected, the students in Kelly's Groups A and B have no trouble completing the five practice questions. They are ready to self-check their answers to determine whether they have understood the new learning.

To facilitate this process and to significantly reduce her own marking load, Kelly leaves the Teacher's Resource Guide open at the appropriate answer guide. Students check their own answers against the Guide and then return to their group to discuss any questions they may have done incorrectly. Since this is practice work, often completed collaboratively, Kelly does not record marks; consequently there is no reason for students to be tempted to cheat on these questions. The practice work serves the sole purpose of letting students know how well they have understood the lesson.

For assessment to support and enhance learning, it must be viewed and designed as an integral part of instruction, not as an addendum or an interruption.

VAN DE WALLE, 2001

8. Review and consolidate learning.

Kelly's intent when providing her students with ten minutes to complete the practice work is that they all finish at approximately the same time, albeit possibly with different levels of understanding. She now takes a couple of minutes to review the learning goal with students and ask them questions to assess their level of understanding.

Groups A and B typically have a solid understanding and are ready to move ahead. Depending on her assessment, she may assign them some additional practice questions for homework, although they have to complete these with no support from their peers. Alternatively, she may deem these students ready to tackle more complex problems. (See Step 9.)

The other groups will likely require further practice and possibly more scaffolding during tomorrow's lesson before their understanding is solidified.

9. Apply new learning to a new context.

By the end of the lesson, Kelly may have evidence that some of her students have achieved the learning goal of being "able to create a stem-and-leaf plot for a set of data." But before she can truly say that her students understand how to use stem-and-leafs plots to analyze data, she needs to see them apply their learning in an unfamiliar context. Not all of her students will be able to do this, so Kelly presents this challenge only to those students who inform her they are ready to try it. For most students, evidence of their ability to apply their learning in an unfamiliar context may not occur until some time later in the term.

Authentic assessment is true assessment of performance because we thereby learn whether students can intelligently use what they have learned in situations that increasingly approximate adult situations, and whether they can innovate in new situations.

WIGGINS, 1998

10. Assess learning.

Because her students are at different stages in their understanding of stem-and-leaf plots, Kelly does not assess understanding of the learning goal at the end of this lesson. Later in the term, however, she may present students with an open-ended mathematics investigation in which she asks them to choose the data management strategies and tools they think are most appropriate to solving a problem. If the students choose to use a stem-and-leaf plot and do so correctly, then Kelly has evidence of understanding.

Eventually, though, Kelly will have to assess students' understanding of this data management tool for grading and reporting purposes. She may use an end-of-unit test, a project, a culminating task, or a combination of these strategies to gather evidence of her students' learning.

Reflecting on the lesson afterwards, Kelly suspects that Steps 7 and 8 of the Ten-Step Lesson Plan—steps she has only recently added to her repertoire—contributed in critical ways to the improvement in mathematics achievement of her students. By assigning less practice work, having students self-assess and peer assess the practice work, and ensuring that she reviews and consolidates new learning before the end of the lesson, Kelly finds that her students have a much deeper understanding of mathematical concepts and procedures and are therefore more confident as they approach a summative assessment.

Summary

- Backward design planning is the preferred approach to unit planning since it clarifies for teachers and students the destination for learning.
- Backward design planning helps teachers manage the often overwhelming number of curriculum outcomes mandated by provincial and local documents.
- Planning templates such as the following provide guidance and support for writing teams:
  - Template 1: Long-Range Assessment Plan
  - Template 2: Unit Curriculum and Assessment Plan
  - Template 3: Culminating Assessment Task Plan
  - Template 4: Instruction Plan/Lesson Sequence
- Lesson planning should begin with the identification of a clear and concise learning goal.
- The Ten-Step Lesson Plan is a purposeful way to teach a lesson. It highlights the need to identify a clear learning goal from which decisions about instruction and assessment flow.
- It is important to use your imagination when planning lessons in order to predict how different students will respond to instruction. Typically, it highlights the need to differentiate certain parts of the lesson to increase the likelihood that all students will learn.

Applying My Learning

UNIT PLANNING

Convene your grade team for an initial unit planning session. To prepare for the first session, you may wish to view Videoclip 4 as well as review this chapter and look ahead to Chapter 14. Examine also sample units in Section 2 of Part 2, the Tools section of this book.

During the first session, use the following questions to guide your discussion:

1. Do we understand the concept of backward design planning?
2. Will Templates 1 through 4 be useful to us in our planning?
3. Do we need to modify any of the templates to better suit our needs?
4. What are we going to plan? A single unit? A long-range plan?
5. What resources do we each need to gather before our first writing session?

LESSON PLANNING

Alternatively, team up with a colleague and plan a lesson using the Ten-Step Lesson Plan. Challenge each other to imagine what each step will actually look like in your classroom, and revisit your plan to maximize the likelihood of success.

If feasible, ask your principal about the possibility of observing each other's lesson. After the lesson, arrange a debriefing session in which you analyze what worked and what might be improved.

Chapter 14

THE PLANNING TEAM

 BIG IDEA 2 Assessment must be planned and purposeful.

Planning is a collaborative process. Nevertheless, little collaboration seems to happen in program planning. Across the country, teachers often work in isolation from each other.

Although long-range planning is part of every teacher's job, it is inefficient to have teachers duplicating the work of unit writing. Instead, schools and school districts should consider

- seeking out those teachers who are enthusiastic and highly skilled in this work
- providing them with incentives to develop exemplary units to serve as models for their colleagues
- ensuring that their work is made available as a database to all teachers in a school or school district.

In this chapter, you will read about two teams who planned collaboratively.

IDENTIFYING BIG IDEAS AND ESSENTIAL SKILLS FOR LEARNING

Video Clip 4:

Grade 6: Backward Planning a Language Unit
16:15 minutes

The first team was comprised of three Grade 6 teachers: Riaz and Alex, experienced teachers, and Janice, a second-year teacher. Together they developed a unit plan for their language arts classes. Let's listen in.

Alex: Have we got all the resources we need to get started? I've got the planning templates.

Janice: I've brought the curriculum guidelines and my language arts materials.

Riaz: I have some resources from units I worked on last year.

Figure 14-1: Template 2: Unit Curriculum and Assessment Plan

Template 2: Unit Curriculum and Assessment Plan			
Unit/Strand:		**Focus for Learning:**	
Big Ideas and Essential Skills:		**Title/Description of Culminating Task:**	
Enabling and/or Other Assessment Tasks			
Learning Habits:	**Title:** Diagnostic/Formative Write/Do/Say		**Curriculum Outcomes/Content Standards:**
Learning Habits:	**Title:** Diagnostic/Formative Write/Do/Say		**Curriculum Outcomes/Content Standards:**
Learning Habits:	**Title:** Diagnostic/Formative Write/Do/Say		**Curriculum Outcomes/Content Standards:**

Copyright © 2007 by Nelson, a division of Thomson Canada Ltd.

2.3 Template 2: Unit Curriculum

TOOL 2.3

Template 2: Unit Curriculum and Assessment Plan, p. 301

Alex: So as you can see, there are two main sections on Template 2, the Unit Curriculum and Assessment Plan. In the first section, we identify the unit and the big ideas and then the essential skills the students focus on, as well as a description of the Culminating Task for the unit. Then, in the second section, we identify the Learning Habits and Curriculum Outcomes/Content Standards that coincide with each task.

The richness of a learning task should be measured in terms of what it invokes, evokes, and provokes... The richer a task, the greater the opportunity for the student to learn and demonstrate learning.

FLEWELLING WITH HIGGINSON, 2000

▲ **The Grade 6 language arts team develops a unit plan.**

Riaz: Does our curriculum guideline identify the big ideas and essential skills?

Janice: Not exactly. But if we begin with the reading strand and examine the outcomes, we can probably pull out the big ideas.

Riaz: How about this one? "Students understand that texts often have meaning beyond the words on the page." In other words, they have to read for meaning—not just decode the words.

Janice: I agree that's important. But what I want to know first is how are the big ideas different from the essential skills?

Alex: I'm not entirely sure, but I think students need to understand the big ideas, and they need to use the essential skills.

Janice: Maybe the big idea is, "Students understand that texts often have meaning beyond the words on the page" and the essential skill would be, "Students use a variety of strategies to read for deep meaning."

Alex: That sounds good to me. Riaz, do you agree?

Riaz: Sure.

After examining their curriculum documents and brainstorming for twenty minutes, the team categorized their list of big ideas and essential skills for reading. Here is their list:

Big Ideas are like suitcases that help students organize and make sense of the myriad of outcomes they are expected to master.

Figure 14-2: Big Ideas and Essential Skills	
Big Ideas	**Essential Skills**
The meaning of texts often goes beyond the words on the page.	Students use a variety of strategies to read for deep meaning.
There are as many interpretations of a text as there are readers. There is no one "right" interpretation.	Readers use their prior knowledge and experience to better understand what they read.
There are a few big stories in literature. They deal with themes such as good versus evil romance versus tragedy, and so on.	Readers know and use specific strategies to help them read.

Many school districts have developed their own sets of big ideas, or enduring understandings (Wiggins & McTighe, 1998). It is ideal to begin planning with these documents.

Using the list in Figure 14-2, the team spent a few minutes completing the unit/strand and the big ideas and essential skills boxes on Template 2.

Identifying Assessment Tasks

Next, the team considered the kinds of assessment tasks that would provide evidence that the students understood the big ideas and could demonstrate the essential skills:

Alex: Let's think about the critical evidence that would show students have learned what was most important.

Riaz: Hold on a minute. What about the more specific outcomes from the curriculum guidelines? Don't we have to deal with those now?

Alex: We'll get to those when we do Template 3. Let's identify the major assessment tasks first. Once we have those, we can match the outcomes to them.

Riaz: I like that idea. I was recently at a workshop where we were told to cluster the outcomes, but I thought, "How do we know what clusters to use?" You're suggesting that we cluster the outcomes according to the assessment tasks, right?

Alex: Right. Let's start by thinking about culminating tasks for the unit. I've brought along a chart called Assessment Targets, Strategies, and Tools. It may be helpful as we do this. (See Figure 14.3.)

Janice: Look at all the different ways besides written work we can use to assess learning!

Riaz: Yes, and that's very important, especially for second-language learners and students with special needs. Last year, I had a young girl from Thailand in my class who was very capable but, because she was still struggling to learn English, her written work was brief and hard to follow. I couldn't draw accurate conclusions about what she could do from any of the written assessments.

Janice: Okay, let's get going. I think a portfolio must be a culminating task, right?

Alex: Yes, but maybe a portfolio is an overall organizer for all of the written tasks throughout the year.

Riaz: Maybe. But a portfolio isn't just a container. I was talking to another teacher at a conference about this question: Is a portfolio a place to keep student work or is it an instructional strategy for helping

A portfolio is a collection of artifacts put together to get at the full story to help students, teachers, and others to understand in-depth one or more aspects of student learning.
STIGGINS IT AL, 2006

students improve their work? We decided that it's both. And we have to remember that we need to include "do" and "say" tasks as well as written ones. If you use portfolios properly in your classroom, then they can be opportunities for write, do, and say.

Janice: What do you mean?

Figure 14-3: Assessment Targets, Strategies, and Tools		
Students need opportunities to demonstrate learning by doing and speaking, as well as writing.		
Achievement Target	**Assessment Method and Strategy**	**Assessment Tool**
	Quiz/Test	
Understanding of Concepts Application of Procedures	- Selected response (matching, multiple choice, true-false) - Short answer	Marking scheme
	Graphic Organizer	
Understanding of Concepts Reasoning Communication	- Mind map - Word web	Rubric
	Extended Writing	
Understanding of Concepts Application of Procedures Reasoning Problem solving Communication	- Article - Report - Brochure - Review - Journal - Portfolio	Checklist Rubric Exemplars Rating scale
	Performance Task	
Understanding of Concepts Inquiry/Design Reasoning Problem solving Application of Procedures Communication	- Design project - Inquiry - Role-play - Investigation - Simulation - Media production - Skills demonstration - Presentation	Checklist Rubric Exemplars Rating scale
	Oral Communication	
Understanding of Concepts Reasoning Communication	- Conference - Informal chat - Informal discussion - Oral questioning	Anecdotal record Checklist

Video Clip 7:

Gr. 2 Language Arts— Using Portfolios to Improve Self- and Peer Assessment
07:55 minutes

Riaz: Think about it. Obviously a portfolio is going to contain samples of a student's written work. But if you conduct regular, in-class portfolio conferences with students, then those conferences would be "say" opportunities because the students would be talking to you about their work.

Janice: I can see that. But what about the "do" piece?

Riaz: Let's say a student chose to do a mime routine as part of the visual communication component of the curriculum. The student could have another student or a parent videotape the performance and include the videotape in the portfolio. That would be a "do" task.

Alex: Great idea, Riaz!

By the time they adjourned their first planning session, Janice, Riaz, and Alex had completed a good portion of their Unit Curriculum and Assessment Plan. (See Figure 14-4.) They still had more work to do, but they were satisfied with their excellent start. Note that they used the Big Ideas to help suggest the culminating task for the unit.

Figure 14-4: Template 2: Unit Curriculum and Assessment Plan—Completed

304 *Tool 2.6*

2.6, Template 2: Sample Unit: Grade 2 Science

Sample Unit: Grade 2 Science—Unit Curriculum and Assessment Plan		
Unit/Strand: Butterflies, Reptiles, and Animals		**Focus for Learning:** Life Systems (Science)/Grade 2
Big Ideas: • All insects, reptiles, and animals go through distinct life cycles. • There are similarities and differences among insects, reptiles, and animals. • Insects, reptiles, and animals react differently to the seasons. **Essential Skills:** • data collection • observation skills • recording information: written, pictorial, charts, and graphs • following directions • using information technology • written, oral, and presentation skills		**Title/Description of Culminating Task:** Your class has been asked to create an exhibit in the Library that will display information about Life Systems, particularly insects, reptiles, and animals. This exhibit will be visited by other students and parents. Your class will be responsible for creating and setting up the displays as well as giving tours of the exhibit. You and your classmates will: • research insects, reptiles, and animals, • create art exhibits, booklets, and posters to present your findings, • create and provide information that will guide visitors through the exhibits.
Enabling and/or Other Assessment Tasks		
Learning Habits: Independence	**Title:** Create a model of a specific type of butterfly with body parts labelled. **Diagnostic/Formative:** F **Write/Do/Say:** W & D	**Curriculum Outcomes/Standards:** • Describe the major physical characteristics of different types of animals (insects, reptiles, mammals). • Produce two- and three-dimensional works of art that communicate ideas. • Identify the characteristics of symmetrical shapes and forms.
Learning Habits: Initiative	**Title:** Create an accordion booklet to illustrate and record the life cycle of a butterfly. **Diagnostic/Formative:** F **Write/Do/Say:** W & D	**Curriculum Outcomes/Standards:** • Describe changes in the appearance and activity of an animal as it goes through its life cycle. • Describe ways that animals respond and adapt to their environment. • Communicate messages, and follow instructions and directions.
Learning Habits: Use of information	**Title:** Construct an observation chamber for watching a chrysalis hatch and keep a journal of events. **Diagnostic/Formative:** F **Write/Do/Say:** W & D	**Curriculum Outcomes/Standards:** • Describe changes in the appearance and activity of an animal as it goes through its life cycle. • Record relevant observations, findings, and measurements, using written language, drawings, and concrete materials.
Learning Habits: Homework completion	**Title:** Create a dialogue that can be used as a guided tour of the exhibit (written and oral).	**Curriculum Outcomes/Standards:** • Describe the major physical characteristics of different types of animals

TOOL 2.6

Template 2: Sample Unit Curriculum and Assessment Plan, p. 304

PLANNING AN INTEGRATED UNIT

Janice, Riaz, and Alex were developing a unit in language arts. But collaborative team work is especially important when planning an integrated unit. Three intermediate math and science teachers, each with three to five years of teaching experience at the Grade 7 and 8 levels, got together to develop an integrated math/science/technology unit.

The three teachers, Rich, Darina, and Jorge, had some prior knowledge of backward design. (See pages 202–205.) Their intent was to design a Grade 7 unit that integrated math and science and addressed the following strands: structural strength and stability, geometry, measurement, and data management. However, as you'll see, their plan evolved as they worked. (Note: The complete unit developed by this team may be found in Part 2, on pages 314-322.)

The powerful collaboration that characterizes professional learning communities is a systematic process in which teachers work together to analyze and improve their classroom practice.

DU FOUR, 2004

Identifying the Unit Focus and Big Ideas

After gathering the relevant provincial and local curriculum guidelines and their own resources, the team pulled out Template 2: Unit Curriculum and Assessment Plan, and started their planning session by agreeing on the unit and focus for learning:

Rich: All we've agreed to at this point is to design a Grade 7 unit that integrates math and science.

Darina: Yes, but what about the artificial limb project we did last year in science? I'm wondering if we can integrate it with math.

Jorge: The testing part of the design process requires data collection and analysis. Measurement skills are also important. And we could introduce some geometry expectations into the unit.

Darina: So, we want students to know that there are many factors and stages involved when designing a product.

Jorge: And that the entire design process requires a lot of math—measurement skills and knowledge of measurement units and metric conversions, not to mention skills in using the appropriate measurement tools.

Darina: There we are: big ideas in science, essential skills in measurement. Let's look at our board's "Enduring Understandings for Math and Science" document so we can write them down.

Rich: Okay, but slow down. I've been thinking about a unit involving a picnic table where students design and construct a model of the table. We could take them to a nearby hardware store to show them what construction materials are available in the market.

Darina: Wow! We could also take them to a local furniture shop to show them current furniture designs.

Jorge: Excellent idea. I'm a fan of experiential learning. But most tables are either round or rectangular, and the geometry curriculum emphasizes triangles, parallelograms, and trapezoids.

Rich: Not a problem. We just tell the students to design a picnic table with no right angle measurements. It will encourage them to create designs using triangles and other shapes besides rectangles and squares.

Darina: A round table wouldn't have a right angle measurement either.

Jorge: Good point. If some students decide to design a round table, then they must do the extra work on their own. It would be an enhancement opportunity for students who are ready to go that far.

Rich: Okay! Picnic table it is. How does this sound? "Your task is to design and construct a scale model of a picnic table with no right angles. You will use your knowledge of data management to test the structural strength and stability of your model."

Although the team had started out discussing the big ideas for learning, they quickly turned to the culminating task for the unit. In switching from their original artificial limb project to the picnic table project, the team was able to expand the scope of the unit to include specific outcomes in 2-D, 3-D, and transformational geometry. However, the scope now appeared to be too wide and the unit too large.

Darina: This is going to be one long unit! Can we cover it all in one term?

Jorge: Sure, we can. Remember, it's an integrated unit. Some lessons will focus on math outcomes, while others will be mostly science. But I see your concern. It may be too close to the end of the term, with report cards and all, by the time we finish the unit.

Rich: Why don't we skip the testing of the product in this unit? That part of the design process can be dealt with in a separate unit immediately following this one.

Darina: Great idea. So now we'll tell students, "Your task is to design and construct a scale model of a picnic table with no right angles."

After reaching agreement on the culminating task, the team again used their board's *Enduring Understandings for Math and Science* document to complete the list of big ideas. They then transcribed the corresponding outcomes for math and science from their provincial curriculum guidelines onto Template 2.

Identifying Enabling and/or Other Assessment Tasks

Jorge: I like the fact that the template reminds us of all the little details in assessment planning. Let me see … we need to use a variety of assessment instruments so students are required to write, do, or say something.

> *… teacher conversations must quickly move beyond "what are we expected to teach?" to "How will we know when each student has learned?"*
>
> Du Four, 2004

Darina: And the learning habits. That's what I like the most. I think they're really important if students are going to become responsible, independent learners.

Rich: Okay. After taking some of the ideas from the old artificial limb project, we have the design-and-construct-a-model component of the culminating task. That would be a "do." We can also ask them to present their model to the class. That would be a "say."

Darina: I always like to ask students to write a reflection on their learning at the end of an activity. We can ask the students to keep a journal or a log. This would be the "write" component of the task.

Jorge: Yes, we can call it the design log. We'll ask them not only to reflect on their learning, but also to include other types of writing, such as their calculations, brainstorming ideas, or information gathered through research.

Jorge: We already have a rubric for each of these components, but we may have to modify them to reflect the added math outcomes.

Rich: And the learning habits? We can get students to self-assess using checklists.

Darina: Right. The design, construction, and presentation components are group work, so cooperation and conflict resolution can be assessed there. The design log is an individual assessment piece, so we can assess the other learning habits from that.

Rich: What about goal setting?

Jorge: We can always add some questions in the design log, maybe an accomplishment chart of some sort, for us to be able to assess that.

Rich: Sure, why not?

At the end of the first planning session, the team had recorded on Template 2

- the unit focus
- learning outcomes
- culminating task for the unit

The team decided to complete Template 3 next, thinking that they would need a thorough understanding of the culminating task before they could tackle the more detailed part of Template 2—identifying the enabling tasks. The tasks of deciding what educational resources to use and how to make the unit more responsive to students with special needs were deferred until the enabling tasks had been identified. Their completed Template 3 is shown in Figure 14-5.

Figure 14-5: Completed Template 3: Unit Culminating Assessment Task Plan

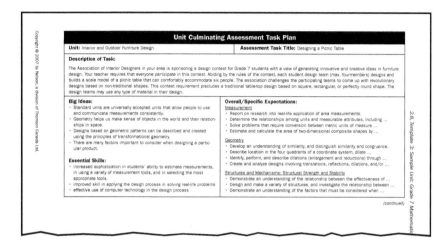

TOOL 2.8

Template 3: Unit Culminating Assessment Task Plan, pp. 317–318

The group's second planning session started with a brainstorming activity, with Darina recording their ideas. As they worked on Template 2, the team took the list of big ideas and discussed different ways of assessing the students' performance for each one. (See Figure 14-6 for Darina's complete record.)

Darina: So, we have the design log. We want them to start writing from the very beginning of the unit. We will ask students to write a brief summary of what they learned from each activity or lesson and how they can use the knowledge or skill to complete the culminating tasks.

Jorge: Remember what we said about goal setting. I guess we can always add specific questions from time to time to address that issue.

Darina: Good, let me write that down.

Rich: I also like giving them daily quizzes to assess their knowledge and understanding. I always find them helpful in assessing students' understanding. It helps me know when I can speed up the pace of lessons, or when to slow down.

Darina: I don't agree with using written quizzes to check for daily understanding.

Rich: What do you use instead?

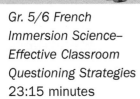

Video Clip 5:

Gr. 5/6 French Immersion Science– Effective Classroom Questioning Strategies 23:15 minutes

Darina: I use a combination of Think/Pair/Share and class discussion to check that everyone understands. (See Chapters 2 and 8 for suggestions about questionning techniques and class discussion to check for understanding.)

Rich: Hmm. I might try that.

Darina: Getting back to my list, we need to know if they can do proper measurements, do metric conversions, and use measurement tools properly.

Rich: There's also proportional reasoning and scaling.

The team continued filling in Template 2, choosing appropriate assessment tasks to prepare students for the culminating task.

From Darina's list, they knew that the big ideas and essential skills they still needed to address included steps in the design process, structures and stability, and expectations in 2-D, 3-D, and transformational geometry.

Darina: Last year, we asked students to construct a bridge using popsicle sticks. Can we use the same task in this unit to address structure and stability?

Jorge: I like the idea, but it doesn't go along with the theme of this unit, which seems to be about outdoor furniture design.

Rich: Good point. How about designing and constructing a doghouse? This can be considered a piece of outdoor furniture, right?

Darina: Maybe, and we can ask the students to present their design first, before the actual construction. The drawings would involve 3-D geometry as they would present the doghouse design in three perspectives: top, side, and front views.

Rich: And transformational geometry?

Jorge: Well, we could expose students to different design ideas for the picnic table. I've seen outdoor tables with mosaic tiles laid out on the surface, and others have stained glass designs. I propose that students design a mural containing elements of transformational geometry—that can be another requirement on the culminating task. This could become part of a summative task—a portfolio of some sort.

Darina: Tell me more about this portfolio.

Jorge: I always ask my Grade 7 students to analyze illustrations by the artist, M.C. Escher. He used elements of transformational geometry in much of his work. For the portfolio, I'm thinking of an assignment where students are asked to present at least five works of art with analysis and some background information about the artist and the artwork.

Rich: Great! A cross-curricular connection to visual arts... Here, I've got the curriculum guidelines. Let's check which outcomes will fit.

Jorge: But I suggest we also require students to present at least five of their own designs using Geometer's Sketchpad, and to analyze their own designs.

Darina: We can include those in the portfolio. I'm impressed. Let's call it a design portfolio.

Building on the portfolio idea, the planning team also decided to include a word-problem portfolio—a summative task that would assess students' achievement in measurement. The word-problem portfolio would be a collection of word problems the students had created and solved, together with explanations of their solution and justification for their strategy choices. This collection would require each student to demonstrate his or her knowledge of conversion algorithms for both linear and square units of measure, their knowledge of ratio and proportion in relation to scaling, and their ability to use area formulas in solving real-life problems. This work would also demonstrate real-life applications of these mathematical concepts and procedures.

To assess students' understanding and application of the key concepts in the structure and stability science strand, the team concluded that a paper-and-pencil assessment such as a written test would be most appro-

Figure 14-6: Darina's Complete Record

Big Ideas/Essential Skills	Suggested Assessment
Standard units are universally accepted units that allow us to use and communicate measurements consistently.	Design Log (ongoing; also used to assess the other Big Ideas on this list) In-class formative assessments (ongoing; may include quizzes and/or other class activities, e.g., Think/Pair/Share, class discussions) Word-problem portfolio
Geometry helps us make sense of the objects in the world and their relationships in space	Design and construction of a product—doghouse, picnic table (3-D-sketches)
Designs based on geometric patterns can be described and created using the principles of transformational geometry.	Design Portfolio (analysis of M.C. Escher's work; creation of designs using GSP software)
There are many factors important to consider when designing a particular product.	Design and construction of a product: construction techniques
We need to consider students' ability to estimate measurements, use a variety of measurement tools, and select the most appropriate tools, and how these abilities increase in sophistication.	Design and construction of a product: actual measurements; metric conversions; proportional reasoning and scaling
Students demonstrate improved skill in applying the design process to solving real-life problems.	Design and construction of a product: (problem solving and application of concepts)
Students demonstrate effective use of computer technology in the design process.	Design Portfolio (Use of Geometer's Sketchpad software to produce designs involving transformational geometry)

Figure 14-7: Completed Template 2: Unit Curriculum and Assessment Plan

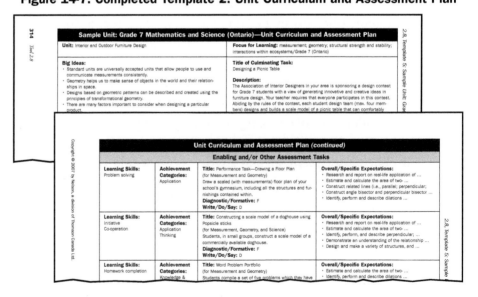

priate. They then used Darina's record (see Figure 14-6) to complete Template 2, which is shown in Figure 14-7.

Identifying the Unit Title

With Templates 2 and 3 almost completed, the team began to look at the finer details of the unit.

Darina: Like Jorge said earlier, we have a recurring theme in the unit— outdoor furniture design. We can make that our unit title or theme.

Rich: I just remembered something, and you probably know this too: our provincial curriculum guidelines require us to integrate career education with some of our units. We can emphasize a career in either architecture or design, or even visual arts.

Darina: Personally, I would emphasize interior design. It's not as academic as architecture, making it more accessible to more students.

Jorge: I agree.

Following further discussion and a few more refinements, Rich, Darina, and Jorge revised their culminating task:

> *The Association of Interior Designers is sponsoring a design contest for Grade 7 students. The goal is to generate innovative and creative ideas in furniture design. Your teacher requires that everyone participate in this contest. Abiding by the rules of the contest, each design team (maximum four members) will design and build a scale model of a picnic table that can comfortably seat six people. The association challenges the participating teams to come up with revolutionary designs based on non-traditional shapes; therefore, the contest requirement is a table-top design based on a shape that is neither square nor rectangular. The design teams may use any type of material in their design.*

Identifying the Lesson Sequence

The team was now ready to work on the last stage: describing the lesson sequence for the unit. They used Template 4: Unit Instruction Plan/Lesson Sequence.

Darina: I think we should start with unit conversions. Students need this skill when they do measurements.

Rich: Okay, we could start with linear measurements, then do area measurements. Do we need to develop the formulas for the area of a triangle, parallelogram, and trapezoid in this unit?

Jorge: I would much rather deal with those outcomes before they begin the unit. They don't go along very well with the theme of the unit. But we can make a notation that if these outcomes have not been addressed prior to the start of the unit: then the most logical time to address them would be at the beginning of the unit: after linear measurements. Oh, by the way, the first thing we need to do is introduce students to the culminating task for the unit. That way, everyone knows where they're headed and how all the work they're going to do connects to the culminating task.

Darina: I agree. But before we move on, why don't we just sequence the enabling tasks on my list, and then make another column for lesson sequence?

Rich: Yes, it would be easier that way.

Darina's suggestion proved prophetic and the team breezed through Template 4.

Figure 14-8: Completed Template 4: Unit Instruction Plan/Lesson Sequence

TOOL 2.8

Template 4: Sample Unit Instruction Plan/Lesson Sequence, pp. 319–322

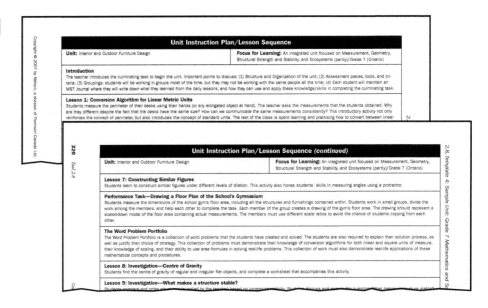

Concluding Remarks

As Rich, Darina, and Jorge were planning their integrated math/science/technology unit, they discussed many excellent ideas, but could not include all of them in the unit. One of these ideas—the testing component of the design process—along with its focus on data management—was moved to the next unit.

Though not included in the preceding text, the team did discuss the choice of materials for the picnic table design. This topic would allow for the integration of sustainable ecosystems, the focus of the life systems strand in Grade 7 science. Students would be made aware of the need for manufacturers to consider how paints, varnishes, thinners, and other chemicals find their way into the water system.

The topic would also connect to pure substances and mixtures, the focus of another Grade 7 science strand: matter and materials.

When they were finished, the team realized that the unit they had planned could be a good introduction to the Grade 7 science program: it could provide a recurring and unifying theme for the entire year in science.

The unit's integrated structure and rich cross-curricular content readily provided students with a variety of applications of the many key science concepts that would be presented throughout the year. The team ended their planning sessions by reviewing Templates 2, 3, and 4 to ensure they had completed all of the sections.

Summary

- The planning process is neither linear nor chronological. It is necessary to move back and forth among the templates as necessary.

- Big Ideas and Essential Skills are the starting point. They help identify what is essential for students to know and be able to do at the end of a unit, term, or year. Some provinces and school boards have identified these in curriculum guidelines.

- Assessment tasks should be identified by answering the question: What evidence do I need to prove that students have learned what is essential?

- Learning outcomes should be embedded in the assessment tasks.

- The culminating task for a unit should be identified first. This makes it easier to identify the other assessments that will build toward the culminating task.

- Assessment tasks should be designed to provide evidence both of students' achievement and their learning habits.

- Once the learning outcomes and assessment tasks have been identified, developing a sequence of lessons is relatively easy. Instructional planning should answer the question: What series of lessons will prepare students to perform successfully on each of the assessments which, in turn, will provide evidence that they have mastered the essential learning of the unit?

Applying My Learning

Before convening the second unit-planning session of your planning team, have each team member read Chapter 14 and jot down questions and observations about the planning sessions described in this chapter. Begin your second session by discussing each member's issues.

Planning sessions can easily become bogged down by relatively insignificant concerns and disagreements. Since time is usually limited, set a clear and specific goal about what the team should accomplish by the end of each planning session. (In other words, follow backward design planning for your meetings as well as for your program!) It is advisable to identify at least one team member to keep the team on track and move everybody along when things get bogged down.

Have one team member take notes about the process, including the discussion. Keeping a record will help everyone become more efficient and effective during subsequent sessions.

8. Grading and reporting student achievement is a caring, sensitive process that requires teachers' professional judgement.

BIG
IDEAS
in Section 4

Grading and Communicating about Student Learning

Although grading and reporting processes and policies are governed by provincial and local mandates, some general principles should be followed. These guidelines form the basis for Section 4.

Chapter 15 describes ways to approach the grading dilemma. It includes a wealth of information about letter grades, percentage grades, and anecdotal comments.

Chapter 16 examines the vital importance of information shared between teachers and parents face-to-face, as well as via phone and email. This sharing of information might be considered reporting *for* learning.

GRADING

 BIG IDEA 8 Grading and reporting student achievement is a caring, sensitive process that requires teachers' professional judgement.

Grading involves taking all the rich data about students' learning that have been gathered over the preceding weeks or months and converting it to a letter grade, achievement level, or percentage. It is often a challenging process because teachers know that report card grades often obscure as much as they reveal about student learning. By its very nature, a grade summarizes many useful pieces of data as one statistic.

Ken O'Connor (2002) notes that grading, *per se*, does not help students learn. Rather, it is like a snapshot of learning that informs parents and guardians about progress and achievement at various points in the learning cycle.

GROWTH, PROGRESS, OR ACHIEVEMENT?

Grading is like a snapshot of learning that informs parents and guardians about progress and achievement at points in the school cycle.

Just as clarity of purpose is important in assessing student learning, clarity about the precise kind of information communicated to students is important during grading and reporting. Is it information about

- how much improvement or growth has occurred from the beginning of the school year or term?
- how much progress a student has made toward an expected standard?
- a current level of achievement with respect to a known standard?

Growth

Growth is the increase in learning that occurs from the beginning of an instructional period to a particular reporting event. It is measured in terms of the gains made by a student from a baseline assessment to the most recent assessment, and is always measured forward from a starting point. Think, for example, how you would describe a child's height: you might say that Nabil has grown five centimetres in the past year and is now 177 cm tall.

Measures of growth are less concerned with established standards than are measures of progress and achievement. So when describing the growth in Nabil's height, there is little concern whether he has reached a standard height that he would be expected to reach.

When describing the gains in student learning that very young children or children who are at risk have made, focusing on growth rather than progress is critical. Growth emphasizes the improvement that has occurred, rather than how far short of a standard the student has fallen.

Growth is always measured forward from a starting point. Progress is measured backward from a desired end point.

Progress

Progress, on the other hand, is measured backward from a desired end point, such as end-of-year outcomes. Just as you would describe progress on a journey in terms of how far you are from your destination ("We're still a hundred kilometres from Vancouver"), student progress is measured in relation to an agreed-upon or known standard.

To illustrate, a local or provincial authority may establish performance standards for mathematics as shown in Figure 15-1. In this example, "Fully Meets Expectations" is the standard. A teacher could report to parents that their child had progressed from "Not Yet Within Expectations" to "Meets Expectations (Minimal Level)" in geometry in the period from September to November, and that it is hoped she will achieve the standard by the end of June.

Figure 15-1: Quick Scale: Grade 2 Numeracy				
Aspect	**Not Yet Within Expectations**	**Meets Expectations (Minimal Level)**	**Fully Meets Expectations**	**Exceeds Expectations**
Snapshot	The student may be unable to complete the task in a reasonable amount of time without one-to-one help.	Most parts of the basic task are correct; some errors or omissions. The student may have difficulty explaining the result. May need some assistance.	In familiar situations, the student completes all parts of the basic task accurately and can explain the result. May need occasional consultation.	The student completes all parts of the task accurately and efficiently and explains the result. May develop an extension or alternative method.
CONCEPTS and APPLICATONS	• Has difficulty seeing the relevance or application of mathematics to everyday problems • Needs one-to-one support to select and apply appropriate processes • Estimates and predictions are often guesses or wishes; may be very illogical	• If prompted, identifies ways to use mathematics in problems similar to those previously encountered • In simple, familiar situations, can select and apply most appropriate processes; some errors • In familiar situations, most estimates and predictions are within the bounds of logic	• With some support, identifies ways to apply mathematics to everyday problems • In familiar situations, selects and applies appropriate processes to solve simple problems; minor errors • In familiar, relatively simple situations, estimates and predictions are logical	• May independently find ways to apply mathematics to everyday problems • Selects and applies appropriate processes to solve simple problems; efficient • Makes logical estimates and predictions in both familiar and unfamiliar situations

Source: British Columbia Performance Standards, Grade 2 Numeracy

Achievement

Achievement is a measure of what a student demonstrates at a given point in time. It may use a scale similar to the one shown in Figure 15-1, but it does not indicate progress from one level to another.

Most report cards indicate only measures of achievement. This can be a source of dismay for parents and guardians of children with special needs who work hard, show plenty of growth relative to where they started, make some progress given their disabilities, yet always achieve far short of the established standard.

Grant Wiggins (1994) has described reporting mechanisms that communicate information about how much growth has occurred, as well as where a child stands relative to a known standard. The problem with these reporting formats is their complexity. Parents understandably demand report cards that are clear and easy to understand. In order to receive information about both growth and achievement—two different but equally important kinds of information—parents would have to wade through much longer report cards.

Why Performance Standards Are Essential to Grading?

...we need developmental standards but we also need absolute standards to educate students about real excellence just as the work of young athletes and musicians is ultimately judged against standards... set by professionals.

WIGGINS, 1998

Regardless of whether student growth, progress, or achievement is being graded, student learning is always described with reference to a performance standard. These standards are illustrated in Figure 15-2. The type of performance standard used will be one of the following:

Self-referenced standard

The student's initial assessment data are used as the reference point to measure how much growth has occurred by the second assessment. This is often the preferred approach in special education where it is expected that students may have difficulty achieving externally set standards such as those set by provincial ministries of education.

Path-referenced standard

The student's performance is compared to the typical path followed by students as they acquire certain knowledge and skills. PRIME, for example, is a path-referenced tool used to track students' knowledge of key concepts and skills. It utilizes a research-based continuum of observable phases of development in mathematical thinking developed by observing a large sample of elementary-aged students. This model is often used with students in core subject areas such as language and mathematics, where the acquisition of an essential set of skills is a prerequisite for later success in school.

Figure 15-2: Comparison of Types of Performance Standards

Self-referenced standard

Norm-referenced standard

Criterion-referenced standard

Norm-referenced standard

One student's performance is compared to a group of students of the same grade level. The sample used may be small (e.g., the rest of the class) or large (e.g., all students who took a standardized test). Today, this approach is used less frequently for classroom assessments since it is incompatible with standards-based methods of grading.

Criterion-referenced standard

The student's performance is measured against a predetermined set of performance indicators. This model is commonly used in skill-based assessments occurring outside of school. The driver's road test and the in-water scuba test are examples of criterion-referenced assessments where the student must demonstrate a predetermined level of proficiency on a specific set of skills in order to pass. Today, this approach is the most prevalent model for classroom assessment. Performance standards and rubrics are tools associated with a criterion-referenced approach to assessment and grading.

Criterion-referenced approaches to assessment measure student performance against a predetermined set of performance indicators.

Video Clip 4:

Grade 6—Backward
Planning a Language
Unit
16:15 minutes

Identifying Critical Evidence for Assessment *of* Learning

When using a criterion-referenced approach to grading, it is important to agree upon the assessment *of* learning tasks: the tasks that will be used for grading and reporting purposes. This requires that teachers of the same grade and subject discuss and agree upon the critical body of evidence—the essential written, oral, and performance tasks—that students need to complete as proof of their learning. This discussion is a natural part of program planning (see Chapters 13 and 14). Once these tasks have been identified, they must be described for parents and students, along with the dates when they will occur or be due.

Figure 15-3 provides a sample of critical tasks in several subjects and grade divisions. Recognize that these serve simply as illustrations since local and provincial curriculum may mandate critical tasks.

Figure 15-3: Critical Evidence: Assessment Tasks by Subject and Division

Language Arts: Grades 1-3

Reading

Read and respond to a:
- poem
- children's story
- folktale
- newspaper article
- directions
  ...

Writing

Create a(n):
- short descriptive paragraph
- short narrative
- letter
- diary entry
- poem
- mind map
- advertisement
  ...

Oral & Visual

Create/present a(n):
- oral retelling of a story
- oral account of a personal experience
- role-play
- telephone conversation
- choral reading
  ...

Science: Grades 4-6

- pose scientific questions and investigate possible answers or solutions
- plan and conduct an investigation
- design and conduct a fair test
- maintain a personal log (e.g., energy use, diet, etc.)
- create a cross-classification chart
- create graphs based on experimental observations
- create a labelled drawing
- make a scientific model
- write a scientific report
- prepare and deliver a presentation on a "science and society" issue (e.g., environmental, sustainable resources)
- investigate and report on connections between science and everyday life
  ...

Social Studies: Grades 7-8

- formulate questions to guide research
- prepare for and participate in a debate*
- role-play historical figures and events*
- conduct an inquiry using primary and secondary sources
- write a report connecting an historical period to the present
- make an oral presentation
- read and respond to information presented graphically (maps, graphs, charts, etc.)

- display information graphically (graphs, maps, Venn diagrams, cross-classifications charts, etc.)
- create maps
- create a media presentation about an issue (e.g., an Historical Minute)
- write a cause and effect report
- write a report analyzing opposing points of view on a major issue
- write an eye witness account of an historical event
- prepare and participate in a global symposium*
- prepare and present a biographical sketch of an historical figure
- participate in a simulation*
- produce labelled diagrams
  ...

* These tasks will involve students working in a co-operative group. Such tasks must include in their design provision for the assessment of individual learning (see Chapter 5).

ENSURING THAT ASSIGNMENTS ARE COMPLETED

Despite good communication between teachers, students, and parents, some students will always have difficulty completing work on time. They are not alone—adults also have difficulty being on time for everything! In reality, being late for some events, such as a plane departure, has more serious consequences than being late for an event such as a movie.

A classroom is not dissimilar. Some due dates are inflexible for good reason, while others can be flexible. For example, if students are creating publicity posters for an upcoming school concert, then they must meet a critical due date. On the other hand, if they are assembling the required elements for a year-long portfolio, they can work according to a flexible schedule—one that recognizes that everyone works at a different pace.

While it is common practice in Grades 7 and 8 to employ late penalties as a strategy for encouraging students to submit work on time, such penalties distort achievement data and are generally ineffective in dealing with tardiness (O'Connor, 2002). It is usually better to

- communicate directly with students and parents about essential assessment tasks
- take a firm but fair approach to task-completion

To illustrate, at the beginning of a new school year, once I had explained to my students all the essential assessment tasks they needed to complete during the year, I gave them a copy of what I called the *Big Ticket Tasks* to take home (see Figure 15-4 on page 246). This list identified for students and their parents the assessment tasks and their due dates. Whenever a student did not submit or complete a task by the suggested date, I would call that student's home to leave a gentle reminder. My purpose was to enlist the parents' collaboration in keeping the student on track, and to alert them to the possibility of the child falling behind in his or her work.

Years and years of lessons using penalties show that they don't work and that they give students excuses to not do the work.

O'CONNOR, 2002

In my classroom, I also posted the *Big Ticket Task* list for each unit on the bulletin board. On the chart, in large letters, was a final date indicating when "the train leaves the station." This date corresponded to the end of the unit when all the essential assessment tasks were to be completed or submitted. I gave constant reminders to the class as a whole, as well as to individual students who owed me Big Ticket Items, such as, "Remember, the train leaves the station in 10 days! Each of you knows which Big Ticket items you still have to complete."

Figure 15-4: Big Ticket Task List

Unit: Beauty and the Beast Train leaves the station on October 14						
Name	**Task** Speech Due: Sept. 12	Reading Response Due: Sept. 18	Personal Letter Due: Sept. 23	Poetry Response Due: Sept. 29	Comparative Essay Due: Oct. 3	Writing Anthology Due: Oct. 6
Maria	✓	✓	✓	✓	✓	✓
Ted	✓	✓		✓	✓	✓
Mia	✓	✓	✓		✓	
Rene	✓		✓	✓	✓	✓

Big Ticket Task lists are an ideal way to alert parents to key assessment tasks their children will need to complete throughout the year.

Did the *Big Ticket Task* list motivate every student to complete his or her work on time? No, but it did motivate most students, and it was particularly effective with students who had previously struggled to complete work. Here are some other actions that can increase the potential for every student's success:

- Communicate to students and their parents, both at the start of the year and each unit, your expectation that assigned work will be completed.
- Provide tools such as rubrics, checklists, and exemplars to clarify the quality standard for each task.
- Provide in-class time for students to work on these tasks, as well as regular conferencing opportunities to meet with you and their peers to receive feedback on their draft work.
- Provide frequent reminders to students and their parents about when work is due.

Responding to Incomplete Assignments

How should you respond when students do not complete one or more of their essential assessment tasks? Unfortunately, this question does not have a simple answer. In the world outside of school, however, there are many examples of criterion-referenced evaluation where the question is both addressed and answered.

Consider the road test everyone takes to get a driver's license. Imagine there are ten competencies that must be demonstrated during the test, including steering, passing, parallel parking, three-point turns, and so on. All competencies must be demonstrated by everyone taking the test. What would happen if you told your examiner, "There's one thing you need to know before we begin: I could never get the hang of three-point turns so would you please leave that competency off my test?" Such a request is, of course, absurd. You cannot be certified as a competent driver unless you demonstrate proficiency in all ten competencies.

Ideally, the standards-based curriculum and grading systems that have become the norm across North America should be no different. If a critical task is missing, then a student is not considered to have completed the requirements for that grade or subject. In practice, this never happens for one simple reason: time. In the road-test example, the required level of achievement is held constant and the time needed to master these competencies varies from person to person. Some may easily master the ten driving competencies and pass the road test on their first attempt, while others may fail at the first and even second attempts and take much longer to achieve success.

In the classroom, holding the level of achievement constant while making time the variable would mean retaining students in a given grade until they demonstrate proficiency in all of the required competencies. However, the research concerning grade retention of students in elementary schools is conclusive: students who are held back suffer academically and socially in the long run and frequently drop out before completing high school (Holmes & Matthews 1984; Jimmerson et al, 2002).

The most common response to dealing with students who have not demonstrated proficiency is to hold time constant and let the level of achievement be variable. In other words, what students are expected to learn is chunked into terms or years and a range of achievement is accepted for advancement to the next grade. Hence, when placement decisions have to be made, teachers rarely, if ever, say, "If any one piece of work is missing, the student will not be promoted." Instead, teachers usually decide whether the completed work comprises sufficient evidence for the student to be promoted to the next grade.

In districts where numerical grades are used for reporting, the decision to pass or fail a student may be made not on the basis of sufficient evidence, but according to whether a student's composite report card

As a society we have tended to place implicit faith in grades as accurate reflections of actual student achievement. Further, we have operated on the belief that grades are productive motivators for students. In fact we may need to be more cautious in making such assumptions.

STIGGINS, 1994

grade is above or below an arbitrarily determined "cut point," such as 50 percent. This decision to pass or fail a student will have been influenced in large part by what happens when a student does not complete an essential assessment task. For example, does the teacher enter "incomplete" in her achievement record or does she enter "zero"? Figure 15-5 illustrates some of the possible responses to missed assignments and the effect on one student's report card grades.

Do not enter missing or invalid evidence of achievement as zero. As Stiggins (1994) states, "Zero implies the total absence of any work… Averaging zeros with other scores to calculate a final grade skews the score and results in an inaccurate picture of student achievement."

Date	% (rubric level)	% Mean Including Zeros	% Mean Excluding Zeros	Level Mean Including Zeros	Level Mean Excluding Zeros
Figure 15-5: Possible Impact of Missed Assignments on Alex's Grade					
Sept. 9	50 (1)	50	50	1	1
Sept. 12	60 (2)	60	60	2	2
Sept. 18	70 (3)	70	70	3	3
Sept. 26	63 (2)	63	63	2	2
Oct. 3	60 (2)	60	60	2	2
Oct. 10	70 (3)	70	70	3	3
Oct. 17	0 (0)	0	NM	0	NM
Nov. 14	0 (0)	0	NM	0	NM
Nov. 21	62 (2)	62	62	2	2
Nov. 28	61 (2)	61	61	2	2
Final Grade		49.6%	62.0%	1.7 = 1+ = 58%	2.1 = 2– = 61%

▲ **This chart indicates the significant impact that marking missed assignments as zero can have on a student's report card grade. (Note: Alex's teacher used the conversion chart shown in Figure 15-9 on page 254 to convert levels to percentage grades.)**

Alex failed to submit the tasks due on October 17 and November 14. Her teacher uses the mean or average to determine report card grades. In the third column, Alex's teacher recorded "0" for each missed task and included the zeros when calculating the mean. In the fourth column, Alex's teacher decided to see what would happen if she recorded "no mark" for the missed tasks and calculated the mean by including only the completed tasks.

In the fifth and sixth columns, Alex's teacher experimented further by using rubric levels instead of percentages. She determined the overall grade by first including the zeros and then by excluding them. If the pass/fail cut point at Alex's school is 50 percent, then the way in which her teacher determines a final grade has critical implications for Alex's future—she either passes or fails!

How can all students be encouraged to complete the set of essential tasks that comprises the critical assessment of learning evidence? How can teachers ensure that final grades offer a fair, accurate representation of overall student achievement? Responses to these two questions must balance flexibility and sensitivity with the need to teach students how to become more responsible. Consequently, guidelines for dealing with late and missed work may vary from grade to grade, with the consequences becoming more serious as students mature. The following guidelines may help you deal with these questions.

Critical Evidence and the Problem of Late/Missed Work

- Identify for students and parents the tasks that are essential as proof of learning.
- Operate on the understanding that all essential tasks must be completed to meet the requirements for a given subject and grade.
- Communicate to students and their parents the timelines for completion of these tasks to facilitate students' and teacher's workload.
- Do not use escalating late penalties.
- If a penalty is used, it should be fixed.
- Returned work must indicate both achieved and reduced marks.
- Late penalties must not change a passing grade to a failing grade.
- Identify strategies for addressing non-completion of essential tasks, for example:
  - completion contract
  - supervised learning centre
  - method for tracking missed tasks
- Develop a clear policy concerning interim and final grade determination. For example, record "incomplete" on the interim report card and provide clear direction to all concerned what the impact of "incomplete" will be on the final report card.

Organizing Assessment of Learning Data

How should assessment *of* learning data be organized and recorded: by strand, by outcome, or by some other category?

In some jurisdictions, local or provincial policy may determine how teachers are required to organize and record assessment *of* learning data. In the absence of such a policy, the decision should be made before the school year begins as part of your long range planning.

Assessment data should be organized and recorded in a manner that yields the most useful information for communicating with students, parents, and guardians about achievement. Ask yourself, "If I were the recipient of this information, would it tell me in which areas of the curriculum my child is having success and in which areas she is having difficulty?" This means organizing and recording assessment of learning data in one of the following ways:

- by strand, for example "geometry"
- by learning process, for example, "problem-solving"
- by learning target, for example, "students construct three-dimensional figures, using two-dimensional shapes"

Regardless of whether or not your school's report card format allows for this level of detail, by organizing your assessment data in one of these ways, you will be able to communicate to students, parents and guardians information that will chart a course toward improvement.

Consider the example shown in Figure 15-6. Although Jason's report card format enabled his teacher to assign only one single grade in mathematics, she recorded Jason's achievement on a matrix that related strands (Number Sense and Numeration, Measurement, and so forth) and mathematical processes (Problem Solving, Understanding of Concepts, and so forth).

Figure 15-6: Assessment of Learning Summary

Student: Jason Costa   Class: Mr. Levy

Category	Problem Solving			Most Consistent Level	Understanding of Concepts				Most Consistent Level	Application of Procedures			Most Consistent Level	Communication	Most Consistent Level	Most Consistent Level Across Strand
Assessment Task and Date	Oct. 7 Inquiry 1	Oct. 20 Problem 1	Oct. 24 Inquiry 2		Oct. 5 Drawing 1	Oct. 13 Journal 1	Oct. 17 Review	Oct. 28 Chap. Task		Oct. 10 Drawing 2	Oct. 17 Review	Oct. 28 Chap. Task		Oct. 28 Chapter Task		
Number Sense and Numeration																
Measurement																
Geometry and Spatial Sense	L2	L2	L3	L2+	L2	L3	6/10	L3	L3-	L2	7/10	L2	L2+	L3	L3	L3-
Patterning and Algebra																
Data Management and Probability																
Comments: Strengths, Areas for Improvement, and Next Steps																

Alternatively, Figure 15-7 illustrates the assessment *of* learning data for Jason matched up with learning targets—or broad learning outcomes. This is far more helpful to Jason and his parents than simply indicating the marks he achieved on "Inquiry 1" or "Problem 1," data that tell Jason and his parents nothing about the specific areas of the mathematics curriculum in which he is having success and those areas where he is struggling.

Figure 15-7: Grading by Outcomes		
Student: Jason Costa	**Class: Mr. Levy**	**Term: 2005-06**
Learning Outcomes:	**Identify and classify quadrilaterals and 3-D figures**	**Construct 3-D figures using 2-D shapes**
Assessment Date & Task		
Oct. 5: Drawing #1	L2	
Oct. 7: Inquiry #1	L2	
Oct. 10: Drawing #2		L2
Oct. 13: Journal #1	L3	
Oct. 17: Review	13/20	L3
Oct. 20: Problem #1		L2
Oct. 24: Inquiry #2		L3
Oct. 28: Chapter Task	L3	L3
Most Consistent Level for Learning Outcome	L3-	L3-
Report Card Grade for Strand	B-	

Note: Levels are based on a 4-point rubric. L4 represents a high level of achievement.

DETERMINING REPORT CARD GRADES

Much has been written about the merits of calculating report card grades mathematically as opposed to determining grades through a combination of estimating and exercising professional judgement. Regardless of the approach taken, grading policy decisions should be made at the very least by school administrators, to ensure consistency among all teachers at a given school but preferably by district administrators, to ensure a consistent approach across schools.

Grading policies often reflect the need to use different methods of grading for different divisions. For example, grading practice in the early years may stress a more anecdotal approach that favours qualitative assessment data and professional judgement by teachers. In later grades, there may be a greater emphasis on quantitative data and exact calculations.

This resource and others that deal with grading (see O'Connor, 2002; Marzano, 2000) will provide you with information on identifying and analyzing possible approaches to grading, along with the strengths and drawbacks of each. Grading policy decisions can then be made by administrators on the basis of sound research. Since grading student achievement is one of the most public actions that teachers perform, it must be governed by policy.

Median, Mean, and Mode

In the example on page 248, Alex's teacher experimented with several methods for determining her final grade. However, each method involved calculating the mean, or average. The mean is just one of several measures of central tendency that may be used to combine a set of marks into a composite grade. Alex's teacher might just as easily have selected the median, the mode, or a combination of the mean and the mode to determine Alex's overall grade. (The median is the middle number in a set of numbers. In other words, there is an equal number of greater and lesser numbers on either side of the median. The mode is the most frequently occurring number in a set of numbers.) Before considering the possible benefits and drawbacks of each method used to calculate Alex's final grades, consider this question: "What *should* the report card grade represent, given that it is a somewhat crude summary of a great deal of information about a student's achievement?"

Ideally, the report card grade should be an accurate summary of the polished work completed by a student; it should reflect the *trend* in achievement. Moreover, the grade should not be a surprise to anyone: not the teacher who determines the grade, not the student whose achievement it summarizes; nor the parent to whom it is communicated. The grade should simply confirm what these three individuals already suspect.

For the sake of simplicity, Figure 15-8 considers assessment data from just six tasks and uses rubric levels only. More information is provided later in this chapter on how to convert scores, letter grades, and rubric levels to a common scale for grading and reporting purposes (see page 254).

Look at columns 3 through 6 and consider the four ways in which Alex's marks were summarized. Which overall score do you think best captures the trend in Alex's achievement: the mean, the median, the mode, or the average of the modes?

The mean is clearly problematic since Alex did not receive a mark of 2.5 on any of the music tasks. The median appears to summarize the marks more accurately. The problem with the mode is that it results in two scores—unacceptable for reporting purposes. Using the average of the two modes is one way to solve that problem.

The report card grade should be an accurate summary of the polished work completed by a student; it should reflect the trend in achievement.

Tips for Teaching

Many teachers use a software program to save time generating report card grades. However, it is important to understand how the program arrives at the summary grades. The software manufacturer should provide you with these details.

Although the decision about which method will be used to determine report card grades should rest with either school or district administrators, it is essential for teachers to understand the method they are using.

Figure 15-8: Alex–Music Class					
Name: Alex	Class: Music				
Assessment Task	Rubric Level (based on a 4-point rubric, 4 is highest level)	Mean Calculation	Median	Mode	Average of Modes
Performance #1	1	Total of rubric points: 15	Rubric scores arranged in ascending order:		Modes: 3, 4
Performance #2	3				
Performance #3	4	Total # of Tasks: 6	0 1 3 3 4 4	3 and 4	Average of Modes: 7/2
Composer Report	3	Mean:15/6			
Performance #4	0				
Composer Presentation	4				
Overall Score		2.5	3.0	3, 4	3.5

Assessment Q & A

Question

There seem to be so many grading software programs on the market. Should I be using one to determine my report card grades?

Answer

You shouldn't have to make this decision alone. School district administrators would benefit from developing a grading policy that includes whether or not grading software is to be used across the schools in a given system. At the very least, I recommend that principals draft such a policy to ensure consistent grading practice among the teachers in one school.

The decision to use grading software should also take into consideration the purposes for which grading data will be used. In secondary schools, where grading data are used for accreditation and admission into colleges and universities, more teachers use grading software than they do at the elementary level. Few teachers of the early grades use grading software; a very small number of Grade 4 to 6 teachers use grading software; and a significant number of middle school teachers use such programs.

When making decisions about using grading software, it is worth remembering the architectural tenet that "form must follow function," and not vice versa. In other words, only those grading programs that conform to established grading policy should be selected. For example, if a district policy stipulates that report card grades are to be determined using the mode, then only grading software that has the capability of determining grades in this way must be selected for use.

When choosing grading software, consider the purposes for which the grading data will be used.

Combining Different Kinds of Assessment Data for Reporting

Jason's assessment *of* learning data in Figure 15-7 included rubric levels and numerical scores. Your assessment records could comprise a combination of numerical scores, letter grades, and rubric scores, depending on the assessment tools you have used to record these data.

To determine Alex's overall grade for Scientific Inquiry, (see Figure 15-10 on page 255) her teacher must convert scores, letter grades, and rubric levels to a common scale. (In Alex's case, rubric levels are suggested.) Then she must convert the overall level to a letter grade (the grading system used at Alex's school). Alex's teacher uses the conversion chart shown in Figure 15-9.

Figure 15-9: Converting Evaluation and Reporting Symbols					
Rubric Descriptor	Rubric Level	Letter Grade	Numerical Score	Percentage Range	Percentage Points
Master	4	A++ A+ A A–	8–10	80–100%	100 95 90 85
Practitioner	3	B+ B B–	7	70–79%	78 75 71
Apprentice	2	C+ C C–	6	60–69%	68 65 61
Novice	1	D+ D D–	5	50–59%	58 55 51
	Below 1		0–4	Below 50%	

Note: This is a sample chart. Grade equivalents will vary from province to province.

Note that specific percentage points are identified in the last column. Many districts have adopted this "pegging" method when determining report card grades. Instead of there being 10 percentage points within the 70–79 percent range, only three possible points are available: 71 percent, 75 percent, and 78 percent.

To determine Alex's grade for yourself, use the conversion chart and follow these steps:

1. Use the conversion chart to convert the data in each column to a rubric level. (For example, 8/10 becomes L4.)
2. Working vertically, determine the most consistent level for each outcome. You may use plus or minus. You will end up with a total of seven levels in the row labelled Most Consistent Level for Outcome.

3. Reading across this row, determine the Most Consistent Level for the Scientific Inquiry strand.
4. Again using the conversion chart, convert this level to a letter grade.
5. Check your calculations against those in Figure 15-11 on the next page.

Topic/ Strand:	Scientific Inquiry							
Outcomes:	Design and conduct scientific investigations	Develop conclusions and explanations	Communicate and defend conclusions	Work safely	Honesty	Critical-mindedness	Questioning	**Most Consistent Level/Total on Task**
Assessment Date & Task								
19/9 Lab 1	L2			L2			L1	
24/9 Report 1		L2	L2			L2		
30/9 Test 1		8/10	6/10			6/10		
2/10 Pres.1		B	B			C		
6/10 Lab 2	L3			L3			L2	
11/10 Report 2		L3	L3		L3			
18/10 Test 2		8/10				8/10	7/10	
24/10 Pres. 2		B	C		B	B		
Most Consistent Level for Outcome								
Most Consistent level for Topic/Strand								
Report Card Grade for Topic/Strand								

Figure 15-10: Determining Alex's Grade for Scientific Inquiry

Note: Levels are based on a 4-point rubric. L4 represents a high level of achievement.

We have looked only briefly at some of the complexities involved in determining report card grades. For an in-depth examination of these issues, see *How to Grade for Learning* by Ken O'Connor or *Transforming Classroom Grading* by Robert Marzano.

Topic/Strand:	Scientific Inquiry							
Outcomes:	Design and conduct scientific investigations	Develop conclusions and explanations	Communicate and defend conclusions	Work safely	Honesty	Critical-mindedness	Questioning	**Most Consistent Level/Total on Task**
Assessment Date & Task								
19/9 Lab 1	L2			L2			L1	L2(-)
24/9 Report 1		L2	L2		L2			L2
30/9 Test 1		8/10 (L3)	6/10 (L1)			6/10 (L1)		20/30 (L2)
2/10 Pres.1(L3)		B (L3)	B (L3)			C (L2		L3 (-)
6/10 Lab 2	L3			L3			L2	L3(-)
11/10 Report 2		L3	L3		L3			L3
18/10 Test 2		8/10 (L3)				8/10 (L3)	7/10 (L2)	23/30 (L3)
24/10 Pres. 2		B (L3)	C (L2)		B (L3)	B (L3)		L3
Most Consistent Level for Outcome	L3(-)	L3	L3(-)	L3(-)	L3	L3(-)	L2 ⟶	
Most Consistent Level for Topic/Strand								L3(-)
Report Card Grade for Topic/Strand								B-

Figure 15-11: Scientific Inquiry: Alex's Calculated Grade

Ten Grading Guidelines

Report card grades cannot possibly summarize all the learning that has occurred in a given subject, which is why it is important to ensure that report card grades represent the trend in a student's achievement.

The report card grade can be described as the "line of best fit" drawn through a set of assessment data. The following grading guidelines will help you derive report card grades that represent this line of best fit. Beginning on page 258, each guideline is illustrated with a case study and commentary.

Guideline 1

Report card grades cannot include all assessment data that you have gathered. Assessment *for* learning data are for instructional purposes only. Report card grades should be based on assessment *of* learning data—the marks students receive for polished work and work that has been improved through practice and feedback.

Guideline 2

Report card grades should be based on an appropriate and balanced sample of student work. The sample should include oral, performance, and written tasks, completed over a period of time.

Guideline 3

Report card grades should capture the trend in a student's achievement over time. They should not be determined by simply calculating the average mark of the student's work. Many districts now require that grades be derived from the mode.

Guideline 4

Report card grades and anecdotal comments should complement each other and provide a consistent picture of each student's strengths and needs.

Guideline 5

Determining report card grades should not be strictly a mathematical calculation. Your professional judgement should play a role, especially in cases where a student has special needs or where extenuating circumstances exist.

Guideline 6

When communicating with students and parents, you must feel confident that you are able to stand behind the grades you have entered on a set of report cards. This confidence results from

- standards that you have discussed with colleagues, and communicated to students, and parents.
- well-maintained records of student achievement and evidence in the form of work samples
- an understanding that students and parents have the right to appeal a mark for a given piece of work or the report card grade

Guideline 7

Report card grades should be based on the most important learning that has occurred, not on the components that are easiest to mark.

Guideline 8

For special needs or ESL students, report card grades must represent fair judgements about these students' strengths and areas of need.

Guideline 9

Many districts require that teachers report separately on achievement and behaviour/learning skills. It is important to distinguish between these two kinds of data accordingly.

Guideline 10

Assessment data used for report card grades must be demonstrated by the individual student and not be distorted by work that other students may or may not have done in a cooperative learning situation.

Looking at the Guidelines Through Case Studies

Use the following case studies to explore implications of these guidelines for your grading practices. Read the case studies and try to answer the *Question* for *Discussion* before you read the commentary.

 CASE STUDY 1 | **Accounting for Marks**

Your kindergarten class is making great progress this year. The students are enthusiastic, and you have posted their work all over the room. Daily story time is going well and, the children are showing an increased level of cooperation during play period. Davinder's expressive and receptive language skills continue to impress you.

During the January interview with Davinder's father, you pull out Davinder's portfolio. His father points out that several of the 18 samples in his son's portfolio are not marked. He reminds you that it is your responsibility to mark all student work and that perhaps there is too much play time and not enough focus on learning in your classroom.

Question for Discussion

How would you respond to a parent who says that you should be marking all student work?

Guideline 1

Report card grades cannot include all assessment data that you have gathered. Assessment for learning data are for instruction only. Report card grades should be based on assessment *of* learning data—the marks students receive for polished work and work that has been improved through practice and feedback.

Commentary

You may wish to point out to Davinder's father that marking work and providing helpful feedback are two related but distinct processes. For Davinder to continue to learn and improve his work, he needs anecdotal information that tells him what he has done well, what he appears to be struggling with, and what he needs to do to improve his work. Marks, on the other hand, are used to indicate the relative quality of a piece of polished work. Hence, not all his work has been marked. (See Chapter 2.)

CASE STUDY 2 | Achieving Balance

Your science program lacks hands-on materials but you have an excellent set of new textbooks. The Grade 5 unit on the body is fun to teach. You ask your students to answer all the textbook questions directly in their science journals. One of your students, Jess, receives all Level 2s on all of his journal work.

Next, you show your students a great video on how food is digested. As a follow-up assignment, you have the students write a story from the perspective of an apple to explain the digestive process. Jeff receives a Level 2.

For another homework assignment, the students write a newspaper ad promoting the organ they think is most important to the body. Jeff receives another Level 2.

Finally, you ask the students to write a letter to you in which they explain what they liked, what they learned, and what they didn't like about this unit of study. Jeff again receives a Level 2.

On Parents' Night, Jeff's mother, a doctor of internal medicine, asks you why her child received a report card grade of only C in science.

Question for Discussion
Are you certain that your assessments are balanced? Why or why not?

Guideline 2
Report card grades should be based on an appropriate and balanced sample of student work. The sample should include oral, performance, and written tasks, completed over a period of time.

Commentary
The sample of science work that you collected from your students was imbalanced in that every task required a written response. Students need to *do* science, in addition to writing about it. A balanced sample of assessment evidence would include oral, performance, and written tasks. (See Chapter 6.)

| CASE STUDY 3 | Adding It Up |

The following are Jason and Joanna's marks for a Grade 7 math unit on number sense and numeration.

Assignment	Jason	Joanna
Pre-test multiplication, 2-digit	18/50	31/50
Title page for number sense	Level 1	Level 4
Homework completed (frequency)	0/5	5/5
Puddle math question	Level 3	Level 1
Number sense application project	Level 4	Level 2-
Need for assistance	Rarely	Daily
Tests signed by parents	0/3	3/3
Quiz	3/10	8/10
Notebook organization	Level 2	Level 2-
Math task package	Level 3+	Level 2-
Post-test multiplication, 2-digit	10/50	38/50
Weekly problem-solving	Level 4	Level 2

Question for Discussion

What grades should Jason and Joanna get for number sense and numeration? Are there any problems using these marks to determine their grades?

Guideline 3

Report card grades should capture the trend in a student's achievement over time. They should not be determined by simply calculating the average mark of the student's work. Many districts now require that grades be derived from the mode.

Commentary

Several of the tasks listed should not be included as part of Jason and Joanna's achievement in mathematics and should be separated from the list before determining their grades (see next page).

Once the data to be included in the grade have been identified, the scores should be converted to a common scale, and the weight of each task should be taken into account.

At this point, each student's grade can be determined.

Note that this set of marks does create a dilemma when reporting procedures require teachers to determine an overall grade. The marks suggest that both students have areas of strength, but also areas of serious need—vital information that is obscured by using the overall "most consistent level" to determine the grades. For example, the data suggest that Jason may suffer from test anxiety. Ideally, the two students and their parents could see the details that appear in these charts so that they, together with their teacher, would work at improving the weak areas.

continued

Tasks Not to Include in Jason and Joanna's Grades			
Include task?	Yes	No	Reason for not including
Pre-test multiplication, 2-digit		✓	Diagnostic assessment to inform instruction, not measure achievement
Title page for number sense		✓	Unrelated to achievement in math
Homework completed (frequency)		✓	Learning skill, unrelated to achievement in math
Puddle math question	✓		
Number sense application project	✓		
Observational assistance		✓	Degree of assistance should be reported anecdotally
Tests signed		✓	Behavioural expectation, unrelated to achievement in math
Quiz	✓		May include, but should carry less weight than tests
Notebook Organization		✓	Learning skill, unrelated to achievement in math
Math task package	✓		
Post-test multiplication, 2-digit	✓		
Weekly problem-solving	✓		

Weighting of Tasks					
Task	Weight	Jason	Jason's Weighted Levels	Joanna	Joanna's Weighted Levels
Puddle math question	1	L3	L3	L1	L1
Number sense application project	2	L4	L4, L4	L2-	L2-, L2-
Quiz	0	3/10	N/A	8/10	N/A
Math task package	2	L3+	L3+, L3+	L2-	L2-, L2-
Post-test multiplication,	2	10/50 (<L1)	< L1, < L1	38/50 (L3-)	L3-, L3-
Weekly problem-solving	2	L4	L4, L4	L2	L2, L2
Most consistent Level & Grade			L4- A-		L2+ C+

Ned has been identified as a learning disabled student. He has an IEP (Individual Education Plan) and struggles in all subjects, especially math. When his parents look at his report card, they are confused.

Ned's Report Card		
Mathematics		
Number Sense	C	Ned is working well in class. Keep it up in the second term.
Measurement	C-	
Geometry	D	
Algebra	N/A	
Data Management	N/A	

Question for Discussion

Can you think of an explanation for the apparent discrepancy between Ned's grades and his teacher's comment?

Guideline 4

Report card grades and anecdotal comments should complement each other and provide a consistent picture of each student's strengths and needs.

Commentary

Ned is struggling in all three of the math strands taught this term. The anecdotal comment is inconsistent with the picture of Ned's achievement and provides little useful information. Anecdotal comments should provide specific details about why Ned received these grades, as well as helpful information about what he needs to do to improve. (See Chapter 16.)

If the rationale behind the comment was to encourage Ned, then the comment might have read, "Ned is working hard but continues to have serious difficulty in each of the strands this term. To improve, he needs to constantly review his number facts, and work with me to complete the extra support materials in measurement and geometry. Please book an interview with me." A comment worded in such a manner provides information about Ned's current achievement, but also indicates that the situation requires intervention.

CASE STUDY 5 | **The Whole Picture**

Aida, an ESL student, took some time to adjust to Grade 2 after the summer vacation. Her first report card grade in reading was a C–. Since the December break, she has made tremendous gains in her language development. Her assessment scores from January's guided reading sessions show that she is now performing at Level 4.

Aida is still at the early-reading phase, but is starting to demonstrate some indicators from the transitional phase. Without any advance warning, her parents inform you that Aida will be accompanying her parents on an extended trip in February and will miss five weeks of school.

Question for Discussion

Based on the data you have, what grade do you think Aida might receive for reading on her March report card?

Guideline 5

Determining report card grades should not be strictly a mathematical calculation. Your professional judgement should play a role, especially in cases where a student has special needs or where extenuating circumstances exist.

Commentary

This case study raises three issues:

1. To what extent should a report card grade reflect the most recent achievement as opposed to achievement over an entire term?

2. How should teachers grade the reading achievement of second-language learners who are integrated into the mainstream?

3. How can report card grades accommodate legitimate, extended periods of absence?

Report card grades should capture both the trend in a student's achievement, but also reflect current achievement. However, if you factor in *all* of a student's achievement results, including first and early attempts, the grade may be skewed by poor performance on the early tries. On the other hand, if you include *only* the most recent achievement data, you may have insufficient data to determine a reliable grade. (See page 244.)

All reporting involves two components: material on which the student has been graded and a symbol (letter grade, numerical score, level, percentage) that captures the student's achievement relative to the standard. In Aida's case, the reading selections chosen for her suit her current level of ability. These materials will almost certainly be less sophisticated than the material that the mainstream students are reading.

The scores that Aida is achieving (C– followed by several Level 4s) represent her achievement on the less sophisticated materials. As her skills improve, you, as her teacher, would substitute these texts with more sophisticated ones so that Aida will gradually be able to handle material at the same level of sophistication as her peers.

Teachers can only report on demonstrated achievement. If Aida's grade on the March report card is based on a smaller sample of work than other students, this fact should be indicated in the anecdotal comment. (See Chapter 3.)

CASE STUDY 6

The Case of the Missing Assessments

Daniel is a Grade 8 student. He has always done well in the writing strand of English so his mother was surprised when he received 55% on his report card. On Parents' Night, Daniel's mother asked the teacher if she could see exactly how the grade for writing had been determined. Daniel's teacher was unable to identify the assessment tasks that contributed to the grade but tried to assure Daniel's mother that she was confident Daniel's grade would improve during the second term.

Question for Discussion
If you were Daniel's mother, how would you respond to Daniel's teacher?

Guideline 6
When communicating with students and parents and guardians, you must feel confident that you are able to stand behind the grades you have

entered on a set of report cards. This confidence results from the following conditions:
• standards that you have discussed with colleagues, and communicated to students, and parents
• well-maintained records of student achievement and evidence in the form of work samples
• an understanding that students and parents have the right to appeal the report card grade

Commentary
All teachers need to maintain careful and thorough records of student achievement. These records should include the tasks used to determine report card grades, as well as the criteria used to assess each task. If assessment tasks have been weighted differentially, then this information should also be available to parents and guardians. Assessment and reporting must be transparent. (See Chapter 16.)

CASE STUDY 7 | Write It Down!

In the chart below, Mrs. Vierou listed the instructional tasks she used in her Grade 4 science class. She then listed the assessments used to determine report card grades.

Question for Discussion
Do you see any problems as you compare the tasks with the assessments?

Guideline 7
Report card grades should be based on the most important learning that has occurred, not on the components that are easiest to mark.

Commentary
The tasks that Mrs. Vierou has assigned her students are rich and engaging; unfortunately, the assessment methods she has used lack balance—all are written tasks—and do not assess essential science skills such as inquiry, observation, and exploration. These science skills require performance assessments. (See Chapter 7.)

Task	Assessment
Field trip to observe plants and animals in their natural habitats	Multiple-choice and matching test to assess knowledge
Research to learn about energy transfer through food chains	Matching and short-answer test to assess knowledge
Experiment to discover how plants respond to varying amounts of sunlight	Lab report summarizing findings
Independent observations to discover how a plant or animal adapts to its natural environment	Test to assess knowledge
Project to discover how humans have contributed to the near extinction of a species	Written report on findings

CASE STUDY 8 | Three Doors

Patrick, a student in your Grade 4 class, has been identified as learning disabled and is on a modified program. He always tries to complete work to the best of his ability, but he has great difficulty meeting the requirements of any written task. He receives daily support from a special education support teacher. While marking his portfolio in preparation for reporting, you suddenly realize how little work he has actually completed.

However, you are required to check off one of the following on his Term 2 report card:
- Progressing well toward promotion
- Progressing with some difficulty toward promotion
- Promotion at risk

Question for Discussion
Which descriptor do you check, and why?

Guideline 8
For students with special needs or ESL students, report card grades must represent fair judgements about these students' strengths and areas of need.

Commentary
When completing Patrick's report card, it is important to consider the information that his parents need to receive. They need to know
- what he has achieved in terms of the prescribed curriculum and how well he has achieved these outcomes
- what he has been unable to achieve, despite modifications to the program, and whether these outcomes are essential
- how much effort he is demonstrating

Ideally, you would have consulted regularly with the special education resource teacher to discuss Patrick's growth. At this time, the two of you need to review his learning over the course of the term. Deciding whether Patrick is on track for promotion must be made on the basis of the second consideration: what has Patrick been unable to achieve and are these outcomes essential preparation for the next grade level? (See Chapter 3.)

CASE STUDY 9 | Two Sides of the Report Card

Marsha is a Grade 8 student who seems mature beyond her years. She has a sister and brother in the junior grades whom she must pick up immediately after school each day.

Marsha never completes any extended homework or long-term assignments. Her daily work in class, however, reflects outstanding performance. She is quick to answer questions and debate in class, and she brings an insightful perspective to classroom discussions. Unfortunately, she never studies for tests. When she does submit work it is always late. She still owes you three social studies assignments for this term; however, the four social studies tasks she did complete were all of Level 4 quality.

Question for Discussion

How will you report on Marsha's work in social studies this term?

Guideline 9

Many districts require that teachers report separately on achievement and behaviour/learning skills. It is important to distinguish between these two kinds of data accordingly.

Commentary

As you write Marsha's report card, you need to ensure that information about her achievement is reported separately from information about her behaviour. All of the work she has completed, as well as her level of understanding in class, demonstrates that she has a solid grasp of the required Grade 8 social studies curriculum. It is also clear that family circumstances combined with some poor study habits are preventing Marsha from completing her work.

The report card must communicate to both Marsha and her parents what she has been able to achieve, and the quality of those achievements, as well as the difficulties she is having as a result of these other circumstances. A parent-teacher-student interview will clarify what important work has not been completed and help to put an action plan in place to enable Marsha to be more successful. (See Chapter 16.)

CASE STUDY 10 | Will the Real Harry Stand Up?

You have planned an engaging integrated science, math, and language arts unit for your Grade 6 class. It includes a culminating task to assess deep understanding. The process component of this task is assessed on a daily basis.

At the start of the unit, you tell students to choose two peers they work well with. Harry picks Zack and Melinda. You let the students and their parents know that the cooperation grade on the report card will be based on students' assessments of each other.

At the end of the unit, both Zack and Melinda agree that Harry deserves an N (needs improvement) because he argues constantly and never completes the assigned tasks on time. You were unaware of this throughout the unit. In all other subjects and interactions, you have noticed Harry's cooperation to be excellent.

Question for Discussion
What descriptor do you place on the report card for "cooperation"?

Guideline 10
Assessment data used for report card grades must be demonstrated by the individual student and not be distorted by work that other students may or may not have done in a cooperative learning situation.

Commentary
There are two principles you should have remembered, which would have prevented this situation from occurring:
1. Although students should be involved in self- and peer assessment, any and all data used to determine report card grades and anecdotal information must come from the teacher's records.
2. Students benefit from assessing the work of their peers since it helps them better understand the criteria for quality work. However, peer assessment must be in the form of feedback that helps students improve; it is not the responsibility of students to evaluate (judge) the work and contributions of their classmates. That is the teacher's responsibility. (See Chapter 5.)

After Thoughts
These case studies illustrate some of the grading dilemmas that often occur at report card time. You may have seen yourself in one or more of these scenarios. No doubt, as well, there are other situations you have encountered that have not been addressed. Nevertheless, it is hoped that these Ten Grading Guidelines will help you navigate the troublesome rapids in which teachers often find themselves each time a reporting period occurs.

THE ROLE OF PROFESSIONAL JUDGEMENT IN GRADING

Teachers must be prepared to stand behind the assessment data they gather and communicate to students and parents and guardians. That said, classroom assessment has been described as more of an art than a science (Sutton, 1992). Since classroom assessment is a human process involving the interaction of teacher and students, it requires professional judgement.

All assessment involves a degree of measurement error, and class-room assessments, by their very nature, tend to be more prone to such error than standardized and provincial assessments. This should not be seen as a problem. Rather, it is a necessary condition of classroom assessment that is more than compensated for by the gains resulting from the one-on-one relationship between teacher and student.

However, professional judgement—an acceptable reality—should never be confused with subjectivity—a major source of assessment bias. Subjectivity in assessment is a different issue and a real problem. It flourishes when the standards for quality work are withheld from students, and when individual teachers develop their own specific assessment criteria, which can stray from established standards. In such situations, students' success has more to do with guessing what their teacher wants than it does with demonstrating proficiency.

The standards movement has seen a move toward clear, public, and shared statements about quality work. The identification of assessment criteria for student work and the sharing of exemplars with students are just two examples of how standards are made public so that teachers, students, and parents have a shared understanding of quality.

Yet even with these components in place, assessing a given task or performance requires that you make a professional judgement, and any judgement includes a degree of measurement error. If the student and parent wish, they may request a second judgement from another teacher in the same way that you may seek a second doctor's opinion regarding your health. A second opinion is helpful and can be viewed as a natural part of the assessment process.

Consider the case of Christine:

Christine and her classmates were asked to write a short report about a play they had read. Their teacher, Miss Keitel, provided a well-written rubric that clearly identified the assessment criteria for the report, as well as indicators at four levels of proficiency for each criterion.

When the report and rubric were returned to Christine, she was both surprised and disappointed. The rubric indicated which elements of her

> **Tips for Teaching**
>
> The weighting of tasks should always be determined as part of your assessment plan and be communicated to students at the beginning of the term.

report were strong and which areas needed improvement. A holistic evaluation of the report, based on her performance on each criterion, should have yielded a mark in the Level 2 range. Instead, Christine received a failing mark of less than Level 1. At her parents' urging, Christine spoke to her teacher about this apparent inconsistency.

Christine was permitted to rewrite the report and took advantage of the opportunity to improve on those criteria where she had performed poorly. Moreover, the rubric for the re-submitted report included an overall evaluation that was consistent with the scores on each criterion.

Christines' Story illustrates several points:

1. Classroom assessment involves the teacher's professional judgement.
2. Teachers must be able to defend their professional judgements.
3. There must be an appeal process that allows students and parents to question those professional judgements if they consider them to be faulty.

Summary

- Different kinds of information are communicated to students and parents and guardians about growth, progress, or achievement. It is important to be clear about which measures have been graded.
- Different reference points that may be used when grading include self-referenced, path-referenced, norm-referenced, and criterion-referenced. It is vital to specify which reference point is being used when grading student learning.
- The Ten Grading Guidelines (pages 257–258) can help with grading and report card completion. The accompanying case studies illustrate the application of each guideline.
- Professional judgement is vital when grading student learning, but should not be confused with subjectivity.

Applying My Learning

Locate *Assessing My School's Current Grading Practices* in Section 6 of Part 2. Examine the grading and reporting practices that are encouraged or mandated in your school or school district. Identify

- strengths in your current practice
- areas where you have concerns
- issues that should be raised with your principal or with other administrators in your district

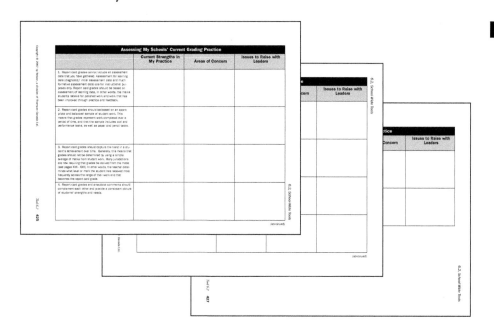

TOOL 6.2

Assessing My School's Current Grading Practices, pp. 425–427

Chapter 16

COMMUNICATING WITH PARENTS ABOUT STUDENT LEARNING

> **BIG IDEA 8** Grading and reporting student achievement is a caring, sensitive process that requires teachers' professional judgement.

GUIDELINES FOR COMMUNICATING WITH PARENTS

Assessment is a collaborative process, not something that teachers *do* to students.

Communicating frequently with students and parents is the best way to establish a climate that promotes learning. In the classroom, teachers are encouraged to communicate frequently with their students through

- informal chats and conferencing
- day-to-day interactions that are integral to the learning environment.

Video Clip 6:

A Three-Way Reporting Conference (Teacher/ Student/Parent)
06:45 minutes

While effective communication with parents requires some pre-planning the results make it worthwhile.

Effective communication with parents requires some effort and planning beyond formal reporting, but the results are clearly worth it. Just as assessment for learning leads to the greatest improvement in student achievement, frequent informal communication with parents about a student's progress offers them the clearest picture of their child's strengths and needs. Think of it this way: ongoing communication with parents about students' learning is assessment for learning; the report card is assessment of learning

How can you keep the communication process manageable? As was the case with classroom assessment, the sampling principle also applies to communication with parents. You may wish to

- draw up a schedule for contacting students' homes
- prioritize your class list according to most needy students and most pressing problems

- work through the class list by making a manageable number of home contacts at a convenient time each week
- set a goal of making contact with every parent at least once before the first reporting period
- keep parents connected by means of a regular newsletter sent home with students or distributed by e-mail

This chapter examines guidelines to follow when communicating formally and informally with parents. These guidelines apply equally to phone, e-mail, and face-to-face communication. Note also that this resource uses the term *parent* to refer to any adult responsible for the student at home, regardless of whether he or she is the child's parent, grandparent, or another legal guardian.

Although you must be realistic about the amount of time you have available to speak with parents, try to communicate more, rather than less frequently. You will never hear a parent complain about being contacted too often! However, principals do hear parents say, "We had no idea our child was having so much difficulty!"

Try to communicate more, rather than less frequently. You will never hear a parent complain about being contacted too often.

BEFORE COMMUNICATION

Any time you contact parents, be clear about the specific purpose for the contact. For example, your overall purpose in speaking with parents before the first report card would be to secure their assistance in facilitating their child's learning and school success. Other purposes for contacting parents might include

- identifying a child's strengths and needs, and sharing your plans to address those needs
- seeking support to help a child overcome difficulties
- celebrating a child's academic or non-academic successes
- helping parents understand their child's growth, progress or achievement

When drawing up your schedule for contacting parents, begin with those students who exhibit the most serious issues. Communicate early and frequently when there are serious learning difficulties such as a significant lack of progress or a failure to complete assigned work.

Prepare thoroughly before initiating communication with parents. This means

- knowing your purpose for communicating
- knowing what you want to say
- having evidence, such as work samples and assessment data, ready and organized to support your comments

> ### Tips for Teaching
>
> It often helps to think of effective communication as the "no surprises" approach. In other words, an important goal of ongoing communication with parents is ensuring there are no surprises at report card time.

- being familiar with the contents of Individualized Education Plans (IEP) for identified students
- being prepared to record the details of the conversation and date of contact

With these preparatory steps completed, you are ready to make contact with parents. The following guidelines will help ensure that the communication is productive for the child, for you, and for the parents.

DURING COMMUNICATION

Keep these three simple criteria in mind when communicating with parents, whether your communication is in person, on the phone, through e-mail, or in a letter:

1. Is the purpose of this communication clear?
2. Is the communication appropriate for the intended audience?
3. Does the communication convey a clear message?

Face-to-Face Meetings

It is usually preferable to talk with, instead of about, a student. Whenever possible, include the child in the communication. These meetings are often referred to as three-way conferences. Share your agenda immediately with parents. However brief the meeting, take time to share your observations and to listen to the parent and child.

Always remain professional, polite, and respectful. Most teachers have experienced meetings with parents where the frustration level has almost boiled over. Nevertheless, it is important to remain calm and, even when provoked, to resist becoming defensive. In potentially contentious situations, well-organized assessment data and carefully chosen student work samples will help support your observations and counter conflicting statements made by parents.

Although it is important to be articulate and professional, some teachers alienate parents by using "teacher-talk." Be mindful of your audience—they are parents, *not* teachers. Avoid using acronyms such as HOTS and USSR, or referring to educational trends such as "brain-compatible learning." These terms are appropriate when communicating with your colleagues, but if used in conversations with parents, they may cause confusion and obscure the important information that parents need to know.

> **Tips for Teaching**
>
> There may be occasions when it is inappropriate to include the child in a parent meeting. When the purpose of the meeting is to discuss a child's exceptionality, it is usually best to meet with the parents alone.

Strengths, Needs, and Next Steps

The "strengths, needs, next steps" agenda is most useful when meeting with parents directly or when communicating with them by phone or e-mail.

This agenda reflects the importance of beginning with the good news—the "strengths." The advantage is obvious: it sets a positive tone, and parents hear first about their child's success. Make reference to a specific piece of work or performance that demonstrates a child's depth of understanding or mastery of skills. For example, you might say the following about Theresa:

> *Theresa delivered an excellent oral report about Canada's First Nations. She included plenty of specific details and spoke in a clear and convincing way. She even handled the questions from her classmates confidently and didn't hesitate to say "I'm not sure" when I asked her a question she didn't know the answer to.*

When selecting performances or samples of work to describe or show to parents, ensure that the work represents their child's achievement of essential learning, not minor aspects of the curriculum.

The "needs" portion of the communication or meeting agenda—discussing the difficulties students are experiencing—is extremely important. Always differentiate between achievement problems (cognition and skills) and problems related to behavioural, social, or learning habits. Although a child's achievement is often highly correlated with these variables, the two areas are distinct. Consider, for example, how this teacher describes the way a child is struggling with achievement and learning habits and how the teacher helps the parents understand the connection between these two kinds of assessment data.

Help parents understand the connection—and difference—between problems arising from achievement and those arising from behaviour, social issues, or learning habits.

> *You can see from Roberto's report card that he has a D in social studies. If you look at his learning habits, you'll see that I've indicated "Needs Improvement" in both "Independent Work" and "Use of Information." What this means is Roberto has not yet acquired the research skills he needs to be able to conduct his own inquiries—things like how to locate information in books and on the Internet. One reason he is falling behind is that he seems reluctant to try for himself the skills that I've been teaching. He generally prefers to ask me for help before attempting to problem solve.*

Combining disparate kinds of results into a single summary should be done cautiously. To the extent possible, achievement, effort, participation, and other behaviours should be graded separately.
Principles for Fair Student Assessment Practices for Education in Canada

When describing a child's progress and achievement, it may be helpful for parents if you make reference to the appropriate standards. Consider, for example, how this teacher quotes the relevant curriculum document almost verbatim to provide Brad's parents with clear and specific information about an area of need:

> *In the Grade 3 Language Arts program, children are expected to consider other's ideas and observations to help them discover and explore their own understanding of books that we read and videos that we watch. Brad is struggling with this outcome because he tends to dominate discussion and is reluctant to listen to what other children have to say.*

(Adapted from *WNCP curriculum*, 1998)

Provincial standards across Canada reflect a criterion-referenced model, not a norm-referenced approach (see pages 242–243.) This means that comparisons between students are not appropriate, nor is it appropriate to label students by either their typical or expected level of performance. Such practices may lead to statements such as, "Elizabeth is an A student; I can't understand why she did so poorly on this project," or, "Sophia was always an A student; I can't believe her brother is so different." There are no A or C students—there are only A and C performances! Any student is capable of producing A-quality work on any given day. Prejudging students according to their histories or past performance, or according to their siblings' performance, can seriously bias your assessment of their performance and distort their actual achievement.

Similarly, no such bias should come into play when communicating with parents. Some of the truly magical moments of teaching occur when a child who has been struggling suddenly produces a piece of excellent work. It is a measure of our skill as teachers to remain constantly open to what each student may achieve, regardless of past performance.

The final phase of communication with parents concerns the "next steps." This is the time to talk to parents about specific suggestions for helping and supporting their children in the areas that have been identified as problematic for them. To make this part of the meeting as productive as possible, quickly and informally assess the parents' ability to help their child. For example, if the parents are not fluent in either English or French, they will be limited in their ability to help their child's progress in language. You may also wish to find out about the suitability of the home learning environment by asking questions such as the following:

It is a measure of our skill as teachers to remain open to what each student may achieve, regardless of past performance.

- Where does Jon do his homework? (This is preferable to "Does Jon have a quiet place to work?" which may not reveal the truth!)
- Does Jon spend time reading at home?
- Do Jon's siblings help him with his math work?

Provide parents with specific, easy-to-understand suggestions about what they can do at home to support their child's learning. For example:

- Set aside a specific time after school each day for your child to do homework. Be available to help your child without doing the work for him or her.
- Demonstrate interest in your child's learning by asking to see what he or she is working on. Talk to young children about their school experiences and discuss what they are learning. Let your child describe what is fun to learn and what is challenging or confusing.
- Ask your child every day, "How was school today? Tell me the most interesting thing that happened." Questions like this might elicit information about bullying situations or general emotional well-being.
- Demonstrate literacy and numeracy in your daily routines, for example, by reading newspapers, writing grocery lists, measuring, or calculating the cost of something.
- Provide hands-on activities for young children such as preparing food, doing arts and crafts, and playing letter and word games.
- Read to and with your child from a variety of materials.
- Keep a fridge calendar that shows important dates about school projects and school events.
- Limit television and other "technology time," especially if your child is having difficulty completing school work.

> **Tips for Teaching**
>
> When making suggestions about improving or altering the home learning environment, be careful to avoid comments that may be in conflict with certain cultural norms.

When meeting with parents, be clear on who is responsible for what: the child, the parents, and you, the teacher, all have different responsibilities.

Occasionally during a parent meeting, you may sense that the discussion is moving into territory that is outside your jurisdiction. If this occurs, do not hesitate to say, "You need to speak to my principal about that."

For example, in districts where new grading and reporting procedures have been introduced, parents may complain about the new system. It is not your responsibility as a classroom teacher to debate the reasons for such changes; you only need to know how the changes affect your own grading and reporting practices and be able to explain how you followed these procedures in determining grades and comments.

> **Tips for Teaching**
>
> Even when you have done everything possible to promote success for a particular student, that child may still refuse to work in a way that is consistent with his or her potential. Always keep a record of the actions you have taken to help this student achieve success.

Report Card Comments

In many parts of the country, teachers have little flexibility when composing report card comments. For example, where computerized comment banks are mandated, the composition process may simply require teachers to "point and click." However, you can still critically examine the process used to generate report cards and how effectively it communicates useful information to parents.

Comments written on the final report cards have less potential to influence student learning, but interim report cards are formative reports that play a critical role in promoting student learning. Therefore, avoid jargon and remember the three criteria to use when communicating to parents:

1. Is the purpose of this communication clear?
2. Is the communication appropriate for the intended audience?
3. Does the communication include a clear message?

Let's use these criteria to assess the quality of the report card comments that might appear as part of a Grade 4 student's science grade, as shown in Figure 16-1.

Figure 16-1: Report Card Comments (Sample 1)

Strengths and Needs

· usually provides nearly complete explanations

· demonstrates some understanding of habitat and community

· identifies factors that could affect habitats and communities of plants and animals

· investigates the dependency of plants and animals on their habitat

Next Steps

· communicate ideas with increased clarity and precision

---

1. Is the purpose of this communication clear?

The purpose of interim report card comments should be to

■ summarize learning up to that point, and

■ indicate to parents any concerns and problems that may exist. Comments should not comprise a list of learning outcomes extracted from provincial curriculum documents.

2. Is the communication appropriate for the intended audience?

Since the intended audience is the student's parents, care must be taken to ensure that the language used is easy to understand and free of educators' professional language.

3. Does the communication convey a clear message?

A report card comment should communicate to parents a clear, general sense of whether their child is progressing well or is struggling, with respect to the standards.

These comments fail on all three counts! Now, apply the same criteria to assess the quality of the report card comments for the same student, shown in Figure 16-2.

Figure 16-2: Report Card Comments (Sample 2)

Strengths and Needs

Tim's journal shows some understanding of the concepts of habitat and community, and factors affecting them. However, his explanations are incomplete. During investigations, Tim used some of the required skills to understand how plants and animals depend on habitat.

Next Steps

Tim needs to use all information available to add clarity and detail to his work. He also needs to pose more questions during investigations.

These comments meet all three criteria:

1. Their purpose is clear; they summarize learning and point out areas of concern.
2. Although the language is specific, both the syntax and diction make the comments easy to understand for parents.
3. The comments convey an overall message about Tim's progress to date.

Although space constraints may seriously limit the amount of detail in your comments, make sure you include a "strength," a "need," and a "next step." The challenge is to do so in a way that refers to the curriculum but uses a lay person's language, not "teacher-talk."

Another problem manifests itself when report card comments make little or no reference to achievement and focus instead on the personality of a child with remarks such as "Cindy is a delightful child and a pleasure to have in the class." Such comments are never appropriate or helpful and, in today's context of curriculum standards and increased accountability, they should be avoided. The following guidelines for communicating with parents will ensure that such comments do not appear on report cards.

1. When composing report card comments or speaking informally to parents, focus on the quality of work completed or the skills demonstrated, not the personality of the student.

2. In all communication with parents, clearly identify whether you are discussing a child's progress and achievement, or behavioural issues.

It is encouraging to note that in many districts report card formats are providing separate areas for the teacher to summarize information about achievement and information about learning/social skills/habits. See Case Study 9, page 267, in Chapter 15 for an illustration of this principle.

AFTER COMMUNICATION

In the "after-communication" phase, the goal is to monitor the extent to which the "next steps" have occurred. To facilitate this monitoring, write down any decisions made as a result of communication with parents, and record any follow-up strategies that you, the parents, or the student agreed to try. This record should describe everyone's responsibilities and include a timeline and a date for the next progress check. Specify also the form of communication that will be used for the next progress check (phone call, email, face-to-face meeting).

The template shown in Figure 16-3 may be useful for keeping track of your communications with parents. (For a reproducible version of this template, see Part 2, page 296.)

TOOL 1.9

Record of Communication.
p. 296

Figure 16-3: Record of Communication

296 *Tool 1.9*

1.9, Chapter 16 Review

Record of Communication

Use this chart to record details of all communication with parents and guardians.

Student	Date	Communication Method	Contact	Strengths, Needs, Next Steps	Follow-up Actions/ Dates

Summary

Before Communication

- Frequent communication with students and parents is the best way to establish collaboration. It is better to err on the side of too much communication, rather than too little.
- The goal of communicating with students and parents is to avoid any surprises at report card time.
- Be clear on the purpose for communicating, whether it be to
  - identify strengths and needs,
  - seek support from parents,
  - celebrate successes, or
  - help parents understand their child's growth, progress or achievement.
- Prepare thoroughly before initiating communication: understand the purpose, know what to say, and have evidence of the student's achievement to back up comments.
- Early and frequent communication is advisable when there are serious learning difficulties.

During Communication

Use the following guidelines to ensure more effective communication with parents:

- Communicate by phone or e-mail before the first report card and between report cards.
- Communicate good news as well as concerns.
- When meeting in person, establish an agenda quickly.
- In report card comments and during informal communications, speak about the quality of the work, not the personality of the student.
- In all communications, differentiate between growth/progress/achievement issues and behavioural issues.
- When speaking about growth, progress or achievement, reference appropriate standards (i.e., provincial curriculum outcomes and performance standards, school and district standards).
- Avoid making any comparisons to other students, including siblings.
- Avoid labelling students.
- Be mindful of your audience; do not use "teacher-talk" in report card comments or when communicating with parents.

- Always be polite and respectful.
- Communicate achievement information about essential learning, not minor aspects of the curriculum.
- Be clear on who—teacher, student, parent—is responsible for what in terms of next steps.
- Provide specific, easy-to-understand suggestions for what parents can do at home to support their child's learning.
- Know your rights and responsibilities as a teacher. Do not hesitate to say, "You need to speak to my principal about that," if issues are raised that exceed your responsibilities.

After Communication

Write down any decisions that have been made or follow-up strategies that will be tried as a result of a meeting with parents.

Applying My Learning

Convene a group of colleagues and, discuss how you might use the *Record of Communication* for one term. Arrange to meet periodically throughout the term to review your experiences.

TOOL 1.9

Record of Communication.
p. 296

Record of Communication

Use this chart to record details of all communication with parents and guardians.

Student	Date	Communication Method	Contact	Strengths, Needs, Next Steps	Follow-up Actions/ Dates

296 Tool 1.9

1.9, Chapter 16 Review

Copyright © 2007 by Nelson, a division of Thomson Canada Ltd.

PART 2:   TOOLS TO IMPROVE STUDENT LEARNING

NOTE

All tools are available in modifiable format on the CD-ROM.

Part 2 Contents

Section 1 Tools

Applying My Learning

In this section, you'll find activities that provide opportunities to apply your learning from *Talk About Assessment*, as well as an Implementation Profile to help you assess your own progress as you try new assessment approaches.

Some of the activities ask that you self-assess your current practices and identify areas where you see the need to make changes, based on suggestions contained in the corresponding chapter. Other activities suggest that you meet with colleagues and either examine together some elements of your current practice or explore a new strategy to improve your practice.

How Does My Current Assessment Toolkit Shape Up?

Criterion	Maintain / Modify / Change Practice
1. Does my assessment toolkit promote student learning?	
2. Is my assessment toolkit responsive to individual student needs?	
3. Do I use data from my assessment toolkit to adjust instruction for individual students and for the whole class?	
4. Do the elements of my assessment toolkit that I use for reporting include a sufficient sample of learning?	
5. Are all of the components in my assessment toolkit valid measures of what I intend to assess?	
6. Are all of the components in my assessment toolkit reliable measures of what I intend to assess?	
7. Is my assessment toolkit for this class manageable for me in terms of workload?	

Implementing Assessment *for* Learning in My Classroom

Use the chart below to examine your current practice. Your responses will likely affirm many of the strategies you are presently using, but you may also discover some areas where you may wish to try different approaches to better meet the needs of your students.

After you have finished checking off your responses, describe on this chart or in a journal what you plan to do to include this strategy in your repertoire.

R = Rarely   S = Sometimes   C = Consistently

Do I?	R ✓	S ✓	C ✓	Notes
1. Do I share learning goals with my students so they know where we are heading?				
2. Do I communicate to students the standards they are aiming for **before** they begin work on a task?				
3. Do I have students self- and peer assess their work in ways that improve their learning?				
4. Does my questioning technique include **all** students and promote increased understanding?				
5. Do I provide individual feedback to students that informs them how to improve?				
6. Do I provide opportunities for students to make use of this feedback to improve specific pieces of work?				

Classroom Observation of a Student with Special Needs

Complete the following anecdotal record for one of your special needs students. When finished, determine how effective you were in assessing that student's strengths and needs, based on what you saw and heard.

To maximize the reliability of your observational assessment, complete this record during the first few days that you are working with a student. Repeat the process periodically throughout the term.

Name: _____	Class: _____	Date: _____
Observations and Notes		

Response to texts:	**Response to assigned tasks:**
Persistence with tasks:	**Organization** (self, time, materials):
Use of oral language (fluency, willingness to speak):	**Work preference** (individual, partner, group):
Response to teacher cues (auditory, visual, proximity):	**Response to authority:**
Interactions with peers:	**Environmental preferences** (desk arrangement, time of day, light, sound, etc.):

Assessing My Current Use of Performance Standards

R = Rarely   S = Sometimes   C = Consistently

Self-Assessment Questions	Current Practice			Maintain / Modify / Change Practice
	R ✓	**S** ✓	**C** ✓	
Before teaching: 1. Do I understand our local/provincial performance standards? (That is, do I have an overall sense of what Level 4 represents as opposed to Level 3, and so on?) 2. Have I created and/or located appropriate assessment tools (rubrics, checklists, etc.) based on the mandated standards? 3. Have I taken steps to ensure that students and parents become familiar with these tools? (For example, have I posted rubrics on the bulletin board, provided students with copies of rubrics, sent rubrics home for parents to see, and so on?) 4. Am I collecting samples and maintaining collections of student work from previous classes that are anchored to the standards? 5. Do I negotiate assessment criteria with my students?				
During teaching: 6. Do I use the tools—rubrics, checklists, exemplars—to provide regular feedback to students? 7. Do I teach students the skills required to use these tools for self- and peer assessment?				
After teaching: 8. Do I use these tools to help make professional judgments about students' achievement? 9. Do I engage in periodic moderation (group marking with other teachers, using work samples, rubrics, and exemplars) to ensure a collective agreement about our performance standards? 10. Do I refer to these standards when communicating with students and parents about achievement?				

Examining My Co-operative Group Learning Assessment Practices

R = Rarely   S = Sometimes   C = Consistently

Guideline	Current Practice			Maintain / Modify / Change Practice
	R ✓	**S** ✓	**C** ✓	
1. Ensure fair and appropriate grouping of students for summative tasks.				
2. Clearly indicate timelines and due dates for the process components and the final products to impress upon students the need to be responsible to the group.				
3. Provide students with appropriate teacher, self- and/or peer assessment tools.				
4. Ensure that each student has fully understood the essential learning included in the task by including a brief written or oral defence as a check for understanding.				
5. Assign an individual mark to each student for a work log or journal used to record learning during the process.				
6. Assess each student individually for work habits demonstrated during the process.				
7. Assign a group mark* to any product that the group is responsible for, such as a model or an audio-visual presentation.				
8. Provide opportunities for students to assess their own work and that of their peers.				
9. *All* marks, scores, or levels for all components of the task are assigned by the teacher, not by the students.				

* Mark may be a rubric level or letter grade.

How Balanced Is My Assessment Toolkit?		
Assessment Mode and Strategy	**Assessment Purpose**	**Assessment Tool**
Oral Communication Conference Informal discussion Oral questioning/defence Structured talk with peer	provide feedback on work assess skills (e.g., reading) assess depth of understanding assess depth of understanding	Anecdotal record
Performance Assessments Skills demonstration	assess level of performance of skills	Checklist/rubric/rating scale
Design project Inquiry/investigation Media product Simulation	assess application of knowledge and skills assess understanding	Checklist/rubric
Presentation Role-play	assess understanding and communication skills	Checklist/rubric
Written Assessments **Quizzes/Tests** Selected response Short answer Extended response	assess knowledge assess knowledge assess knowledge and understanding	Scoring guide Scoring guide Marking scheme
Graphic Organizers Mind map Word web	assess understanding assess understanding	Rubric Rubric
Extended Writing Article Brochure Report Review	assess depth of understanding assess communication skills	Rubric/checklist
Journal Portfolio	assess metacognition	Rubric/checklist

Evaluating the Quality of a Performance Task		
Quality Criterion	**Evaluation of Task*** **(✓) or (✗)**	**Maintain / Modify / Change**
Task provides evidence of essential learning		
Task demands innovation and creativity on the part of the student		
Task presents students with an engaging challenge that requires persistence to complete		
Task engages students in problem solving and decision making		
Task is appropriate for all students		
If task involves co-operative groups, there is provision for individual accountability		
Assessment criteria for task reflect the essential learning		
Assessment criteria are communicated in student-friendly language before students begin work		

* Meets individual criterion or is substandard

Professional Learning in Assessment: Implementation Profile

Use this profile to track your improvement as you implement new assessment practices. You may wish to assess your practice three times: currently (Initial), after several months (Formative), and at the end of the year (Summative). To record your data, simply write I, F, or S in the space provided under the appropriate column to indicate whether it is an **I**nitial, **F**ormative, or **S**ummative assessment. Ideally, all "S" indicators will be in the last column. Once you've completed the checklist, review the pattern of indicators you have entered. Determine which description best summarizes your practice at this time.

	Beginning	On My Way	I'm There!
	I am just beginning to use the following practices and strategies as I try to improve the quality and effectiveness of my assessment practice, but I am tentative and still need a lot of support	I am feeling more comfortable using the following practices and strategies to improve the quality and effectiveness of my assessment practice, and I need only minimal support	I have mastered the following practices and strategies for improving the quality and effectiveness of my assessment practice, and I routinely use them
Planning			
· Design down from big ideas and essential skills when planning units			
· Design down from learning goals when lesson planning			
Assessment for Learning			
· Adjust assessment processes appropriately to meet the needs of all students			
· Include regular opportunities for students to demonstrate their learning through performance and oral tasks, as well as written tasks			
· Adjust instruction for groups of students based on assessment data			
· Provide regular and specific feedback to students to help them improve			
· Provide students with assessment criteria before they begin work on a task			
· Provide opportunities for students to redo their work, incorporating feedback			
Assessment of Learning			
· Identify a sufficient and appropriate sample of essential learning for purposes of grading			
· Use an effective process for tracking and recording achievement			

Record of Communication

Use this chart to record details of all communication with parents and guardians.

Student	Date	Communication Method	Contact	Strengths, Needs, Next Steps	Follow-up Actions / Dates

Program Planning Templates and Sample Units

Sample Units

In this section, you'll find the four program planning templates that are described in detail in Chapter 13. You will also find several sample units created by teachers using these templates.

Feel free to modify the templates to suit your own needs, or to use only one or two of them if you are pressed for time. A template is only helpful if it meets your particular needs, so experiment, modify, and play with these materials until they enable you to plan effectively and efficiently.

Overview: The Program Planning Process

Template 1

Includes Units/Strands for Whole Year
For each unit, includes:
- Big Ideas/Essential Skills
- Culminating Task

Template 2

Provides Overview of One Unit
Includes:
- Big Ideas/Essential Skills
- Culminating Task
- Formative/Enabling Tasks
- Curriculum Outcomes
- Learning Skills

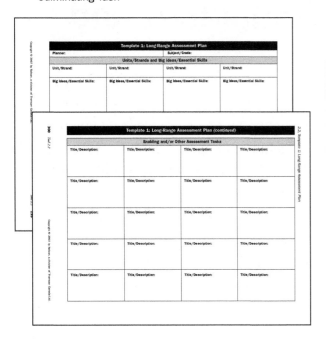

Template 3

Provides One Culminating Task in Detail
Includes:
- Description of Task
- Big Ideas/Essential Skills
- Curriculum Outcomes
- Learning Skills
- Student Products and Assessment Criteria

Template 4

Lists Sequence of Lessons for One Unit
Includes:
- Lesson sequence
- Resources and Accommodations

Note: While the numbering of the templates suggests a chronological sequence, teachers typically find that they move back and forth between the templates as they plan. For example, you may find it necessary to complete work on Template 3: Culminating Assessment Task Plan before identifying the Enabling Tasks on Template 2. You may also leave your Long Range Assessment Plan until you've developed all of your units in detail using Templates 2 through 4.

Template 1: Long-Range Assessment Plan

Planner: **Subject/Grade:**

Units/Strands and Big Ideas/Essential Skills

Unit/Strand:

Big Ideas/Essential Skills:

Unit/Strand:

Big Ideas/Essential Skills:

Unit/Strand:

Big Ideas/Essential Skills:

Unit/Strand:

Big Ideas/Essential Skills:

Culminating Tasks

Title/Description:

Title/Description:

Title/Description:

Title/Description:

(continued)

Template 1: Long-Range Assessment Plan (*continued*)

Enabling and/or Other Assessment Tasks

Title/Description:	Title/Description:	Title/Description:
Title/Description:	Title/Description:	Title/Description:
Title/Description:	Title/Description:	Title/Description:
Title/Description:	Title/Description:	Title/Description:
Title/Description:	Title/Description:	Title/Description:

Template 2: Unit Curriculum and Assessment Plan

Unit/Strand:

Focus for Learning:

Big Ideas and Essential Skills:

Title/Description of Culminating Task:

Enabling and/or Other Assessment Tasks

Learning Habits:

Title:		Curriculum Outcomes/Content Standards:
Diagnostic/Formative	Write/Do/Say	

Learning Habits:

Title:		Curriculum Outcomes/Content Standards:
Diagnostic/Formative	Write/Do/Say	

Learning Habits:

Title:		Curriculum Outcomes/Content Standards:
Diagnostic/Formative	Write/Do/Say	

Learning Habits:

Title:		Curriculum Outcomes/Content Standards:
Diagnostic/Formative	Write/Do/Say	

Template 3: Unit Culminating Assessment Task Plan

Unit:

Assessment Task Title:

Description of Task:

Curriculum Outcomes/Content Standards:

Big Ideas:

Essential Skills:

Student Products and Processes

Assessment Strategy 1:

Assessment Tool:

Assessment Criteria:

Assessment Strategy 2:

Assessment Tool:

Assessment Criteria:

Assessment Strategy 3:

Assessment Tool:

Assessment Criteria:

Resources/Technology Integration:

Accommodations/Modifications:

Cross-Curricular Integration:

Template 4: Unit Instruction Plan/Lesson Sequence

Unit:	Focus for Learning:
Introduction	
Lesson 2:	
Lesson 3:	
Lesson 4:	
Lesson 5:	
Lesson 6:	
Lesson 7:	
Lesson 8:	
Culminating Task	

Sample Unit: Grade 2 Science—Unit Curriculum and Assessment Plan

Unit/Strand: Butterflies, Reptiles, and Animals

Focus for Learning: Life Systems (Science)/Grade 2

Big Ideas:
- All insects, reptiles, and animals go through distinct life cycles.
- There are similarities and differences among insects, reptiles, and animals.
- Insects, reptiles, and animals react differently to the seasons.

Essential Skills:
- data collection
- observation skills
- recording information: written, pictorial, charts, and graphs
- following directions
- using information technology
- written, oral, and presentation skills

Title/Description of Culminating Task:

Your class has been asked to create an exhibit in the Library that will display information about Life Systems, particularly insects, reptiles, and animals. This exhibit will be visited by other students and parents.

Your class will be responsible for creating and setting up the displays as well as giving tours of the exhibit.

You and your classmates will:
- research insects, reptiles, and animals,
- create art exhibits, booklets, and posters to present your findings,
- create and provide information that will guide visitors through the exhibits.

Enabling and/or Other Assessment Tasks

Learning Habits	Task	Curriculum Outcomes/Standards
Learning Habits: Independence	**Title:** Create a model of a specific type of butterfly with body parts labelled. **Diagnostic/Formative:** F **Write/Do/Say:** W & D	**Curriculum Outcomes/Standards:** · Describe the major physical characteristics of different types of animals (insects, reptiles, mammals). · Produce two- and three-dimensional works of art that communicate ideas. · Identify the characteristics of symmetrical shapes and forms.
Learning Habits: Initiative	**Title:** Create an accordion booklet to illustrate and record the life cycle of a butterfly. **Diagnostic/Formative:** F **Write/Do/Say:** W & D	**Curriculum Outcomes/Standards:** · Describe changes in the appearance and activity of an animal as it goes through its life cycle. · Describe ways that animals respond and adapt to their environment. · Communicate messages, and follow instructions and directions.
Learning Habits: Use of information	**Title:** Construct an observation chamber for watching a chrysalis hatch and keep a journal of events. **Diagnostic/Formative:** F **Write/Do/Say:** W & D	**Curriculum Outcomes/Standards:** · Describe changes in the appearance and activity of an animal as it goes through its life cycle. · Record relevant observations, findings, and measurements, using written language, drawings, and concrete materials.
Learning Habits: Homework completion	**Title:** Create a dialogue that can be used as a guided tour of the exhibit (written and oral). **Diagnostic/Formative:** F **Write/Do/Say:** W & S	**Curriculum Outcomes/Standards:** · Describe the major physical characteristics of different types of animals (insects, reptiles, mammals). · Describe ways that animals respond and adapt to their environment. · Communicate messages, and follow instructions and directions.

(continued)

Unit Curriculum and Assessment Plan (*continued*)

Enabling and/or Other Assessment Tasks

Learning Habits	Enabling and/or Other Assessment Tasks	Curriculum Outcomes/Standards
Learning Habits: Use of information	**Title:** Use a graphic organizer to gather information about the life cycle of a reptile. **Diagnostic/Formative:** D **Write/Do/Say:** W	**Curriculum Outcomes/Standards:** · Identify and use a variety of sources of science information and ideas. · Record relevant observations, findings, and measurements, using written language, drawings, and concrete materials.
Learning Habits: Initiative	**Title:** Create and present a poster highlighting significant features of the life cycle of their reptile. **Diagnostic/Formative:** F **Write/Do/Say:** W, D, & S	**Curriculum Outcomes/Standards:** · Describe changes in the appearance and activity of an animal as it goes through its life cycle. · Describe ways that animals respond and adapt to their environment. · Communicate procedures and results using drawings, demonstrations, and written and oral descriptions.
Learning Habits: Use of information	**Title:** Use a different graphic organizer to gather information about a selected animal. **Diagnostic/Formative:** F **Write/Do/Say:** W	**Curriculum Outcomes/Standards:** · Identify and use a variety of sources of science information and ideas. · Record relevant observations, findings, and measurements, using written language, drawings, and concrete materials.
Learning Habits: Independent work	**Title:** Create a pop-up book as a means to present the information about the animal they researched. **Diagnostic/Formative:** F **Write/Do/Say:** W & D	**Curriculum Outcomes/Standards:** · Produce two- and three-dimensional works of art that communicate ideas. · Describe the major physical characteristics of different types of animals (insects, reptiles, mammals). · Describe ways that animals respond and adapt to their environment. · Communicate messages, and follow instructions and directions.
Learning Habits: Co-operation	**Title:** The students will work in groups of five to prepare a chart that will compare the similarities and differences of their animals. **Diagnostic/Formative:** F **Write/Do/Say:** W & S	**Curriculum Outcomes/Standards:** · Describe the major physical characteristics of different types of animals (insects, reptiles, mammals). · Compare ways different animals care for their young. · Compare the life cycles of familiar animals and describe the major physical characteristics; classify them according to their similarities and differences. · Describe ways that animals respond and adapt to their environment.

Unit Culminating Assessment Task Plan

Unit/Strand: Butterflies, Reptiles, and Animals

Assessment Task Title: The Library Exhibit

Description of Task: Your class has been asked to create an exhibit in the library that will display information about Life Systems, particularly insects, reptiles, and animals. This exhibit will be visited by other students and parents.

Your class will be responsible for creating and setting up the displays, as well as giving tours of the exhibit.

You and your classmates will:
- research insects, reptiles, and animals,
- create art exhibits, booklets, and posters to present your findings,
- create and provide information that will guide visitors through the exhibits.

Big Ideas:
- All insects, reptiles, and animals go through distinct life cycles.
- There are similarities and differences among insects, reptiles, and animals.
- Insects, reptiles, and animals react differently to the seasons.

Essential Skills:
- data collection
- observation skills
- recording information: written, pictorial, charts, and graphs
- following directions
- using information technology
- written, oral, and presentation skills

Curriculum Outcomes/Standards:
- Describe the major physical characteristics of different types of animals (insects, reptiles, mammals).
- Describe changes in the appearance and activity of an animal as it goes through its life cycle.
- Describe ways that animals respond and adapt to their environment.
- Communicate procedures and results using drawings, demonstrations, and written and oral descriptions.
- Produce two- and three-dimensional works of art that communicate ideas.
- Communicate messages, and follow instructions and directions.

Student Products and Processes

Assessment Strategy 1: Students select one of their products for summative assessment (butterfly model, accordion booklet, poster, or pop-up book)

Assessment Tool: Self-assessment checklist and rubric

Assessment Criteria: understanding concepts, written and visual communication skills, attention to detail, and overall quality

Assessment Strategy 2: Dialogue for Guided Tour

Assessment Tool: Self-assessment checklist and rubric

Assessment Criteria: understanding concepts, oral communication skills (organization, diction), quality of recorded or spoken communication (fluency, audibility, intonation)

Unit Instruction Plan/Lesson Sequence

Unit/Strand: Butterflies, Reptiles, and Animals

Focus for Learning: Life Systems (Science)/Grade 2

Introduction

The teacher introduces the Life Systems unit, describing its three major parts: Butterflies, Reptiles, and Animals. The teacher emphasizes that the unit will end with a culminating exhibit in the library to which other students, teachers, and parents will be invited.

As each section of the unit is introduced, the teacher describes what will be completed and assessed in preparation for the culminating task.

Lesson 1:

The teacher introduces the topic of butterflies using a "What We Know About Butterflies" chart. The teacher records the students' ideas. A large poster of a butterfly is posted. Word cards with butterfly body parts are also presented. Together, the class labels the butterfly beginning with the most logical parts. Definitions are provided by the teacher as more sophisticated parts are labelled (antenna, thorax, abdomen, proboscis). The students spend the remainder of the class looking at a wide variety of books about butterflies in order to select one that they will recreate as a model in art period.

Lesson 2:

The teacher removes the labels from the butterfly and has the class work together to re-label the parts of the butterfly, this time eliciting the definitions from the students. The teacher introduces the concept of symmetry by showing the students how the butterfly can be folded in half lengthwise and each side will be the same, or symmetrical. On a previous day, the students have used a variety of widths of brushes and colours of paint to completely cover large pieces of white paper. Using Eric Carle illustrations such as those found in *Brown Bear, Brown Bear* as a model, the teacher shows the class how shapes can be cut from the paper and glued on to a template to make a butterfly. The students then take a large piece of white paper and fold it in half. After they have drawn half a butterfly they cut it out to be used as a template. Referring to the picture they chose from a book, the students cut and paste pieces to create the designs of the wings symmetrically. Finally the head, eyes, thorax, abdomen, and antenna are added. Once named and labelled, the finished products will make a colourful part of the culminating butterfly exhibit. As students are completing their pieces, the teacher is circulating and asking each student to name the butterfly parts. Results are recorded on an "At-a-Glance" page.

Lesson 3:

The teacher reads *The Very Hungry Caterpillar* by Eric Carle. The teacher has the students recall the stages in the life cycle and records them on chart paper. The students then discuss each stage in the life cycle. The teacher provides a cut-and-paste page with the stages of development recorded in words and in pictures. The students are to cut out the pieces and match the words to the correct stage of development in the correct order. They then glue them to paper and colour the pictures. The whole class has a choral reading of the finished products to reinforce the vocabulary and the sequence of a butterfly's development.

Lesson 4:

Students follow directions from the teacher to create an accordion book that has four sections with four flaps that lift up. (Illustration can be included here.) Each flap will be labelled with a stage in the cycle in order (egg, larva, pupa, adult). Students draw a picture to illustrate each stage in the cycle. Under each flap they record in their own words facts about that stage.

Lesson 5:

The teacher introduces the concept of watching a butterfly hatch from its chrysalis. She or he has collected or purchased a chrysalis for each student. Students will need to construct a place to keep the chrysalis safe yet be able to watch it hatch. The teacher posts step-by-step instructions and models each step in constructing a box. Each student constructs a box. The teacher circulates and provides assistance as needed. The teacher also keeps notes on each student's ability to follow the illustrated instructions and work independently or with another student. Journals will be kept as the students observe the butterfly hatching.

(continued)

Unit Instruction Plan/Lesson Sequence (continued)

Unit/Strand: Butterflies, Reptiles, and Animals | **Focus For Learning:** Life Systems (Science)/Grade 2

Lesson 6:
Time will be provided for the teacher to guide the students in a discussion about how to display the information in the exhibit. This may be reserved for the completed exhibit with the reptile and animal sections. Once the material has been posted, the students create their own tour commentary based on the way they will move through the exhibit and what information they want to feature. The teacher has a conference with each student to assess the content of their "tour" and to provide any necessary feedback. The students can practise together, or the teacher may choose to have a few exemplary "tours" given for the class as models.

Lesson 7:
The teacher introduces the topic of reptiles and the task of gathering information about a variety of different reptiles to be presented in the exhibition. Through discussion the class decides what information should be reported on. This would include appearance, habitat, food, and life cycle. Each student has the opportunity to look through a variety of resources and select a reptile on which to gather information.

Lesson 8:
A graphic organizer is presented with the headings determined from the last lesson. The teacher models how to use a table of contents and chapter headings to locate relevant information. Making point-form or jot notes is also modelled. With the assistance of the teacher and the teacher librarian, the students gather information about their reptile. A conference is held with each student to check that all necessary information has been recorded.

Lesson 9:
A variety of posters are provided for the students to examine. A discussion follows about the important features of a good poster. These would include layout, size and number of words, visual illustrations, and overall appeal. Based on the information the students gathered on their reptiles, the students have a clear idea of what will be presented on their poster. Appropriate time is given to design and create the posters.

Lesson 10:
Students are guided in a discussion about how to appropriately present their information to the class. Time is given for the students to plan and rehearse their presentation. Each student has the opportunity to present their poster and the information about their reptile. Feedback is provided from the teacher and the class as the students prepare for the exhibit tours.

Lesson 11:
To introduce this portion of the Life Systems unit, the teacher asks the class to think about animals native to Canada that would be interesting to present in the exhibit. The students brainstorm many but decide that the bear, wolf, raccoon, moose, and beaver would be the most popular animals to research. The class decides that they want to report on appearance, habitat, eating habits, babies, and what the animal does in the winter. The students go to the library where the teacher librarian reviews the Dewey Decimal system and how to locate information about specific animals. A new graphic organizer is presented; the teacher reviews where to look for specific information in a resource and how to take point-form notes. The students choose an animal, locate appropriate resources in the library, and record data on the graphic organizer. This process will be completed as independently as possible for each student. A conference will be held with either the teacher librarian or the teacher to assess the data that has been collected by each student.

Lesson 12:
Students examine a variety of pop-up books. The teacher models how a pop-up book can be made. Students are directed to have one page for each of the specific topics that were researched. The students will record their findings for each topic and accompany each page with an appropriate pop-up picture.

(continued)

Unit Instruction Plan/Lesson Sequence (continued)

Unit: Butterflies, Reptiles, and Animals

Focus for Learning: Life Systems (Science)/Grade 2

Lesson 13:

Students are placed into groups so that each member has researched a different animal. They are given a large piece of chart paper or piece of mural paper. Using the headings that were determined for research, the students complete the chart. Discussion about similarities and differences should be encouraged as the students work.

	Bear	Wolf	Raccoon	Moose	Beaver
Appearance					
Habitat					
Eating Habits					
Babies					
How it winters					

As a group, the students will decide how to present the information from their chart. They will be directed to point out distinct characteristics, as well as similarities and differences in all the animals.

Lesson 14:

Time will be provided for the teacher to guide the students in a discussion about how to display the information in the culminating library exhibit. Once the material has been posted, the students create their own tour commentary based on the way they will move through the exhibit and what information they want to feature. The teacher has a conference with each student to assess the content of their "tour" and to provide any necessary feedback. The students can practise together, or the teacher may choose to have a few exemplary "tours" given for the class as models.

Sample Unit: Grade 6 Language—Unit Curriculum and Assessment Plan

Unit/Strand: Story Writing (using the big book *The Napping House* by Audrey Wood as a model)

Big Ideas:
- Storytelling is as old as language itself and serves a vital function in societies.
- Rhythm and repetition facilitate memorization.
- Young children learn more effectively when they can associate words with pictures.

Essential Skills:
- narrative writing
- using the writing process
- oral reading for various audiences
- producing illustrations

Focus for Learning: story elements (plot, stetting, and characters); writing descriptively to engage very young readers; producing a children's book/Grade 6

Title/Description of Culminating Task:
Students will produce their own big book mimicking *The Napping House* focusing on word choice (use of adjectives). Students will be in groups of 3. Each student will have a task in the group.

Group member #1: writer
Group member #2: editor
Group member #3: graphic artist

They will write a draft copy, have it edited by two other editors in the class, and then by the teacher. The illustrations will be drawn by hand or computer-generated and coloured.

Enabling and/or Other Assessment Tasks

Learning Habits: Initiative Co-operation	**Title:** Oral sharing activity Students bring in their favourite storybook from home and share it with the class. They read it as if they are reading to a small child, using appropriate expression and gestures. (If students do not have a favourite book, they may choose a library book, a comic book, or any piece of writing they would like to share.) **Diagnostic/Formative:** F **Write/Do/Say:** D & S	**Curriculum Outcomes/Standards:** - Use tone of voice and gestures to enhance the message and help convince or persuade listeners in conversations, discussions, or presentations. - Use constructive strategies in small-group discussions. - Read aloud, showing understanding of the material and awareness of the audience. - Read a variety of fiction and non-fiction materials for different purposes. - Decide on a specific purpose for reading and select the material that they need from a variety of appropriate sources. - Identify the elements of a story and explain how they relate to each other.
Learning Habits: Independent work	**Title:** Writing sample Students write a descriptive paragraph using their choice of picture, photo, or object. They must use as many adjectives as possible, using the list generated together. Students highlight all adjectives in their writing sample. **Diagnostic/Formative:** D **Write/Do/Say:** W	**Curriculum Outcomes/Standards:** - Use writing for various purposes and in a range of contexts. - Use a variety of sentence types. - Use adjectives correctly and effectively. - Use conventions correctly. - Revise and edit work in collaboration with others, seeking feedback, focusing on content, organization, and appropriate vocabulary.
Learning Habits: Independent work	**Title:** Drawing activity Students draw pictures (cartoon-like characters) using samples from any source of their choice (magazines, computer, books, etc.). They will colour them using different materials and techniques used in previous art classes (pastel, paint, charcoal). **Diagnostic/Formative:** F **Write/Do/Say:** D	**Curriculum Outcomes/Standards:** - Produce 2-D and 3-D works of art using the appropriate materials and techniques for the grade level.

Unit Culminating Assessment Task Plan

Unit/Strand: Story Writing (using the big book *The Napping House* by Audrey Wood as a model)

Assessment Task Title: Creating a big book mimicking the format of *The Napping House* by Audrey Wood and presenting it to an early primary class

Description of Task:

Students will produce their own big book version of *The Napping House* focusing on word choice (use of adjectives). The students will be in groups of 3. Each student will have a task in the group.

Group member #1: writer
Group member #2: editor
Group member #3: graphic artist

They will write a draft copy, have it edited by two other editors in the class, and then by the teacher. The illustrations will be drawn by hand or computer-generated and coloured, using materials and techniques taught in previous lessons.

Big Ideas:

- Storytelling is as old as language itself and serves a vital function in societies.
- Rhythm and repetition facilitate memorization.
- Young children learn more effectively when they can associate words with pictures.

Essential Skills:

- narrative writing
- using the writing process
- oral reading for various audiences
- producing illustrations

Curriculum Outcomes/Standards:

- Read aloud, showing understanding of the material and awareness of the audience.
- Read a variety of fiction and non-fiction materials for different purposes.
- Decide on a specific purpose for reading and select the material that they need from a variety of appropriate sources.
- Identify the elements of a story and explain how they relate to each other.
- Use writing for various purposes and in a range of contexts.
- Use a variety of sentence types.
- Use adjectives correctly and effectively.
- Use conventions correctly.
- Revise and edit work in collaboration with others, seeking feedback, focusing on content, organization and appropriate vocabulary.
- Use tone of voice and gestures to enhance the message and help convince or persuade listeners in conversations, discussions, or presentations.
- Use constructive strategies in small-group discussions.
- Produce 2-D and 3-D works of art using the appropriate materials and techniques for the grade level.

Student Products and Processes

Assessment Strategy 1: (Write) a Big Book
Assessment Tool: Self-assessment checklist; teacher/student-generated writing rubric
Assessment Criteria: creativity, descriptive language, quality of illustrations, conventions, professionalism

Assessment Strategy 2: (Do, Say,) Class presentation /primary class presentation
Assessment Tool: Self-assessment checklist; teacher/student-generated oral presentation rubric
Assessment Criteria: Quality of oral reading, Expressiveness, Engagement with audience

Resources/Technology Integration: We will use the *The Napping House* by Audrey Wood, similar stories such a *The Lady Who Swallowed a Fly*, and other storybooks brought in by the students. Students will use art programs on the computer if they wish to generate their illustrations.
Accommodations/Modifications: Made as necessary, according to individual needs.
Cross-Curricular Integration: Art; Social Studies.

Unit Instruction Plan/Lesson Sequence

Unit: Story Writing (using the big book: *The Napping House* by Audrey Wood as a model)

Focus for Learning: Story elements (plot, stetting, characters); writing descriptively to engage very young readers; producing a children's book/Grade 6

Introduction

The teacher uses the big book, *The Napping House* by Audrey Wood for a read-aloud, focusing on the structure of the story. It is a repetitive story using many descriptive words, which builds as the story progresses. The teacher introduces the focus of the lesson: to have students create their own version of the story using the same format.

Lesson 1: Activation of Prior Knowledge

Students will be instructed to close their eyes and imagine an outdoor scene while classical music plays in the background. Students then turn to their elbow partner and describe what they saw and discuss their word choices. (Question examples: "What season is it? Where are you? What are you doing? What do you see in your backyard in the winter, summer?" etc.) In small groups of three or four students, one student will record the adjectives on sticky notes. Working as a whole group, all the sticky notes will be placed on large paper where the class can discuss the choices of words and add to it or make changes.

Lesson 2: Mini-Lesson on Adjectives

Large-group discussion: definition of an adjective, why they are used, and how they work in a sentence. Students choose an object in the class and are instructed to use as many adjectives as possible to describe the object. They then draw a picture of the object in the centre of white paper and make a web using the adjectives to describe their object.

In small groups, students have a few minutes to share their work. What were the similarities, differences? Are there any other words another group member could offer? If any student chose the same object, pair them up so they can compare their choice of words.

Lesson 3: Noun/Adjective Word Chart

On large chart paper, the teacher makes a chart labellingone column "nouns" and the other column "adjectives." Have the students come up and enter their responses to the object they chose during the second lesson. Post the chart paper for future reference.

Lesson 4: Read Aloud

1st reading of *The Napping House*: Read the story, focusing on text form. Ask students to make connections to what the story reminds them of. of (e.g., *The Old Lady Who Swallowed a Fly*).

Lesson 5: Shared Reading

2nd reading of *The Napping House*: Before reading, hide all the adjectives with sticky notes. As a focus for reading, instruct students that they will be asked to substitute their own adjectives when they come to a hidden word. This activity is done orally.

Formative Assessment: Oral Sharing Activity

Students bring in their favourite storybook from home and share it with the class. They read it as if they are reading to a small child, using appropriate expression and gestures. (If students do not have a favourite book, they may choose a library book, a comic book, or any piece of writing they would like to share.) Peers provide feedback regarding the quality of readings.

(continued)

Unit Instruction Plan/Lesson Sequence (*continued*)

Unit: Story Writing (using the big book: *The Napping House* by Audrey Wood as a model)

Focus for Learning: Story elements (plot, stetting, characters); writing descriptively to engage very young readers; producing a children's book/Grade 6

Diagnostic Assessment: Writing Sample

Write a descriptive paragraph using the students' choice of picture, photo, or object. Students must use as many adjectives possible, using the list generated together. Have students highlight all adjectives in their writing sample. The teacher assesses students' strengths and needs.

Lesson 6: Review

In a large-group setting, ask orally about the characters, plot, and setting in the story, *The Napping House*. Record students' responses on chart paper so students can start to see the connections being made between the use of descriptive language and establishing these elements.

Use the "show me your thumbs" assessment strategy to determine students' understanding of these elements.

Lesson 7: Character/Plot/Setting (small group)

Hand each student a chart with three headings: Character, Plot, and Setting. Using their own book selections and working in groups of three or four, students select one of the books and complete the chart by recording the adjectives each author used to help create each element.

Lesson 8: Independent Art Activity

Working independently, students choose the character, the plot, or the setting of *The Napping House*. They may choose either to draw or build their own version of one of the elements of the story. Students will write their adjectives on pieces of paper (cut out to represent an object in the story) and tie them to a coat hanger using thread or yarn.

Lesson 9: Three-Ring Circus

In the Three-Ring Circus format, students present their "Napping House Hangers" to the rest of the class. Peers will provide feedback to the presenter (something they did well, something they need to improve upon, and a question). Presenters will be practising their oral presentation skills, focusing on expression and voice. The teacher is in the centre of the three groups using a checklist to assess each group member's progress during their oral presentations.

Lesson 10: Re-read

The teacher re-reads the *The Napping House* in its original form. Students will then be asked to replace the characters, plot, or setting of the story, using their own ideas. As the teacher reads the story once again, students replace the nouns in the story on lined sticky notes. The teacher asks different students to volunteer to read the story to the whole class, changing the characters, plot, or setting.

The Culminating Task: Children's Big Book

Students produce their own Big Book, applying all the knowledge and skills they have acquired. This will require several class periods. Depending on access and arrangements made by the teacher, students will read and present their Big Books to an audience of K–3 students.

Sample Unit: Grade 7 Mathematics and Science (Ontario)—Unit Curriculum and Assessment Plan

Unit: Interior and Outdoor Furniture Design

Focus for Learning: measurement; geometry; structural strength and stability; interactions within ecosystems/Grade 7 (Ontario)

Big Ideas:
- Standard units are universally accepted units that allow people to use and communicate measurements consistently.
- Geometry helps us to make sense of objects in the world and their relationships in space.
- Designs based on geometric patterns can be described and created using the principles of transformational geometry.
- There are many factors important to consider when designing a particular product.

Essential Skills:
- increased sophistication in the students' ability to estimate measurements, in using a variety of measurement tools, and in selecting the most appropriate tools.
- improved skill in applying the design process in solving real-life problems
- effective use of computer technology in the design process

Title of Culminating Task:
Designing a Picnic Table

Description:
The Association of Interior Designers in your area is sponsoring a design contest for Grade 7 students with a view of generating innovative and creative ideas in furniture design. Your teacher requires that everyone participates in this contest. Abiding by the rules of the contest, each student design team (max. four members) designs and builds a scale model of a picnic table that can comfortably accommodate six people. The association challenges the participating design teams to come up with revolutionary designs based on non-traditional shapes. This contest requirement precludes a traditional table-top design based on square, rectangular, or perfectly round shape. The design teams may use any type of material in their design.

Enabling and/or Other Assessment Tasks

Learning Skills: Independent work	**Achievement Categories:** Thinking Application	**Title:** Math/Science/Technology Journal (for Measurement, Geometry, and Science) Each student maintains a design log with daily entries on the question: "What did you learn today and how can you use or apply these knowledge/skills in designing, and/or constructing a model of a picnic table?" **Diagnostic/Formative:** F **Write/Do/Say:** W
		Overall/Specific Expectations: · Geometry helps us make sense of objects in the world and their relationships in space. · There are many factors important to consider when designing a particular product.
Learning Skills: Use of information	**Achievement Categories:** Knowledge & Understanding	**Title:** Daily Quizzes (or Worksheets) on Metric Conversion, Area Measurement, Scaling, Structural Strength and Stability, and Ecosystems (for Measurement, Geometry, and/or Science) **Diagnostic/Formative:** F **Write/Do/Say:** W
		Overall/Specific Expectations: · Solve problems that require conversion between … · Estimate and calculate the area of two- … · Identify, perform, and describe dilations …

(continued)

Unit Curriculum and Assessment Plan *(continued)*

Enabling and/or Other Assessment Tasks

Learning Skills	Achievement Categories	Task	Overall/Specific Expectations
Learning Skills: Problem solving	**Achievement Categories:** Application	**Title:** Performance Task—Drawing a Floor Plan (for Measurement and Geometry) Draw a scaled (with measurements) floor plan of your school's gymnasium, including all the structures and furnishings contained within. **Diagnostic/Formative:** F **Write/Do/Say:** D	**Overall/Specific Expectations:** · Research and report on real-life application of … · Estimate and calculate the area of two- … · Construct related lines (i.e., parallel; perpendicular; · Construct angle bisector and perpendicular bisector … · Identify, perform and describe dilations …
Learning Skills: Initiative Co-operation	**Achievement Categories:** Application Thinking	**Title:** Constructing a scale model of a doghouse using Popsicle sticks (for Measurement, Geometry, and Science) Students, in small groups, construct a scale model of a commercially available doghouse. **Diagnostic/Formative:** F **Write/Do/Say:** D	**Overall/Specific Expectations:** · Research and report on real-life application of … · Estimate and calculate the area of two- … · Identify, perform, and describe perpendicular; … · Demonstrate an understanding of the relationship … · Design and make a variety of structures, and …
Learning Skills: Homework completion	**Achievement Categories:** Knowledge & Understanding Application	**Title:** Word Problem Portfolio (for Measurement and Geometry) Students compile a set of five problems which they have created, solved, and explained according to a set of criteria designed to assess their knowledge and application of key measurement concepts. **Diagnostic/Formative:** Summative **Write/Do/Say:** W	**Overall/Specific Expectations:** · Estimate and calculate the area of two- … · Identify, perform and describe dilations …
Learning Skills: Use of information	**Achievement Categories:** Knowledge & Understanding	**Title:** Long Quiz—Structural Strength and Stability (for Science) Students write a Long Quiz on the Science Strand: Structural Strength and Stability **Diagnostic/Formative:** F **Write/Do/Say:** W	**Overall/Specific Expectations:** · Demonstrate an understanding of the relationship …

(continued)

Unit Curriculum and Assessment Plan (continued)

Enabling and/or Other Assessment Tasks

Learning Skills: Independent work Initiative	**Achievement Categories:** Thinking Communication	**Title:** Designing a Mural (for Geometry) Students create a tiling pattern composed of three to six repeating shapes using Geometer's Sketchpad. Then, they perform the necessary calculations to enlarge the design to fit a wall 3 m x 4 m in size. Each student presents and describes his or her design, highlighting the concepts of similar and congruent figures, as well as the elements and types of movement present in the pattern. **Diagnostic/Formative:** F **Write/Do/Say:** D & S	**Overall/Specific Expectations:** · Develop an understanding of similarity, and … · Describe location in the four quadrants of a … · Demonstrates an understanding that enlarging or … · Distinguish between and compare similar shapes … · Identify, perform, and describe dilations … · Create and analyze designs involving translations …
Learning Skills: Initiative Use of information Problem solving	**Achievement Categories:** Knowledge & Understanding Thinking Communication	**Title:** Art and Design Portfolio (for Geometry) Part 1: Students create a set of five designs, described and analyzed based on their knowledge of transformations. Part 2: Students use the Internet to find five pieces of artwork showing transformations (e.g., artwork by Escher). They will research about the history of each art piece, as well as analyze and describe the content of each work on the basis of their knowledge of transformational geometry. **Diagnostic/Formative:** Summative **Write/Do/Say:** W & D	**Overall/Specific Expectations:** · Create and analyze designs involving translations …

Unit Culminating Assessment Task Plan

Unit: Interior and Outdoor Furniture Design

Assessment Task Title: Designing a Picnic Table

Description of Task:

The Association of Interior Designers in your area is sponsoring a design contest for Grade 7 students with a view of generating innovative and creative ideas in furniture design. Your teacher requires that everyone participate in this contest. Abiding by the rules of the contest, each student design team (max. fourmembers) designs and builds a scale model of a picnic table that can comfortably accommodate six people. The association challenges the participating teams to come up with revolutionary designs based on non-traditional shapes. This contest requirement precludes a traditional table-top design based on square, rectangular, or perfectly round shape. The design teams may use any type of material in their design.

Big Ideas:

- Standard units are universally accepted units that allow people to use and communicate measurements consistently.
- Geometry helps us make sense of objects in the world and their relation-ships in space.
- Designs based on geometric patterns can be described and created using the principles of transformational geometry.
- There are many factors important to consider when designing a partic-ular product.

Essential Skills:

- increased sophistication in students' ability to estimate measurements, in using a variety of measurement tools, and in selecting the most appropriate tools.
- improved skill in applying the design process in solving real-life problems
- effective use of computer technology in the design process

Overall/Specific Expectations:

Measurement

- Report on research into real-life application of area measurements.
- Determine the relationships among units and measurable attributes, including …
- Solve problems that require conversion between metric units of measure …
- Estimate and calculate the area of two-dimensional composite shapes by …

Geometry

- Develop an understanding of similarity, and distinguish similarity and congruence.
- Describe location in the four quadrants of a coordinate system, dilate …
- Identify, perform, and describe dilations (enlargement and reductions) through …
- Create and analyze designs involving translations, reflections, dilations, and/or …

Structures and Mechanisms: Structural Strength and Stability

- Demonstrate an understanding of the relationship between the effectiveness of …
- Design and make a variety of structures, and investigate the relationship between …
- Demonstrate an understanding of the factors that must be considered when …

(continued)

Unit Culminating Assessment Task Plan (continued)

Student Products and Processes

Assessment Strategy and Tool: (Do)
Design and Scale Model (Rubric)
Achievement Categories/Assessment Criteria
K/U: Depth of Understanding (Math & Science)
T: Creativity of Design (Math)
A: Accuracy of Measurement (Math)
A: Accuracy of transformation (Math)
A: Craftsmanship—Construction Technique (Science)
A: Choice of Materials (Science)

Learning Skills:
Co-operation
Conflict resolution

Assessment Strategy and Tool: (Write)
Design Log—Written or Audio-taped (Rubric)
Achievement Categories/Assessment Criteria
K/U: Depth of Understanding (Math & Science)
T: Use of planning and processing skills (Math & Science)
T: Use of problem solving strategies (Math)
A: Accuracy of Calculations (Math)

A: Making Connections between concepts (Math & Science)
C: Use of conventions and terminologies (Math & Science)

Learning Skills:
Independent Work
Use of information
Problem solving

Assessment Strategy and Tool: (Say)
Class Presentation or Group Interview (Rubric)
Achievement Categories/Assessment Criteria
K/U: Depth of Understanding (Science and Math)
C: Use of appropriate visuals/media (Math & Science)
C: Organization of Ideas (Math & Science)
C: Clarity of Expression (Math & Science)
C: Use of appropriate terminologies (Math & Science)

Learning Skills:
Co-operation
Class participation

Resources/Technology Integration:
· Materials for models: cardboard boxes; old newspapers; Popsicle sticks; glue
· Computer technology: the Internet; Geometer's Sketchpad, a presentation software
· Others: furniture store catalogues, design magazines, store websites

Accommodations/Modifications:
· Heterogeneous groupings, co-operative and peer-assisted learning
· Use of a variety of visual aids, manipulatives, and computer technology
· Open-ended problem allowing advanced learning or scaled-down curriculum content

Cross-Curricular Integration: entire unit is integrated

Unit Instruction Plan/Lesson Sequence

Unit: Interior and Outdoor Furniture Design

Focus for Learning: An integrated unit focused on Measurement, Geometry, Structural Strength and Stability, and Ecosystems (partly)/Grade 7 (Ontario)

Introduction

The teacher introduces the culminating task to begin the unit. Important points to discuss: (1) Structure and Organization of the unit; (2) Assessment pieces, tools, and criteria; (3) Groupings: students will be working in groups most of the time, but they may not be working with the same people all the time; (4) Each student will maintain an MST Journal where they will write down what they learned from the daily lessons, and how they can use and apply these knowledge/skills in completing the culminating task.

Lesson 1: Conversion Algorithm for Linear Metric Units

Students measure the perimeter of their desks using their hands (or any elongated object at hand). The teacher asks the measurements that the students obtained. Why are they different despite the fact that the desks have the same size? How can we communicate the same measurements consistently? This introductory activity not only reinforces the concept of perimeter, but also introduces the concept of standard units. The rest of the class is spent learning and practising how to convert between linear metric units.

Lesson 2: Area of Simple Two-Dimensional Figures—Using Formulas for Calculation

Students are asked to cut a piece of paper and find how many of the same piece of paper is needed to completely cover the top of their desk. How accurate and consistent are their measurements? What shape can yield the most accurate result? This introductory activity re-introduces the concept of unit square and square units, and introduces the standard unit for area, the "m^2". Note: If the area formulas for triangles, parallelograms, and trapezoids have not been developed in previous units, then now is the best time to do so. Otherwise, students proceed by completing a worksheet designed to help students practise their skills on how to use area formulas for each of the above-mentioned two-dimensional shapes.

Lesson 3: Conversion Algorithm for Square Metric Units

Students complete a worksheet aimed at improving their skill in converting between square metric units.

Lesson 4: Area of Composite Two-Dimensional Figures

Students learn and practise decomposing composite two-dimensional figures into simple shapes, calculating the area of the component simple shapes, and adding them together to find the area of the composite figure. Alternative solutions should also be discussed, since there are many ways to decompose composite shapes.

Lesson 5: Similar versus Congruent Figures

Concept Formation Activity: Each group of three or four students is given a set of 20 cut-out 2-D shapes. The group divides the shapes into groups based on a set of criteria that only the members of the group know. The rest of the class will guess the set of criteria used by the group to classify the shapes. Once a correct guess is obtained, and the criteria used explained, the second group presents their own scheme of classification and the process repeats until all the groups have had their chance of presenting their own way of classifying the shapes. In the students' explanations and subsequent class discussions, the concept of similar and congruent figures will be clarified.

Lesson 6: Map Reading—How do we calculate the actual distance between any two points or locations in a map?

Students learn to read distances in maps, and relate this knowledge to the concept of similar figures. What relates the map distances to actual distances? How can we describe mathematically the relationship between and among similar figures?

(continued)

Unit Instruction Plan/Lesson Sequence *(continued)*

Unit: Interior and Outdoor Furniture Design

Focus for Learning: An integrated unit focused on Measurement, Geometry, Structural Strength and Stability, and Ecosystems (partly)/Grade 7 (Ontario)

Lesson 7: Constructing Similar Figures
Students learn to construct similar figures under different levels of dilation. This activity also hones students' skills in measuring angles using a protractor.

Performance Task—Drawing a Floor Plan of the School's Gymnasium
Students measure the dimensions of the school gym's floor area, including all the structures and furnishings contained within. Students work in small groups, divide the work among the members, and help each other to complete the task. Each member of the group creates a drawing of the gym's floor area. The drawing should represent a scaled-down model of the floor area containing actual measurements. The members must use different scale ratios to avoid the chance of students copying from each other.

The Word Problem Portfolio
The Word Problem Portfolio is a collection of word problems that the students have created and solved. The students are also required to explain their solution process, as well as justify their choice of strategy. This collection of problems must demonstrate their knowledge of conversion algorithms for both linear and square units of measure, their knowledge of scaling, and their ability to use area formulas in solving real-life problems. This collection of work must also demonstrate real-life applications of these mathematical concepts and procedures.

Lesson 8: Investigation—Centre of Gravity
Students find the centre of gravity of regular and irregular flat objects, and complete a worksheet that accompanies this activity.

Lesson 9: Investigation—What makes a structure stable?
Students compare and order structures (supplied by the teacher) based on increasing stability. Students discuss and answer the question: What makes a structure stable?

Lesson 10: What are the different forces acting upon a structure?
Students use structures found in the classroom (e.g., desks, chairs) as examples to examine the different forces acting upon a structure. Discussions may centre on the following questions: How do we describe forces? How does a force, or a combination of forces, affect a structure? How are these structures designed, or constructed, to withstand these forces?

Lesson 11: Concept Formation Activity—Classifying Structures
In small groups, students think of a category (or categories) that the first group used in classifying those structures. The second group takes their turn and the process is repeated until all the groups have presented their classification scheme. This activity introduces the three types of structures: shell, frame, and solid. Group and class discussions should answer the following questions: How are they different or the same? What are pros and cons of having each of these structures? What are the factors to consider when deciding what type of structure to use? How is each type affected by different types of forces?

Lesson 12: How can we make "this" structure stronger?
The teacher presents an unstable piece of furniture (e.g., a chair, a table) in class. Students work in groups to discuss how they can strengthen the structure. Each group shares their suggestions in class. This activity introduces the different methods of strengthening structures, including the different types of fasteners available in the market.

(continued)

Unit Instruction Plan/Lesson Sequence (*continued*)

Unit: Interior and Outdoor Furniture Design

Focus for Learning: An integrated unit focused on Measurement, Geometry, Structural Strength and Stability, and Ecosystems (partly)/Grade 7 (Ontario)

Performance Task—Designing and Constructing a Doghouse made of Popsicle Sticks

In small groups, students design and create a doghouse made of Popsicle sticks using glue as fastener. Note that this project requires that students draw a blueprint of their design showing the top, side, and front views, with measurements, of the real-life structure.

Long Quiz—Structural Strength and Stability

Lesson 13: Geometer's Sketchpad—Basic Functions and Commands

Students learn the basic functions and commands of the program. Using an LCD projector, the teacher models how to create designs that incorporate translation, reflection, and rotation. Students use the rest of the period to familiarize themselves with the GSP program.

Lesson 14: Translation

Students use grid paper to plot figures on the Cartesian plane, as well as the images of the figures under different translation movements. How do we describe movement of figures under translation? How do we use the translation function of GSP? What are the variables in this function? How do we create designs composed solely of translated images?

Lesson 15: Reflection

Students use grid paper to plot figures on the Cartesian plane, as well as the reflected images of the figures using different axes. How do we describe movement of figures under reflection? How do we use the reflection function of GSP? What are the variables in this function? How do we create designs composed solely or predominantly of reflected images?

Lesson 16: Rotation

Students use grid paper to plot figures on the Cartesian plane, as well as the image of the figures under different degrees of rotation. How do we describe movement of figures under rotation? How do we use the rotation function of GSP? What are the variables in this function? How do we create designs composed solely or predominantly of images?

The Design Portfolio

The teacher shows slides of representative work of Escher demonstrating translation, reflection, and dilation. The teacher models how to analyze the patterns and how to describe the various movements (translation, reflection, rotation, and dilation) in each art piece. Then, the design portfolio is introduced together with the requirements and assessment of the project.

Work on the Culminating Task Begins

· Final student grouping is assigned.
· Students end their MST Journal. The journal, if done well, becomes an important resource for the final project.
· Students begin their design log. The log must contain all the work accomplished by the group and those contributed by the author. It should also contain calculations, measurements, information obtained from research, ideas adopted from the author's MST Journal, drawings, GSP prints, sketches, etc.

(*continued*)

Unit Instruction Plan/Lesson Sequence *(continued)*

Unit: Interior and Outdoor Furniture Design

Focus for Learning: An integrated unit focused on Measurement, Geometry, Structural Strength and Stability, and Ecosystems (partly)/Grade 7 (Ontario)

Lesson 17: Contemporary Furniture Design

The teacher makes available design magazines, furniture store catalogues, and a list of websites that the students can browse through to give them ideas on what is currently available in the market. The students particularly make notes of the following: (1) shape of table tops, (2) shape of table legs, (3) dimensions, (4) the materials being used, and (5) the colour of materials used. These represent most of the issues that the group needs to discuss and agree on. Then, they take their list of materials and research them, including the presence of toxic elements in the materials, method of disposal, and if they can be recycled.

Lesson 18: Is it possible to use less materials for more seating space (Perimeter versus Area)?

Students investigate how to minimize the area of a rectangle with the perimeter being held constant. In this activity, the dimensions (length and width) of the rectangle will be varied in such a way that the perimeter remains the same. What dimensions yield the least area? How can this knowledge be applied to your design?

Lesson 19: Front, Side, and Top Views of 3-D Objects

Students learn and practise how to draw the front, side, and top views of 3-D figures on grid paper.

Lesson 20: Review of Safety Procedures and the Design Process

Each group records at least 10 safety rules to follow during construction. This is a safety contract that all members must sign. The whole class reviews the steps in the design process. The teacher creates a poster to be hung on the wall.

Students complete their blueprint and prepare a brief written proposal containing their plans on how to construct their models, as well as the list of materials to be used in the model construction. The proposal must first be approved by the teacher before model construction begins. Construction and presentation follows.

Lesson 21: Self- and Group Assessment

Each student prepares a pie graph with sectors corresponding to the percentage of work each member has contributed to the completion of the culminating task.

Sample Unit: Grade 8 Geography—Long-Range Assessment Plan

Planner: J. Mendoza

Subject/Grade: Geography (Human)/Grade 8

Units and Big Ideas

Unit 1: Canada from the Eyes of a Foreigner	**Unit 2:** Immigrating to Canada	**Unit 3:** Migration within Canada	**Unit 4:** The Canadian Mosaic
Big Ideas: · Human activities are affected by changing global patterns. · Sites and situation influence human settlement. · Factors that affect population distribution also affect population density. · Changes in human development patterns influence our choices. · Why are there different levels of development or rich and poor countries?	**Big Ideas:** · People move for a variety of reasons. · There are patterns and trends in migration that affect the people, culture, and communities of Canada. · People have moved around the world throughout history. · A changing world economy is one of the most important factors in international migration.	**Big Ideas:** · Economic resources influence economic success of a region. · There are three major types of industries, and these sectors are continually changing. · How does sustainable development promote responsible use of land and responsible human development? · What are the job trends and skills for the future?	**Big Ideas:** · Language and culture are the two most important considerations for new migrants when deciding on where to relocate within Canada. · Ethnic communities create a demand for new (international) products. Note: This unit is designed to integrate most or all of the key ideas/concepts presented in the previous units.

Essential Skills (for all units):
· use of qualitative and quantitative data to understand patterns, trends, and concepts in Social Sciences
· use and application of technology (the Internet, databases, spreadsheets, presentation software) in research and analysis of maps, quantitative and qualitative data presented in a variety of formats (tables, graphs, written form, etc.)
· written and oral communication and presentation skills

(continued)

Long-Range Assessment Plan (*continued*)

Culminating Tasks

Title: Unit 1 – The Canadian Student Exchange Program

The Canadian government hopes to promote international peace and understanding by offering Grade 8 students from foreign countries opportunities to study in Canada for six months. Because of their young age, Grade 8 applicants are requested to form small groups of three or four interested students. Each student group will submit one application only.

You belong to a group of four Grade 8 students in a foreign country who wishes to be considered for the Canadian Student Exchange Program. One of the application requirements (your group's TASK) is to create a storybook or a website about Canada and your own country focusing on four questions:

(1) Why is Canada a great place to live?
(2) If chosen for the program, where in Canada would you choose to live and study, and why?
(3) How is your country different from Canada?
(4) What would you tell your Canadian friends about your country?

Title: Unit 2 – Life and Aspirations of a Migrant Family

Your group (with four members) will play the role of a family (father, mother, two children) from a foreign country applying to immigrate to Canada.

You will create your own family history and background, your birthdates, birth places, education, careers, and so on with only one purpose in mind:

· So that your whole family will be approved for immigration to Canada according to the existing Canadian immigration laws and procedures.

Your tasks include the following:

(1) Prepare a narrative of your family history/background.
(2) Prepare a resume/bio-data for each member of the family.
(3) Complete an Immigration Canada application form for the whole family.
(4) Pass an interview with an Immigration Canada visa officer in a Canadian embassy or consulate abroad.

Title: Unit 3 – Searching for a Greener Pasture: My Life's Goals and Dreams

You are about to graduate from high school, and you are wondering what to do with your life.

If you had the chance to live anywhere in Canada, and build your career and your future life and family there, then:

(1) What career would you choose and why?
(2) What do you need to do (education, experience, apprenticeship, etc.) to get there?
(3) Where would you settle to build your career, and why?

NOTE: This is a goal-setting and career-planning exercise. You need to be able to justify your choices based on the patterns, trends, and other key concepts that you learned in present and past units.

Title: Unit 4 – Venturing into an Ethnic Retail Business

Your research team works for a food retail company that operates across Canada. The company would like to investigate the feasibility of opening a "specialty" grocery stores that would cater to the needs specific and unique to each of the many ethnic communities comprising the Canadian mosaic (e.g., Italian, Latin American, Chinese). Your team will conduct a research study focused on one ethnic community, and determine the most promising Canadian location (city) for a grocery (or other product) store specific to your chosen community.

Your research team will prepare a PowerPoint presentation of your recommendations (location and rationale) to the company's Board of Directors.

(continued)

Long-Range Assessment Plan (continued)

Enabling and/or Other Assessment Tasks

Title: Unit 1 – Response Paper No. 1 If you had the choice where to live in Canada, where (city or town) would it be and why? Use the materials presented in the previous lessons to justify your answers.	**Title:** Unit 2 – Presentation 1 (An Interview with a Recent Immigrant) Students, in small groups, will interview a recent immigrant (individual or family) to gain first-hand understanding of the phenomenon of international migration: the reasons and consequences. Groups will present their findings as a news report.	**Title:** Unit 4 – Ethnic Composition of Canadian Communities Students will analyze the ethnic composition of one Canadian city or town, and analyze the demographic characteristics and economic contributions of the 10 largest ethnic groups in the chosen community.
Title: Response Paper No. 2 If you had to live in another country (other than the country of origin of your ancestors), where would it be and why? Use the materials presented in the previous lessons to justify your answers.	**Title:** Presentation 2 (Forced or Political Migration) Groups will prepare a short PowerPoint presentation about a topic on forced or political migration (e.g., slavery, formation of Israel, partition of India, aftermath of the Vietnam War, etc.).	**Title:** Market Analysis of One Ethnic Product Students will research one ethnic product that has experienced increased demand in the Canadian market. How and where is this product being produced? How does it reach the Canadian market? How is it marketed in Canada? What is its future in the Canadian market?
Title: Short Quizzes	**Title:** Information Technology Students will analyze the effect of information technology in one sector of the economy and predict how it will affect the nature of jobs in this economic sector. In what cities or communities in Canada will these changes be felt the most?	
	Title: Unit 3 – Resource-dependent Communities Students will analyze demographic and economic data on one resource-dependent community in Canada and write a short report on characteristics of its population, available jobs, and future economic trends.	
	Title: Short Quizzes	

Unit Curriculum and Assessment Plan

Unit 1: Canada from the Eyes of a Foreigner

Focus for Learning: GEOG (Patterns in Human Geography, Population Distribution, Population Characteristics, Human Development Index)/Grade 8

Big Ideas:

- Human activities are affected by changing global patterns.
- Sites and situation influence human settlement.
- Factors that affect population distribution also affect population density.
- Changes in human development patterns influence our choices.
- Why are there different levels of development or rich and poor countries?

Essential Skills:

- use of qualitative and quantitative data to understand patterns, trends, and concepts in Social Sciences
- use and application of technology ...
- written and oral communication and presentation skills

Description of Task:

The Canadian government hopes to promote international peace and understanding by offering Grade 8 students from foreign countries opportunities to study in Canada for six months. Because of their young age, Grade 8 applicants are requested to form groups of three or four interested students. Each student group will submit one application only.

You belong to a group of four Grade 8 students in a foreign country who would like to be considered for the Canadian Student Exchange Program. One of the application requirements (your group's TASK) is to create a storybook or a website about Canada and your own country focusing on four questions:

(1) Why is Canada a great place to live?
(2) If chosen for the program, where in Canada would you choose to live and study, and why?
(3) How is your country different from Canada?
(4) What would you tell your Canadian friends about your country?

Enabling and/or Other Assessment Tasks

Learning Habits:
Use of information
Homework completion

Title: Response Paper No. 1

If you had the choice where to live in Canada, where (city or town) will it be and why? Use the materials presented in the previous lessons to justify your answers. (Students with special needs may use photographs, or audiotapes, together with numerical data in tabular or graph forms, to form their responses and support their answers.)

Diagnostic/Formative: F
Write/Do/Say: Choice

Curriculum Outcomes/Standards:

- Identify the main patterns of human settlement and ...
- Explain how site and situation influence settlement ...
- Compare the characteristics of places with high and low ...
- Identify and explain the factors affecting population ...
- Summarize the factors that affect patterns of ...
- Explain how the availability of particular economic ...
- Identify and give examples of the major types of ...

(continued)

Unit Curriculum and Assessment Plan (continued)

Enabling and/or Other Assessment Tasks

Unit 1 (continued)

Learning Habits: Use of information Homework completion	**Title:** Response Paper No. 2 If you had to live in another country (other than the country of origin of your ancestors), where would it be and why? Use the materials presented in the previous lessons to justify your answers. (Students with special needs may use photographs, or audiotapes, together with numerical data in tabular or graph forms, to form their responses and support their answers.) **Diagnostic/Formative:** F **Write/Do/Say:** Choice	**Curriculum Outcomes/Standards:** · Compare the living and working conditions in countries … · Compare key characteristics of a number of developed … · Compare the economies of different communities, … · Compare the economies of some of the top trading …
Learning Habits: Use of information	**Title/Description:** A Series of Short Quizzes **Diagnostic/Formative:** F **Write/Do/Say:** W	**Curriculum Outcomes/Standards:** · Identify the main patterns of human settlement and … · Compare the characteristics of places with high and low … · Identify and explain the factors affecting population … · Identify and give examples of the major types of …

Unit Culminating Assessment Task Plan

Unit 1: Canada from the Eyes of a Foreigner

Assessment Task Title: The Canadian Student Exchange Program

Description of Task: The Canadian government hopes to promote international peace and understanding by offering Grade 8 students from foreign countries opportunities to study in Canada for six months. Because of their young age, Grade 8 applicants are requested to form groups of three or four interested students. Each student group will submit one application only.

You belong to a group of four Grade 8 students in a foreign country who would like to be considered for the Canadian Student Exchange Program. One of the application requirements (your group's TASK) is to create a storybook or a website about Canada and your own country focusing on four questions:

(1) Why is Canada a great place to live?
(2) If chosen for the program, where in Canada would you choose to live and study, and why?
(3) How is your country different from Canada?
(4) What would you tell your Canadian friends about your country?

Big Ideas:
- Human activities are affected by changing global patterns.
- Sites and situation influence human settlement.
- Factors that affect population distribution also affect population density.
- Changes in human development patterns influence our choices.
- Why are there different levels of development or rich and poor countries?

Essential Skills:
- use of qualitative and quantitative data to understand patterns, trends, and concepts in Social Sciences
- use and application of technology …
- written and oral communication and presentation skills

Curriculum Outcomes/Standards:
- Explain how site and situation influence settlement …
- Compare the characteristics of places with high and low …
- Identify and explain the factors affecting population …
- Use a variety of geographic representations, resources, …
- Summarize the factors that affect patterns of …
- Explain how the availability of particular economic …
- Identify and give examples of the major types of …
- Use thematic maps to identify economic patterns …
- Compare the living and working conditions in countries …
- Compare key characteristics of a number of developed …
- Compare the economies of different communities, …
- Compare the economies of some of the top trading …

Student Products and Processes

Assessment Strategy 1: (Do, Write) Scrapbook, website or other in consultation with the teacher
Assessment Tool: Self-assessment checklist and rubric
Assessment Criteria: Depth of understanding, Persuasiveness, Attention to detail

Assessment Strategy 2: (Do, Say, Write) Class Presentation
Assessment Tool: Self-assessment checklist and Oral Presentation Rubric
Assessment Criteria: Depth of understanding, Persuasiveness, Communication skills

(continued)

Unit Culminating Assessment Task Plan (continued)

Student Products and Processes

Unit 1 (continued)

Resources/Technology Integration: Statistics Canada website and databases; Fathom; a word processing, spreadsheet, and presentation program; Internet search engines; the Canadian Geographic website; Canadian and world atlases; human geography textbooks (introductory/basic level); other related sources, such as magazine articles, and so on.

Accommodations/Modifications: Co-operative, peer-assisted and reflective learning; use of appropriate technologies; open-ended questions/problems/tasks

Multicultural Integration: Promotes better understanding of other cultures and the significant contributions of immigrants in Canada's past, present, and future development.

Cross-Curricular Integration: Projects, class activities, and other assignments promote language and mathematical literacy

Unit Instruction Plan/Lesson Sequence

Unit 1: Canada from the Eyes of a Foreigner

Focus for Learning: GEOG (Patterns in Human Geography, Population Distribution, Population Characteristics, Human Development Index)/Grade 8

Introduction

The teacher introduces the Structure and Organization of the program, emphasizing that each unit ends with a culminating task.

The first unit is then introduced by: (1) describing the culminating task for the current unit, (2) assessment pieces, tools, and criteria, and (3) groupings: students will be working in heterogeneous groups. Each student will maintain a Geography Journal, either in print or digital, and must bring a floppy disc to each class for submitting work.

Lesson 1: Patterns of Human Settlement

Students will be instructed to stand randomly anywhere in the classroom. From this random arrangement, the whole class will define the three patterns of human settlement: linear, clustered, and scattered. The whole class will describe how they are distributed in the classroom in terms of high and low number of students standing in different areas of the classroom. This will be followed by a slide show of areas with high and low densities in Canada and around the world (e.g., apartment high rise buildings in Toronto, farmlands in the prairies, slums in Calcutta, inner-city housing in major cities, mansions and sprawling estates in Beverly Hills). In small groups, students will examine different thematic maps of Canada (people and society, economic, etc.) with the purpose of identifying the different characteristics of areas with high and low population densities, and the factors that affect people's decision on where to live. The teacher will model how to relate information from one map to those from the other maps. Each student group will report and share their observations with the rest of the class.

Lesson 2: The Statistics Canada Database and the Google Earth website

The teacher will model how to access the Statistics Canada website and database, how to find the population and area of each province and territory of Canada, how to enter or import data sets into a spreadsheet program, and how to use the "formula" feature of the spreadsheet program to calculate the population density of each Canadian province and territory. Working in small groups of three or four, students will focus their study on one province. They will use the same technique to find the 20 most populous communities/towns/cities in their assigned province or territory, to find its area, and to calculate its population density. What makes these areas more attractive to settlers than others? Students will use the online Atlas of Canada at the Statistics Canada website and other related sites (e.g., Digital Globe at the Google Earth website) to find answers to this question.

Lesson 3: Rural Land Use Planning—Northern Ontario Communities

What are the so-called primary industries, as opposed to secondary, tertiary, and quaternary industries? Where in Canada do we see primary industries? How can we ensure sustainability in developing our resource-rich communities? What are the effects of transportation and technology in the development of these communities? How does the Canadian Government respond to the increasing demand for rural recreational facilities (ski slopes, camping grounds, etc.) and at the same time ensure the preservation of our wetlands, lakes, and wilderness areas? The lesson presents the rural areas of Northern Ontario, its resource-dependent communities, and its various tourist facilities and recreational areas including, but not limited to, the provincial and national parks, using many of the online resources already mentioned above.

Lesson 4: Urban Land Use Planning—Selected Cities of Southern Ontario

Students will study the effects of various manufacturing and other secondary industries (e.g., population, urban sprawl, destruction of natural habitats for other species, conversion of fertile agricultural lands to other uses) in urban communities when poor decisions are made. The lesson presents the land use experiences of selected cities in Southern Ontario and how changes in technology and the communities' environmental consciousness effect changes in the present and future land use policy and zoning by-laws of these cities.

(continued)

Unit Instruction Plan/Lesson Sequence (continued)

Focus For Learning: GEOG8 (Patterns in Human Geography, Population Distribution, Population Characteristics, Human Development Index)

Unit 1 (continute): Canada from the Eyes of a Foreigner

Lesson 5: Case Study—The City of Mississauga

Students will trace the settlement history of the city and its evolution into the sprawling and progressive city that it is today. They will explain how site and situation affected the early settlement of the city, and how transportation and technology affect significant growth and development in its economy. Then, students will study the city's land use policy and the city plan to learn how the city intends to sustain its present and future growth and development.

Response Paper No. 1:

If you had the choice where to live in Canada, where (city or town) would it be and why? Use the materials presented in the previous lessons to justify your answers. (Students with special needs may use photographs and numerical data in tabular or graph forms to form their responses and support their answers.)

Lesson 6: Scatter Plot and Correlation Studies—Population Characteristics

Using a spreadsheet program, students will work in small groups to study the correlation between pairs of pre-assigned sets of population characteristics, using data sets from selected countries provided by the teacher. Each group will share their results with the rest of the class.

Lesson 7: Population Pyramids

Students will compare the population pyramids of selected countries and, in groups, discuss and interpret the meaning of the patterns that they observe. How does the population pyramid reveal information about the future trends in the population characteristics of a country?

Lesson 8: Economic Indicators and the Human Development Index

How do we measure the economic performance of a country? Students will learn the definition of key economic concepts such as GNP, GDP, per-capita income, and the Human Development Index (HDI). What does the HDI score measure? Students will analyze the HDI scores of selected countries, and will use their observations to understand the main differences between the population characteristics of the developed and developing worlds.

Lesson 9: Command vs. Mixed Economy—China's Experience

Students will analyze data sets on China's economic performance in the last 30 years, particularly focusing on the effect of China's change in economic policy from a command to a mixed economy. What are the pros and cons of command, mixed, and market-driven economies? How was Canada's economic performance compared to China's during the same period?

Lesson 10: Mixed vs. Free-Market Economy—Canada vs. the USA

What are the economic sectors (e.g., health care services, tertiary education, public transportation) that are being controlled in Canada? What are the consequences of these controls to Canadians? How do the lives of Canadians differ from those of Americans as consequence of these controls?

Response Paper No. 2:

If you had to relocate to another country in order to further your career, and were given a free choice by your company on where to relocate, where would it be and why? Use the materials presented in the previous lessons to justify your answers.

The Culminating Task: presentation of students' products

INTRODUCTION

Space constraints limit the number of assessment tools that can be included in this resource. In the following pages you will find a representative sample of assessment tools for Kindergarten to Grade 9. The *Talk About Assessment* website contains additional tools. All of the tools in Sections 3 – 5 are referred to in Part 1 of *Talk About Assessment*.

The tools are organized according to the following grade and subject groupings. A complete Table of Contents appears at the beginning of each section.

Section 3—Assessment Tools for K to Grade 3
· Language Arts
· Mathematics
· Science
· Generic Tools

Section 4—Assessment Tools for Grades 4 to 6
· Language Arts
· Mathematics
· Social Studies
· Generic Tools

Section 5—Assessment Tools for Grades 7 to 9
· Language Arts
· Science
· Generic Tools
· Learning Skills

TIPS FOR THE EFFECTIVE USE OF ASSESSMENT TOOLS

1. **Share your assessment tools with students so they know what your standards for quality work look like.**

   Tools such as rubrics serve to clearly outline for students, and parents, what you expect in terms of quality work. For this reason, students should be provided with a rubric when you first introduce a task or learning process. For example, it is important to take the time to carefully examine and discuss the Writing Process Rubric when first introducing students to this approach. Teach students about the criteria and indicators on the rubric, and continue to refer to these on a regular basis. Your goal is to have students internalize these criteria and indicators so they are able to judge for themselves when their work meets the expected standard. They should be able to justify the level they select for their work.

2. **Assessment is a collaborative process involving students, peers, and teachers.**

   While it is the teacher's job to be the ultimate judge of quality in terms of evaluating work, everyone needs to be involved in the assessment process. For example, students should be instructed in the use of checklists and/or rubrics to self- and/or peer assess their own work, before it is submitted to the teacher for assessment.

   Too often, teachers spend countless hours marking work that students have not spent much time on, and certainly have not critically self-assessed before submitting it. Encourage students to develop the habit of using the appropriate checklist to ensure that their work is up to standard before it is assessed by you. This will help convince students that *they* are being held accountable for producing quality work.

   Assessment *for* learning places the focus squarely on the indicators of quality work, as opposed to numerical marks. The intent of checklists is not to have the student assign a numerical mark or a level to their own or their peer's work. Rather, it is to encourage students to examine in a critical, objective way the extent to which the work they have produced meets the required criteria.

3. **Assessment is all about sampling.**

   A rubric contains all of the criteria required by a given task. However, when students are learning the skills associated with a new task, you should focus only on selected criteria. Only when students have had the chance to practise, make mistakes, and get helpful feedback should they be assessed on all of the criteria for a given task. Put another way, focus on selected criteria when conducting assessment *for* learning; focus on all the criteria when conducting assessment *of* learning.

4. **Organize during your long-range planning what critical evidence of achievement you will gather, as well as the tools you will use to assess this learning.**

   Effective assessment *of* learning involves determining the set of critical tasks that will be used to gather evidence of the essential learning in a given subject. Decide during your planning which tasks and assessment tools you will use to gather the evidence you need. For example, a quiz may be an excellent task for gathering evidence of students' knowledge of key terms, and a simple marking key will suffice to assess student responses. However, to gather evidence of students' problem-solving skills in mathematics, you will assign open-ended tasks for them to solve and assess their skills using the Problem-Solving Rubric.

5. **Conferencing is critical.**

   Students benefit far more from face-to-face feedback about their work than from written comments on work that is simply returned after marking. For this reason, you are strongly encouraged to build regular student conferencing time into their lesson planning so that there are opportunities to provide students with immediate feedback about their work. Tools such as rubrics and checklists are excellent vehicles for assessment discussions between teachers and students, or students and their peers.

6. **Assessment tools make your expectations regarding quality clear—don't accept work that doesn't meet these criteria.**

   If you have done your part in terms of providing clear and meaningful assessment tasks, as well as tools to guide students toward quality such as rubrics, checklists, and exemplars, then do not accept work from students that does not meet these standards.

Poor work habits are reinforced by spending time marking work that does not represent students' best efforts.

7. **Rubrics are qualitative tools and demand the teacher's professional judgement.**

   Some of the things that you teach and students learn can be readily quantified—knowledge of terms, simple quiz questions, etc. Rubrics, on the other hand, are qualitative tools that enable you to assess much more complex learning such as research skills or depth of conceptual understanding. Because such learning is complex, it does not lend itself to measurement on a 10- or 25-point scale. A well-designed rubric, therefore, demands that the teacher exercise his/her professional judgement to determine which level on the rubric best describes a given piece of work or performance. Rubric assessment involves matching the performance with the indicators on the scale. A computer cannot perform this function because it involves professional judgement. For this reason, students and teachers need to engage in discussion about the match between the rubric and samples of work at every opportunity so that, over time, the standards for quality will become internalized.

8. **Anchors are as critical as rubrics.**

   No matter how well-written a rubric is, it remains a piece of paper with sets of indicators that must match a wide array of student work. In order to help students and teachers become clear about what the indicators represent, anchors (samples of student work anchored to the levels) are necessary. Create your own bank of local anchors by saving student work from year to year. The necessary permissions must be sought from students and their parents.

   A word of caution! Always have multiple anchors at each level to reflect the wide range of possible performances corresponding to that achievement level.

Section 3 Tools

A Sample of Assessment Tools for Grades K to 3

In this section, you will find a variety of assessment tools that will help you to record and track the development of young children's learning. Many of these tools are *developmental* in their design. For example, we expect most children to pass through *emergent, early,* and *fluent* phases as they acquire the skills and knowledge associated with reading and writing.

Many of the tools in this section reflect the fact that learning in the early years of school is best *described* rather than *evaluated*. Teachers in the early grades observe and describe children's learning by referring to research-based, developmental or path-referenced tools, such as reading and writing continua. These same continua also provide a foundation for instruction.

Language Arts

Mathematics

Science

Generic Tools

Developmental Stages of Reading

Children in any grade have many learning needs in common. However, children acquire language skills and strategies at an individual pace and in unique ways. Every child arrives at school with different experiences and abilities—as well as different family and cultural backgrounds, likes and dislikes, and knowledge of books and reading. For a child to experience success in reading and to be encouraged to read further there needs to be a focus on knowing each learner and the general characteristics of learners at the three main literacy-learning stages: Emergent, Early, and Fluent. Also, children need to be provided with text that offers both support and challenge.

The following charts identify these general characteristics of learners; however, it should be noted that within each of these three broad categories there will be overlap, and it is unlikely that any one child could be matched against all the characteristics listed in a group. The characteristics listed are a guide to a child's general stages of development.

The Emergent Reader		
Characteristics	**Understandings**	**Skills and Behaviours**
• enjoys hearing and using new language • shows pleasure in rhythm and rhyme of language • enjoys playing at reading • likes listening to stories, poems, and rhymes • is willing to work at reading and writing • expects text to make sense • enjoys having books reread • wants to read and see self as a reader • is confident in making attempts at reading	• knows that language can be recorded and revisited • knows how stories and books work—understands that text, as well as illustrations, carries the story • is aware that print in books and his or her own writing hold meaning • recognizes book language and sometimes uses this in speech, retellings, etc. • understands the importance of background knowledge and uses this to get meaning • knows the rewards of reading and rereading • is aware of some print conventions • is beginning to be aware of the difference between fiction and nonfiction	• "plays" at reading and writing • handles books confidently • interprets pictures • uses pictures to predict text • retells a known story in sequence • develops a memory for text • finger-points to locate specific words • begins to realize that words are always spelled the same • focuses on word after word in sequence • identifies some words • explores new books and returns to favourites • chooses to read independently at times • recognizes and reads familiar signs, symbols, and labels • chooses work to be published and shared with others

(continued)

Developmental Stages of Reading *(continued)*

The Early Reader

Characteristics	Understandings	Skills and Behaviours
• is eager to listen to and read longer texts • is eager to read for information and pleasure from an increasing range of texts • expects to get meaning from text • likes to explore new words, language features, and patterns • wants to write on a range of topics • shows confidence in taking risks and making approximations • expects own writing to be enjoyed by others • sustains independent reading for longer periods	• shows an increasing knowledge of print conventions • associates sounds with letter clusters as well as with individual letters • accepts miscues as a part of striving to get meaning • understands the importance of self-monitoring to get meaning • knows that own real and imaginary experiences can influence the meaning gained form books • increases sight vocabulary rapidly	• makes greater use of context for predictions • makes more accurate predictions • uses letter-sound relationships as clues to meaning • selects and integrates appropriate strategies more frequently • uses illustrations for checking rather than for predicting • reads on and rereads to regain meaning • confirms by cross-checking to known items • chooses to read more frequently • copes with a greater variety of genres and forms • copes with more characters, scene changes, and episodes • builds up pace

(continued)

Developmental Stages of Reading *(continued)*

The Fluent Reader

Characteristics	Understandings	Skills and Behaviours
• expects to take a more active part in interacting with the author's message • expects to meet challenges but is more confident in overcoming them • is eager to extend reading interests • gains satisfaction from writing in a range of genres • does not expect to agree with everything that is read • sees books as providing answers to many questions • expects books to be a part of daily life and seeks time to read	• knows how to search for more visual information when having difficulty • understands that taking risks and making approximations are essential parts of reading • knows that texts are constructed for different purposes and different audiences • understands that authors and illustrators have different voices and styles • understands how to adjust reading pace to accommodate purpose, style, and difficulty of material • knows some features of factual texts such as letters, instructions, and explanations	• samples text rather than focusing on every detail • uses an increasing knowledge of letter clusters, affixes, roots, and compound words to confirm predictions • uses a range of strategies to solve problems when reading and writing • integrates sources of information efficiently • sets own purpose for reading • makes inferences from text and illustrations • rereads own writing and edits to maintain meaning • compares styles and forms • uses a range of print conventions in own writing • maintains meaning over longer and more complex structures • copes with longer time sequences and more complex characters • copes with less predictable text • frequently explores books independently • chooses to read for pleasure and for information • summarizes texts for retelling • responds to text in various ways, including critically • expects others to respond to his or her own writing

Running Record Sheet

Name: _____ **Date:** _____

Book/Selection: _____

$$\frac{\text{Number of words correct}}{\text{Number of words in selection}} \times 100 = \underline{\hspace{2cm}} \ \% \ \text{(accuracy)}$$

Easy 96%–100%   Instructional 90%–95%   Hard 89% and below

Page	Title _____ Level _____	Comments

(continued)

Running Record Sheet (*continued*)

Scoring a Running Record

A running record is scored by dividing the total number of words the child reads correctly (including self-corrections, which are not counted as errors) by the total number of words in the selection (called the running word count).

The accuracy (in percent) is calculated as follows:

$$\frac{\text{Number of words correct (includes self-corrections)}}{\text{Number of words in selection}} \times 100 = \underline{\hspace{2cm}} \%$$

Example:

Number of words read correctly:	18
Self-corrections:	2
Total number of correct words:	20
Total number of words in selection:	25

$20/25 \times 100 = 80\%$ accuracy

The following chart indicates the instructional level of the text as it relates to the accuracy rate of the child's reading. In the example above, an 80% accuracy indicates the text is too difficult for that child.

Accuracy Rate	Text Level	Support Level
96% to 100%	Easy	Little new learning taking place; text appropriate for independent reading
90% to 95%	Instructional	Text that requires the reader to problem solve (independently) new challenges while reading, while maintaining the meaning of the text
89% and below	Hard	Text requires too much reading work; the child has to focus on word-by-word analysis and loses the meaning of the text

Concepts About Books and Print:
Class Assessment Summary Sheet

Date: _____

Teacher: _____ **School:** _____

The purpose of this class assessment summary sheet is to provide the teacher with an overall picture of their "class at a glance." This summary also helps teachers get to know their students individually (strengths and needs), and assists them in the formation of flexible learning groups.

	Student Name														
Understands concept of a book (what it is)															
Understands purpose of a book															
Understands content of a book (words, pictures, story, information)															
Understands front of a book (orientation)															
Understands top of a book (orientation)															
Knows where to find title (terminology)															
Recognizes author's name (terminology)															
Knows where to begin reading (opening the book; orientation)															
Knows where on the page to start reading															
Knows which way to read (directionality)															
Knows how to turn the pages (orientation)															
Knows where the story ends (last page, last word)															
Matches spoken words to printed words															
Understands concept of a word (terminology)															
Understands concept of a letter (terminology)															
Understands concept of a period															
Understands concept of a question mark															
Understands concept of a first letter															
Understands concept of a last letter															
Understands concept of upper case (capital) letter															
Understands concept of lower case (small) letter															
Recognizes uppercase letters (fluently)															
Recognizes lowercase letters (fluently)															
Recognizes sight words (high-frequency) 1–50															
Recognizes sight words (51–100+)															

Source: Language Arts Grades 1-2 Teacher's Resource Book, Trehearne 2004, 261.

Self-Assessment: Comprehension Strategies

Name: _____ Date: _____

Today I read: _____ Author: _____

This book was   Easy   Just Right   Hard   (Circle one)

I know this because:

_____

_____

_____

Today I:	Yes	No
1. read the title and author's name and looked at the cover before I began reading		
2. thought about what I already knew about the topic		
3. made a prediction before I began reading		
4. used strategies to help me understand		
5. enjoyed this book		

I retold the story/book to _____

My prediction was: Right On   Close   Not Close   (Circle one)

☺   ☺   ☹

Here is a picture I made in my head.

_____

Source: Language Arts Grades 1-2 Teacher's Resource Book, Trehearne 2004, 529.

Writing Benchmarks: Grade 1

Name: _____ Grade: _____ Date: _____

Teacher: _____ School: _____

Ideas: Message Is Clear
__ Creates pictures to support the text
__ Creates text that others can understand
__ Creates text of five or more related sentences
__ Develops one main idea using important details
__ Writes on different topics

Organization
__ Uses a beginning sentence to introduce the topic
__ Provides a title
__ Uses organizational words (first, then, next, last, finally) to sequence ideas
__ Uses connecting words (then, and, because, etc.)
__ Creates five or more sentences that are generally sequenced effectively
__ Writes an appropriate sentence to end the piece

Voice
__ Shows beginning sense of audience: tries different forms for different purposes (e.g., letter, procedural text, persuasive writing)
__ Creates pictures and text that express personality, mood, individuality
__ Uses !, ?, big or bold letters, repetition, and underlining to make a point
__ Moves the reader

Word Choice
__ Uses a variety of words
__ "Stretches" in an attempt to use new words
__ Attempting (beginning) use of descriptive adjectives and strong verbs

Sentence Fluency
__ Uses a mixture of shorter and longer sentences, mostly shorter
__ Is beginning to vary lead sentences
__ Is beginning to use dialogue
__ Creates a text that others can easily read aloud

Conventions/Presentation
__ Correctly spells many high-frequency words
__ Uses logically invented spelling including vowels in most syllables (may not be correct ones)
__ Capitalizes beginning word in sentences, names, and the pronoun "I"
__ Correctly uses periods and question marks
__ Uses appropriate subject/verb agreement
__ Grammar is generally appropriate
__ Printing, spacing, and drawings make text readable
__ Puts name on work
__ Begins to edit independently

Source: Language Arts Grades 1-2 Teacher's Resource Book, Trehearne 2004, 410.

Writing Scale: Grade 2

	Level 1	Level 2	Level 3	Level 4
Narrative	• unfocused story; limited attention given to plot, setting, and character	• simple, somewhat focused story; limited connection between plot, setting, and character	• logically sequenced story; plot, setting, and character connected with some development	• well sequenced story; plot, setting, and character connected and developed
Expository	• text has limited organization; ideas unclear; details irrelevant; fails to support ideas or give evidence; message, if evident, is unclear	• text organized with some simple ideas; ideas clear but details limited; inconsistently supports ideas with evidence; message is vague	• text organized; ideas are clear; main ideas supported with some evidence; conveys a message	• text well organized; most main ideas well supported with evidence; conveys a clear message
Style	• writes for self almost exclusively; limited attention paid to text form; limited evidence of voice; lacks awareness of audience	• unsure of purpose for writing; applies basic knowledge of text form; relies on one voice; limited awareness of audience	• has purpose for writing; applies most features of text form; voice and audience awareness usually appropriate	• expresses ideas with clarity; applies conventions of text form; voice and audience awareness evident; personal style developing
	• shows limited sentence variety; vocabulary limited and inappropriate	• uses some sentence variety; vocabulary simple but generally appropriate	• uses good sentence variety; vocabulary varied and appropriate	• varies sentences; vocabulary well selected and appropriate; experiments with words for positive effect
Writing Process	• has limited awareness of stages of preparing a written piece (text added rather than integrated for editing; revisions usually added at the end)	• engages in writing and revising stages; edits and proofreads with some success when prompted (misses spelling errors; often repeats the error)	• applies prewriting (thinking, organizing, outlining), writing, revising, editing, and proofreading to many writing tasks	• consistently applies stages of prewriting, writing, revising, editing, and proofreading to most writing tasks
Conventions	• limited control of sentence structure; numerous errors in grade-level grammar, punctuation, capitalization, spelling often interfere with communication; no use of dictionary	• relies on simple sentence structure; some errors in grade-level grammar, punctuation, capitalization, spelling may interfere with communication; little use of dictionary	• has basic control of sentence structure; minor errors in grade-level grammar, punctuation, capitalization, spelling; errors do not interfere with communication; uses dictionary	• shows good control of sentence structure; few, if any errors in grade-level grammar, punctuation, capitalization, spelling; uses dictionary

Self-Assessment: My Writing Ideas

Name: _____ Date: _____

Title: _____

	Yes ☺	No ☹
1. **Are my sentences on topic?**		
All my sentences are about _____ This is my topic: _____		
2. **Did I use good information (details)?**		
I gave many details		
I gave too few details		
Two details I gave are: 1. _____ 2. _____		
My details are interesting.		
3. **Does my picture match my writing?**		

Yes, because my picture shows _____

_____

No, because my picture shows _____

_____

But my writing shows _____

_____

Source: Language Arts Grades 1-2 Teacher's Resource Book, Trehearne 2004, 413.

Teacher/Peer Rubric: Grade 2 Narrative

Criteria	Level 1	Level 2	Level 3	Level 4
A Good Story (Reasoning)	• You need to add more events that will make your story more interesting. For example …	• Some parts are interesting but some parts are not. For example …	• Your story has many interesting events.	• What a great story!
Sounds Real (Communication)	• You need to read your story and make changes that will make it sound like a real story. For example …	• Some parts sound like a real story but some parts do not. For example …	• Your story almost sounds like a real story.	• Your story sounds just like a real story.
Organized (Organization)	• You need to read your story and make changes that will make it easy for the reader to follow. For example …	• Some parts are easy to follow but some parts are confusing. For example …	• Your story is easy to follow.	• Your story is very well organized.
No Mistakes (Conventions)	• You need to read your story and correct the errors that make it difficult to understand. For example …	• You need to read your story and correct the errors that make some parts difficult to understand. For example …	• You need to do a final check and correct the small errors in your story.	• Your story has no errors.

High-Frequency Word Test (End of Grade 1)

Date: _____   School: _____

Name: _____   Teacher: _____

Grade: _____   Test Score: _____/103

Record any incorrect responses. Check off correct responses. Correct responses must be automatic. If the response was not automatic or fluent, mark (h) for hesitation. These words represent approximately 70 percent of all reading for Grade 1–2 students.

Practice word: _____ (student's name)

Word	Attempt	Word	Attempt	Word	Attempt	Word	Attempt
1. the		27. have		53. two		79. my	
2. of		28. this		54. than		80. back	
3. and		29. but		55. no		81. how	
4. to		30. by		56. me		82. did	
5. a		31. were		57. look		83. then	
6. in		32. one		58. him		84. will	
7. is		33. all		59. am		85. over	
8. that		34. she		60. go		86. now	
9. it		35. when		61. see		87. just	
10. was		36. an		62. man		88. after	
11. for		37. their		63. do		89. little	
12. you		38. there		64. us		90. put	
13. he		39. her		65. saw		91. I'm	
14. on		40. can		66. has		92. away	
15. as		41. we		67. day		93. came	
16. are		42. what		68. into		94. going	
17. they		43. about		69. play		95. make	
18. with		44. up		70. mother		96. before	
19. be		45. said		71. get		97. your	
20. his		46. out		72. big		98. don't	
21. at		47. if		73. like		99. because	
22. or		48. some		74. come		100. our	
23. from		49. would		75. went		101. too	
24. had		50. so		76. here		102. could	
25. I		51. who		77. them		103. where	
26. not		52. very		78. asked			

Source: Language Arts Grades 1-2 Teacher's Resource Book, Trehearne 2004, 289.

Oral Language Checklist

Name: _____ Grade: _____ Date: _____

Teacher: _____ School: _____

The following language skills can generally be observed during a variety of classroom activities throughout the school day. Oral language observations can be organized on this checklist. Use a ✓ or an ✗.

	Not Yet	Some of the Time	Most of the Time
Speaking and Listening Behaviours			
1. Participates in whole-group language activities (e.g., discussion, shared reading, read-aloud)			
2. Contributes to small-group discussions			
3. Shares personal experiences and feelings			
4. Relates what is read or heard to personal experiences			
5. Speaks clearly and fluently			
6. Knows when and how to take a turn in conversation			
7. Begins to use language that is sensitive to others' feelings			
8. Is learning to interrupt appropriately			
9. Understands and uses appropriate body language			
• in conversations			
• in oral presentations			
10. Understands classroom language and follows classroom routines			
11. Ignores distractions and focuses on listening task			
12. Recognizes when he/she is not understanding			
13. Begins to ask for clarification or help when necessary			

(continued)

Source: Language Arts Grades 1-2 Teacher's Resource Book, Trehearne 2004, 112-113.

Oral Language Checklist (continued)

	Not Yet	Some of the Time	Most of the Time
Speaking and Listening Behaviours			
14. Asks appropriate questions in response to what was heard			
15. Shows flexibility with communication (e.g., matching language style and language used to the audience, topic, or situation)			
Knowledge of Language Meaning			
16. Understands how to categorize items			
17. Uses descriptive language (e.g., size, shape, colour, number, function, part/whole, action)			
18. Uses language to compare and contrast items and ideas (e.g., same, different)			
19. Gives clear directions using spatial concepts (e.g., right/left, up/down)			
20. Follows two- and three-step directions			
21. Retells story information including characters and key story events			
22. Shares news using "who, what, where, when, why, and how" format			
23. Uses language to make predictions			
24. Begins to make inferences from what is read			
25. Begins to reflect on own learning			
Knowledge of Language Structure			
26. Uses complete sentences when speaking			
27. Uses compound sentences (e.g., joining ideas with *and*, *or*, and *but*)			
28. Uses complex sentences (e.g., joining ideas with *because*, *if*, *when*, *after*, *before*, and *although*)			
Knowledge of Language Sounds			
29. Uses all sounds correctly in oral language			
30. Demonstrates phonological awareness skills			

Self-Assessment Checklist: Me as a Speaker

Name: _____ Date: _____

Grade: _____

This self-assessment is read to and discussed with students initially. Students use the form independently over time.

Self-Assessment—Speaking Behaviours	No ☹	Sometimes 😐	Yes ☺
I look at the person I'm speaking to.			
I speak clearly.			
I speak loudly enough, but not too loud.			
I try to stay on the same topic.			
I know how to take a speaking turn.			
I let the person know when I am finished speaking.			
I interrupt by using the "GAG" strategy.*			

* **G**et the person's attention
Apologize for interrupting
Give the reason for interrupting

Source: Language Arts Grades 1-2 Teacher's Resource Book, Trehearne 2004, 123.

Listening Skills Checklist

Name: _____   Grade: _____   Date: _____

Teacher:_____   School: _____

Hearing History	Yes	No
Student has a history of hearing loss.	☐	☐
Student has a history of middle ear infections.	☐	☐
Student has had a recent hearing assessment.	☐	☐

Date: _____   Result: _____

	Not Yet	Some of the Time	Most of the Time
Listening Environment			
1. Listens effectively one-to-one			
2. Listens effectively in small-group situations			
3. Listens effectively in whole-class activities			
4. Recognizes classroom cues for listening			
5. Responds to specific cues to focus listening behaviour List specific cues used to signal "focus": _____			
Purpose for Listening			
6. Identifies purpose for listening			
7. Listens effectively when - listening to a story			
- listening to factual information			
- listening to instructions			
- other: _____			
Listening Behaviours			
8. Looks at speaker			
9. Uses appropriate body language (e.g., nodding head, leaning forward)			
10. Acknowledges speaker by saying "uh, huh" or "hmm"			
11. Responds by offering a comment or question			
12. Identifies listening distractions			
13. Has strategies to deal with listening distractions			

Source: Language Arts Grades 1-2 Teacher's Resource Book, Trehearne 2004, 116.

Self-Assessment Checklist: Me as a Listener

Name: _____ Date: _____

Grade: _____

This self-assessment is read to and discussed with students initially. Students use the form independently over time.

Self-Assessment-Listening Behaviours	No ☹	Sometimes 😐	Yes ☺
I look at the speaker.			
I think about what is being said.			
I know the things that distract me when I listen.			
I try to ignore the distractions.			
I know what I'm listening for (my purpose).			
I ask when I don't understand something.			
I show respect to the speaker.			

I listen best when:

_____

_____

_____

Source: Language Arts Grades 1-2 Teacher's Resource Book, Trehearne 2004, 124.

Sample Chapter Task Rubric for Patterning

	Level 1	Level 2	Level 3	Level 4
Problem Solving	chooses an **inappropriate** strategy to solve the problem	chooses an **appropriate** strategy	chooses **appropriate** strategies	chooses an **efficient** or **innovative** strategy
			may show more than one way to solve the problem	demonstrates more than one way to solve the problem
	provides an **inaccurate** or **illogical** solution	provides an **inaccurate** or **partial** solution	provides an **accurate** and **complete** solution	provides an **accurate** and **complete** solution
Understanding of Concepts	demonstrates a **limited** understanding of patterning by modelling a small part of the problem situation	demonstrates **some** understanding of patterning by partially modelling the problem situation	demonstrates **an understanding** of patterning by modelling the problem situation	demonstrates **an in-depth** understanding of patterning by thoroughly modelling the problem situation; may use symbols and/or labels
	provides a **limited description** of the pattern created when more shapes are added	**partially describes** the pattern created when more shapes are added	**describes** the pattern created when more shapes are added	provides an **in-depth description** of the pattern created when more cars/trailers are added
Application of Mathematical Procedures	continues the pattern, making **major errors**	continues the pattern, making **some errors**	continues the pattern, making **very few errors**	continues the pattern **accurately**
Communication of Required Knowledge Related to Procedures and Problem Solving	demonstrates a **limited** ability to communicate strategies used	communicates strategies with **some clarity**	communicates strategies and reasoning **with clarity**	communicates strategies and reasoning **with clarity and precision**
	records **very little**	provides **partial** recordings	provides a **complete** recording using words, numbers, and pictures	provides a **thorough** recording using words, numbers, and pictures
	demonstrates a **limited** ability to use math terminology appropriately	demonstrates **some** ability to use math terminology appropriately	**generally uses** math terminology appropriately	**uses** math terminology skillfully

Sample Chapter Interview Questions and Prompts:
Grade 2 Mathematics

Patterning

Interview Questions/Prompts	Watch and Listen
Part 1 Place a pile of attribute blocks on the table in front of the student. Ask the student to make a pattern and describe it. If the student has made a pattern with 2 attributes, ask what the 2 attributes are. If not, make a new 2-attribute pattern. Ask: **How is my pattern different from yours?** Ask: **How can you use actions to describe my pattern?** **How can you change it to make a different pattern?**	☐ recognizes that an object has more than 1 attribute ☐ creates a pattern using a single attribute ☐ creates and extends a pattern that shows change in 1 attribute ☐ translates a pattern into other forms ☐ combines 2 attributes in creating a pattern ☐ explains a pattern rule
Part 2 Place toothpicks on the table in front of the student. Draw a circle on a piece of paper. Place 1 toothpick out from the edge. **Here is a flower with one petal.** Draw another circle and add 2 toothpick petals. Here is a flower with 2 petals. Then make a flower with 3 petals. Ask the student to make the next flower. Ask: **How did you know what to do?** **How many petals are on the next flower? on the next?** **What is the pattern rule?** Repeat as above, this time showing 3 flowers that grow by 3 petals (3, 6, 9). Have the student make the next flower. Observe, then ask how the student determined the number of petals. **What is the pattern rule?** Show the student a blank t-chart. Label the columns Flowers and Petals. Point to the first 3-petal toothpick flower. Print 1 in the left column and 3 in the right. Point to the second flower. Print 2 in the left and 6 in the right. Ask: **What will I print next? Why?** **Print the next 2 numbers for me.** Give the student a calculator. Ask: **How can the calculator and the chart help you figure out the number of petals on 7 flowers?** Allow the student to demonstrate with the calculator and chart.	☐ describes a growing pattern as skip counting or repeated addition ☐ explains the relationship between counting patterns on a t-chart ☐ uses a calculator to extend a growing number pattern ☐ organizes data on a chart to extend a pattern

Sample Chapter Interview Recording Sheet: Grade 2 Mathematics

Sorting and Patterning

Student:	Date:
Part 1	Comments:
☐ recognizes that an object has more than 1 attribute	
☐ creates a pattern using a single attribute	
☐ creates and extends a pattern that shows change in 1 attribute	
☐ translates a pattern into other forms	
☐ combines 2 attributes in creating a pattern	
☐ explains a pattern rule	
Part 2	
☐ describes a growing pattern as skip counting or repeated addition	
☐ explains the relationship between counting patterns on a t-chart	
☐ uses a calculator to extend a growing number pattern	
☐ organizes data on a chart to extend a pattern	

Student:	Date:
Part 1	Comments:
☐ recognizes that an object has more than 1 attribute	
☐ creates a pattern using a single attribute	
☐ creates and extends a pattern that shows change in 1 attribute	
☐ translates a pattern into other forms	
☐ combines 2 attributes in creating a pattern	
☐ explains a pattern rule	
Part 2	
☐ describes a growing pattern as skip counting or repeated addition	
☐ explains the relationship between counting patterns on a t-chart	
☐ uses a calculator to extend a growing number pattern	
☐ organizes data on a chart to extend a pattern	

Sample Chapter Checklist: Sorting and Patterning

Throughout the chapter, observe individual students for evidence that they show an understanding of key knowledge and can perform key skills.

Student:	Sorts objects by more than 1 attribute	Identifies and describes patterns using 1 or 2 attributes	Creates, extends, compares, and translates patterns	Uses charts and/or calculator to display and extend a pattern	Solves problems using patterns	Uses pattern rules

Probing Questions

- What letters can you use to describe this pattern? What is another way you can show the same pattern?
- How many attributes change in this pattern? How do they change? What will come next?

Assessment of Learning Summary

Student Name: _____

Date: _____

Sorting and Patterning

Chapter Goals		
Sorts objects by more than 1 attribute		
Identifies and describes patterns using 1 or 2 attributes		
Creates, extends, compares, and translates patterns		
Uses charts and/or a calculator to display and extend a pattern		
Solves problems using patterns		
Uses pattern rules		

Chapter Task Summary:

☐ Problem Solving

☐ Understanding of Concepts

☐ Application of Procedures

☐ Communication

Summary of Anecdotal Records:

REPORT CARD COMMENTS

Strengths:

Areas of Need:

Next Steps:

Summary of Interview(s):

Rubric for "Design a Dream Bedroom" Task: Grade 3

Criteria	Level 1	Level 2	Level 3	Level 4
Depth of Understanding	• demonstrates a **superficial or inaccurate** understanding of congruency, symmetry, and patterning	• demonstrates a **growing but still incomplete** understanding of congruency, symmetry, and patterning	• demonstrates a **grade-appropriate** understanding of standard units of congruency, symmetry, and patterning	• demonstrates an **in-depth** understanding of standard units of congruency, symmetry, and patterning
	• demonstrates a **superficial or inaccurate** understanding of 2-D shapes and 3-D figures	• demonstrates a **growing but still incomplete** understanding of 2-D shapes and 3-D figures	• demonstrates a **grade-appropriate** understanding of 2-D shapes and 3-D figures	• demonstrates an **in-depth** understanding of 2-D shapes and 3-D figures
	• design reflects **limited** creativity	• design reflects **some** creativity	• design reflects **some** creativity and innovation	• design reflects a **high degree** of creativity and innovation
Applying Procedures	• makes **major errors and/or omissions** when measuring or drawing geometric shapes	• makes **several errors and/or omissions** when measuring or drawing geometric shapes	• makes only a **few minor errors and/or omissions** when measuring and drawing geometric shapes	• makes **almost no errors** when measuring or drawing geometric shapes
Explanation and Justification of Mathematical Thinking	• provides an **incomplete or inaccurate** description of their bedroom design using few words, figures, or numbers	• provides a **partial** description of their bedroom design using some words and/or figures and/or numbers	• provides a **grade-appropriate** description of their bedroom design using a range of words and/or figures and/or numbers	• provides a **thorough and clear** description of their bedroom design using a range of words and/or figures and/or numbers
Use of Mathematical Vocabulary	• uses **very little** mathematical vocabulary in describing their design	• uses **some** mathematical vocabulary in describing their design	• uses **grade-appropriate** mathematical vocabulary in describing their design	• uses a **broad range** of mathematical vocabulary in describing their design

Rubric for "Plants" Culminating Task: Grade 3

Criteria	Level 1	Level 2	Level 3	Level 4
Inquiry Question	· has difficulty posing an inquiry question	· needs some help to pose an inquiry question	· independently poses an inquiry question	· poses a thoughtful inquiry question
Gathering Data/ Record Keeping	· has difficulty gathering, recording, and organizing data	· needs some help to gather, record, and organize data	· independently gathers, records, and organizes data	· gathers, records, and organizes data effectively
Communication	· has difficulty organizing ideas and presenting information	· needs some help to present information so it is clear and organized	· independently presents information	· presents information clearly and precisely
	· ideas are incomplete or unclear	· ideas are simple but are in order	· ideas are clear and make sense	· ideas are well-expressed and are interesting
Information Supported with Data	· has difficulty using data collected to support ideas presented	· needs some help to use data collected to support ideas presented	· independently uses data collected to support ideas presented	· effectively uses data collected to support ideas presented so they are clear and informative

At-a-Glance Recording Sheet

Use this chart to record observations about students' skills and/or level of understanding when moving around the class or conferencing one-on-one.

NAME	NAME	NAME	NAME	NAME
NAME	NAME	NAME	NAME	NAME
NAME	NAME	NAME	NAME	NAME
NAME	NAME	NAME	NAME	NAME
NAME	NAME	NAME	NAME	NAME

K-W-L-M Chart

Name: _____ Date: _____

Topic: _____

What We Know	What We Want to Learn	What We Learned	What More Do We Want to Know

Source: Language Arts Grades 1-2 Teacher's Resource Book, Trehearne 2004, 103.

How We Worked Together

Name: _____ Date: _____

Who is in our group:

_____

_____

_____

Circle the answer that tells about your group.

We got our work done.	No	Some of it	Most of it	Completely
We took turns talking.	No	Some of the time	Most of the time	All of the time
We shared the work.	No	Some of the time	Most of the time	All of the time
We helped each other.	No	Some of the time	Most of the time	All of the time
We encouraged each other.	No	Some of the time	Most of the time	All of the time
We were polite to each other.	No	Some of the time	Most of the time	All of the time
We feel good about our work.	No	Some of it	Most of it	All of it

Thinking About My Work

Name: _____   Date: _____

Something I am proud of:

Something I learned:

Something I wonder about:

Something I want to do better:

Something I liked about someone else's work:

A Sample of Assessment Tools for Grades 4 to 6

In this section, you will find a range of assessment tools designed for classroom use. There are rubrics intended for teacher, self-, and peer assessment, as well as checklists designed for self- and peer assessment. All of these tools may be used to assess *for* learning, and they may be used to gather assessment *of* learning data. These tools should be shared with students and parents so that everyone is aware of the standards used to define quality work.

The rubrics for Grades 4–6 enable the assessor to *rate* achievement on a 4-point scale*. We do not expect students to pass through each of these four levels in the normal course of their learning. Instead, Levels 3 and 4 represent quality performance and a major goal of our teaching is to have as many students as possible performing at these levels.

Language Arts

* THESE TOOLS ARE ALSO AVAILABLE IN A MODIFIABLE FORMAT ON THE CD-ROM.

Mathematics

Page	Resource
380	4.13 Initial Assessment Summary
381	4.14 What to Look for When Assessing Student Achievement
382	4.15 Coaching Students Toward Success
383	4.16 Student Interview Form (with prompts)
385	4.17 Student Interview Form (without prompts)
386	4.18 Problem-Solving Rubric
387	4.19 Knowledge and Understanding Rubric
388	4.20 Application of Learning Rubric
389	4.21 Communication Rubric—Mathematics
390	4.22 Using the Assessment of Learning Summary
391	4.23 Assessment of Learning Summary
392	4.24 Assessment of Learning Summary (Sample)
393	4.25 Rubric for Identifying Student Levels of Response (Teacher's Version)
395	4.26 How Am I Doing in Mathematics? (Student's Version)

Social Studies

Page	Resource
396	4.27 Grade 6 Social Studies Performance Task Rubric

Generic Tools

Page	Resource
397	4.28 Diagnostic Assessment: Understanding Key Concepts
398	4.29 Self-Assessment Checklist: Problem-Solving Tasks

Sample Rubric: Reading Conference

Name: _____ Date: _____

Criteria	1 - Developing	2 - Basic	3 - Proficient	4 - Strong
Fluency	• pauses frequently, sometimes for extended periods	• reads slowly and deliberately with some hesitation	• reads most of the text smoothly	• reads confidently and expressively
Miscues/Use of Cues	• makes several miscues that do not make sense	• makes some miscues; some may be illogical	• makes few miscues; most are logical in the context	• makes few, if any, miscues; all are logical in the context
	• often unaware that correction is needed	• corrects most miscues, but may occasionally get "stuck"	• self-corrects, often relying on the context	• self-corrects quickly
	• tends to rely on one type of cue (e.g., phonetic)	• uses cues, but may not be effective or efficient	• uses a variety of cues effectively and efficiently	• uses a variety of cues effectively and efficiently
Understanding and Recall of Main Ideas	• may omit or misunderstand main ideas or key events	• includes most main ideas or key events	• able to state main ideas or key events, and shows some understanding of their relationships	• focuses on main ideas and key events, and explains their relationships
Understanding and Recall of Detail	• recalls some details	• includes some details in retelling or discussion but may be inconsistent	• offers some accurate and relevant details in retelling or discussions	• offers relevant details and examples in retelling or discussion
	• may be unable to find relevant details in response to questions	• able to find details in response to specific questions or prompts	• may cite specific evidence to support an answer	• cites specific evidence to support an answer
Personal Response	• may not connect the selection to own experiences or other works	• makes general or obvious connections to own experiences or other works	• makes connections to own experiences or other works	• makes connections to experiences or other works that show some insight (goes beyond the obvious)
	• expresses unsupported opinions or preferences	• expresses preferences with some general support	• offers some support for opinions or preferences	• provides logical reasons and explanations for opinions or preferences

Teacher Rubric: Assessing Writing Ideas

Name: _____   **Date:** _____

4	• The paper is clear and focused from beginning to end. The topic is small and very well defined, so it's easy for the writer to manage. • The message/story is both engaging and memorable. • The writer seems to have a thorough understanding of the topic. • The writer is selective, sharing beyond-the-obvious details that are informing, entertaining, or both.
3	• The reader can identify the writer's main idea. The topic is well defined, and is small enough to handle in the scope of the paper. • The message/story has many engaging moments. • The writer knows enough about the topic to do a good job. • The writer has chosen many interesting details.
2	• The reader can discern the main idea. The topic is defined to some extent, but it needs to be more narrow and more manageable. • The message/story has some engaging moments. • The writer has some understanding of the topic; more information is needed to make this writing more interesting and/or helpful. • The writing contains some interesting or unusual details.
1	• The main idea is unclear. What is the writer trying to say? • The message/story lacks engaging moments. • The writer has a limited understanding of the topic. There is not enough information to make the writing interesting or helpful. • Details are very sketchy. The reader can only guess at the writer's meaning.

Student Rubric: Assessing Writing Ideas

Name: _____   **Date:** _____

4	**My paper has plenty of details that make my main idea clear.** • My readers will really enjoy and remember my paper/story. • Readers can tell that I know a lot about this topic. • I chose my details carefully. They are important and interesting.
3	**My main idea is clear and well thought out.** • Readers will enjoy my story/paper. • I know enough about the topic to keep my readers interested. • My details make my topic interesting.
2	**My main idea is clear in some parts, but in others it's a little scattered.** • Readers will enjoy some parts of my story/paper. • I know some things about this topic. I wish I knew more so that I could keep my readers interested. • Some of my details are interesting, but some of them are things most people already know.
1	**My main idea isn't clear. I don't know what I want to say.** • I doubt my readers will want to finish reading my story/paper. • I don't know enough about this topic to write about it. My story/paper is not interesting. • I need better details. My readers won't be able to understand what I'm saying.

Teacher Rubric: Assessing Writing Conventions

Name: _____   **Date:** _____

4	**If there are any errors, they are insignificant. Their impact on the text is minor.**
	• The writer uses conventions skillfully to bring out meaning and/or voice.
	• The writer shows control over a wide range of conventions for this grade level.
	• This piece is ready to publish.
3	**A few minor errors are noticeable; however, they do not affect the clarity.**
	• The writer often uses conventions to enhance meaning or voice.
	• The writer shows control over most conventions appropriate for this grade level.
	• This piece is ready to publish with minor touch-ups.
2	**There are several minor errors, some of which may interfere with meaning or slow a reader down.**
	• Errors in the use of conventions affect readability.
	• The writer uses some conventions appropriate for the grade level, but is not fully in control of them.
	• Thorough, careful editing is needed prior to publication.
1	**Serious, frequent errors make this text hard to read.**
	• Though a few things are done correctly, serious errors impair readability.
	• This writer does not appear to be in control of many conventions appropriate for this grade level.
	• Thorough, word-by-word editing is required for publication.

Student Rubric: Assessing Writing Conventions

Name: _____   **Date:** _____

4	**A reader would have a hard time finding errors in my paper. If he/she does, those mistakes won't change the meaning at all.** • I used conventions correctly, which made the meaning very clear. • I checked the spelling, punctuation, grammar, and capitalization. They are all correct. • My paper is ready to publish.
3	**I made a few minor mistakes that the reader will likely notice, but my meaning is still clear.** • I used conventions correctly and this helps the reader understand the meaning. • I checked the spelling, punctuation, grammar, and capitalization. I believe most if it is correct. • Once I make a few small changes, my paper will be ready to publish.
2	**The reader will notice some errors. These errors may make my meaning harder to understand.** • I did a lot of things right, but I also made some errors. The reader might slow down once or twice because of the errors. • I checked my spelling, punctuation, grammar, and capitalization. I corrected things I knew were wrong, but I wasn't sure if some things were right or wrong. • I have to reread and carefully edit my paper before it will be ready to publish.
1	**The reader will notice lots of errors. These errors make my meaning very hard to understand.** • All of the errors make my paper very hard to read. • I did not check a lot of my spelling, punctuation, grammar, and capitalization. I did not really edit this piece. • My paper is far from being ready to publish. I have to reread it very carefully, one word at a time, and make all necessary corrections before it will be ready to publish.

Writing Process Rubric

Name: _____   **Date:** _____

- *This rubric is appropriate to assess any or all stages in the writing process.*
- *It may be used while conferencing with individual students, with groups of students, or while observing students as they work.*
- *Use only those criteria that are appropriate to a given stage in the writing process.*
- *Focus on the indicators when conducting assessment for learning; focus on the indicators and performance levels when conducting assessment of learning.*

Categories/Criteria	Level 1	Level 2	Level 3	Level 4
Prewriting	• **shows reluctance** to brainstorm ideas and approaches with peers and/or teacher	• **attempts** to brainstorm ideas and approaches with peers and/or teacher	• **brainstorms** ideas and approaches with peers and/or teacher	• **shows insight and creativity** when brainstorming ideas and approaches with peers and/or teacher
	• has difficulty **generating ideas for the task**	• generates **some** ideas for the task	• generates **workable** ideas for the task	• generates **rich** ideas for the task
	• **has difficulty** conducting research on the topic (if required)	• **attempts** to conduct research on the topic (if required)	• conducts **sufficient** research on the topic (if required)	• conducts **thorough** research on the topic (if required)
Drafting	• **produces a limited** first draft that meets **few** of the criteria for the task	• **produces** a first draft that meets **some** of the criteria for the task	• **produces an acceptable** first draft that meets **most** of the criteria for the task	• **produces a creative and original** first draft that meets **all** of the criteria for the task
Revising	• reads draft but **has difficulty** identifying the need to make improvements	• reads draft and makes **some** necessary improvements	• reads draft **critically** and makes **appropriate** improvements	• reads draft **critically** and makes **significant** improvements
Editing	• **shows reluctance/has difficulty** editing for content, sentence structure, paragraph structure, spelling, grammar, punctuation	• makes **some** edits for content, sentence structure, paragraph structure, spelling, grammar, punctuation	• edits **sufficiently** for content, sentence structure, paragraph structure, spelling, grammar, punctuation	• **routinely** and **thoroughly** edits for content, sentence structure, paragraph structure, spelling, grammar, punctuation
Proofreading	• reads final draft but **misses many** errors	• reads final draft but **misses some** errors	• reads final draft **carefully**	• reads final draft **critically and carefully**
Conferencing	• **has difficulty** identifying strengths and weaknesses in own work	• **attempts** to identify strengths and weaknesses in own work	• **identifies** several strengths and weaknesses in own work	• **shows insight and objectivity** about strengths and weaknesses in own work
	• **shows reluctance** to incorporate feedback from others	• **attempts** to incorporate feedback from others	• **willingly incorporates** feedback from others to improve the piece	• **seeks** to understand and incorporate feedback from others to improve the piece
	• **has difficulty** providing feedback to others about their writing	• **attempts** to provide feedback to others about their writing	• **offers helpful** feedback to others about their writing	• **routinely offers insightful** feedback to others about their writing

Descriptive Writing Rubric

Name: _____

Date: _____

- This rubric is appropriate to assess a variety of descriptive writing tasks.
- Use only those criteria that are appropriate for a given assessment task, at a given time.
- Focus on the indicators when conducting assessment for learning; focus on the indicators and performance levels when conducting assessment of learning.

Categories/Criteria	Level 1	Level 2	Level 3	Level 4
Style	• includes **insufficient** details to create mental images	• includes **some** details that create partial mental images	• piece includes **sufficient** details to create mental images	• piece includes **rich and sophisticated** details to create mental images
	• figurative language (similes, personification, etc.) is **lacking** or used **ineffectively**	• figurative language (similes, personification, etc.) is used **somewhat effectively**	• figurative language (similes, personification, etc.) is used **effectively**	• figurative language (similes, personification, etc.) is used **skillfully**
	• sentence type and length show **little variation**	• sentence type and length show **some variation**	• sentence type and length are **varied**	• sentence type and length are **varied skillfully to engage the reader**
Communication	• piece does **not engage** reader	• piece engages reader **to some extent**	• piece **engages** reader	• piece **engages** reader **thoroughly**
	• choice of words has **little appeal** to the senses	• choice of words has **some appeal** to the senses	• choice of words **appeals** to the senses	• **skillful** choice of words results in **wide appeal** to the senses
	• writer's voice is **lacking**	• writer's voice is **sometimes evident**	• writer's voice is **evident**	• writer's voice is **consistently evident**
Conventions	• **numerous errors** in spelling and/or grammar and/or punctuation **seriously interfere** with communication	• **several errors** in spelling and/or grammar and/or punctuation **interfere** with communication **to some degree**	• there are **minor errors** in spelling and/or grammar and/or punctuation, but not sufficient to interfere with communication	• **few if any errors** in spelling, grammar, or punctuation

Producing a Children's Book Rubric

Name: _____ Date: _____

Criteria	Limited	Acceptable	Proficient	Excellent
Creativity	• theme is **not original**	• theme shows **some originality**	• theme is **original**	• theme is **original** and **clever**
Writing Style	• theme **may not engage** children	• theme **may engage some children**	• theme is **engaging** for children	• theme is **highly engaging** for children
	• vocabulary and sentence structure **show little variety**	• vocabulary and sentence structure show **some variety**	• vocabulary and sentence structure are **effective**	• vocabulary and sentence structure are **highly effective**
	• dialogue is **lacking**	• dialogue shows **some realism**	• dialogue is **realistic**	• dialogue is **life-like** and **engaging**
Illustrations	• pictures or artwork are **ineffective**	• pictures or artwork add to the story to **some degree**	• pictures or artwork are **effective**	• pictures or artwork are **visually striking**
Professionalism	• book **lacks polish**	• book shows **some attention to final polishing**	• book is **polished**	• book is **polished and professional looking**
Conventions	• errors **seriously interfere** with the story	• errors **interfere with the story to some extent**	• book contains **minimal errors**	• book is **free of errors**

Informal Speaking and Listening Rubric

Name: _____   Date: _____

Categories/Criteria	Level 1	Level 2	Level 3	Level 4
Thinking	• demonstrates **limited ability** to explore/express thoughts when speaking to others • demonstrates **limited** ability to build on the ideas of others	• demonstrates **some ability** to explore/express thoughts when speaking to others (e.g., is beginning to reflect, analyze, hypothesize) • demonstrates **some** ability to build on the ideas of others	• **explores/expresses own thoughts** when speaking to others (e.g., reflects, analyzes, hypothesizes) • **builds on** the ideas of others when speaking	• **explores/expresses original/creative thoughts** when speaking to others (e.g., reflects, analyzes, hypothesizes) • **integrates and extends** the ideas of others when speaking

Communication	• expresses ideas, opinions, feelings with **limited clarity** when speaking to others in terms of:
	  • fluency
	  • volume
	  • speed
	  • intonation
	  • inflection
	• uses a **limited** vocabulary
	• has **difficulty** maintaining appropriate eye contact when speaking
	• makes **limited** use of gestures when speaking
		• expresses ideas, opinions, feelings with **partial clarity** when speaking to others in terms of:
		  • fluency
		  • volume
		  • speed
		  • intonation
		  • inflection
		• **attempts to use** new vocabulary
		• maintains eye contact **some of** the time when speaking
		• makes **some** use of gestures when speaking
			• expresses ideas, opinions, feelings **clearly** when speaking to others in terms of:
			  • fluency
			  • volume
			  • speed
			  • intonation
			  • inflection
			• uses new vocabulary **effectively**
			• maintains **appropriate** eye contact when speaking
			• uses gestures **effectively** when speaking
				• expresses ideas, opinions, feelings **clearly and in an engaging manner** when speaking to others in terms of:
				  • fluency
				  • volume
				  • speed
				  • intonation
				  • inflection
				• **explores** new vocabulary **successfully**
				• **establishes and maintains** eye contact when speaking
				• uses gestures **naturally and effectively** when speaking

Active Listening	• demonstrates **limited ability** to listen to others' ideas, opinions, points of view • challenges to others' ideas, opinions, points of view **may be inappropriate** • asks **few** questions • has **difficulty** demonstrating appropriate posture and body language when listening to others	• listens **some of the time** to others' ideas, opinions, points of view • **attempts to** challenge others' ideas, opinions, points of view appropriately • **attempts to** ask appropriate questions • demonstrates appropriate posture and body language **some of the time** when listening to others	• listens **attentively** to others' ideas, opinions, points of view • challenges others' ideas, opinions, points of view **appropriately** • asks **appropriate** questions • demonstrates **appropriate** posture and body language when listening to others	• listens **attentively and respectfully** to others' ideas, opinions, points of view • challenges others' ideas, opinions, points of view **appropriately and constructively** • asks **insightful** questions • **encourages** speaker through appropriate use of posture and body language

Presentation and Speech Rubric

Name: _____   **Date:** _____

- *This rubric is appropriate to assess a variety of oral presentations.*
- *Use only those criteria that are appropriate for a given assessment task, at a given time.*
- *Focus on the indicators when conducting assessment for learning; focus on the indicators and performance levels when conducting assessment of learning.*

Categories/Criteria	Level 1	Level 2	Level 3	Level 4
Content	· ideas are **derived from another source or cliché** OR · material **lacks depth** and **may include many inaccuracies**	· ideas show **some original** thinking OR · material shows **some depth** but **may include inaccuracies**	· ideas are **creative and original** OR · material is **well researched** and **accurate**	· ideas are **creative, original, and sophisticated** OR · material is **thoroughly researched** and **accurate**
	· responses to questions are **hesitant or unclear** and **may not be appropriate**	· responses to questions are **somewhat clear** and generally **appropriate**	· responses to questions are **clear** and **appropriate**	· responses to questions are **clear, appropriate, and insightful**
Organization	· opening **lacks clarity**	· opening attempts to **introduce** topic	· opening **clearly** introduces topic	· opening is **engaging, original,** and clearly introduces topic
	· ideas are presented with **significant lapses** in logic	· ideas are presented with **some lapses** in logic	· ideas are presented in a **logical** sequence	· ideas are presented **logically** and in an **original** way
	· conclusion **lacks clarity**	· conclusion is **partially clear**	· conclusion is **clear**	· conclusion is **clear, effective,** and **original**
Communication	· word choice and level of language reflect a **limited sense** of the intended purpose or audience	· word choice and level of language **attempt to suit** the purpose and audience	· word choice and level of language are **appropriate** to the purpose and audience	· word choice and level of language are **skillfully suited** to the purpose and audience
	· speech **lacks** fluency, expressiveness, and/or audibility	· speech is **somewhat** fluent, expressive, and generally audible	· speech is **fluent, expressive, and audible**	· speech is fluent, **highly** expressive, and audible
	· gestures and facial expressions **add little** to the effectiveness of the presentation	· gestures and facial expressions **add somewhat** to the effectiveness of the presentation	· gestures and facial expressions **add to the effectiveness** of the presentation	· gestures and facial expressions are used **skillfully** to increase the effectiveness of the presentation

Peer Assessment Checklist: Oral Report

Assessor: _____   **Class:** _____

	Yes	No
Content		
1. The presentation included sufficient details.		
2. The material presented was interesting to listen to.		
Communication		
3. The speaker's voice was loud enough to hear easily.		
4. The speaker's voice was clear so that I could understand easily.		
5. The speaker delivered the presentation at an appropriate speed.		
6. The speaker made eye contact with the audience.		
7. The speaker used gestures to help make points clear.		
Organization		
8. The presentation had a clear beginning that caught my interest.		
9. The presentation had a clear conclusion.		
10. The speaker connected the ideas so that I could follow easily.		

What you did well:

_____

_____

_____

What you did not do well:

_____

_____

_____

Next time, I suggest that you

_____

_____

_____

Role-Play and Dramatization Rubric

Name: _____   **Date:** _____

- *Focus on only selected criteria and their corresponding indicators when conducting assessment for learning; focus on all criteria, corresponding indicators and performance levels when conducting assessment of learning.*

Categories/Criteria	Level 1	Level 2	Level 3	Level 4
Creativity	· ideas are **derived from another source or cliché**	· ideas show **some original** thinking	· ideas are **creative and original**	· ideas are **creative, original, and sophisticated**
	· characters **lack believability**	· characters are **convincing some of the time,** or to some degree	· characters are **convincing**	· characters are **convincing and engaging**
	· humour (if applicable) is **lacking or ineffective**	· humour (if applicable) is **somewhat effective**	· humour (if applicable) is **effective**	· humour (if applicable) is **effective and sophisticated**
	· props **add little** to the overall effect	· props are **effective to some extent**	· props are **appropriate** and add to the overall effect	· props are used **skillfully** and **creatively** to add to the overall effect
Communication	· piece holds **little engagement** for the audience	· audience is engaged **to some degree**	· audience is **engaged**	· audience is **captivated**
	· dialogue bears **little resemblance** to real conversation	· dialogue bears **some resemblance** to real conversation	· dialogue is **realistic and believable**	· dialogue is **realistic** and **convincing**
	· piece reflects a **limited** sense of the intended purpose or audience	· piece **attempts** to suit the purpose and audience	· piece is **appropriate** to the purpose and audience	· piece is **skillfully suited** to the purpose and audience
	· speech **lacks** fluency, expressiveness, and/or audibility	· speech shows **some** fluency, expressiveness, and is **mostly** audible	· speech is **fluent, expressive,** and **audible**	· speech is fluent, **highly** expressive and audible
	· gestures and facial expressions **add little** to the piece	· gestures and facial expressions **contribute somewhat** to the piece	· gestures and facial expressions are **appropriate**	· gestures and facial expressions are used **skillfully** to deepen character and engage the audience
Staging	· dramatic conventions are used to **little effect** (e.g., blocking, entrances, and exits)	· dramatic conventions are **somewhat effective** (e.g., blocking, entrances, and exits)	· dramatic conventions are used **effectively** (e.g., blocking, entrances, and exits)	· dramatic conventions are used to **great effect** throughout (e.g., blocking, entrances, and exits)

Initial Assessment Summary

Student: _____ **Class:** _____ **Term:** _____

- Use this tool to assess students' prior knowledge, as well as those concepts and skills requiring intervention.
- Enter assessment data from initial assessment activities that you choose.
- Record anecdotal comments rather than levels or scores, since these data are not for reporting purposes.

Date	Chapter	Skills/Concepts	Observations/Next Steps/Intervention

What to Look for When Assessing Student Achievement

When observing students as they work, or when examining completed work, look for the following kinds of evidence.

Knowledge and Understanding	Application of Learning	Problem Solving/Thinking	Communication

• assess the completeness and depth of the learner's knowledge of mathematics content (e.g., facts, terms, procedural skills, use of tools)
 	
 • assess the depth of the learner's understanding of concepts (i.e., how deep is the student's grasp of concepts?)
 	
 • assess the learner's ability to make observations about their own learning, as reflected in their work and during discussions and one-on-one conferences
	• assess the learner's ability to apply mathematical knowledge and skills in familiar contexts (i.e., the ability to apply new learning to solve familiar or routine problems)
	
	 • assess the learner's ability to transfer mathematical knowledge and skills to new contexts (i.e., to what extent is it evident that the learner is making the connections that demonstrate he or she "gets it"?)
	
	 • assess the learner's ability to make connections:
	    • between new mathematical concepts and prior learning
	    • between new mathematical concepts and other subject areas
	    • between their learning in mathematics and contexts outside the classroom
		You may focus on one or all of the following steps:
		
		 Understand the Problem
		 • assess the learner's depth of understanding of the problem (i.e., the ability to differentiate between relevant and irrelevant information and the ability to restate/rephrase the problem)
		
		 Make a Plan
		 • assess the completeness of the plan developed by the learner to solve the problem
		
		 Carry Out the Plan
		 • assess the ability of the learner to use one or more strategies to solve the problem, and the flexibility shown by the learner when using the strategy(ies)
		 • assess the ability of the learner to revise the plan, when necessary, to solve the problem
		 • assess the correctness with which the learner selects and uses procedures in terms of frequency of errors/omissions
		
		 Look Back
		 • assess the learner's identification of procedural and computational errors and omissions within a solution
		 • assess the degree to which the learner reflects on the reasonableness of his or her solution
		
		 Communicate
		 • assess the completeness of the learner's explanation of his or her solution
		 • assess the clarity and precision of the explanation
		 • assess the use of mathematical language and representations in the solution
			• assess the completeness, clarity, and logic of the learner's explanations and justifications of their understanding through oral, visual, and written modes
			
			 • assess expressive communication (i.e., to what extent is the learner's communication clear and precise to the reader/listener?)
			
			 • assess the clarity and precision of the learner's use of mathematical vocabulary
			
			 • assess the degree to which the learner organizes written, spoken, and drawn work in order to communicate effectively
			
			 • assess the degree to which the learner uses mathematical units, symbols, and labels correctly and effectively

Coaching Students Toward Success

- *Use the following prompts when providing students with feedback to help them improve their learning.*
- *Provide each student with a copy of this chart*

Knowledge and Understanding	Application of Learning	Problem Solving/Thinking	Communication
- "Ink your thinking." - Talk me through what you did. - Make it short but say enough that I can see what you were thinking. - Explain with more detail. - Describe the math idea; explain how the idea relates to another math idea; provide an example to explain the idea. - Is there a counter-example?	- What knowledge are you going to use to answer this question/complete this task/solve this problem? - What procedure(s) are you going to use to answer this question/complete this task/solve this problem? - How is this question/task/problem similar to/different from ones you have done before? - What strategies could help you? - How is the concept we learned today similar to a previous concept? - How could you use this concept in science (or another subject)? - Why/how is this skill/concept important outside of school?	- What information is given? What information is important? What information is not important? - What are you asked to find out? - What do you need to know? - What information is important to solve this problem? - What information is missing? - Show your mathematical thinking at every stage (Understand, Plan, Do, Look Back, Communicate) - Do you notice any patterns? - Is there a rule that you could share and explain? - Show the materials and representations that helped you solve the problem. - Use different ways to show what you did. - Justify your answer. Tell what you were thinking. - How do you know you are right? (reasonableness, looking back)	- Read over what you have written - Does it make sense? - Could another person follow what you did? - Do you need to explain more fully? - Have you used precise, correct mathematical terms? - Have you used correct mathematical symbols?

Student Interview Form (with prompts)

Name: _____   **Date:** _____

You may want to use one or more of the four generic rubrics as a focus for the interviews. This will help students to understand areas of strength and need. Additional bullets are provided for your own prompts.

Problem Solving/Thinking
*Focus on selection and use of **appropriate strategies**.*

Sample Prompts:

• What are you asked?

_____

• How did you decide what information is important?

_____

• What strategies did you try?

_____

• Show me what you did.

_____

• How do you know if it's right?

_____

Knowledge and Understanding
*Focus on the questions "**Does the student know _____?**" and "**Does the student understand _____?**"*

Sample Prompts:

• Can you explain to me …?

_____

• How is …like …?

_____

• Talk me through what you did.

_____

(continued)

Student Interview Form (with prompts) *(continued)*

Name: _____   **Date:** _____

Application of Learning
*Focus on ability to **apply**, **transfer**, and **connect learning** in a variety of contexts.*

Sample Prompts:

- What knowledge/skill did you use to answer this question/complete this task/solve this problem?

  _____

- How is this question/task/problem similar to ones you have done before?

  _____

- How is this concept similar to a previous concept?

  _____

- Why is this skill important outside of school?

  _____

Communication
*Focus on **clarity**, **organization**, and **precision**.*

Sample Prompts:

- Is your explanation easy for others to understand?

  _____

- Have you used terms and symbols correctly?

  _____

- Is there a more precise way to explain this?

  _____

Observations/Next Steps/Intervention

_____

_____

_____

_____

Student Interview Form (without prompts)

Name: _____ **Date:** _____

You may want to use one or more of the four generic rubrics as a focus for the interviews. This will help students to understand areas of strength and need.

Problem Solving/Thinking
*Focus on selection and use of **appropriate strategies**.*

_____

_____

_____

Knowledge and Understanding
*Focus on the questions "**Does the student know _____?**" and "**Does the student understand _____?**"*

_____

_____

_____

Application of Learning
*Focus on ability to **apply**, **transfer**, and **connect learning** in a variety of contexts.*

_____

_____

_____

Communication
*Focus on **clarity**, **organization**, and **precision**.*

_____

_____

_____

Observations/Next Steps/Intervention

_____

_____

_____

_____

Problem-Solving Rubric

Name: _____   Date: _____

Criteria	Level 1	Level 2	Level 3	Level 4
Think: Understand the Problem	• shows **limited** understanding of the problem (e.g., is unable to identify sufficient information or to restate problem)	• shows **some** understanding of the problem (e.g., is able to identify some of the relevant information but may have difficulty restating problem)	• shows **complete** understanding of the problem (e.g., is able to identify relevant information and to restate problem)	• Shows **thorough** understanding of the problem (e.g., is able to differentiate between relevant and irrelevant information and is able to rephrase problem)
Plan: Make a Plan	• shows **little or no evidence** of a plan	• shows **some** evidence of a plan	• shows evidence of an **appropriate** plan	• shows evidence of a **thorough** plan
Do: Carry Out the Plan	• uses a strategy and **attempts** to solve problem but **does not arrive at a solution**	• carries out the plan **to some extent**, using a strategy, and develops a **partial and/or incorrect solution**	• carries out the plan **effectively** by using an **appropriate** strategy and **solving the problem**	• shows **flexibility** and **insight** when carrying out the plan by **trying** and **adapting**, when necessary, **one or more** strategies to **solve the problem**
	• shows **little evidence** of revising plan when necessary	• shows **some evidence** of revising plan when necessary	• shows **strong evidence** of revising plan if necessary	• revises plan in **insightful ways,** if necessary
	• use of procedures includes **major errors and/or omissions**	• use of procedures includes **several errors and/or omissions**	• use of procedures is mostly correct, but there may be a **few minor errors and/or omissions**	• use of procedures includes **almost no errors or omissions**
Review: Look Back	• has **difficulty** identifying either errors or omissions in the plan or in the attempted solution	• shows **some ability to check** the plan and attempted solution for errors and/or omissions	• **checks** the plan and solution for procedural errors and omissions	• **thoroughly reviews** the plan and solution for effectiveness of strategies chosen and for procedural errors and omissions
	• draws **faulty** conclusions based on **insufficient** evidence	• draws **partial** conclusions based on **some** evidence	• draws **appropriate** conclusions based on **sufficient** evidence	• draws **thoughtful** conclusions based on **all available** evidence
Communicate	• provides a **limited** explanation of the strategy/solution that **lacks clarity** (e.g., uses very little mathematical language; makes very little use of mathematical representations—models, diagrams, graphs, tables)	• provides a **partial** explanation of the strategy/solution that shows **some clarity** (e.g., uses some mathematical language correctly; makes some use of mathematical representations—models, diagrams, graphs, tables—as required/as necessary)	• provides a **complete** and **clear** explanation of the strategy/solution (e.g., uses mathematical language correctly; makes appropriate use of mathematical representations—models, diagrams, graphs, tables—as required/as necessary)	• provides a **thorough, clear,** and **insightful** explanation of the strategy/solution (e.g., uses precise mathematical language; makes most appropriate use of mathematical representations—models, diagrams, graphs, tables—as required/as necessary)

Knowledge and Understanding Rubric

Name: _____   **Date:** _____

- This is a generic assessment tool. Not all criteria are necessarily appropriate to a given task.
- This rubric is well suited to assessing understanding orally in a teacher-student conference, or when assessing journal responses.
- Level 1 represents a limited performance but one in which the student has engaged with the prescribed task to some extent. Some students will perform below Level 1.

Criteria	Level 1	Level 2	Level 3	Level 4
Depth of Knowledge	• demonstrates a **limited** or **inaccurate** knowledge of the specific math facts, terms, or procedural skills that have been taught	• demonstrates **some** knowledge of the specific math facts, terms, or procedural skills that have been taught	• demonstrates **considerable** knowledge of the specific math facts, terms, or procedural skills that have been taught	• demonstrates **thorough** knowledge of the specific math facts, terms, or procedural skills that have been taught
Depth of Understanding	• demonstrates a **limited** or **inaccurate** understanding of concept(s) (e.g., restates what has been taught but with inaccuracies)	• demonstrates **some** understanding of concept(s) (e.g., provides incomplete explanation of thinking)	• demonstrates **considerable** understanding of concept(s) (e.g., provides appropriate and complete explanation of thinking)	• demonstrates **thorough** understanding of concept(s) (e.g., provides a clear, complete, and logical explanation that may go beyond what was taught)
Reflective Thinking (Metacognition)	• makes **very simple** observations about completed work and/or new learning (e.g., demonstrates **limited** ability to justify answers/solutions during discussions, during a teacher-student conference, or in a journal)	• makes **simple** observations about completed work and/or new learning (e.g., demonstrates **some** ability to justify answers/solutions during discussions, during a teacher-student conference, or in a journal)	• makes **grade-appropriate** observations about completed work and/or new learning in order to clarify thinking and increase understanding (e.g., demonstrates **considerable** ability to justify answers/solutions during discussions, during a teacher-student conference, or in a journal)	• makes **insightful** observations about completed work and/or new learning in order to clarify thinking and increase understanding (e.g., demonstrates **sophisticated** ability to justify answers/solutions during discussions, during a teacher-student conference, or in a journal)

Application of Learning Rubric

Name: _____   **Date:** _____

- *This is a generic assessment tool. Not all criteria are necessarily appropriate to a given task.*
- *This scale may be used to observe students as they are working, or it may be used to assess completed work.*
- *Level 1 represents a limited performance but one in which the student has engaged with the prescribed task to some extent. Some students will perform below Level 1.*

Criteria	Level 1	Level 2	Level 3	Level 4
Applying Knowledge and Skills in Familiar Contexts	• demonstrates **limited** ability to apply mathematical knowledge and skills in familiar contexts (e.g., has difficulty using new learning to solve routine problems)	• demonstrates **some** ability to apply mathematical knowledge and skills in familiar contexts (e.g., demonstrates some ability to use new learning to solve routine problems)	• demonstrates **considerable** ability to apply mathematical knowledge and skills in familiar contexts (e.g., uses new learning to solve routine problems)	• demonstrates **sophisticated** ability to apply mathematical knowledge and skills in familiar contexts (e.g., demonstrates sophisticated ability to use new learning to solve routine problems)
Transferring Knowledge and Skills to New Contexts	• demonstrates **limited** ability to transfer mathematical knowledge and skills to new contexts (e.g., has difficulty using new learning to solve non-routine problems)	• demonstrates **some** ability to transfer mathematical knowledge and skills to new contexts (e.g., demonstrates some ability to use new learning to solve non-routine problems)	• demonstrates **considerable** ability to transfer mathematical knowledge and skills to new contexts (e.g., uses new learning to solve non-routine problems)	• demonstrates **sophisticated** ability to transfer mathematical knowledge and skills to new contexts (e.g., demonstrates sophisticated ability to use new learning to solve non-routine problems)
Making Connections Within and Between Various Contexts	• demonstrates **limited** ability to connect new concept(s) to prior learning	• demonstrates **some** ability to connect new concept(s) to prior learning	• demonstrates **considerable** ability to connect new concept(s) to prior learning	• demonstrates **sophisticated** ability to connect new concept(s) to prior learning
	• demonstrates **limited** ability to connect mathematics concepts/procedures to other subject areas (e.g., has difficulty thinking flexibly)	• demonstrates **some** ability to connect mathematics concepts/procedures to other subject areas (e.g., has some ability to think flexibly)	• demonstrates **considerable** ability to connect mathematics concepts/procedures to other subject areas (e.g., shows ability to think flexibly)	• demonstrates **sophisticated** ability to connect mathematics concepts/procedures to other subject areas (e.g., demonstrates flexible and adaptive thinking)
	• demonstrates **limited** ability to connect mathematics learning and the real world (e.g., has difficulty relating classroom learning to the outside world)	• demonstrates **some** ability to connect mathematics learning and the real world (e.g., demonstrates some ability to relate classroom learning to the outside world)	• demonstrates **considerable** ability to connect mathematics learning and the real world (e.g., relates classroom learning to the outside world)	• demonstrates **sophisticated** ability to connect mathematics learning and the real world (e.g., demonstrates sophisticated ability to relate classroom learning to the outside world)

Communication Rubric—Mathematics

Expressive Communication: (Speaking, Writing, and Representation)

Name: _____ Date: _____

- This is a generic assessment tool. Not all criteria are necessarily appropriate to a given task.
- This scale should be used to assess the degree to which students are able to communicate about their understanding of concepts, procedures, and problem-solving strategies. Use only those criteria that are appropriate to a given task.
- Level 1 represents a limited performance but one in which the student has engaged with the prescribed task to some extent. Some students will perform below Level 1.

Criteria	Level 1	Level 2	Level 3	Level 4
Explanation and Justification of Mathematical Concepts, Procedures, and Problem Solving	· provides **limited or inaccurate** explanations/justifications that **lack clarity or logical thought**, using **minimal** words, pictures, symbols, and/or numbers	· provides **partial** explanations/ justifications that exhibit **some clarity** and **logical thought**, using **simple** words, pictures, symbols, and/or numbers	· provides **complete, clear,** and **logical** explanations/ justifications, using **appropriate** words, pictures, symbols, and/or numbers	· provides **thorough, clear,** and **insightful** explanations/ justifications, using a range of words, pictures, symbols, and/or numbers
Organization of Material (written, spoken, or drawn)	· organization is **limited** and **seriously impedes** communication	· **some** organization is evident	· organization is **effective** and **supports** communication	· organization is **highly effective** and **aids** communication
Use of Mathematical Vocabulary	· **uses very little** mathematical vocabulary, and vocabulary used **lacks clarity and precision**	· **uses some** mathematical vocabulary with **some degree of clarity and precision**	· **uses** mathematical vocabulary with **considerable clarity and precision**	· **uses a broad range** of mathematical vocabulary to communicate **clearly and precisely**
Use of Mathematical Representations (graphs, charts, diagrams)	· uses representations that exhibit **limited clarity** and **accuracy** and are **ineffective** in communicating	· uses representations that exhibit **some clarity and accuracy**	· uses representations that are **clear** and **accurately** communicate information	· uses representations that are **clear, precise,** and **effective** in communicating
Use of Mathematical Conventions (units, symbols, labels)	· **few** conventions are used correctly	· **some** conventions are used correctly	· **most** conventions are used correctly	· **almost all** conventions are used correctly

Using the Assessment of Learning Summary

(See partially completed sample on page 392.)

The *Assessment of Learning Summary* is used to generate the student's report card grade.

For this reason, it should include no data from *Initial Assessment* or *Assessment for Learning* tasks.

1. Use this chart to record all assessment data that will be used to generate a student's report card grade.

2. You may enter numerical marks, rubric levels, and/or letter grades on the chart (e.g., 6/10, 3, B, etc.).

3. Enter all required information on the chart as follows:
   - enter the date and assessment task under the appropriate category, for example, *Sept. 10; Pattern Block Puzzle* under Problem Solving (some tasks may be entered under several categories)
   - enter the mark (score, level, or letter grade) in the appropriate row
   - make anecdotal comments about both student achievement in the curriculum and learning skills in the Strengths, Areas, For Improvement, and Next Steps box

4. As a reporting period approaches, you will need to use your professional judgment to summarize each student's achievement according to his/her most consistent level of performance for each category and then for the whole strand. To help you do this, you will need
   - the assessment rubrics for *Problem Solving, Knowledge and Understanding, Application of Learning,* and *Communication* (Assessment Tools 4.18, 4.19, 4.20, and 4.21)

5. For a given category (e.g., Problem Solving)
   - review the student's marks, for example, 3, 6/10, 3–, 2+, 14/20, 3
   - refer to the *Problem Solving Rubric* and ask the question, "Which set of indicators best characterizes this particular student's achievement at this time?"
   - enter the corresponding level in the Most Consistent Level column, for example, Level 3 for the marks listed in the first bullet above
   - if appropriate, convert to a percentage equivalent
   - repeat this process for the other three categories

6. To determine the most consistent level across a whole strand, such as Patterning and Algebra, look at the most consistent level for each category. Then determine the most consistent level overall.

Assessment of Learning Summary

Student: _____   Class: _____   Term: _____

Category	Problem Solving				Most Consistent Level	Understanding of Concepts				Most Consistent Level	Application of Procedure				Most Consistent Level	Communication						Most Consistent Level	Most Consistent Level Across Strand
Assessment Task Date																								
Number Sense and Numeration																								
Measurement																								
Geometry and Spatial Sense																								
Patterning and Algebra																								
Data Management and Probability																								

Comments: Strengths, Areas for Improvement, and Next Steps

Assessment of Learning Summary (Sample)

Student: Jason Costa C. **Class:** Mr. Levy **Term:** 2005-2006

Category	Problem Solving	Most Consistent Level	Understanding of Concepts	Most Consistent Level	Application of Procedure	Most Consistent Level	Communication	Most Consistent Level	Most Consistent Level Across Strand
Assessment Task Date	Oct. 24 Inquiry 2 / Oct. 20 Problem 1 / Oct. 7 Inquiry 1		Oct. 28 Chap. Task / Oct. 17 Review / Oct. 13 Journal 1 / Oct. 5 Drawing 1		Oct. 28 Chap. Task / Oct. 17 Review / Oct. 10 Drawing 2		Oct. 28 Chapter Task		
Number Sense and Numeration									
Measurement									
Geometry and Spatial Sense	L3 / L2 / L2	L2+	L3 / $\frac{6}{10}$ / L3 / L2	L3-	L2 / $\frac{7}{10}$ / L2	L2+	L3	L3	L3-
Patterning and Algebra									
Data Management and Probability									

Comments: Strengths, Areas for Improvement, and Next Steps

Rubric *for* Identifying Student Levels of Response (Teacher's Version)

		Level 1	Level 2	Level 3	Level 4
Knowledge	**conceptual knowledge**	• limited understanding of concepts	• incomplete understanding of concepts	• reasonable understanding of concepts	• deep understanding of concepts
	procedural knowledge	• limited knowledge of steps in procedures	• incomplete knowledge of steps in procedures	• knows steps in procedures	• high level of procedural knowledge
Connections	**linking concepts and procedures**	• limited understanding of procedures	• partial understanding of procedures	• understands procedures	• deep understanding of procedures
	linking concepts and procedures to world	• has difficulty making connections	• needs encouragement to make connections	• makes and describes connections	• makes and articulates insightful connections
Problem Solving	**problem understanding**	• needs assistance to understand problem or task	• partial understanding of problem or task	• comes to understand problem or task independently	• complete and insightful understanding of problem
	solution plan	• needs assistance to select appropriate strategy from limited number of strategies	• needs some assistance to select appropriate strategy from limited number of strategies	• selects/develops effective strategy, evaluating strategy when encouraged	• selects, develops, and analyzes highly effective strategies
	applying concepts/procedures/strategies	• needs assistance to apply given procedures/strategies	• applies procedures/strategies in situations of moderate difficulty	• applies procedures/strategies to solve problems of reasonable difficulty	• applies, often creatively, procedures/strategies to solve problem which are often complex/non-routine
	self-monitoring/reflection	• little reflection on solution process or reasonableness of conclusion	• reflects on solution process and reasonableness of conclusion when asked	• reflects on solution process and reasonableness of conclusion	• monitors progress of solution and reflects on implications; often generalizes solutions
Reasoning	**conjectures/arguments**	• makes unsupported statements, illogical arguments	• supports assertions/conclusions with evidence, when encouraged	• makes convincing arguments, makes/tests conjectures	• makes convincing/alternative arguments; insightful conjectures
	questioning skills	• has difficulty formulating clarifying questions	• needs encouragement to formulate clarifying questions	• formulates clarifying questions	• asks "what if", or extending questions
	explanatory skills	• incomplete explanation of an idea, strategy, or solution	• gives incomplete explanation of idea/answer/solution	• gives complete explanation of idea/answer/solution	• gives complete and compelling explanation of an idea/answer/solution

(continued)

Rubric for Identifying Student Levels of Response (Teacher's Version) (continued)

		Level 1	Level 2	Level 3	Level 4
Communication	**interaction**	• avoids/resists interacting to share ideas/strategies	• with encouragement/ assistance, interacts to share ideas/strategies	• interacts to share/ create ideas and strategies; uses feedback	• initiates interaction to share and create ideas/strategies
	reading/listening/input skills	• needs assistance to gain understanding from written/spoken input	• gets partial understanding from written/spoken input	• gains effective understanding from written/spoken input	• gains understanding and insight from written/spoken input
	reporting/output skills	• needs assistance to communicate solution processes and results in oral, written, or other forms of reporting	• needs some assistance to communicate solution processes and results in oral, written, or other forms of reporting	• clearly communicates solution processes and results in oral, written, or other forms of reporting	• communicates solution processes and results precisely and persuasively in all forms of reporting
Technology	**selection/use of tools**	• limited skills in the selection/use of appropriate tools	• inconsistency in selection and use of appropriate tools	• proficient in the selection/use of appropriate tools	• uses sophisticated skills in selection and use of tools

How Am I Doing in Mathematics? (Student's Version)

		Level 1	Level 2	Level 3	Level 4
What I Know	Do I understand the ideas?	I don't really understand the ideas.	I understand the ideas a little bit.	I understand the ideas.	I understand the ideas very well.
	Do I know all the steps to do something?	I need help to remember all the steps.	I know some of the steps.	I know all of the steps.	I know all the steps, and some shortcuts.
Making Connections	Do I understand all the steps to do something?	I don't really understand what I'm doing.	I sort of understand what I'm doing.	I understand what I'm doing.	I understand what I'm doing and I can teach others.
	Do I connect what I know to the world?	I need help to connect what I know to the world.	I sometimes connect what I know to the world.	I connect a lot of what I know to the world.	I make lots of great connections from what I know to the world.
Solving Problems	Do I understand the problem?	I need a lot of help to understand the problem.	I understand some parts of the problem.	I understand the problem.	I understand the problem really easily.
	Do I think of a plan?	I need help to come up with a plan.	I come up with a plan if I have a bit of help.	I come up with a good plan.	I come up with a really neat plan.
	Do I follow my plan?	I don't usually follow my plan.	I carry out some of my plan.	I carry out my whole plan.	I carry out my plan very well.
	Do I check my work?	I don't usually review my work.	I review my work when my teacher asks me to.	I review my work carefully.	I review my work carefully, and think about better ways to do it.
Reasoning	Do I give good reasons for my answers?	I don't give any reasons for my answers.	I give a reason for my answer when I'm asked.	I give good reasons for my answers.	I give great reasons for my answers.
	Do I ask good questions?	I don't know what questions to ask.	I ask questions sometimes.	I ask good questions.	I ask really good questions.
	Do I explain my ideas well?	I need help to explain my ideas.	I explain some of my ideas.	I explain my ideas clearly.	I explain my ideas in an interesting way.
Communicating	Do I work well with others?	I don't share or take part.	I share ideas and take part if I'm asked.	I share and take part well.	I help make the group work better.
	Do I read and listen well?	I need help to read and listen.	I read and listen pretty well.	I read and listen well.	I read easily and listen hard.
	Do I report my ideas well?	I need help to report my ideas.	I make simple reports.	I report my ideas clearly and completely.	I make awesome reports.
Using Technology	Do I pick the right tool and use it well?	I need help to choose the right tool and help to use it.	Sometimes I use the right tools.	I use the right tools to complete the task.	I use a variety of tools with lots of success.

Grade 6 Social Studies Performance Task Rubric

Name: _____ Date: _____

Criteria	Level 1	Level 2	Level 3	Level 4
Depth of Understanding	• products and/or performances demonstrate a **limited** or **shallow understanding** of how the environment helped to mould Canadian Aboriginal cultures (i.e., role of climate, hunting, geography, etc.)	• products and/or performances demonstrate a **partial understanding** of how the environment helped to mould Canadian Aboriginal cultures (i.e., role of climate, hunting, geography, etc.)	• products and/or performances demonstrate a **solid understanding** of how the environment helped to mould Canadian Aboriginal cultures (i.e., role of climate, hunting, geography, etc.)	• products and/or performances demonstrate a **thorough understanding** of how the environment helped to mould Canadian Aboriginal cultures (i.e., role of climate, hunting, geography, etc.)
	• products and/or performances demonstrate a **limited** or **shallow understanding** of social, political, or economic issues facing Aboriginal peoples today (i.e., technology, language, self-government, land claims, etc.)	• products and/or performances demonstrate a **partial understanding** of social, political, or economic issues facing Aboriginal peoples today (i.e., technology, language, self-government, land claims, etc.)	• products and/or performances demonstrate a **solid understanding** of social, political, or economic issues facing Aboriginal peoples today (i.e., technology, language, self-government, land claims, etc.)	• products and/or performances demonstrate a **thorough understanding** of social, political, or economic issues facing Aboriginal peoples today (i.e., technology, language, self-government, land claims, etc.)
Quality of Performance or Product	• performance demonstrates **very little planning and practice** OR • product exhibits **very little attention** to detail and craftsmanship	• performance demonstrates **some planning and practice** OR • product exhibits **some attention** to detail and craftsmanship	• performance demonstrates **sufficient planning and practice** OR • product exhibits **sufficient attention** to detail and craftsmanship	• performance demonstrates **extensive planning and practice** OR • product exhibits **extensive attention** to detail and craftsmanship
Quality of Research	Note: Use the Research Skills Rubric to assess skills **during** the research process. (see Tool 5.11)			

Diagnostic Assessment: Understanding Key Concepts

Unit: _____   **Date:** _____

Your teacher will give you a list of the key concepts you will be learning about in this unit. Write one of the concepts in each of the bubbles. For each concept, write the things you already know about it around the outside of the bubble.

Self-Assessment Checklist: Problem-Solving Tasks

Name: _____ **Class:** _____

Place a ✓ or ✗ to indicate "yes" or "no" for each question.

	Date	Date	Date	Date	Date
Understanding the Problem					
1. Do I understand the problem I have to solve? Can I restate it in my own words?					
2. Do I understand the information I have been given?					
Making a Plan					
3. Do I know what strategies and procedures might help me solve this problem?					
4. Am I able to select from these and develop a plan to solve this problem?					
Carrying Out the Plan					
5. Do I know which strategy to try first?					
6. Do I know what to do when I get stuck?					
7. Am I recording data or information as I proceed?					
8. Am I following my plan, or revisiting if I need to?					
9. Have I checked any written work related to solving this problem?					
Solving the Problem					
10. Have I checked whether my solution is reasonable?					
11. Have I checked my work for correctness?					
12. Am I able to reach a conclusion?					
Communicating					
13. Am I prepared to communicate my findings orally or in writing?					
14. Is my work complete and correct?					
15. Is my work organized to help others understand it?					

A Sample of Assessment Tools for Grades 7 to 9

In this section, you will find a range of assessment tools designed for immediate classroom use. There are rubrics intended for teacher, self-, and peer assessment, as well as checklists designed for self- and peer assessment. All of these tools may be used to assess *for* learning, and they may be used to gather assessment *of* learning data. These tools should be shared with students and parents so that everyone is aware of the standards used to define quality work.

The rubrics for Grades 7–9 enable the assessor to *rate* achievement on a 4-point scale.* We do not expect students to pass through each of these four levels in the normal course of their learning. Instead, Levels 3 and 4 represent quality performance and a major goal of our teaching is to have as many students as possible performing at these levels.

* THESE TOOLS ARE ALSO AVAILABLE IN A MODIFIABLE FORMAT ON THE CD-ROM.

Generic Tools

Page	Resource
410	5.10 Assessing Prior Knowledge: Diagnostic Assessment
411	5.11 Research Skills Rubric
412	5.12 Research Skills: Self-Assessment Checklist
413	5.13 Research Projects: Peer Feedback Form
414	5.14 Anecdotal Record for Conferencing
415	5.15 Portfolio Product Rubric
416	5.16 Reflection Strip for Portfolio Entries
417	5.17 Portfolio: Self-Assessment Checklist

Learning Skills—Samples

(Additional checklists are available on the *Talk About Assessment* website.)

Page	Resource
418	5.18 Independent Work: Self-Assessment Checklist
419	5.19 Initiative: Self-Assessment Checklist
420	5.20 Work Habits and Homework Completion: Self-Assessment Checklist

Expository and Persuasive Writing Rubric

Name: _____   **Date:** _____

- *This rubric is appropriate to assess a variety of reports and opinion pieces.*
- *Use only those criteria that are appropriate for a given assessment task, at a given time.*
- *Focus on the indicators when conducting assessment for learning; focus on the indicators and performance levels when conducting assessment of learning.*

Categories/Criteria	Level 1	Level 2	Level 3	Level 4
Content	• main ideas are **difficult to discern**	• main ideas **lack clarity**	• main ideas are **clear**	• main ideas are **clear and sophisticated**
	• support for main ideas is **insufficient**	• includes **some** support for main ideas	• includes **sufficient** support for main ideas	• includes **thorough** support for main ideas
Communication	• argument **lacks clarity**	• argument is **sometimes** or **partially clear**	• argument is **clear**	• argument is **clear and convincing**
	• diction, tone, and level of language show a **limited** sense of purpose and audience	• diction, tone, and level of language suit the specific purpose and audience to **some degree**	• diction, tone, and level of language are **appropriate** to the specific purpose and audience	• diction, tone, and level of language are used **artfully** to suit the specific purpose and audience
	• sentence type and length show **little** variation	• sentence type and length show **some** variation.	• sentence type and length are **varied**	• sentence type and length are **varied skillfully** to engage the reader
Organization	• paragraph organization is **ineffective**	• paragraph organization is **inconsistent**	• paragraph organization is **effective**	• paragraph organization is **highly effective**
	• overall organization is **ineffective**: unclear beginning, middle, and end; little evidence of transitions between paragraphs	• overall organization is **inconsistent**: some problems with beginning and/or middle and/or end; few transitions between paragraphs	• overall organization is **effective**: clear beginning, middle, and end; some transitions between paragraphs	• overall organization is **highly effective**: clear beginning, middle, and end; smooth transitions between paragraphs
Conventions	• **numerous errors** in spelling and/or grammar and/or punctuation **seriously interfere** with communication	• **several errors** in spelling and/or grammar and/or punctuation **interfere** with communication **to some degree**	• **minor errors** in spelling and/or grammar and/or punctuation, but not sufficient to interfere with communication	• **few if any errors** in spelling, grammar, or punctuation

Narrative Rubric

Name: _____   Date: _____

Categories/Criteria	Level 1	Level 2	Level 3	Level 4
Storytelling	• logic of plot is **faulty** • narrator's point of view is **unclear or inconsistent** • stylistic devices are **lacking or ineffective** (e.g., use of foreshadowing, varying sentence length to create suspense)	• logic of plot is **inconsistent** • narrator's point of view may **change** and **cause some confusion** • stylistic devices are **effective some of the time** (e.g., use of foreshadowing, varying sentence length to create suspense)	• plot develops **logically** • narrator's point of view is **clear and consistent** • stylistic devices are **effective** (e.g., use of foreshadowing, varying sentence length to create suspense)	• plot develops in a **clever way** • narrator's point of view is **clear, consistent, and highly effective** • stylistic devices are used in **sophisticated** ways (e.g., use of foreshadowing, varying sentence length to create suspense)
Creativity	• ideas **lack originality** • characters are **undeveloped and/or unconvincing** • humour (if appropriate) is **lacking or ineffective** • theme is **unclear** or lacking	• ideas show **some original thinking** • characters are **developed and/or convincing to some degree** • humour (if appropriate) is **somewhat effective** (e.g., use of exaggeration) • theme is **not fully developed**	• ideas are **creative and original** • characters are **well-developed and convincing** • humour (if appropriate) is **effective** (e.g., use of exaggeration) • theme is **clear**	• ideas are **creative, original, clever** • characters are **thoroughly developed** and **highly convincing** • humour (if appropriate) is **effective and clever** (e.g., use of exaggeration) • theme is **clear and sophisticated**
Style	• introduction is **ineffective** in presenting main character, conflict and/or setting effectively • description of setting is **ineffective** in creating a mental image	• introduction presents **some of the** following elements effectively: main character, conflict, setting • description of setting is **somewhat effective** in creating a mental image	• introduction presents main character, conflict, and setting **effectively** • description of setting is **effective** in creating a mental image	• introduction presents main character, conflict, and setting in a **creative or original way** • description of setting is **highly effective** in creating a mental image
Style	• ending is **ineffective** • organization is **confusing** (e.g., paragraph structure, transitions) • diction, tone, and level of language show a **limited** sense of the intended audience • dialogue (if applicable) is **unconvincing**	• ending is **effective to some degree** • organization is **inconsistent** (e.g., paragraph structure, transitions) • organization is **effective** (e.g., • diction, tone, and level of language suit the intended audience to **some degree** • dialogue (if applicable) is convincing **some of the time**	• ending is **effective** • paragraph structure, transitions) • diction, tone, and level of language are **appropriate** to the intended audience • dialogue (if applicable) is **convincing**	• ending is **effective and original** • organization is **highly** effective (e.g., paragraph structure, transitions) • diction, tone, and level of language are used **skillfully** to suit the intended audience • dialogue (if applicable) **adds significantly** to the narrative
Conventions	• **numerous errors** in spelling and/or grammar and/or punctuation **interfere seriously** with communication	• **several errors** in spelling and/or grammar and/or punctuation **may interfere** with communication to some degree	• **minor errors** in spelling and/or grammar and/or punctuation **do not interfere** with communication	• **few, if any, errors** in spelling and/or grammar and/or punctuation

Letter to the Editor Rubric

Name: _____   Date: _____

- Focus on only selected criteria and their corresponding indicators when conducting assessment for learning; focus on all criteria, corresponding indicators, and performance levels when conducting assessment of learning.

Categories/Criteria	Level 1	Level 2	Level 3	Level 4
Content	• purpose of letter is **unclear**	• purpose of letter is **questionable**	• purpose of letter is **clear** (e.g., to criticize, question)	• purpose of letter is **clear** (e.g., to criticize, question)
	• includes **little** information or **few** ideas	• includes **some** information and/or ideas but not sufficient to accomplish purpose	• includes **sufficient** information and/or ideas to accomplish purpose	• includes **rich** information and/or **plentiful** ideas to accomplish purpose
	• message **lacks clarity**	• message is **inconsistent**	• message is **clear**	• message is **clear** and **convincing**
	• diction, tone, and level of language show a **limited** sense of purpose and audience (i.e., lacks formality)	• diction, tone, and level of language suit the specific purpose and audience **to some degree** (i.e., level of formality)	• diction, tone, and level of language are **appropriate** to the specific purpose and audience (i.e., level of formality)	• diction, tone, and level of language are used **artfully** to suit the specific purpose and audience (i.e., level of formality)
Organization	• introduction is **ineffective** (e.g., issue and/or opinion are unclear)	• introduction is **somewhat effective** (i.e., identifies issue or expresses opinion)	• introduction is **effective** (i.e., identifies issue and expresses opinion)	• introduction is **highly effective** (i.e., clearly identifies issue and expresses strong opinion)
	• paragraph organization is **ineffective**	• paragraph organization is **inconsistent**	• paragraph organization is **effective**	• paragraph organization is **highly effective**
	• overall organization is **ineffective**: unclear beginning, middle, and end; little evidence of transitions between paragraphs	• overall organization is **inconsistent**: some problems with beginning and/or middle and/or end; few transitions between paragraphs	• overall organization is **effective**: clear beginning, middle, and end; some transitions between paragraphs	• overall organization is **highly effective**: clear beginning, middle, and end; smooth transitions between paragraphs
	• conclusion is **ineffective**	• conclusion is **somewhat effective** (e.g., call to action, summary)	• conclusion is **effective** (e.g., call to action, summary)	• conclusion is **powerful** (e.g., call to action, summary)
Conventions	• correct letter format is used (e.g., block, semi-block) but with **numerous errors**	• correct letter format is used (e.g., block, semi-block) but with **several errors**	• correct letter format is used (e.g., block, semi-block) with only **minor errors**	• correct letter format is used (e.g., block, semi-block) with **no errors**
	• **numerous errors** in spelling and/or grammar and/or punctuation **seriously interfere** with communication	• **several errors** in spelling and/or grammar and/or punctuation **interfere** with communication **to some degree**	• **minor errors** in spelling and/or grammar and/or punctuation, but not sufficient to interfere with communication	• **few if any errors** in spelling, grammar, or punctuation

Newspaper Article Rubric

Name: _____ **Date:** _____

- Focus on only selected criteria and their corresponding indicators when conducting assessment for learning; focus on all criteria, corresponding indicators and performance levels when conducting assessment of learning.

Categories/Criteria	Level 1	Level 2	Level 3	Level 4
Content	• headline is of **limited** effectiveness in engaging reader	• headline is **appropriate**	• headline is **catchy**	• headline is **catchy and original**
	• article includes **insufficient** facts or descriptive details to maintain reader's interest	• article includes **some** facts and descriptive details that maintain reader's interest to some degree	• article includes **sufficient** facts and descriptive details to maintain reader's interest	• article includes **highly engaging** facts and descriptive details to maintain reader's interest
	• purpose of article **is unclear**	• purpose of article is **somewhat clear** (e.g., specific human interest)	• purpose of article is **clear** (e.g., specific human interest)	• purpose of article is **clear and engaging** (e.g., specific human interest)
	• lead answers **at least 3** of the 5 W's	• lead answers the 5 W's but in a **stilted way**	• lead answers the 5 W's **adequately**	• lead answers the 5 W's **concisely and effectively**
Organization	• paragraph organization is **ineffective**	• paragraph organization is **inconsistent**	• paragraph organization is **effective**	• paragraph organization is **highly effective**
	• overall organization is **ineffective**: unclear beginning, middle, and end; little evidence of transitions between paragraphs	• overall organization is **inconsistent**: some problems with beginning and/or middle, and/or end; few transitions between paragraphs	• overall organization is **effective**: clear beginning, middle, and end; some transitions between paragraphs	• overall organization is **highly effective**: clear beginning, middle, and end; smooth transitions between paragraphs
Conventions	• visual aspects bear **little resemblance** to a newspaper article (e.g., type size, font, columns)	• visual aspects bear **some resemblance** to a newspaper article (e.g., type size, font, columns)	• visual aspects **resemble** a newspaper article (e.g., type size, font, columns)	• visual aspects bear **strong resemblance** to a newspaper article (e.g., type size, font, columns)
	• **numerous errors** in spelling and/or grammar and/or punctuation seriously interfere with communication	• **several errors** in spelling and/or grammar and/or punctuation interfere with communication to some degree	• **minor errors** in spelling and/or grammar and/or punctuation, but not sufficient to interfere with communication	• **few if any errors** in spelling, grammar, or punctuation

Personal Response Writing Rubric

Name: _____   **Date:** _____

- This rubric is appropriate to asses a variety of personal and response writing forms including journals, diaries, and learning logs.
- Note that this rubric does not encourage the assessment of writing conventions; the focus is on depth of students' responses.

Categories/Criteria	Level 1	Level 2	Level 3	Level 4
Writing Habits	• demonstrates **reluctance** to write on a daily basis	• writes on a daily basis **if prompted**	• **writes** on a daily basis	• **chooses to write** on a daily basis
Quality of Thinking	• uses **little** information from a text to support personal interpretations	• uses **some** information from a text to support personal interpretations	• uses **specific** information from a text to support personal interpretations	• uses **rich and detailed** information from a text to support **insightful** personal interpretations
	• **has difficulty comparing** personal ideas and values with those in a text	• makes **simple comparisons** between personal ideas and values with those in a text	• **compares** personal ideas and values with those in a text	• compares in **insightful** ways personal ideas and values with those in a text
	• **has difficulty analyzing** and synthesizing ideas and information from a text, and communicating it	• **analyzes, in simple ways,** ideas and information from a text, synthesizes it, and communicates it	• **analyzes** ideas and information from a text, synthesizes it, and communicates it	• **analyzes, in insightful ways,** ideas and information from a text, synthesizes it skillfully, and communicates it

Science Design Product Rubric

Name: _____ **Date:** _____

Use this rubric:
· to inform students before they begin work of the criteria and indicators for their science design products,
· to assess the quality of students' design products.

Criteria	Level 1	Level 2	Level 3	Level 4
Understanding of Science Concepts	· design/model reflects a **superficial understanding** of relevant science concepts	· design/model reflects a **partial understanding** of relevant science concepts	· design/model reflects a **solid understanding** of relevant science concepts	· design/model reflects a **deep understanding** of relevant science concepts
Quality of Design	· design/model meets **few** of the required criteria	· design/model meets **some** of the required criteria	· design/model meets **all** of the required criteria	· design/model meets **all** of the required criteria and **may exceed** some
	· design/model demonstrates **ineffective or inappropriate** use of materials	· design/model uses **some** materials appropriately	· design/model demonstrates **appropriate** use of materials	· design/model demonstrates **innovative** use of materials
	· design/model reflects a **minimal** level of draftsmanship and/or craftsmanship	· level of draftsmanship and/or craftsmanship of design/model **requires improvement** to meet standard	· design/model reflects an **acceptable** level of draftsmanship and/or craftsmanship	· design/model reflects a **superior** level of draftsmanship and/or craftsmanship
Performance (if applicable)	· model **meets few** of the required performance criteria	· model **meets some** of the required performance criteria	· model **meets** required performance criteria	· model **meets all** of the required performance criteria and **may exceed** some
Communication (oral or written)	· designer(s) provide(s) **superficial** explanation of the design and performance of design/model	· designer(s) provide(s) **partial** explanation of the design and performance of design/model	· designer(s) provide(s) **solid** explanation of the design and performance of design/model	· designer(s) provide(s) **thorough** explanation of the design and performance of design/model
	· designer(s) provide(s) **superficial** explanation of environmental and/or societal issues related to design/model	· designer(s) provide(s) **partial** explanation of environmental and/or societal issues related to design/model	· designer(s) provide(s) **solid** explanation of environmental and/or societal issues related to design/model	· designer(s) provide(s) **thorough** explanation of environmental and/or societal issues related to design/model

Science Performance Skills: Teacher Checklist

Class: _____

- *Use this checklist to observe students while they are demonstrating science skills.*
- *Observe a manageable number of students during one class. Observe all students over time. Make sufficient copies of this checklist for your class.*
- *Place a ✓ or an ✗ to indicate "yes" or "no" for each question.*

Name/Date					
Understanding the Task					
· Asks relevant questions to clarify the task					
· Understands the concepts related to the task					
Planning					
· Selects appropriate procedures to complete the task					
· Identifies and controls variables					
Carrying Out the Plan					
· Follows appropriate procedures					
· Demonstrates appropriate level of skill					
· Records data appropriately					
· Follows necessary safety procedures					
· Makes required observations					
Analyzing and Interpreting Data					
· Analyzes and interprets data logically					
· Draws appropriate conclusions					
· Evaluates quality of procedures used					
Communicating					
· Prepares to communicate findings orally or in writing					

Notes and Observations:

_____

_____

Science Design Projects: Self-Assessment Checklist

Name: _____   Class: _____

Place a ✓ or an X to indicate "yes" or "no" for each question.

Date					
Understanding the Task					
Do I understand the task I have been given?					
Do I understand which science concepts relate to this task?					
Planning					
Have I developed a complete plan for this project?					
Designing/Building					
Have I assembled the materials and tools required to complete the task?					
Am I following my plan, or revising it if I need to?					
Do I know what to do when I get stuck?					
Do I know what safety procedures I must follow?					
Testing, Recording, and Evaluating					
Do I know how to test the design/model?					
Have I conducted enough tests?					
Have I recorded enough data from these tests?					
Have I analyzed the data from these tests?					
Do I know how to modify the design/model to improve it?					
Communicating					
Am I prepared to communicate my findings orally or in writing?					
Is my work complete and correct?					
Is my work organized to help others understand it?					

Things I still have to do:

_____

_____

Inquiry Investigation Skills: Self-Assessment Checklist

Name: _____   Class: _____

Place a ✓ or an ✗ to indicate "yes" or "no" for each question.

Date					
Initiating (Questioning and Hypothesizing):					
Do I understand the task?					
Do I have a testable hypothesis?					
Planning:					
Have I developed a clear set of procedures to follow?					
Do I know what variables I need to control?					
Conducting and Recording:					
Have I followed the procedures that I set out in my plan?					
Do I know how to perform all of the procedures safely?					
Do I know how to use all of the tools, equipment, and materials?					
Have I made enough observations to produce good data?					
Have I recorded the relevant data in an organized way?					
Did I modify my plan when I needed to?					
Analyzing and Interpreting:					
Have I analyzed the data correctly?					
Do my conclusions match the data?					
If I didn't get the results I was expecting, can I say what I should have done differently?					
Communicating:					
Is the information complete and detailed enough?					
Is the information organized so others can understand it?					
Have I used the correct units of measure and terminology?					

Assessing Prior Knowledge: Diagnostic Assessment

Name: _____   **Class:** _____

At the beginning of this unit, your teacher will ask you to answer three Big Questions. You will probably have some ideas already about how to answer the questions, but as you work through this unit, you will learn much more. Write the best answers you can right now in the second column. Before the end of the unit, write your revised answers in the third column.

Question	My Answers at the Beginning of the Unit	My Revised Answers Near the End of the Unit
1. (a)		
(b)		
(c)		
2. (a)		
(b)		
(c)		
3. (a)		
(b)		
(c)		

Record any additional questions you want to have answered as you learn during this unit.

_____

_____

_____

Research Skills Rubric

Name: _____   **Date:** _____

Use this rubric to
- *inform students of the criteria on which they will be assessed each time they conduct research,*
- *provide ongoing feedback to students as they conduct research,*
- *evaluate the quality of students' research skills at the end of a unit.*

Categories/Criteria	Level 1	Level 2	Level 3	Level 4
Use of Resources	• has **difficulty** formulating a research question and tries to use a **single** strategy for locating and selecting information	• formulates a **tentative** research question and uses a **limited range** of strategies for locating and selecting information	• formulates a **clear** research question and uses **several** strategies for locating and selecting information	• formulates an **insightful** research question and uses **a full range** of strategies for locating and selecting information
	• accesses information from **only one** resource	• is able to access information from **more than one** resource	• is able to access information from a **variety of** resources (print, electronic, human)	• is able to access information from a **full range of** resources (print, electronic, human)
Quality of Information	• has **difficulty** distinguishing between fact and opinion	• collects information which represents a **single** point of view	• collects information which represents **different** points of view	• collects information which represents **all relevant** points of view
	• has **difficulty** locating information that is related to the issue, concept, or topic	• locates **some** information that is related to the issue, concept, or topic and some that is not	• **locates** information that is clearly related to the issue, concept, or topic	• locates information that reflects a **sophisticated understanding** of the issue, concept, or topic
Recording Information	• **copies** main ideas from resources	• **summarizes some** main ideas from resources in own words	• **summarizes** main ideas from resources in own words	• **integrates** main ideas from resources with own ideas on the topic
	• only acknowledges sources **when prompted**	• **attempts to** acknowledge sources correctly	• **acknowledges** sources correctly	• **routinely acknowledges** all sources
	• has **difficulty** recording and organizing information	• uses a **limited number** of strategies to record and organize information with some success	• uses **strategies** to record and organize information	• uses a **range of strategies** to record and organize information effectively
Use of Information	• shows **little evidence** of having formulated own ideas/opinions	• **attempts to** combine research with own ideas/opinions	• **combines** research with own ideas/opinions	• **combines** research with own ideas/opinions in a **fluent and skillful manner**
Use of Information	• presents information with **limited evidence** of organization	• presents information with **some evidence** of organization	• presents information in an **organized manner**	• presents information which is **skillfully organized**
	• has **difficulty** handling questions and discussion with classmates	• demonstrates **some competence** in handling questions and discussion with classmates	• handles questions and discussion with classmates **competently**	• handles questions and discussion with classmates **insightfully**

Research Skills: Self-Assessment Checklist

Name: _____   Class: _____

Place a ✓ or an ✗ to indicate "yes" or "no" for each question.

Date					
Use of Resources:					
Do I have a plan for researching my topic?					
Have I researched print (books, magazines), electronic (Internet), and human (an expert) resources?					
Quality of Information:					
Have I considered different points of view while researching my topic (e.g., different opinions on an environmental issue)?					
Is all my information clearly related to my research question?					
Recording Information:					
Have I summarized the main ideas in my own words?					
Have I identified the sources of my information (i.e., used footnotes and bibliography correctly)?					
Have I summarized the information in an organized way?					
Use of Information:					
Have I included my own ideas and opinions and supported them with the information I researched?					
Is my information organized so others can understand it?					

Things I still need to do:

_____

_____

_____

_____

Research Projects: Peer Feedback Form

Name: _____   **Date:** _____

When listening to students deliver their presentation, refer to the Presentation and Speech Rubric (4.10, p. 377) to help you note the strengths, weaknesses, and suggestions for improvement.

Presenter(s):_____ **Topic:**_____

Strengths:

_____

_____

_____

_____

_____

_____

Weaknesses:

_____

_____

_____

_____

_____

_____

Suggestions for How to Improve the Presentation:

_____

_____

_____

_____

_____

_____

Anecdotal Record for Conferencing

Name:

Date	Focus for Conference	Strengths	Needs	Next Steps

Additional Notes:

_____

_____

_____

_____

_____

_____

Portfolio Product Rubric

Name: _____ **Date:** _____

- Use this rubric to assess the contents of individual students' portfolios.
- Ideally, assess the portfolio with the student present.
- Do not attempt to assess everything in the portfolio. Remember, you are looking for evidence of the student's learning and growth.
- Each portfolio should be individualized by the student. Avoid looking for sameness or consistency.

Categories/Criteria	Level 1	Level 2	Level 3	Level 4
Contents	• **few** required pieces are included	• **most** required pieces are included	• **all** required pieces are included	
	• **few** student-selected pieces are included	• **some** student-selected pieces are included	• **required number** of student-selected pieces are included	
Thinking/Reflecting	• reflection sheets are **incomplete** and/or attached to **few** selections	• reflection sheets are partially complete and/or attached to **some** selections	• reflection sheets are complete and attached to **all** selections	• reflection sheets are detailed and attached to **all** selections
	• reflection sheets show **limited** evidence of thoughtfulness or insight	• reflection sheets show **some** evidence of thoughtfulness and/or insight	• reflection sheets show **clear** evidence of thoughtfulness and insight	• reflection sheets show **rich** evidence of thoughtfulness and insight
	• selections reflect a **limited** understanding of the portfolio process (i.e., purposeful collecting, selecting, and reflecting on pieces to improve learning	• selections demonstrate **some** understanding of the portfolio process (i.e., purposeful collecting, selecting, and reflecting on pieces to improve learning)	• selections demonstrate a **solid** understanding of the portfolio process (i.e., purposeful collecting, selecting, and reflecting on pieces to improve learning)	• selections demonstrate a **thorough** understanding of the portfolio process (i.e., purposeful collecting, selecting, and reflecting on pieces to improve learning)
	• selections demonstrate **little** originality or creativity	• selections demonstrate **some** originality and/or creativity (e.g., a creative mind map)	• selections **demonstrate** originality and/or creativity (e.g., a creative mind map)	• selections demonstrate a **high degree** of originality and/or creativity (e.g., a creative mind map)
	• selections demonstrate **little** evidence of growth and learning over time (e.g., initial and revised responses to questions; first and revised written drafts)	• some selections **demonstrate** growth and learning over time (e.g., initial and revised responses to questions; first and revised written drafts)	• **several** selections **demonstrate** growth and learning over time (e.g., initial and revised responses to questions; first and revised written drafts)	• **many** selections **clearly demonstrate** growth and learning over time (e.g., initial and revised responses to questions; first and revised written drafts)
Organization	• portfolio contents **lack organization** into the required sections and sections are not labelled clearly (e.g., first drafts, personal reflections)	• portfolio contents are **partially organized** into the required sections and sections are labelled to some degree (e.g., first drafts, personal reflections)	• portfolio contents are **appropriately organized** into the required sections and sections are labelled appropriately (e.g., first drafts, personal reflections)	• portfolio contents are **highly organized** into the required sections and sections are clearly labelled for ease of use (e.g., first drafts, personal reflections)

Reflection Strip for Portfolio Entries

Reflection Strip	Reflection Strip
Complete and attach this Reflection Strip to each item you choose to include in your portfolio.	*Complete and attach this Reflection Strip to each item you choose to include in your portfolio.*
Name: _____ **Date:** _____	**Name:** _____ **Date:** _____

Reflection Strip (left)

This piece of work shows:
☐ how I have improved an earlier draft
☐ something important that I learned
☐ something I need to work on
☐ something I need help with
☐ something I am proud of
☐ what I do outside of school
☐ how well I have learned something

1. I choose to include this item because:

2. How does this item demonstrate the thing(s) I've checked above?

3. Other important things about me that this item shows:

Reflection Strip (right)

This piece of work shows:
☐ how I have improved an earlier draft
☐ something important that I learned
☐ something I need to work on
☐ something I need help with
☐ something I am proud of
☐ what I do outside of school
☐ how well I have learned something

1. I choose to include this item because:

2. How does this item demonstrate the thing(s) I've checked above?

3. Other important things about me that this item shows:

Portfolio: Self-Assessment Checklist

Name: _____   Term: _____

Enter the date each time you use this checklist to assess the contents of your portfolio. Place a ✓ or an ✗ to indicate "yes" or "no" for each question.

Contents: Have I ... Date:					
• made sure that I've included all required pieces?					
• made sure that I've included my own selections?					
Thinking/Reflecting: Have I ...					
• completed and attached a Reflection Strip to each piece?					
• read over my Reflection Strips to check that they show evidence of my thinking and learning?					
• thought carefully about the purpose of each piece that I have included in my portfolio?					
• included some pieces that demonstrate creative and original work?					
• made sure that there are some early and later drafts of the same piece to show how my work has improved?					
Organization: Have I ...					
• ensured that the container for my work is suitable and appropriate?					
• made sure that the contents of my portfolio are well-organized?					
• made sure that each piece is placed in the correct section of my portfolio?					
• checked to see that each section is clearly labelled?					

Summary of things I need to do to bring my portfolio up to standard:

_____

_____

_____

Independent Work: Self-Assessment Checklist

Name: _____ **Term:** _____

Enter the date each time you use this checklist to assess your ability to work independently. Place a ✓ or an ✗ to indicate "yes" or "no" for each question. **Date:**										**Overall Assessment**
Did I accomplish tasks independently today?										
Did I accept responsibility for completing tasks today?										
Did I follow instructions today?										
Did I complete required homework or assignments today?										
Did I demonstrate self-direction today (e.g., selecting and using materials and resources)?										
Did I demonstrate persistence by completing tasks today?										
Did I use my time effectively today?										
Did I rely on what I already know and can do to solve problems and make decisions today?										
Did I reflect on what I did today in order to improve my learning?										

Summary of things I need to do to improve my ability to work independently:

_____

_____

_____

_____

_____

Initiative: Self-Assessment Checklist

Name: _____   **Term:** _____

Enter the date each time you use this checklist to assess your ability to demonstrate initiative. Place a ✓ or an ✗ to indicate "yes" or "no" for each question.

											Overall Assessment
Date:											
Did I seek out new opportunities to learn today?											
Did I respond well to a challenge, or take an appropriate risk to improve my learning today?											
Did I demonstrate a particular interest or curiosity about an idea, concept, event, or object today?											
Did I seek out additional information from print, electronic media, or human resources today?											
Did I generate a problem, question, or inquiry about a topic that interests me today?											
Did I demonstrate self-motivation or self-direction today?											
Did I approach a new learning situation with a positive attitude today?											
Did I develop an innovative approach or an original idea today?											
Did I attempt a variety of learning activities today?											
Did I seek assistance when I needed it today?											
Did I use information technologies in creative ways today?											

Summary of things I need to do to improve my level of initiative:

_____

_____

Work Habits and Homework Completion: Self-Assessment Checklist

Name: _____   Term: _____

Enter the date each time you use this checklist to assess your ability to demonstrate good work habits or to complete homework. Place a ✓ or an X to indicate "yes" or "no" for each question. **Date:**										**Overall Assessment**
Did I complete my homework for today on time and with care?										
Did I make a consistent effort in class today?										
Did I follow directions today?										
Did I show attention to detail when polishing my work for today?										
Did I use materials and equipment appropriately and effectively today?										
Did I begin work promptly and use my time effectively today?										
Did I persevere with a complex task today, despite difficulties?										
Did I demonstrate effective home study habits to prepare for what I had to do today?										

Summary of things I need to do to improve my work habits:

_____

_____

_____

_____

_____

_____

Tools to Examine School-Wide Practices

In this section, you will find tools that address school-wide assessment issues, such as portfolio use and grading processes. They will be useful to gather data to inform school-wide assessment reform.

Examining Portfolio Use in My School

With colleagues, examine current portfolio use in your school and explore ways to learn more about this powerful process. Consider assembling a Portfolio Team to reflect upon and implement best practice. (Refer to Chapter 11 in this resource.) Your team could fulfill one or more of the following functions:

- Research how portfolios are currently used by teachers in your school.
- Research the latest professional literature on portfolios and make it available to colleagues.
- Meet on a regular basis to share best practices with team members in order to refine portfolio practices in your school.

Note: Ask for a lead teacher/principal's support in facilitating meetings (e.g., release time, resources).

You could begin by conducting this survey at a staff meeting.

1. Do you use portfolios as an integral part of your classroom routines? _____

2. What do you consider to be the purpose(s) of using portfolios with students?

   _____

   _____

3. How frequently do students work on their portfolios?

   _____

   _____

4. What kind of physical containers do students use to store the contents of their portfolios?

   _____

5. For which of these assessment purposes do you use portfolios:
   - initial/diagnostic assessment?
   - ongoing/formative assessment?
   - summative assessment?

   _____

6. What kind of assessment information do you record from students' portfolios?

   _____

7. How do you record assessment information from students' portfolios?

   _____

   _____

8. What specific responsibilities do students have with respect to the contents of their portfolios?

   _____

   _____

9. Are students required to self-assess the contents of their portfolio?

   _____

10. How do they do this?

    _____

    _____

11. Do you conduct one-on-one conferences with students about their portfolios?

    _____

    _____

12. If "yes," how often?

    _____

13. How do students use the information shared during conferences to improve the work in their portfolio?

    _____

    _____

14. Are parents involved in the portfolio process? If "yes," how are they involved?

_____

_____

15. Do you use the "Collect, Select, Reflect, Inspect" process to structure your portfolio program?

_____

_____

16. If "yes," how well are these steps working? If "no," do you plan to try this approach?

_____

_____

17. What aspects of your current portfolio program are working very well?

_____

_____

18. What aspects of your current portfolio program are not working very well?

_____

_____

19. Do you have the information and resources that you need to improve the things that are not working well?

_____

_____

20. At the end of a school year, how is information from student portfolios summarized and passed on?

_____

Assessing My School's Current Grading Practice

	Current Strengths in My Practice	Areas of Concern	Issues to Raise with Leaders
1. Report card grades cannot include all assessment data that you have gathered. Assessment for learning data (diagnostic/ initial assessment data and much formative assessment data) are for instructional purposes only. Report card grades should be based on assessment of learning data, in other words, the marks students receive for polished work and work that has been improved through practice and feedback.			
2. Report card grades should be based on an appropriate and balanced sample of student work. This means that grades represent work completed over a period of time, and that the sample includes oral and performance tasks, as well as paper and pencil tasks.			
3. Report card grades should capture the trend in a student's achievement over time. Generally, this means that grades should not be determined by using a simple average of marks from student work. Many jurisdictions are now requiring that grades be derived from the mode (see pages XXX - XXX). In other words, the teacher determines what level or mark the student has received most frequently across the range of their work and that becomes the report card grade.			
4. Report card grades and anecdotal comments should complement each other and provide a consistent picture of students' strengths and needs.			

(continued)

(continued)

Assessing My School's Current Grading Practice

	Current Strengths in My Practice	Areas of Concern	Issues to Raise with Leaders
5. Determining a report card grade should not be a straight mathematical calculation. Teachers' professional judgment should play a role, especially in cases where a student has special needs or where extenuating circumstances exist.			
6. When communicating with students and parents, teachers must feel confident that they are able to stand behind the grades they have entered on a set of report cards. This confidence results from standards that have been shared with their colleagues, with students and with parents, well-maintained records of student achievement, and the understanding that parents have the right to question report card grades and/or to ask for a re-evaluation.			
7. Report card grades should be based on the most important learning that has occurred, not on those components that are easiest to mark.			
8. For students with special needs, or for students whose first language is not the predominant language of the school, report card grades must represent fair judgments about these students' strengths and areas of need.			

Assessing My School's Current Grading Practice

	Current Strengths in My Practice	Areas of Concern	Issues to Raise with Leaders
9. Most jurisdictions require that teachers record a report separately on achievement and behaviour/learning skills. It is important to separate these two kinds of data accordingly.			
10. Assessment data derived from co-operative group learning situations should reflect individual student performance and not be distorted by work that other students may or may not have done.			

Converting Grading and Reporting Symbols

Note: This chart is only a guide. Locally developed guidelines may prescribe different interpretations.

Description of Knowledge and Skills	Rubric Descriptor	Rubric Level	Letter Grade	Numerical Score	% Grade Range
Demonstrates: • mastery of thinking and problem-solving strategies • an in-depth knowledge and understanding of content and concepts • consistent and appropriate application of procedures • mastery of both receptive and expressive communication skills	Exceeds Standard	4	A+ A A–	8–10	80–100%
Demonstrates: • considerable skill in thinking and using problem-solving strategies • considerable knowledge and understanding of content • considerable competence in applying learning in a variety of contexts • considerable skill in both receptive and expressive communication	At Standard	3	B+ B B–	7	70–79%
Demonstrates: • some proficiency in thinking and using problem-solving strategies • some knowledge and understanding of content and concepts • some proficiency in applying learning in a variety of contexts • some proficiency in both receptive and expressive communication skills	Developing	2	C+ C C–	6	60–69%
Demonstrates: • limited competence in using problem-solving strategies • limited understanding of concepts • limited competence in the application of procedures • limited competence in both receptive and expressive communication skills	Limited	1	D+ D D–	5	50–59%
Demonstrates insufficient understanding and skills to be graded on the scales		Below 1		0–4 (–)	Below 50%

CONTINUING YOUR PROFESSIONAL LEARNING IN ASSESSMENT

Introduction

How can we ensure the new learning you acquire through your reading and the professional development sessions you attend translate into long-term, meaningful changes in classroom practice? Current research indicates that the following conditions need to be in place to maximize the effectiveness of professional learning programs:

- Incentives for teachers to change and improve their practice
- A clear focus for improvement (Joyce and Showers, 2002; Guskey, 2000)
- Pressure as well as support from administration (Fullan, 2001)
- Opportunities to collaborate with peers on improvement initiatives (Hargreaves, 2003; Stiggins et al., 2004)
- Sufficient time to learn, apply and evaluate the effectiveness of an initiative (Guskey, 2000; Stiggins et al., 2004)
- Measures of accountability (Guskey, 2000)

It is clear from this research that for professional learning to be effective, it is necessary to have incentives to change and improve practice; a clear focus for learning; pressure as well as support from administration; the opportunity to collaborate with peers; sufficient time to learn, apply, and evaluate the effectiveness of an initiative; and a measure of accountability.

Just as students need to be active participants in their own learning, teachers need opportunities to practise what they are learning.

Think Big, Start Small

Talk About Assessment contains sixteen chapters. How are you going to decide what areas of assessment to focus on improving? To help answer this question, many of these chapters include a self-assessment tool for reflecting on your current practice. These include:

- How Does My Current Assessment Toolkit Shape Up?
- Implementing Assessment for Learning in My Classroom
- Classroom Observation of a Student with Special Needs

Many conventional forms of professional development are seen as too top-down and too isolated from school and classroom realities to have much impact on practice. As a result, hoped-for improvements are seldom realized.

GUSKEY, 2000

- Assessing My Current Use of Performance Standards
- Examining My Co-operative Group Learning Assessment Practices
- How Balanced Is My Assessment Toolkit?

The choice of a focus for improvement should be driven by data that you, your colleagues, and your principal have gathered. Any one of these tools can help you and your colleagues determine areas of need and lead to an examination of the relevant sections in *Talk About Assessment*. To maximize the likelihood of success, limit the number of areas you are going to pursue, develop a plan for your learning in these areas, and set clear and achievable timelines. (See self-improvement tools in Part 2 of this resource.)

Once you have embarked on a focus for improvement (for example, integrating performance assessment into your repertoire), allow sufficient time to "work out the bugs." Remember that a new approach is rarely successful the first time a teacher introduces it. Only with practice, ongoing monitoring of what works and what doesn't, and adjustments to refine the innovation will improvements in student learning and teacher effectiveness begin to show. For this reason, too, working with colleagues will benefit your practice as you share with one another successes and sources of frustration.

Creating a Learning Team

Whenever and wherever possible, learn with colleagues rather than alone. Working collaboratively affords the opportunity to discuss and reflect upon a richer bank of ideas and possible approaches. Only by working with colleagues can you benefit from planning a lesson together, having a peer observe that lesson, and then having a colleague critique that lesson. When implementing a new strategy, if two or more of you try the innovation, you can learn from one another about what works and what might need modification.

A learning team can be assembled at the grade level, school level, or district level. The learning team serves to foster learning about best practice and to provide support in the implementation of best practice.

Richard DuFour reminds us that three principles should drive the work of learning teams:

- Ensuring that the focus is student learning: the ultimate purpose for a learning team convening is to find ways to improve student learning.

Harsh lessons from the past have taught educators that fragmented, piecemeal approaches to professional development do not work. Neither do one-shot workshops based on the most current educational fad. One reason for their failure is that, as a rule, they offer no guidance on how the new strategies fit with those advocated in years past.

GUSKEY, 2000

Professional learning communities lead to strong and measurable improvements in students' learning. Instead of bringing about 'quick fixes' of superficial change, they create and support sustainable improvements that last over time, because they build the professional skill and capacity to keep the school progressing.

HARGREAVES, 2003

- Ensuring that collaboration characterizes the work of the team: as we shall see below, collaboration is essential if teachers are going to improve their practice.
- Ensuring that the success of the team is measured by results: merely sensing that an innovation has improved learning for students is not sufficient; you need to gather data as evidence that the innovation is successful.

ADAPTED FROM DUFOUR, ED. LEADERSHIP, MAY, 2004.

How should learning teams be set up? To answer this question, we need to consider the desired result. If the goal is to improve assessment and instruction at a specific grade level or division, then the team should comprise teachers who have a similar teaching assignment. Teachers can then create or refine program units that they will all teach, while at the same time learn how to integrate new assessment, instructional strategies, or both. I have found that grade or divisional teams should be relatively small—three or four teachers. The Unit Planning Templates described in Chapter 13 provide an excellent starting point for such teams. The descriptions of typical planning meetings that appear in Chapter 14 provide insights into the work of two teams.

If, on the other hand, the goal of a learning team is to implement change across a whole school, then representation from all grades is essential, including the presence and support of the principal or vice-principal. The most effective school- and district-level learning teams include both teachers and an administrator. When a principal or vice-principal is part of a team, the necessary support (as well as the pressure!) is far more likely to occur.

Let's suppose that a learning team decides to explore the extent to which assessment for learning strategies are currently used in a school. Based on the data gathered, the team intends to develop a plan for increasing the use of these strategies in all grades. A good place to start would be to have all teachers complete the "Implementing Assessment for Learning in My Classroom" survey at the end of Chapter 2. This would provide one source of school-wide data to help the team determine specific strategies on which to focus improvement. Notice that I specified *one source*. Since this survey relies on teachers self-reporting, it should be supplemented by observational data gathered by

Professional learning communities in schools emphasize three key components: collaborative work and discussion among the school's professionals; a strong and consistent focus on teaching and learning...; and gathering assessment and other data to inquire into and evaluate progress and problems over time.
HARGREAVES, 2003

...a learning team: a group of three to six individuals who have committed to meet regularly for an agreed amount of time guided by a common purpose.
STIGGINS ET AL, 2004

Our experience is that many districts engage in 'adoption cycles' without a design that makes a difference. The teachers feel (and are) buffeted by initiatives that ask them to change without adequate support.
JOYCE AND SHOWERS, 2002

peers or a school administrator from a representative sample of class-rooms in the school.

With the data available, the team can begin to formulate its improvement plan. They may wish to select material from Chapters 4 through 12 of *Talk About Assessment*, as well as material from other excellent sources such as Rick Stiggins' *Classroom Assessment for Student Learning: Doing It Right; Using It Well* (2004) to help accomplish their goal.

Working Alone

Attending workshops, reading journals and books, and observing others' classrooms all provide access to new ideas and strategies. However, if our professional development actions stop there, research and experience tell us the new information has little chance of changing our classroom practice. We also need opportunities and support for experimentation in the classroom, coupled with the time to reflect on the results of what we tried.

STIGGINS ET AL, 2004

In a small school, it may be difficult to assemble a team of colleagues with whom to work. This need not be a problem. First, you have probably already discovered that *Talk About Assessment* provides plenty of material for self-study and numerous strategies and tools to experiment with in your classroom. Begin by identifying one or more specific areas for improvement. Choose from the self-assessment tools listed under *Think Big, Start Small* to help you determine areas of need in your current practice.

Second, technology facilitates distance communication with colleagues. The most obvious is e-mail for sharing ideas, lesson plans, and assessment tools with colleagues, and asking them to provide feedback and suggestions for improvement. In my work with remote school districts, I have found that the rapidly increasing availability of video conferencing is enabling teachers to communicate over distance, with the added advantage of seeing one another. This technology makes it possible for teachers to observe each other's classroom practice and to ask questions about strategies they are using, all in real time. Try to establish a long-term partnership with one or more colleagues. This will enable you to work through the complete improvement cycle from identifying areas of need, learning about strategies and tools you may wish to explore, sharing successes and challenges, and gathering data about the effectiveness of your initiatives.

An Improvement Model

To increase the chances of success—meaning that your classroom practice improves, thereby increasing student learning—I recommend the following model:

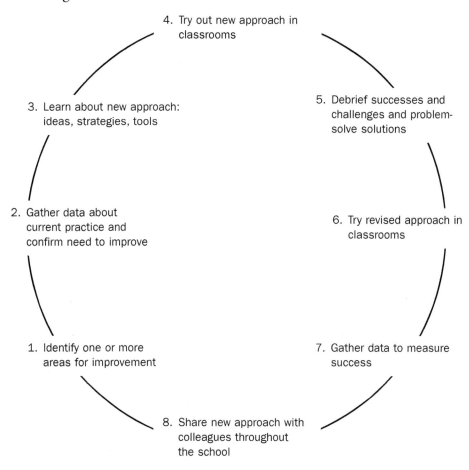

4. Try out new approach in classrooms

3. Learn about new approach: ideas, strategies, tools

2. Gather data about current practice and confirm need to improve

1. Identify one or more areas for improvement

8. Share new approach with colleagues throughout the school

5. Debrief successes and challenges and problem-solve solutions

6. Try revised approach in classrooms

7. Gather data to measure success

Peer Coaching and Mentoring

If you have decided to experiment with one or more new strategies in your classroom (for example, trying a number of new oral questioning techniques that will include all students), you will benefit most if you can arrange for a colleague or an administrator to observe you while you teach. I have found the following model for peer coaching and mentoring highly effective since it involves collaborative planning, in-class demonstrations and observation, and reflective analysis.

No matter how good the content of staff development, making things happen for students is the ultimate goal. To do so, we need to study the changes we make and the effects on the capacity of our students.

JOYCE AND SHOWERS, 2002

Teacher A is planning the change in practice; Teacher B is the coach/mentor:

- Teachers A and B meet to discuss the area for improvement and plan a lesson for Teacher A to deliver. Their discussion includes agreeing on a feedback sheet to focus observation and subsequent debriefing.
- Teacher A delivers the lesson, observed by Teacher B.
- Teachers A and B meet to debrief the lesson, focusing on what worked and what might have been done differently. They then plan a similar lesson for Teacher B to deliver, highlighting improvements that Teacher A may wish to consider.
- Teacher B delivers lesson, observed by Teacher A, using the same feedback sheet.
- Teachers A and B meet to debrief Teacher B's lesson using the agreed-upon feedback form to focus discussion. They then discuss next steps.

I strongly recommend that you keep a professional journal to log your experiences throughout this process. By reflecting on your experiences during a quiet half hour at home, you will often gain insights that may have eluded you during the hustle and bustle of the school day.

Assessing My Progress in Professional Learning

Review the *Professional Learning in Assessment: Implementation Profile* on page 295 (see reduced copy below). This tool will help you and your colleagues track your progress as you learn about and implement new practices and strategies.

...all workshops and presentations must be accompanied by appropriate follow-up activities. In addition, they are but one of a wide variety of highly effective approaches to professional development.

GUSKEY, 2000

TOOL 1.8

Professional Learning in Assessment: Implementation Profile, p. 295

Professional Learning in Assessment: Implementation Profile

Use this profile to track your improvement as you implement new assessment practices. You may wish to assess your practice three times: currently (Initial), after several months (Formative), and at the end of the year (Summative). To record your data, simply write I, F, or S in the space provided under the appropriate column to indicate whether it is an Initial, Formative, or Summative assessment. Ideally, all "S" indicators will be in the last column. Once you've completed the checklist, review the pattern of indicators you have entered. Determine which description best summarizes your practice at this time.

	Beginning	On My Way	I'm There!
	I am just beginning to use the following practices and strategies as I try to improve the quality and effectiveness of my assessment practice, but I am tentative and still need a lot of support	I am feeling more comfortable using the following practices and strategies to improve the quality and effectiveness of my assessment practice, and I need only minimal support	I have mastered the following practices and strategies for improving the quality and effectiveness of my assessment practice, and I routinely use them
Planning			
· Design down from big ideas and essential skills when planning units			
· Design down from learning goals when lesson planning			
Assessment for Learning			
· Adjust assessment processes appropriately to meet the needs of all students			
· Include regular opportunities for students to demonstrate their learning through performance and oral tasks, as well as written tasks			
· Adjust instruction for groups of students based on assessment data			
· Provide regular and specific feedback to students to help them improve			
· Provide students with assessment criteria before they begin work on a task			
· Provide opportunities for students to redo their work, incorporating			

accommodations strategies and supports that may be applied to the curriculum, assessment strategies, and/or instruction to enable students to be successful; providing extra time, different resources, and/or an alternative mode of demonstrating learning are all examples of accommodations (see also *modifications*)

achievement demonstrated student learning at a given point in time

analytic assessment assessment that focuses on discrete aspects of knowledge or skills

anchor sample of student work that is matched to a specific level of performance (see also *exemplar*)

anecdotal record short account of observed student behaviour on a given task or set of skills

assessment gathering of data about student knowledge and/or skills, either through informal methods, such as observation, or formal methods, such as testing

assessment for learning assessment that is designed primarily to promote learning; early drafts, first tries, and practice assignments are all examples of assessment for learning

assessment of learning assessment that is designed primarily to determine student achievement at a given point in time; report-card grades should be comprised of data from assessments of learning

authentic assessment performance assessment that involves a real-world context, where the tasks are either replicas of or analogous to the kinds of problems faced by adults, consumers, and professionals in the field

conferencing informal assessment in which the teacher discusses work or progress with a student

content standards prescribed or mandated public statements about curriculum

correlation measure of the relationship between two sets of data, with a scale range from -1.0 to 1.0

criterion-referenced assessment assessment based on a prescribed set of learning expectations

culminating performance assessment task that requires students to synthesize learning at the end of a unit or other instructional period

diagnostic assessment assessment to determine appropriate starting points for instruction

evaluation making judgments about student-demonstrated knowledge and/or skills

exemplar sample of student work that represents either the best or expected level of performance on a given task

formative assessment assessment that gathers data during the learning process, and provides feedback to both students and teachers to help improve learning

grade equivalent indicates the theoretical grade level, in years and months, for which an obtained score on a norm-referenced test compares with the average score for the norm group; for example, when a Grade 3 student scores a grade equivalent of 4.8, it means that, for the questions presented on the norm-referenced test, the student achieved a score that was in the average range for students in the eighth month of Grade 4. Based on these results, this does not mean that this Grade 3 student is operating at a Grade 4 level

grading summarizing assessment data in the form of a letter or numerical grade

growth measure of the increase in student learning that has occurred over time, compared to baseline data (see also *progress*)

holistic assessment assessment that provides an overall impression of what has been learned

ipsative assessment assessment that compares a student's recent performance with the results of that student's earlier performance

levels of performance scale, often ranging from 1 to 4, used in many criterion-referenced assessments

margin of error difference between results based on the selected sample and results that would have been obtained if the whole population had been tested

mean arithmetic average of a group of marks/scores

median middle mark/score in a group of ascending or descending marks/scores

miscue analysis form of running record used in oral reading assessment that identifies the specific types of errors made by a student

mode most frequently occurring mark/score in a group of marks/scores

moderation collaborative process in which a group of teachers examine and mark a set of student work samples according to agreed-upon standards; moderation fosters consensus about performance standards and leads to greater reliability

modifications changes made to the curriculum to enable a student to be successful; permitting a student to work at a different grade level is an example of a modification

normal distribution symmetrical distribution of scores with the mean, median, and mode all being equal, and 95 percent of all scores falling within two standard deviations of the mean

norm-referenced assessment assessment that compares students' performance to a normed sample of students who have taken the same test

opportunity-to-learn standards standards that describe the resources, learning conditions, and other considerations that should be available to all students in a specified jurisdiction; these standards are a key element to ensuring equity

path-referenced assessment assessment that compares students' performance to the typical path by which most students acquire such learning

percentile rank measure of relative standing within a defined group where scores range from 1 to 99; this type of score should not be confused with the percent correct on a teacher test; 35 percent correct on a teacher test may indicate serious problems while a PR of 35 indicates that the student has done better than more than one-third of the group

performance assessment assessment that requires students to perform a task, as opposed to merely writing about it

performance standards pre-determined statements that describe expected levels of performance on a given task or set of learning targets; a rubric is an example of a classroom performance standard

population all students possessing a certain set of characteristics

progress measure of the improvement that has occurred from a starting point or baseline towards a specified standard

qualitative data data that is anecdotal or descriptive; rubric descriptors and anecdotal comments are examples of qualitative data

quantitative data data that is numerical; scores out of 10, 25, and 100 are examples of quantitative data

raw score number of items a student answered correctly on a test

reliability measure of the consistency or stability of an assessment instrument when used repeatedly

rubric assessment tool that includes a set of performance indicators, often organized into several levels, for a given task or set of skills

running record ongoing assessment, in which the teacher tracks student responses to learning

sample selected group of students drawn from the population

screening process to gather initial information about the performance of students for the purpose of special programming

significance level measure of whether differences in test scores represent meaningful variation (significant) or may be due only to measurement error

standard public and agreed-upon statement about what is expected in terms of curriculum, student performance, or conditions for learning.

standardized test empirically developed test that includes specific directions for administration and scoring; test includes evidence of reliability, validity, and information about how the test was normed

standards-based test test that is based on a set of curriculum and/or performance standards, such as those developed by provincial ministries

summative assessment assessment that occurs at the end of a significant period of learning and summarizes student achievement of that learning

validity measure of how well an assessment instrument measures what it is intended to measure

Alberta Education. *WNCP Curriculum: Language Arts.* Edmonton, Alberta: Alberta Learning, 1998.

Bereiter, Carl, and Marlene Scardamalia. *Rethinking learning.* Cambridge, MA: Basil Blackwell, 1996.

Black, Paul, and Dylan Wiliam. "Inside the Black Box: Raising Standards Through Classroom Assessment." *Phi Delta Kappan* October 1998: 139-144, 146-148.

Booth, David, and Carol Thornley-Hall, eds. *Classroom Talk.* Markham, ON: Pembroke, 1991.

British Columbia Ministry of Education. "British Columbia Performance Standards: Grade 2 Numeracy." Online. World Wide Web. Available http://www.bced.gov.bc.ca/perf_stands/numerg2.pdf. 15 Aug. 2006.

Butler, R. "Enhancing and Undermining Intrinsic Motivation: The Effects of Task-Involving and Ego-Enhancing Evaluation on Interest and Performance." *British Journal of Educational Psychology* 58(1988): 1–14.

Covey, Stephen. *The Seven Habits of Highly Effective People.* New York: Fireside, 1990.

Davies, Anne. *Making Classroom Assessment Work.* Merville, BC: Classroom Connections, 2000.

Dewey, J. *Experience and Education.* New York: Touchstone, 1938.

DuFour, Richard. "What is a 'Professional Learning Community'?" *Educational Leadership* May 2004: 61(8). Alexandria, VA: ASCD.

Eaker, Robert, Richard DuFour, and Rebecca Burnette. *Getting Started: Reculturizing Schools to Become Professional Learning Communities.* Bloomington, IN: National Education Service, 2002.

Flewelling, Gary, and William Higginson. *A Handbook on Rich Learning Tasks.* Kingston, ON: Centre for Mathematics, Science & Technology Education, Queen's University, 2000.

Fullan, Michael. *Leading in a Culture of Change.* San Francisco, CA: Jossey-Bass, 2001.

Fullan, Michael. *The New Meaning of Educational Change.* Toronto, ON: Irwin, 2001.

Gardner, Howard. *Frames of Mind: The Theory of Multiple Intelligences.* New York: Basic Books, 1983.

"Grade 3 Sample Questions Spring 2006: Mathematics" *EQAO Educator Resources Link.* Online. World Wide Web. Available http://www.eqao.com/pdf_e/06/06P020e.pdf. 21 August 2006.

Graves, Donald H. *Writing: Teachers and children at work.* Exeter, NH: Helnemann Educational Books, 1983.

Guskey, Thomas. *Evaluating Professional Development.* Thousand Oaks, CA: Corwin, 2000.

Guskey, Thomas. "How Classroom Assessment Improves Learning." *Educational Leadership* 60, (5): Feb. 2003.

Hargreaves, Andy. *Teaching in the Knowledge Society: Education in the Age of Insecurity.* New York: Teachers College Press, 2003.

Hattie, J.A. "Measuring the effects of schooling." *Australian Journal of Education* 36(1), 5-13.

Holmes, C. T., and K.M. Matthews. "The effects of non-promotion on elementary and junior high school pupils: A meta-analysis." *Review of Educational Research* 54 (1984).

Inhelder B., and J. Piaget. *The Growth of Logical Thinking from Childhood to Adolescence.* New York: Basic Books, 1958.

Jimmerson, Shane R., Phillip Ferguson, Angela D. Whipple, Gabrielle E. Anderson, and Michael J. Dalton. "Exploring the Association Between Grade Retention and Dropout: A Longitudinal Study Examining Socio-Emotional, Behavioural, and Achievement Characteristics of Retained Students." *The California School Psychologist* 7 (2002).

Joint Advisory Committee. *Principles of Fair Student Assessment Practices for Education in Canada.* Edmonton, Alberta: University of Alberta, 1993.

Joyce, Bruce, and Beverley Showers. *Student Achievement through Staff Development.* 3rd ed. Alexandria, VA: ASCD, 2002.

Kagan, S. *Cooperative Learning Resources for Teachers.* San Juan Capistrano, CA: Resources for Teachers, 1990.

Kestell, Mary Lou, and Marian Small. *Nelson Mathematics K–8 Series.* Toronto, ON: Thomson Nelson, 2004–2006.

Lazear, David. *Seven Ways of Knowing: Understanding Multiple Intelligences.* 2nd ed. Palatine, IL: Skylight, 1991.

Marzano, Robert J. *Transforming Classroom Grading.* Alexandria, VA: ASCD, 2000.

O'Connor, Ken. *How to Grade for Learning.* Arlington Heights, IL: Skylight, 2002.

Ontario Ministry of Education and Training. *The Ontario Curriculum Grades 1–8: Language.* Ontario: Ministry of Education and Training, 1997.

References

Scardamalia, M., and C. Bereiter. "Schools as Knowledge Building Organizations." *Today's Children, Tomorrow's Society: The Developmental Health and Wealth of Nations.*" Keating and C. Hertzman, eds. New York: Guilford, 1999.

Small, Marian. *PRIME – Professional resources and Instruction for Mathematics Educators Series.* Toronto, ON: Thomson Professional Learning, 2005–2006.

Stiggins, Richard, Judith A. Arber, Jan Chappuis, and Stephen Chappuis. *Classroom Assessment for Student Learning: Doing it right – using it well.* Portland, OR: Assessment Training Institute, 2004.

Strong, Richard, Harvey Silver, and Matthew Perini. "Keeping it Simple and Deep." *Educational Leadership* Mar. 1999: 56–6. Alexandria, VA: ASCD.

Sutton, Ruth. *Assessment: A framework for teachers.* Oxford, London: Routledge, 1992.

Sutton, Ruth. Unpublished document, 2001.

Tomlinson, Carol Ann. *How to Differentiate Instruction in Mixed-Ability Classrooms.* 2nd ed. Alexandria, VA: ASCD, 2001.

Trehearne, Miriam P. *Nelson Language Arts Grades 1–2 Teacher's Resource Book.* Toronto, ON: Thomson Nelson, 2004.

Van De Walle. John A. *Elementary and Middle School Mathematics: Teaching Developmentally.* 4th ed. Longman, New York: Addison Wesley, 2001.

Vygotsky, L. *Thought and Language.* Cambridge, MA: Massachusetts Institute of Technology, 1986.

Wiggins, Grant. *Assessing Student Performance: Exploring the purpose and limits of testing.* San Francisco, CA: Jossey-Bass, 1993.

Wiggins, Grant. *Educative Assessment.* San Francisco, CA: Jossey-Bass, 1998.

Wiggins, Grant. "Toward Better Report Card Grades." *Educational Leadership* 52(2): Oct. 1994.

Wiggins, Grant. *Standards, Not Standardization: A video and print curriculum on performance-based student assessment.* Genesee, NY: CLATS, 1994.

Wiggins, Grant. *Understanding by Design* Workshop. Cherry Hills, NJ, 1999.

Wiggins, Grant, and Jay McTighe. *Understanding by Design.* Alexandria, VA: ASCD, 1998.

We have made every effort to trace the ownership of all copyrighted material and to secure permission from copyright holders. In the event of any question arising as to the use of any material, we will be pleased to make the necessary corrections in future printings. Thanks are due to the following for permission to use the material indicated.

Cover

Photo Credits

Top David Young-Wolff/Photo Edit; bottom left Michael Prince/Corbis Canada; bottom right LWA-Dann Tardif/Corbis Canada.
Back: Marilyn MacLennan

Part 1: Strategies to Improve Student Learning

Section 1: Photos

2: ©Bill Aron/Photo Edit; **4:** Al Harvey/The Slide Farm, www.slidefarm.com; **6:** PhotoDisk/Getty Images; **13:** Corbis Canada; **15:** LWA-Dann Tardif/Corbis Canada; **21:** Thomson Nelson; **27:** Eyewire Images; **29:** ©Michael Newman/Photo Edit; **43:** Amanda Davis/Thomson Nelson; **54:** © Gideon Mendel/Corbis Canada; **57:** Amanda Davis/Thomson Nelson; **59:** LWA-Dann Tardif/CORBIS Canada.

Section 2: Photos

66: Tony Freeman/Photo Edit; **71:** Michael Newman/Photo Edit; **82:** Mark Peterson/Corbis Canada; **83:** Photos.com; **85:** Holger Winkler/zefa/Corbis Canada; **96:** Thomson Nelson; **98:** Bonnie Kamin/Photo Edit; **99:** Michael Newman/Photo Edit; **102:** Corbis Canada; **106:** Corbis Canada; **111:** Thomson Nelson; **118:** Thomson Nelson; **122:** Mary Kate Denny/Photo Edit; **126:** Tony

Freeman/Photo Edit; **136:** Koval/Shutterstock; **141:** Lisa F. Young/Shutterstock; **144:** Mikhail Lavrenov/Shutterstock; **149:** Bill Freeman/Photo Edit; **151:** Shutterstock; **158:** Myrleen Ferguson Cate/Photo Edit; **161:** David Young-Wolff/Photo Edit; **166:** © Liquidlibrary/Alamy; **168:** Corbis Canada; **174:** Larry Williams/Corbis Canada; **186:** ©Mary Kate Denny/Photo Edit.

Section 2: Text

79, 113, 140: Student Samples by Jessica Pegis; **122**: British Broadcasting Corporation © 2002-2005; **123**: From David Lazear, *Seven Ways of Knowing-Understanding Multiple Intelligences* (Palatine, IL: Skylight Publishing, 1991).

Section 3: Photos

200: Bill Aron/Photo Edit; **214:** Michael Newman/Photo Edit; **221:** Damian Cooper.

Section 4: Photos

238: Bill Aron/Photo Edit; **274:** Bob Daemmrich/Photo Edit.

Section 4: Text

241 Copyright © 2001, Province of British Columbia. All rights reserved.

Part 2: Tools to Improve Student Learning

Section 3: Text

343-345, 347, 349-354, and 363: © reprinted by permission of Miriam P. Trehearne: Copyright 2004. All rights reserved.

DVD Music: composed and performed by Chris Smith

Index

Notes